The Background of Napoleonic Warfare

NUMBER 596

COLUMBIA STUDIES IN THE SOCIAL SCIENCES

EDITED BY THE FACULTY OF POLITICAL SCIENCE

OF COLUMBIA UNIVERSITY

AMS PRESS
NEW YORK

Robert S. Quimby

THE BACKGROUND

OF

NAPOLEONIC WARFARE

THE THEORY OF MILITARY TACTICS IN

EIGHTEENTH-CENTURY FRANCE

The Library of Congress cataloged this title as follows:

Quimby, Robert S.
    The background of Napoleonic warfare; the
theory of military tactics in eighteenth–
century France [by] Robert S. Quimby. [1st
AMS ed.] New York, AMS Press [1968]
    viii, 385 p. illus. 23 cm. (Columbia
studies in the social sciences, no. 596)
    Reprint of the 1957 ed. Bibliography: p.
[371]–375.
    1. France. Armée—History.   2. Military
art and science—History.   3. Tactics—
History.   4. France—History, Military—18th
century.   I. Title. (Series)
UA702 .05   1968   68–59257
                          355.4/09/033

UA
702
. Q5
1968

Reprinted from the edition of 1957, New York.
First AMS edition published in 1968.
Second AMS printing: 1979.

Manufactured in the United States of America

AMS PRESS, INC.
NEW YORK, N.Y.

Acknowledgments

It is not possible to mention here all those who have given assistance to the author in the preparation of this book. The author gratefully acknowledges special indebtedness to Professors Garrett Mattingly and Stebelton Nulle who have read the whole manuscript, to Professor Shepard Clough who has read parts of it, and who have all made many valuable suggestions; to Lura M. Quimby who has also made many helpful suggestions; to Professor Paul Evans, Professor Walter Dorn, and President Charles Cole for encouragement and aid at various stages in the undertaking; and to Professors Marjorie Gesner, Martha Layman, and John Reinoehl who have helped in the tedious task of manuscript revision and proofreading. The author has benefited much from the courtesy and assistance which he received at the Harvard University Libraries, the Library of Congress, the National War College Library, and, above all, at the Library of the United States Military Academy. Colonel Morton and his staff by their warm welcome and unfailing helpfulness make research at West Point a great pleasure. It is necessary to point out that the author is solely responsible for the conclusions and any errors in the text. Finally, Albert V. Quimby and Christopher S. Quimby helped in the preparation of the drawings for the figures.

R.S.Q.

East Lansing, Michigan
June 24, 1956

Contents

CONTENTS

The Background of Napoleonic Warfare

Introduction

The period from the opening of the War of the Spanish Succession to the meeting of the Estates-General is generally looked upon as a period of decadence in the history of the French Army. Compared with the great days of Louis XIV or with those of the Revolution and Napoleon this estimate seems correct enough. It was a period of many humiliations. The disasters inflicted upon France by Marlborough and Prince Eugene were followed by the much more humiliating failures of the Seven Years' War. Yet the record is not without its glorious moments. During the War of the Austrian Succession, a series of brilliant successes was won under the leadership of the great Saxe.

If the combat record of the French Army was, to say the least, uneven during the eighteenth century, such was not the case with its intellectual achievements. The French Army stood foremost among all those of Europe in this respect. Throughout most of the years of the century, there was a great intellectual ferment within the Army leading to major developments in ideas and in material improvement.

The reasons for this intellectual activity are to be sought in the fact that progress in military developments, tactical and material, is most frequently made by defeated armies. The victorious army remains content with the organization and methods which have given it victory. The victory is proof of their excellence. The defeated army, however, left with nothing but the memory of failure, seeks to analyze the causes of its defeats, the defects within itself, and to consider possible remedies. Developments in the Prussian Army after 1806 and in the German Army after 1919 are cases in point, but the outstanding example of this is to be found in the history of the French Army during the eighteenth century.

Within a few years after the War of the Spanish Succession,

books began to appear, pointing out defects in the tactics then in use and proposing changes. After the Seven Years' War, the number of such books greatly increased. The result was to stimulate an ardent and at times acrimonious debate. Book countered book; pamphlets and memorials multiplied. Gradually, through the abandonment of more extreme ideas, a compromise was worked out. Embodied in the Ordinance of 1791, this became the basis for the tactics of the Wars of the French Revolution and of Napoleon.

There is another probable reason for the activity in the field of military ideas. It is a natural outgrowth of the intellectual climate of the times. It would be curious if a century which devoted itself so strongly to better government and legislation did not turn to military questions.[1] The great interest in ideas, characteristic of the times, carried over into the field of military science, leading to a prolonged and intensive examination of the military institutions of France. The military writers are characteristic of the Age of Enlightenment. The marks of the doctrinaire spirit of the Age are very much apparent in some of them. Others reflect the keen interest of the Age in experimentation, wishing to try out various ideas and accept those which proved workable. Military writing which regarded tactical problems as mere problems of geometry also showed the influence of the mathematical ideas of the time. Mathematics was also applied more appropriately to the special problems of artillery, a field in which the French came to preeminence during the course of the century.

Tactical ideas were debated vigorously in the Army. They influenced the large number of drill regulations which were issued after the middle of the century. Before adoption some of these ideas were tested in camps of instruction. They were current, therefore, among a very large number of officers in the Army. This fact is important because it helps to explain the tactical developments in the Revolutionary armies.

The sharp break alleged to have existed between the Army of the Old Regime and that of the Revolution is greatly exaggerated. There was a very large degree of continuity. For example, the old regiments were retained, though many of the foreign ones were recalled or disbanded. The basic drill book, the Ordinance of 1791, was drawn up after the outbreak of the Revolution, and contained the results of three-quarters of a century of tactical debate. The Volunteers of 1791 were trained under this ordinance, as well as the line regiments with which they were subsequently brigaded. The soldiers of the Revolutionary and Napoleonic Wars did not feel that this ordinance differed much from the tactics which were used in the field. Although the ordinance was the subject of many criticisms, these were so diverse that no current of opinion developed, strong enough to bring about a change.[2] It was not until 1831 that a new drill book appeared.

All the tactical innovations which have so impressed many writers, especially English, on the Revolutionary and Napoleonic Wars are to be found in the writings of the eighteenth century. They were familiar to the officers who led the armies of the early campaigns and to those who led the subordinate units. It is in this that the importance of these works lies. They form the foundation of the ideas and practices of the generals who led the French armies from 1792 to 1815.

The books written on military theory in eighteenth-century France dealt with two lines of development corresponding to actual changes within the French Army. The first was the proper size, composition, and armament of the battalion leading to the unspectacular, but exceedingly important, changes in petty tactics. By 1770 these had produced a battalion having very great flexibility when compared with the battalion of 1715. Since the developments in petty tactics formed the essential basis without which the developments in grand tactics could not have been made, it is necessary to consider the details of the changes in order to understand the handicaps of armies engaged in combat at the outset of the century and to understand how these handicaps were overcome.

The second line of development resulted from the subdivision of armies into permanent large units or divisions. This opened the way to greatly extended grand tactics. The later works, therefore, deal also with the tactics of armies, the employment of divisions, and all the advantages which the new flexibility provided.   These new tactics made possible the bolder strategy also sketched by some of the later works.

The essential tactical issue involved in the controversy which raged in the French Army over the *ordre profond* and the *ordre mince* during the eighteenth century boiled down to whether the bayonet joined to the fusil [3] was primarily a shock weapon or a fire weapon.   Those who maintained the former advocated formation in depth as the basic combat order with deployment into lines for fire purposes as secondary, or on the part of the more extreme members, the dispensing with this formation altogether. Those who felt that this combination was primarily a fire weapon, and only secondarily a shock weapon, naturally advocated a thin order which would allow them to bring into action the maximum fire power.   The more extreme members of this group maintained that such a formation was adequate for shock action as well as fire action.   Since the thin order had developed as a result of combat experience, it is not surprising that the course of the controversy led to a gradual modification of position on the part of the advocates of the order in depth.   The ultimate compromise came much closer to the views of the advocates of the thin order than to those of the partisans of the order in depth.   In other words, the idea that the fusil with bayonet is primarily a fire weapon came to prevail over the doctrinaire ideas of the more opinionated disciples of the *ordre profond*.

Tactics of the Early Eighteenth Century

BACKGROUND DEVELOPMENTS

During most of the Middle Ages, the basis of military forces was the heavy cavalry. A change began in the fourteenth century as a result of the experience of the English with the longbow combined with dismounted men-at-arms, and that of the Swiss with the halberd and the pike. This last weapon led the Swiss to adopt a formation in heavy columns, strongly reminiscent of the phalanx of Philip of Macedon.

During the fifteenth century, the Swiss pike columns were practically invincible, and gained one triumph after another,[1] almost entirely by shock tactics. They rushed forward, usually in an echelon of three columns, meeting the enemy head on and smashing them. Missile or fire tactics were used in an auxiliary manner by light infantry armed with crossbows, or later, handguns. These troops went before the columns, and sought to distract attention from them as long as possible by their fire. The basis of the army and the reliance for victory, however, was the pike column.

The Swiss received the sincerest form of flattery. Large numbers of them were hired as mercenaries by neighboring princes, especially by the kings of France after the future Louis XI had experience with them at the battle of St. Jacob in 1444. The Swiss were imitated also. The most successful of these imitations were the German *Landsknechts,* first raised, apparently, by the Emperor Maximilian I.

In the sixteenth century, much thought was devoted to the problem of coping with the Swiss pike column. Several methods were found. The first was the sword-and-buckler infantry of Spain which gained an unexpected victory over the Swiss by deflecting the blows of the pikes with their bucklers and rushing in to engage the pikemen at close quarters where the latter were at a hopeless disadvantage. This repetition of the Roman legion versus the Macedonian phalanx occurred several times during the Italian Wars. A second method, employed by the French at the battle of Marignano in 1515, consisted in repeated cavalry attacks upon the flanks of the pike columns which forced them to halt and face outwards in their hedgehog formation, while the French field artillery plowed great gaps in their ranks. A third method was employed at the battle of Bicocca in 1522. This was to man an entrenchment with artillery and arquebusiers, backed by a strong force of pikemen who were to be employed in case the attackers were able to cross the obstacle. Each of these methods led to severe Swiss defeats.

The growing efficacy of fire power was of increasing importance in the wars of the sixteenth century, but the pike did not disappear, in spite of the deficiencies which it had displayed. Machiavelli had expected the pike to give way after its defeats by the sword and buckler, yet it was the latter which yielded, even in the Spanish armies. One does not have to look very far for the reason. The sword-and-buckler men were helpless against cavalry, while pikemen could easily defend themselves against it, if it were not supported by other arms.

So the pike was retained, but in the typical battalion of the later sixteenth and seventeenth centuries it was combined with firearms. The center of the battalion, when drawn up in combat array, was composed of pikemen and was long called the "battle." On each flank were the fire troops. These arquebusiers, and later the musketeers, like the sword-and-buckler men, were helpless against cavalry. Sent out as skirmishers to harass the enemy, they had to retire when attacked by mounted troops. The pikemen were therefore necessary to give solidity and resistance to the battle line.

At first the pikemen predominated, and the arquebusiers were used chiefly as skirmishers. With the development of the musket, a heavier but more efficient weapon, fire became more effective and fire troops became more important in action. One result of this was the gradual reduction in the number of pikemen and the increase in that of musketeers. In the French Army the pikemen were first reduced to one-half of the total, then to one-third in 1651, to one-fourth in 1677, and to one-fifth in 1688. They were entirely suppressed in 1703. (All statements and discussions in this work refer to the French Army unless otherwise noted.)

An army composed of two kinds of infantry was awkward to deploy. There were other inconveniences, too, though these were not very apparent so long as the pikemen formed the bulk of the battalion. As the central core of the battalion shrank in size, the space between these cores, filled by the wings of musketeers, increased and could be defended only by the fire of the troops, for as yet there was no effective bayonet. This meant that the battle line tended to be vulnerable to cavalry attacks, but this did not prevent the decline in the number of pikes.

The adoption of the fusil, a flintlock weapon which was much lighter and more effective, brought a still greater increase in the efficacy of fire. It was this that led to the final suppression of the pike. The latter weapon had almost completely disappeared before the socket bayonet was adopted. The gradual reduction and final suppression of the pike was the result of experience in the field, and not of theoretical speculation.[2]

Another tactical effect of the growing fire power of infantry was the gradual diminution of the depth of infantry formations. The combat formation of troops is, or should be, dictated by its principal arm. When the troops are armed for shock action, with pikes, for instance, the formations are normally in considerable depth. When they are armed for fire action, the ideal formation is one which makes possible the fullest use of the battalion's weapons, i.e., a shallow line.

At first the musketeers were drawn up in ten or eight ranks like the pikemen. This made it impossible for the rear ranks to fire while they were in formation. The ranks behind the first had to come through to the front, deliver their volley, and return to their place, unless they were advancing, in which case the ranks successively advanced and fired without returning to their former position. This was, at best, a slow and cumbersome operation. So, as the musket came gradually to prevail over the pike in the battalion, there was a concomitant reduction in the number of ranks in order to make better use of the increased fire power. This took place over a period of years, first from ten to eight ranks, then to six, and eventually to five ranks. This last reduction was accomplished in the French Army by the Ordinance of March 2, 1703. During the War of the Spanish Succession, the number was, in practice, reduced to four. This number became customary henceforth, though it fell on occasion to three during the war. These reductions were made as the result of actual combat experience. The later diminutions resulted from the adoption of the more rapidly firing fusil which permitted the thinner formations to deliver the same or a greater volume of fire than the deeper ones armed with muskets. Thus there gradually developed the practice of deploying battalions in a long, thin firing line.

Two great developments followed the adoption of the socket bayonet and the suppression of the pike. The first was a single, uniform type of line infantry which greatly simplified the order of battle. This had not been possible since portable firearms had first made their influence felt on the battlefield. The second was the combination of a fire weapon and a shock weapon in one arm. As a result, infantry that was equipped to fight primarily with fire power could now fight in either manner and could resist successfully the attacks of cavalry. From this time, the preponderance of infantry gradually grew, and the slow decline of cavalry's battlefield importance began.

TACTICS DURING THE WAR OF THE SPANISH SUCCESSION

At the beginning of the eighteenth century, in spite of the suppression of the pike and the consequent uniformity of the infantry, the movements of armies were still slow and ponderous, their formations cumbersome. Though the regulation specified that the formation of the battalion should be on five ranks, it was, in practice, actually four. Between each rank an interval of four yards (five to six paces) was maintained at all times during both the march and maneuvers. Since there was no cadenced step, it was almost impossible to maintain the intervals between ranks or, more important, those between units in a column of march. Furthermore, an army marched in columns of at least twenty files,[3] a formation too wide to move on roads. Marches across country had to be prepared at least a day in advance by special pioneer units. Such wide columns greatly slowed the movement of armies, but they alone made it possible for armies to deploy within a few hours.

A battalion at the beginning of the century was composed of twelve or sixteen companies of fusiliers and a company of grenadiers. The latter were no longer what the name implies but rather a group of picked men, used either for special enterprises or as a reserve for a last effort. The fusilier companies were also known as sections for maneuvering purposes. Two such companies formed a platoon, and two platoons formed a *manche* (a survival of the days when the term referred to one-third of a battalion). The battalion was also divided into halves called *demi-rangs* composed of six or eight companies. Such was the interior composition of the basic infantry unit of an army.

It was not possible even to dream of deploying a column of such battalions promptly.[4] The order of march had to correspond to the order of battle, else hopeless confusion would result. The army came on the field in an open column of march, the only kind in general use in that day. There were normally two great columns corresponding to the two lines of battle which the army would assume on the battlefield. In what the French called a processional movement, it marched across the position which it was to occupy in its open columns—that is, columns in which there were intervals between each section of the battalion exactly equal to the front of the section. The deployment was then achieved by having all sections perform simultaneously a right quarter-wheel. If the deployment was to be made to the left, it was even more cumbersome, for in order to avoid inversion of the units, each section had to wheel separately after having passed behind those which had been ahead of it in column and which had already wheeled. Because of this awkward maneuver, deployment was made to the right if possible. It was this latter maneuver which made the exact intervals so necessary. Since there were no fixed rules for maintaining the intervals and no cadenced or regulated step, it was obviously necessary to halt and arrange the column before the deployment could begin. Add to the intervals between sections those between the ranks of each section, which complicated matters still further, and it becomes apparent why the movements and deployments of an army were so deliberate.

It was, therefore, usually impossible for a general to force a battle. A battle normally took place when both generals desired it, or were at least prepared to risk it. One of them took up a position in which he felt that he could repulse the attack of his opponent. The latter reconnoitered, and, if he observed points which he felt he could attack with success, a battle resulted. Even in the case of an able general like Marlborough, however, the long period of deployment was necessary. In three of his four major battles, serious action did not begin until three in the afternoon. The single exception was Malplaquet where both armies were in position by nightfall on the day before the battle.

Once an army was drawn up in position, it was usually impossible for any but minor changes to be made in its order, because of the slow, deliberate maneuvers which were necessary. Battles in that day were usually delivered in parallel, that is, engaged along the full length of the line, unless a topographical obstacle prevented it on some portion of the front. The usual battle formation consisted of an order in two lines, perhaps three hundred yards apart, with the infantry stationed in the center. The army formed an almost continuous line, with only a very slight interval between battalions. The cavalry was divided between the two wings and was also drawn up in two lines. Since the flanks of such an array were very weak, one of the cardinal requirements of a position was support for the flanks. This could be supplied by a fortified village, an inaccessible slope, a marsh, or any barrier which prevented access to the flanks. Normally woods were quite acceptable support, since they were usually considered impassable for an army in formation. A battle such as Malplaquet, where more than eighty battalions plunged into the woods on the Allied right to attack the French positions, was extremely rare.

Maneuver battles were delivered only by the most able generals, and here Marlborough stands out in preeminence. Ramillies is an example of such a battle. Marlborough feinted vigorously at the French left with the English infantry, drawing the French high command and many additional troops to that area, and then delivered his main attack on the French right, transferring the bulk of his right-wing cavalry, thirty-nine squadrons, to his left to reinforce this attack which was the decisive event of the battle. It uncovered the right wing of the French infantry, once the cavalry had been defeated and driven off. There followed another maneuver notable for that day. Having defeated the French cavalry, the Allied cavalry, composed of more than one hundred squadrons disordered by the prolonged mêlée, were reformed on a new front to attack the rear and flanks of the French infantry. This latter, assailed in front, flanks, and rear, broke and fled.

This engagement illustrates another characteristic of the battles of that day. The decisive stroke was delivered by the cavalry, which was usually the case. The infantry normally had a more passive role. They advanced slowly, exerting a steady pressure upon the enemy and preventing the transfer of troops to counter the decisive stroke of the cavalry. There was a prejudice, especially in the French Army, against delivering decisive strokes with the infantry. At the battle of Malplaquet, the infantry of the French right stopped the Allied attack completely with its fire, repulsing the Dutch infantry with great slaughter. "At this moment, our soldiers had the feeling that the battle was won, and that it would be sufficient for an offensive movement by our right to effect the defeat of the battalions that had just been decimated by their fire. But one was not yet accustomed to the idea of winning a great victory by an infantry charge." [5] In two battles of the war there were exceptions to this general rule. These were the battles of Spires in 1703 and Denain in 1712, where the French infantry advancing in columns played the principal role and gained the victory.

Such was the nature of maneuver and the general characteristics of battles during the War of the Spanish Succession. There was no general drill regulation in the French Army until the middle of the century. Such matters were left to each regiment, which established a tradition unto itself. This naturally led to great variety in evolutions, some of which were of no utility in the field. There was, therefore, no uniformity in the Army. This was to be an achievement of the eighteenth century.

There was considerable dissatisfaction in the French Army with its methods of combat and with the thin order, the *ordre mince*. It was impossible to move the long, thin lines of infantry with celerity. They moved forward with great deliberation and even minor obstacles caused great difficulties. The absence of a uniform, cadenced step left these lines subject to wavering and fluctuation. There was a tendency for them to crowd together in some places and to open gaps in others. The slowness of movement resulted in the advancing troops having to suffer from the defending fire for considerable periods. The almost irresistible urge of the troops was to stop and return the fire they found so galling. The fight would stabilize into a motionless fire combat until one side or the other, unable to endure it longer, either gave ground or broke. There was a widespread feeling within the French Army that, in such a combat, the advantage was all with the more "phlegmatic nations," such as the Dutch or Germans. The French, by their "national genius," needed a more vigorous method of combat and, consequently, a new battle array which would make it possible. These sentiments were repeated with great frequency in the works on tactics which appeared in the course of the century.[6]

Many writers have condemned the warfare of the eighteenth century as pusillanimous and dilatory. They have represented its generals as being unwilling to engage in battle, wishing to gain their ends by the less dangerous method of maneuvering. Thus whole campaigns went by without a battle and without any decisive results. Most of these writers were steeped in the spirit of nineteenth-century warfare, and especially the doctrine of the offensive *à outrance*. They contrast the short, sharp, decisive nature of most nineteenth-century wars with the long-drawn-out and indecisive nature of those of the preceding century.

This attitude ignores the practice of the best leadership of that century. No general ever desired battle more consistently than Marlborough, although he succeeded in bringing off only four battles during the ten campaigns that he conducted. What is neglected here is the fact that, with the armies and tactics of that day, one could not force battle upon an unwilling opponent.

The practice of the best generalship of the late seventeenth and early eighteenth centuries is concentrated in the *Mémoires* of the Marquis de Feuquières (1648-1711), a distinguished soldier of Louis XIV. The *Mémoires* present one of the best available views of the art of war in 1700. Feuquières was a strong advocate of the offensive and of battle for the purpose of deciding a war. He was all for striking hard with one's whole force when undertaking an offensive war. "A battle at the beginning of a war, delivered *à propos*, almost always decides its success. Therefore, one should not hesitate to fight, if the enemy . . . places himself in range." [7]

Feuquières felt that it was necessary to attack a country in a quarter which would give access to the capital and the heart of the interior. One should penetrate as deeply as possible for the purpose of demoralizing the enemy and causing him to expose his vital areas. If a general was successful in surprising his enemy, he must exploit his advantage to the utmost.

This is very different from the long-prevailing concept of eighteenth-century ideas about warfare. The will to short decisive action was present among its able generals, and the doctrine is here stated. There are qualifications expressed to be sure. Battle is not sought merely for battle's sake. There must be good prospects for success, and some tangible results to be gained from that success, to justify the risk which any battle entails. Since they are fraught with such important consequences, they should not be lightly undertaken. This is the meaning of Feuquières's seemingly contradictory statement, "Battles being general actions of one army against another, often deciding the success of the whole war, or at least, and almost always that of the campaign, they ought to be given only under necessity and for important reasons." [8]

The warfare of the later seventeenth and early eighteenth centuries, as revealed in the pages of Feuquières, seems curiously stiff and formal to us. The danger is that it may seem unreal because of this formality, and many have fallen into the mistake of thinking that it was only a sort of game. No one can read Feuquières without realizing that the purposes and objectives were not only real but sound. The best generals of the day had the same instinct for destroying the forces of the enemy that those of later times had, although they realized that this could only be accomplished with a certain preponderance of power, either in quantity or quality. Unlike some of their successors, they understood that if this preponderance were lacking, they had to use other means. If they were seldom or never able to destroy the enemy's forces, the reason was the defective nature of the instruments with which they had to work. The nature of these defects will become more apparent in the following pages. Feuquières's value lies in having concentrated in his work the scope and practice of the military art as it was in his day.

PUYSÉGUR

In his *Art de la guerre par principes et par règles,* Marshal Puységur (1656-1743), a distinguished soldier whose career, begun during the Franco-Dutch War in 1677, extended through the War of the Polish Succession to 1735, undertook a systematic treatment of the art of war, reducing it to a basis of rules and standard practice. He was not interested in establishing a new system, nor in making marked changes in existing practice, as were so many of the writers of the period, although he did not hesitate to suggest improvements which were adopted in some cases. The great value of his work is historical rather than theoretical. It did not exercise a great influence on subsequent tactical development, by no means so much as the works of Folard, for example. There is no place, however, where one can obtain a clearer picture of the tactics of the French Army during the first half of the eighteenth century, and of the difficulties which those tactics entailed.

The main thesis of Puységur was that it is not necessary to learn war by experience only, that it is, in fact, highly undesirable to do so. It was his intention to reduce field warfare to rules and principles, as had already been done with sieges. While he was doing this, Puységur repeatedly demonstrated his clear understanding of the actualities of warfare. An example was his discussion of the suppression of the pike. This weapon, he declared, was used almost entirely for resisting cavalry.[9] It was always employed, during the first two wars in which he served, massed in the center of the battalion front as the *corps de bataille*. Even if the pikemen held firm, he pointed out, they could do nothing to protect the *manches* from the cavalry in their front. If the *manches* were overthrown, the pikemen could be outflanked and attacked from the rear, in which case they could hardly defend themselves. Therefore, in such a disposition, they were of no utility against cavalry, their principal employment and justification. They were not used in any other manner under Louis XIV. Puységur concluded that the suppression was justified because pikes were very rarely useful.

This same practical approach was demonstrated in his attitude towards fire power. "It is a fact known to everyone in war that the greater fire silences the other." [10] While this greater volume would usually be delivered by superiority in numbers, he believed that a smaller force trained to fire more rapidly *and accurately* could gain fire superiority over a larger one. It is significant that this veteran soldier, writing at the end of a long career, had a much sounder understanding of fire than many of his contemporaries, including Saxe and Frederick the Great, had at this period. The latter came to recognize the importance of fire power only after having conducted many campaigns.

Puységur stated clearly the facts concerning fire power, which Folard and his successors ignored.

But not merely in such places [broken and rough country], can actions occur only by fire, but in all the posts that one defends, where assailants can frequently advance only on a small front. Thus it is necessary that he [the enemy] be made to quit his post by the superiority of one's fire; and when you have succeeded, then you can seek to come to hand-to-hand conflict. Thus one improperly neglects in our troops to learn thoroughly how to employ firearms effectively. Nevertheless, it is easy to correct this, and to know how to use effectively all the kinds of arms which we ought to use in the various actions of war;

but because we do not know how to instruct the soldiers well, we believe we can exonerate ourselves from this by making use of an advantageous pretext, i.e., that it is not necessary to accustom the French soldier to fire, and that it is necessary to make him charge sword in hand. Such an idea is not accepted by people who study war by principles, and that surprises only those who are not trained in it. I am quite aware one ought to strive for hand-to-hand conflict wherever the situation permits.

But since you have an enemy opposed to you, who is always against letting you do that which is profitable to you: if on his side he believes himself superior in fighting with firearms, he will seek the means of avoiding combats in the open; and if you wish to attack him, you will often be compelled to do it in some posts, which he has studied [in order] to profit from the location, or will have procured the advantages for himself by works; and then it is necessary to resort to fire action, before being able to come to shock action. Moreover, firearms destroy the most men, especially today. . . . My proposition is not advanced lightly but with knowledge. Thus it is necessary to seek superiority in everything to our enemies neglecting nothing to that end, informing ourselves how the foreign nations train their troops, adopting from them that which is recognized as better than our practice.[11]

This is sound doctrine and would have been considered obvious had not the writings of Folard obscured the issue. He and Mesnil-Durand ignored completely the problem of the enemy's dispositions in drawing up their systems. Puységur stood out among the writers of his day in his understanding of the importance of fire and the necessity of fire action in many, if not most, battles. Moreover, he recognized as fallacious the idea that French troops were unsuitable for fire combat and need not be trained for it.

Puységur discussed infantry drill and maneuver at considerable length [12] in a portion of his work originally composed for the instruction of the Duke of Burgundy, grandson of Louis XIV. This discussion is of great value historically for its exposition of contemporary tactics with all the complications which open ranks and the non-cadenced step involved. Puységur used the standard battalion of twelve companies of fusiliers and one of grenadiers, each of fifty men, providing a total of six hundred fifty drawn up on a depth of five. His own preference, however, was for a battalion about 50 percent greater in strength.

He declared that since the length of the halberds had been fixed at six and a half feet, there was a means of regulating the distance between ranks to two halberd lengths. Thus the twelve-foot intervals actually measured thirteen feet, which made no practical difference. There was still no standard means of regulating the distance between files, two feet, nor from the rear of one division to the head of the next in column. Each regiment regulated this matter to suit itself.

He emphasized the great importance of uniformity for all the intervals both in battle and in marching, and among all the battalions and squadrons. He opposed all useless complications in drill, saying that "it is necessary to simplify things as much as one can." Also, a little further on he said, "Thus all our drills ought to have only the end of rendering the troops disciplined and drilled to know how to move themselves and to fight in all places. It is this to which one must adhere uniquely, and omit all that which is superfluous." [13]

What Puységur had to say demonstrated the complications which maneuvering then involved. The manner of performing the "simplest" maneuver, defiling, further demonstrated these complications. Defiling means breaking the battalion to right or left for the purpose of marching forward from the respective flank of its position. After the closed ranks were adopted, this was done by a simultaneous quarter-wheel of all the divisions of the battalion. (Division is here used to refer to any subordinate unit of the battalion which might form the element for maneuver; the required front would determine which unit would be used.) Companies with open ranks could not defile by this method because their depth exceeded their front. Thus, if the battalion performed the maneuver in ten divisions, these would have a front of twelve men each.[14] Since there was an interval of twelve feet between each rank, however, the depth of the formation was forty-eight feet, or twenty-four paces, while the front was only twelve paces (counting one pace for each file), so that it was obviously impossible to perform this maneuver by simultaneous wheels. The depth of each division in marching would exceed the front by twenty-four paces (counting intervals) and the whole column, instead of occupying the one hundred thirty paces of the battalion's front, would occupy three hundred ninety-six paces, more than three times as much ground.

Puységur laid down the rule that in order for the intervals to be correct, it was absolutely necessary for the second division to

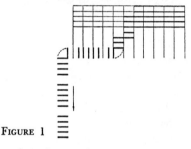

FIGURE 1

move forward at the precise moment when the fifth rank of the first division was abreast of its first rank. This maneuver is shown in Figure 1.[15]

This is not the end of the complications, for if the number of divisions was changed, then the arrangements had also to be changed; otherwise the correct intervals would not result. If the maneuver was performed in eight divisions, the front of each was fifteen men. The second division had then to step off when the fourth rank of the first division had passed three paces beyond its first rank. If the number of divisions was five, giving a front of twenty-four men, then they all had to wheel simultaneously, for their front was long enough to permit it. To keep the files straight, however, the ranks had to displace to the left a distance equal to the intervals between them. There was a further complication in that there was not room enough for the fourth and fifth ranks to do this, and so they had to divide and file to the right to leave the ground free for the following division.

A common occurrence among the troops, when the move was being made in ten divisions, was for the second division's first rank to fail to move off when the first division's fifth rank was abreast of it. If it moved out only after the first division had passed, say eight or ten paces beyond it, then at the completion of the turn the interval instead of being twelve paces would be twenty or more, and it would need to hurry its march in order to close up to the correct interval. If all the divisions did the same, the lengthening became progressive, and in a line of thirty battalions (one line of an army of sixty) this would be a very serious matter.

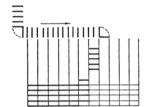

FIGURE 2

Puységur estimated that the last division of the thirtieth battalion would have to march more than two thousand paces at a rapid rate before it could resume its proper interval. This was no hypothetical case, for such occurrences were frequent in the days before the cadence was adopted.

Because the resulting columns were much longer than the front which they would occupy when deployed, forming an order of battle was extremely slow and ponderous. The method was that shown in Figure 2.[16] The time necessary to form a line of battle of thirty battalions is obvious, for the figure represents only one battalion. In order to shorten this time one had to develop a column whose length was equal to its deployed front and permitted deployment by simultaneous wheels. This was a simple matter when the ranks were closed, but with the open ranks of Puységur's time it was not so easy.

It was necessary, he said, in order to form a column of the same length as its battle front, to do so on two, three, or not more than four divisions. The complications involved were those already mentioned in connection with defiling. They are shown in Figure 3.[17] Because of the depth of the formation, there was insufficient room for the second, third, and fourth ranks to complete the movement without their left sides breaking. Puységur declared that the left part of each of these ranks must move straight ahead until they had cleared the pivots of the divisions to their left, after which they could move to their left in order to redress their files and then complete the movement.

FIGURE 3

It was possible to form such a column with eight divisions, if the intervals between ranks and between divisions were cut in half. Puységur's comment on this is enlightening and clearly indicates one of the difficulties which the absence of cadence entailed.

But it is very difficult for battalions to march a long time with such small intervals from one rank to another without confounding themselves, so much the more since the ground is frequently uneven, and often the ranks, even with the greatest intervals, must become confused. . . . Independent of these considerations, as I have often studied troops in their march, I have recognized that there was only one interval large enough from one rank to another which facilitated marching, and that it was the only means of avoiding confusion in it, seeing that marching in order, when the ranks are so closed up, demands of the soldier a great concentration which one cannot expect from him over a long time.[18]

Puységur concluded, consequently, that one must keep the six-pace interval. He pointed out that the bulk of the French troops closed to sword's point (the point of the swords of the preceding rank) for wheeling in eight, ten, or twelve divisions. This added a further complication, for the troops must halt at the completion of the wheel, after which each rank stepped off at three- or four-pace intervals to resume the necessary space for marching. To form a battle line, the troops had to close up again, and upon completing their movement, the four rear ranks had to about-face, resume their former intervals, and then about-face again. Puységur believed that this not only spoiled the troops' appearance at reviews, but was very dangerous in the presence of the enemy.

It is perfectly clear from the foregoing discussion that the complications of even the simplest maneuver were numerous and time consuming. These complications largely explained the deliberate and indecisive nature of warfare down to the middle of the eighteenth century. Within a period of some twenty years they were to be eliminated by the, to us, simple invention of the cadenced step. This ended the necessity for open ranks and slow, deliberate maneuvers. It further eliminated many complications in marching which will shortly become evident. Puységur never conceived of this solution.

The problem of making marches in the period before the adoption of the cadenced step was a serious one, requiring careful planning and precise rules. It must be remembered that the order of march of these unitary armies had to have an exact relation to the order of battle so that if contact was made unexpectedly with the enemy the army could take up its combat order as expeditiously as the tactics of the day permitted. A long passage [19] described with extreme clarity the difficulties of such marches. Puységur supposed a line of forty battalions marching in a column. Such a line alternately lengthened and shortened as the battalions first ran to overtake those ahead and then halted to allow them to resume their proper intervals. By the time the fortieth battalion arrived on the ground from which the first had left, the latter was some fifty-five hundred to six thousand *toises* (some six or seven miles) on its way. The former would arrive at the new camp three and a half to four hours after the latter, having made perhaps two hundred halts in a march of three leagues.

Puységur devoted much space to giving the rules for the various types of marches and situations which one would meet on a campaign. He supposed an army of forty-eight battalions and eighty squadrons in two full lines on standard formation, infantry in the center and cavalry divided between the wings, the two lines being two hundred to four hundred yards apart. The marches were made in eight columns, into which the army naturally divided, the right and left wings of cavalry and the right and left of the infantry of each line forming the eight columns.[20]

The marches, to be ideal, should approach as nearly as possible that of an army by its front. Each division should have the shortest possible route to its new camp. All should leave at the same time, and all parts of each division should get under way at the same time. The column should put itself on the march by the right, its right battalion or squadron marching straight forward. The rest should wheel to the right and, on reaching the ground from which the first departed, wheel successively to the left to place themselves in column behind it. The column should arrive at the left of the position which it was to occupy in the new camp. On reaching the left of the new position, the lead battalion would make a right quarter-wheel and move off, with each following battalion doing the same on the same ground in order to move to its position. Upon the completion of this maneuver, they all should wheel to the left and would be in the correct position.

If the column arrived at the right of its new position instead of the left, it would be compelled to defile in the manner shown in Figure 2. This consumed much time and must be avoided if it was at all possible. The same was true if one started with the right battalion but marched from the left of the position. Thus if there were fifteen battalions in the column, the first would have to cross the front of fourteen battalions, the second that of thirteen, etc.[21]

To show the composition of a march, organized as Puységur described, the following diagram will be useful. The army is formed on two lines, each of which is composed of four divisions. These divisions are each composed of twenty squadrons or twelve battalions. Each division is subdivided into brigades of four battalions or squardons. Using figures to designate cavalry brigades and letters for infantry brigades, the army is drawn up as shown below.[22]

| 2 | 10 | 18 | 14 | 6 | B | F | L | | I | E | A | | 5 | 13 | 17 | 9 | 1 |
| 4 | 12 | 20 | 16 | 8 | D | H | N | | M | G | C | | 7 | 15 | 19 | 11 | 3 |

Each wing of cavalry forms two columns and the infantry forms four. In order of march, the army would appear as shown below.

6	8	L	N	A	C	1	3
14	16	F	H	E	G	9	11
18	20	B	D	I	M	17	19
10	12					13	15
2	4					5	7

Enough has been said to give an idea of the formal nature of marches in the eighteenth century and the complications which greatly inhibited the rapid movement of armies. The limitations of the maneuvers available to eighteenth-century infantry rendered it very inflexible. It was essential, therefore, that its order of march be exactly calculated to enable it to take its order of battle as rapidly as those maneuvers would permit. This could never be done instantaneously, as it was at the end of the century, so one needed to be sure that no countermarches were required to put the order of march into order of battle. Puységur showed this and the complications involved more clearly than any other writer of the time.

Puységur was the first writer to submit war to such systematic treatment and he was recognized and commended for it, especially for the actual demonstrations of his principles in a hypothetical war between the Seine and the Loire. His work must have been extremely valuable to serious young officers of his day who wished to learn their profession. It is certainly a valuable source today on the military practices and conditions of the first half of the eighteenth century. No other work so clearly indicates the complications of the still rather primitive tactics of the French Army down to the Seven Years' War.

The Makers of Systems

FOLARD

It was in the atmosphere of self-criticism and search for improvement, brought on by the unsuccessful War of the Spanish Succession, that the Chevalier de Folard (1669-1752), first of the great tactical writers, published his works. He was himself a veteran of that war, having served with distinction in the Italian campaigns and later on in Flanders. After the conclusion of the war, he served under Charles XII of Sweden. His ideas were strongly influenced by the experiences of his various campaigns, both in French and Swedish service. He was also a student of classical military history, and it was in connection with his determination to publish a new and accurate translation of Polybius' works that his military ideas were made public.

Folard published his *Nouvelles découvertes sur la guerre* in 1724. This work combined the exposition of some of his military views with a prospectus of the greater work to come. Folard, like Puységur, rejected the idea that war is a trade to be learned only through practical experience as French officers strongly believed, for there are occasions where experience will not serve.[1] The implication is that study, similar to his, is also necessary.

Folard went on to discuss the tactics of the Greeks and Romans which he claimed as the source of his own. It becomes clear in this that he did not understand the implications of the subject. He much preferred the tactics of the Greeks. "The troops of the Romans were not exempt from defects in regard to the manner in which they ranged themselves in battle. The order of the Greeks was, without doubt, simpler and more nearly perfect; but defective, if one examines the nature of the arms of their infantry."[2] This is the source of his preference for the massive and rigid formations of the Greeks, rather than for the flexibility of the Romans. He did recognize the difficulties of the former in broken ground, which he attributed to their uniformity of arms.

He turned from this subject to the discussion of his forthcoming major work. Here he mentioned the column, the discovery of which he declared he owed to what Polybius had to say on the Macedonian phalanx. "This manner of fighting by column is, in my opinion, superior to all others. It also forms the fundamental principle of my tactics; for it does not appear to me that any force would be capable of resisting it. The whole world talks today about the column; few understand it, and still less the manner of forming it systematically." [3]

This fundamental article of Folard's tactical faith formed one of the bases of his system. The column was first used, he declared, by Epaminondas, "the greatest man of infantry there ever was." He declared mistakenly [4] that Epaminondas owed his victories of Leuctra and Mantinea to the column. Finally Folard concluded with a dissertation on orders of battle which subject formed an important part of his system.

Folard's major work was the *Histoire de Polybe . . . avec un commentaire* which began to appear in 1727. His part was the commentary on the military operations described in the text with frequent discussions of the different types in terms of modern warfare and with adaptations of his own tactical system to the various situations. This work was prefaced by a *Traité de la colonne, la manière de la former, & de combattre dans cet ordre,* which set forth the major elements of his system of columns.

The essential elements of Folard's system of tactics are two in number: the column and the mixed order of battle. The great importance which he laid upon the column was based upon his famous principle of shock.

Our battalions know neither how to attack nor [how to] defend themselves independently of one another, because they fight on so little depth that they can easily be pierced and broken, [an] essential violation of the rules of tactics. The true force of a corps lies in its weight; or in the depth of its files, in their union, in their pressing [together], and that of its ranks at sword's point. That weight renders the flanks as strong, or almost as strong, as the front. By that method a battalion is in a state to resist, to overthrow every battalion which does not fight on this principle, and to move with more facility and agility than the others, whereas a corps, which fights on a great front and little depth, maneuvers with difficulty, and cannot avoid the wavering so ordinary in corps ranged on too great an extent. In war, the weight of the files remedies all, and augments the force and the rapidity of shock. One ought to regard it as a maxim, that every battalion which attacks, ranged on a very great deal of depth and little front, although weaker, ought to overcome another stronger one, ranged according to the ordinary method, although that one extends beyond it on the wings. In fighting in this manner, all the force of a battalion is in itself, without its defeat influencing those which it has alongside.

I believe, however, that this is not sufficient. Something more solid is necessary, which secures us more against the great numbers which can crush us and envelop us. It is necessary to support and cover the small corps by larger ones, capable of acting by themselves, and to hinder the ruin of a line by distributing them on all its front, particularly at the wings and at the center.[5]

Having thus set forth what he considered to be the true principle of infantry action, Folard proceeded to define a column.

The column is a corps of infantry, closed and *suppressed*,[6] that is to say, a corps ranged on a rectangle, of which the front is much less than the depth, which is not less formidable by the weight of its shock, than by the force with which it pierces and resists everywhere equally, and against all sorts of efforts. The ranks and the files ought to be so closed and condensed that the soldiers conserve only as much space as is necessary for them for marching, and for using their weapons.[7]

Folard thus wished a solid column in which the intervals were suppressed and all the troops formed in a heavy mass. The column was to be composed of from one to six battalions, depending upon the ground on which it was to act. It would always be best to form two columns, rather than one which was too large. The front of the column was to be composed of twenty, twenty-four, or, at most, thirty files on open unobstructed ground; although in broken or forested ground, the number could be as high as sixty, but not more. He felt that anything less than twenty or more than sixty was defective. In action, there would be no intervals between the various battalions which formed the sections of the columns. The officers would be at the head and along the flanks. Folard called the flanks faces because flank implies weakness, and there was no weak side to a column. The grenadier companies would not be a part of the column, but would rather form at its rear or along the faces. The battalions were to have a strength of five hundred, four hundred fusiliers and one hundred men armed with partisans.

The column was to be divided down the middle into a right and a left *manche*. "I subdivide further each *manche* into groups of five files each; I call the three to the right, *Divisions of the*

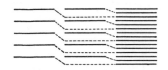

FIGURE 4

right, the three of the left, *Divisions of the left.* The two first of the wings, *Divisions of the wings;* the two following, *first division of the right, second of the left;* the two last of the center, *third of the right, third of the left;* which makes thirty files." [8] (It would appear to the author that there is a misprint in this quotation. Where Folard says "first division of the right, second of the left," it would seem to make sense only as "second of the right, second of the left." The italics are Folard's.) This division was absolutely necessary, Folard said, in order to resume position in line, or in combat to divide the column into two from head to tail, in order to fall on the right and the left flanks of enemy battalions, when one had pierced his line.

To form a column from a battalion, Folard would have the latter double, triple, quadruple, and quintuple its files. The battalion being of five hundred fifty men, including grenadiers, on a depth of five, at the command to triple the files, the *manche* of the center would file to the right into the right *manche,* first center rank behind first right rank, second behind second, etc. The left *manche* would do likewise at the same time, its first rank filing to the right behind the first rank of the center *manche,* the second behind the second, etc. The grenadiers would go to their position at the tail or face of the column.[9] See Figure 4. (The intervals are exaggerated for clarity, and the grenadiers are not shown.)

Such was the composition and formation of Folard's famous column. What were its properties, and how was it to be used in combat? Folard was most emphatic about this.

The column formed according to our principles is more prompt and more disposed to all sorts of maneuvers. It can make them as a unit, and by sections. It decomposes and reforms itself in an instant, divides from head to tail, and doubles according to events by rapid and unexpected movements, even in action and in the warmest affairs.

All ground is proper for it; it defiles and forms itself by a single command, without the movements which it makes giving the enemy the time and the opportunity to charge it, so great is the promptness of its maneuvers. The corps which compose it can attack and defend themselves independently of one another. Finally, the column has more activity and more force in its shock than any formation which has been invented. It has the solidity and the impulsion of the doubled phalanx, of which Polybius speaks, without having its weakness. Its arms are perfect, as we will make evident in its place. We make that perfection to consist in their diversity, in their intermixture, so that one [arm] finds itself supported by the other.

It is morally impossible that a column can ever be broken. Where is the corps of cavalry, however superior it may be, which dares to hurl and commit itself on a mass armed and formed in such a manner, and to penetrate that forest of spontoons, of halberds, of partisans, and of bayonets on the end of fusils, and sustain in addition a prodigious fire, regulated and uniform, which does not change? The column has nothing weak; it can make head to all sides and reform itself easily. It is a bundle of spines that one does not know how to grasp, and of which the shock, the solidity, the weight, and the force is so violent, that there is nothing which can refuse it passage; nothing that it does not open and that it does not break; moreover, as I have so often repeated, all ground, every situation is proper for it. It undergoes all kinds of changes. One varies it, one changes it according to different circumstances, and its force is in itself; its movements are simple, active, and rapid. It is the only order which reveals the strength of infantry.[10]

Thus in Folard's conception, these heavy columns had all the properties which critics found lacking in lines. They were the answer to the tactical problems which were then occupying the best minds in the Army.

A battle would involve the advance of the columns which would rupture the enemy's line in several places. They would then roll it up, dividing from head to tail for that purpose. In his dogmatic way, Folard denied that there was any recourse whatever for an enemy, drawn up in the customary manner, to counter such an attack. He would be helpless before it.[11] Folard did not mind if his columns were outflanked, or even if they were surrounded. Such were their properties that they could meet these situations without peril. A column in such a position would not remain motionless, but would hurl itself forward and break through the outflanking troops. In the second situation, it would split along its length, and the two *manches* would attack the troops which surrounded them.

For those who accused his column of excessive weakness on the sides, Folard had only scorn. A corps of twenty-four or thirty files on a depth of forty-six would have a depth of at least twenty-four if attacked on a side. "Where then is *that excess of weakness?* Where are *these thin sides?*" [12] The attackers would be on a depth of four or five, if formed in the customary manner, and Folard asked if it wouldn't be a marvel if these files of five should break those of twenty-four. Even if the column was surrounded, the files would still be twelve or fifteen deep.

No situation, therefore, found the column without resource. But Folard was not satisfied with this. Although he stated repeatedly that the force of infantry is in its shock and in the weight of the bodies composing it, he claimed that the column was a formation proper for fire and that it could actually deliver a better furnished fire than deployed lines. This is the more astonishing in that every other man on the front and faces of the column was a pikeman. Such a formation was obviously improper for fire.

In his first references to fire,[13] Folard would fire in the Dutch fashion by platoons or divisions, which is superior to the fire by ranks.[14] He admitted that this method was less proper to the column than "to the battalion otherwise disposed." Later Folard became less modest in his claims. Discussing a hypothetical case where four columns, of two sections each, attacked an enemy line, he said:

I go further . . . If the four columns advance on the front E [see Figure 5] which intercepts their advance, not only will they pierce

[it], but I claim, moreover, that their fire is triple that of the enemy. One will be surprised, but the matter is, nevertheless, incontestable.

Let us consider the different fires of these columns ordered in the manner that I range them and opposed to the line, EG. Is the fire of E (for it is unnecessary to speak of that of the line G, which cannot furnish any) comparable to the fire which emanates from the heads and the sides, HL, of my columns: fire so much more terrible, more deadly and more dangerous, since the shots or discharges are oblique, crossed and concentrated as at M; so that that which appears and which presents itself between the intervals or the gaps between the columns, would never know how to sustain the quantity and the violence of this direct and oblique fire, which has no end according to my method.

I suppose that the enemy endures all that gust of shots, without budging and without losing patience. I wish even that these lines of fire be not such as I represent (for although they are such in reality, it is here only a supposition), and that the battalions, EG, in order to protect themselves from such a storm, or thinking to avoid it, attack the columns, and that the corps opposed to the heads of the columns fold themselves upon, embrace, and encompass them to the points N. Will these battalions, and those which outflank them on their wings be at their ease between the several fires of these columns? Will the contest be very equal between these thin battalions which attack them, and corps of such formidable depth, with arms of length [pikes], with which the enemy finds himself unprovided? How can that be possible? I do not see it.[15]

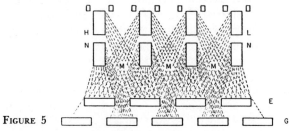

FIGURE 5

This is an example of one of Folard's "proofs." That the battalions will receive a fire three times as great as they deliver he proved by his diagram, which shows that each battalion, save those on the flank, would receive fire from the head of the column opposite, and from the faces of the columns to the right and left of it. There was no mention of how many ranks and files would fire;

no mention of the fact that every other man in the front rank and outer files was armed with a pike and was, consequently, unable to fire; no mention of the difficulty which the men would have in delivering this oblique fire, which required them to march in one direction while shooting in another. It is obvious, as critics were quick to point out, that the adjacent columns were more apt to suffer from this oblique fire than the enemy. The columns were likely to have their leading angles shot away.

Folard claimed that there was not a single useless man in his column, "whether for shock, whether for fire, whether for swiftness of his movements." [16] He did not at any time make it apparent how he intended to make use of the fire of the men in the interior.

The last point about Folard's column concerns the use of pikes, or rather partisans, twelve and a half feet long.[17] The suppression of pikes was not the result of a sudden decision by the War Ministry, nor was it the result of theory. It was rather the result of the growing effectiveness of firearms which made their increased number more valuable than the defensive power of pikes. Yet Folard railed against this suppression and wished to restore the use of pikes, although he adduced no apparent advantage for them, save their greater length. His argument against the very practical reason for suppressing the pike is typical.

The strongest argument against the pike is a pure sophism. Those who do not approve of this arm say that a third or a fifth of pikemen would eliminate a third or a fifth of the fire of the infantry. Bad argument which proves nothing, if one knows a little of the character of the French nation, and which scarcely proves more in regard to the others. True valor consists not in combats which are made at a distance; but in shock and sudden attacks. That is the only road which brings us to victory.[18]

After stating the sound reason for dispensing with pikes, he tried to becloud the issue by resorting to flights of rhetoric and totally unrelated examples, instead of answering the argument. His dislike of the fire battle with its heavy losses led him to seek an alternative. He felt that he had found it in charging rapidly upon the enemy in his heavy columns. Mistaken or not this is legitimate enough, but nowhere does Folard indicate in what way the bayonet was deficient for this purpose. Folard was apparently so opposed to fire action that he wished to gain the slight advantage of the pike's additional length, though how it could be very effective with only alternate pikemen and fusiliers is somewhat difficult to see. In spite of the contradiction involved, he was at great pains to show the intense fire power of his column!

The second major element in Folard's system of tactics was the mixture of arms.[19]   He did not mean by this merely the mixture of infantry weapons, such as fusils, pikes, and spontoons, although he did insist upon the importance of this too. He had in mind something more, namely, the mixture, in line, of infantry with cavalry, which he regarded as an arm of the infantry.

The contemporary system of arranging armies was all wrong, said Folard, even if it was practiced by the Greeks and the Romans as well as by modern nations. He did not believe that anyone had noted the "absurdities and faults" of the contemporary order of battle. This he attributed to failure, through sloth, prejudice, or usage, to use their minds. Cavalry placed on the wings was separated from the infantry, and the two arms could no longer sustain each other. Each fought its separate action in battle. If the cavalry was beaten, then the infantry, finding itself alone, was certain to be defeated also, as at the battle of Rocroi which he cited. He asked what could be done if one or both cavalry wings was attacked and in danger. It was possible to despatch some squadrons from the reserve, which seldom contained any infantry. If this failed then all was lost, for it was not possible to draw troops from some part of the line if the battle was engaged over all the front. To do so was a delicate maneuver which a vigilant opponent would not fail to note and exploit. This condition was the result of the failure to sustain each of the arms by the other.

The purpose of the mixed order of battle was to obtain a mutual support of the two arms. Folard did not claim to be the originator of this type of battle order whose modern origin he attributed to Montecuccoli. He attributed to the mixed order the victory of the Imperialists at Pavia in 1525 where, he says, they mixed 1,500 to 2,000 arquebusiers among the cavalry. Many of the great generals of more recent times had made use of this method, said Folard, such generals as Coligny, Gustavus Adolphus, the Prince (Condé apparently), and especially Gassion and Turenne. Folard did not claim that the mixed order would absolutely prevent defeat at the hands of a vigorous and well-handled cavalry, especially if one's own cavalry was feeble.

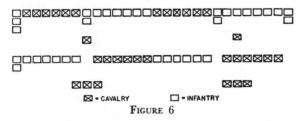

FIGURE 6

This figure represents the center brigade and left-wing brigades only of Folard's line of battle. The right wing reproduces the formation of the left wing, i.e., with three more brigades in each line.

In Folard's order of battle (see Figure 6), the army was drawn up in the usual two lines. The infantry would be on a depth of eight ranks. He would alternate cavalry and infantry by brigades in the line, the cavalry by half or whole brigades between the infantry. He would support each of the wing brigades of cavalry by a column composed of three or four battalions on a depth of twelve or sixteen ranks. Each column would be hedged with pikes. Similar columns would be placed in the center of the line on both sides of the center brigade of infantry. The squadrons would be interlaced with platoons of twenty-five grenadiers or élite fusiliers. These would, at first, remain at the rear of the squadrons, ready, on the instant that one reached the enemy, to slip into his intervals and take him in the flank with fire and bayonet.

The second line would be the same as the first, except that behind each first-line infantry brigade, Folard would place a cavalry brigade, and behind each first-line cavalry brigade, one of infantry. The reserve, composed of dragoons, would be in third line, divided into three corps at the wings and center.   Between the lines, at wings and center, would be the hussars.

What advantages did Folard advance for his order of battle? They are many and varied.   He said that a line of alternate squadrons and battalions was undesirable because these units were too small.   If they were as large as they had been a hundred and fifty years before, he would prefer such lines, but to obtain units large enough for this purpose would require overthrowing the whole existing system of tactics.   Therefore, he based his order on the alternating brigades.   With each cavalry brigade supported by an infantry brigade in second line and vice versa, each arm would sustain the other reciprocally and yet be in large enough units to maintain itself firmly, independently of the others.

He strongly justified his platoons of infantry interlaced with the squadrons (not shown in the figure).   He declared that they had nothing to fear if their squadrons were routed for they could join either the columns or the second-line infantry.   The latter should advance as soon as they see the action in balance, however, and restore the situation instead of waiting until matters were in their last extremity.

An even greater advantage of this order was, Folard claimed, that the enemy could not fall upon a brigade of infantry without engaging a cavalry brigade at the same time.   With the infantry bristling with pikes, the enemy cavalry (or infantry) could hardly avoid being terrified, if it fought in the ordinary manner.   The mixture of arms would also simplify the general-in-chief's task, largely freeing him from the details of the action and allowing him to concentrate on overall supervision.

Folard believed his order had yet another great advantage. He did not have to resort to the feeble resource of felled trees, wagons, or *chevaux de frise* to cover the flanks of his army.   He covered them instead with columns, "capable of resisting and rendering vain and useless every effort of the most vigorous cavalry. The wings being so well flanked, they have nothing to fear even if the enemy outflanks them or envelops them with a great number of squadrons." [20]

This is one of the roles of his columns.   The other is to reinforce the first line especially at the center "in order to make an effort at this point, as the principal blow whence depends the victory; for all is lost when an army is ruptured at the center, as I have so often repeated." [21]

There will be some, Folard declared, who will say that the enemy, finding one drawn up in such an order, will himself oppose a similar order to it. This is not an objection to his order, but rather an avowal of its strength, Folard asserted. Such a procedure will not be easy to accomplish, as the enemy general must overthrow all his dispositions—a very delicate maneuver. The result would not be any more fortunate for him, as he would have only fire and bayonets to oppose to troops also armed with pikes.

If the enemy fights in conformity to the usual practice, cavalry on the wings and infantry in the center, he will be unable to avoid being beaten and ruptured on nearly the entire front of his line. If the cavalry attacks the wings, it will be unable to attack a squadron without having infantry before it as the same time. If the rest of the cavalry falls on the brigade of infantry alongside, I ask if it will find what it expects there, having to deal with two different arms at the same time. It is necessary that it consider, moreover, disengaging itself from platoons, among which I would like to see a number of partisans, the platoons harassing it and turning it from all sides, without its having anything to oppose to them. It sees itself exposed to the combined fire of the battalions, which being thick and making front to all sides without wavering and without breaking, moving with facility, and attacking at point of pike, fearing nothing, while the columns, somewhat extended beyond the line, taking all in the flank and making a hail of fire, fall on the flanks of the opposing squadrons and battalions.[22]

Thus it is that Folard conceived of his battle line in action, and such were the advantages which he attributed to it. The objection which Folard had to the standard order of battle was well taken. It would indeed be desirable to provide greater mutual support between the arms than the old order permitted. It is an open question, however, whether Folard's order gave the answer. Infantry and cavalry fight in different ways. While infantry can fight either by advancing to the attack or by receiving it in its post, cavalry is lost if it gives combat in any other way than by charging. To receive an attack motionless is fatal as the French were to find out at the battle of Minden in 1759. Just how was this intermixed line to fight? If the cavalry advanced to charge by itself, it would present a line of fragments for the enemy to take in the many exposed flanks and leave the infantry line in similar case. If the cavalry, which depended upon its velocity, slowed its pace to that of the infantry, it would lose much of its force. In this formation, the cavalry is chained to the infantry rather than supported by it. As to the platoons placed in the cavalry intervals, the same objection seems to hold. Unless the cavalry advanced at the slowest pace, it is not apparent just how the foot could keep up with it.

Another pretension which Folard maintained about this formation was the claim that its flanks, being covered by his columns, were absolutely secure and could accept with confidence any attack made upon them. In other words, Folard claimed that an army in his formation could be outflanked and enveloped without any untoward results, a claim not generally conceded by his contemporaries.

During his own lifetime, Folard was subjected to vigorous criticism, as might well be expected, considering how far he departed from the current tactical ideas and practices. He devoted considerable space in his various works to "proving" the correctness of his views in answer to various objections which he said had been made against his system. He admitted, or implied, that his critics were men of rank and reputation but was scathing in his replies to them. From his language, it is clearly apparent that he was highly incensed at having his creation subjected to criticism. One of the proposals was to replace his column by fully-deployed battalions placed one behind another with intervals between them.

I appeal to the experts whether these objections are very forcible, and whether these means of improvement which they propose are actually reasonable, sound, and worthy of serious debate; they would doubtless answer no, and that they merit no reply. It is necessary to reply here, however, although we are entirely convinced that those who propose them have understood nothing in our system. It would appear evident by all that they say that, in regard to infantry, they understand infinitely less about it than the generality of officers.

When one listens to them (that is to say the majority) without any regard to who they are and without even taking into account their rank and reputation, one no longer regards them with so much respect in their decisions.

And further on:

In truth, we are ashamed to refute such quibbles, we will have still more of them in that which remains to reply to in our adversaries, who spend their time criticizing a demonstrated method which ought to be a perpetual subject of meditation for them, rather than of dispute.[23]

More serious criticisms were stated by a Colonel Terson and General de Savornin. Both officers prefaced their criticisms by giving general praise to Folard's system and then proceeded to criticize it devastatingly in detail. Both pointed out the liability to being outflanked which Folard's system involved, since the increased depth could only be gained by contracting the front. Both insisted that the flank columns were not enough to guarantee the flanks. The former reported that while Folard blamed generals who allowed themselves to be outflanked, "he falls into the same fault with gaiety of heart [a phrase which aroused Folard's ire] and that he even declares that he does not care about being outflanked," [24] which is contradictory. Both pointed out that attacks upon the flank columns would compel them to halt and face outwards which in turn would compel the whole line to halt or lose its flank protection. Repeated attacks would hold the whole line motionless under the combined infantry and artillery fire of the defense and thus deny to Folard's attack its vaunted shock, its one and only resource. This was the method used by the French at Marignano in 1515.

Folard never, at any point, met squarely the objection of halting his line by attacking the flank columns. He "proved" that he did not have to fear attacks on his flanks, by reasserting that his columns, being unbreakable, protected them completely. This was just the point to which his critics objected. Reiteration did not answer the criticism, for it was not a question of whether his columns could repulse all attacks, but, that in doing so, they and his line must halt under hostile fire.

Savornin also criticized Folard's system [25] for its inability to use fire, for he denied that it could do so. He also advanced the accurate criticism that once in range of the enemy it could make no change whatever in its formations because of its method of ployment. In both cases, he sustained his criticism by unanswerable arguments. He concluded his article by wishing that there was nothing to criticize in Folard's column or tactics, for he did not agree with those who found no good in Folard's system. His estimate did not differ much from the more pungently expressed judgment of Frederick the Great who said that Folard "had buried diamonds in a dung heap."

What then can be concluded about Folard's system? Folard was apparently the first to propose the use of columns in battle, to increase the offensive power of troops, and to increase their mobility and maneuverability. There is little or no dispute about the advantage which the column has in ease of movement over the line. This was a secondary point with Folard, however. He was far more interested in the offensive and defensive power of columns. He had reacted from one extreme and fallen into the contrary one of ignoring, or missing completely, the lessons of the recent wars on the preponderance of fire power.[26]

The major faults of his system become apparent to anyone who studies it, and all critics, contemporary and subsequent, are pretty much agreed upon them. The first is that his column was too heavy and massive to be controlled, directed, and rallied—a point in which Folard was not interested, since he did not expect it ever to be repulsed. Secondly, his column had little fire power, and was not proper for that form of combat, however much Folard refused to admit it. Thirdly, his orders of battle were too short and were subject to flanking, an evil which his critics could not dismiss with the lack of concern which Folard showed. It is interesting that nowhere, as far as I know, did Folard face the objection that flank attacks would halt his battle line. His answer was always that such attacks would not break the flank columns.

In spite of all this, Folard exercised considerable and continual influence. There was a group of officers which accepted his system, and a far larger group which, like Savornin, accepted his basic ideas, while rejecting his specific system. Though the former group long existed, being renewed in the next generation by a new version of his system, it had only a transitory influence on actual practice in French tactics. Its influence on theoretical discussion, however, long continued. The larger group, composed of those who were not extreme partisans of the *ordre profond,* but representing all those who were dissatisfied with existing tactics, continued to seek a practical application of Folard's ideas, or rather a more flexible system of battle tactics than that which was then in existence.

S A X E

Mes rêveries by Marshal Maurice de Saxe (1696-1750), by far the most distinguished soldier among eighteenth-century French military authors, is one of the great military classics. It has a vigor of language which matches the freshness of its ideas. This is because one of Saxe's strongest characteristics was a disdain of routine and an interest in obtaining new methods or improvements upon current practices. It is not a systematic treatment of war, but rather a presentation of Saxe's ideas wherever he thought that they were new or original.

Saxe had suggestions on a great variety of matters from improved clothing for the troops to improved methods of fortification. He was an inventor and had developed a series of breech-loading weapons, a new pike, a new accompanying gun, and a new suit of armor. This same enterprising spirit showed itself in other ways. He rejected the conventional methods of making fire and indicated some marked advances in this field, although to a considerable degree he disliked fire action and distrusted it. Yet his empirical mind would not let him go to the extremes of his friend, Folard. He was a strong advocate of the use of skirmishers at a time when they had long fallen into disuse. He was the first military writer to advocate a vigorous pursuit of a defeated enemy in order to complete the victory won on the battlefield. He was the first to emphasize the importance of the troops' morale on operations, and its variable and uncertain quality.[27]

In short, Saxe is by far the most stimulating military writer of the period with the single exception of Guibert, and one of the very few whose work still has a practical message for soldiers of today. The contrast with the work of Puységur, which was contemporary in composition, is extreme. The one attempted to systematize existing practice, albeit with much sound common sense; the other wished to sweep away those practices which seemed illogical to him, and to suggest improvements. The reason for the long obscurity of Saxe and his work was, no doubt, the over-shadowing of his reputation by that of Frederick the Great whose greatest campaigns came almost immediately after Saxe's death and absorbed the attention of all military men. Shortly after came Napoleon, who was to dominate the military thought of succeeding generations. Those who did study Saxe in some cases misunderstood him as Liddell Hart points out in the case of Marshal Foch,[28] or misunderstood eighteenth-century warfare.

Saxe opened his work with a general discussion of war in his foreword. He declared, "War is a science covered with darkness, in the obscurity of which one cannot move with assured step: habit and prejudices make up its base, the natural result of ignorance." [29] Other sciences are based upon fixed principles, he said. War alone is not. One has to be really capable to understand the writings of the great captains on war for their works are deficient in respect to rules and also "intricate and undigested." The mechanical part of war is dry and dull, he continued, and those works which deal with it are mediocre.

The Chevalier Follard [sic] has been the only one who has dared to cross the limits of prejudice: I approve his noble boldness. Nothing is so contemptible as being its slave: it is, moreover, a result of ignorance, and nothing proves it so much. But he goes too far: he advances an opinion and determines it success, without taking notice that this success depends upon an infinity of circumstances that human prudence knows not how to foresee. He supposes all men [to be] always brave, without taking notice that the courage of troops varies daily; that nothing is so variable; and that the true ability of a general consists in knowing how to guarantee it, by his dispositions, by his positions, and by those traits of insight which characterize the great captains. Perhaps he avoided that subject which is so immense; perhaps also he had not paid attention [to it]. It is however, of all the parts of war, the most necessary to study.[30]

Following his opening remarks, Saxe turned to the problems of raising and equipping troops. Here he showed his originality, for he advocated raising the army by compulsory military service. All men of whatever station of life should be required to serve their monarch and country for five years.[31] This was not mere conscription—already, in the period in which he wrote, the principal method for the wartime recruiting of French armies. It was rather the basic principle of universal military service used much later by Continental armies. Saxe declared that it was natural and just for citizens to take part in the defense of the state, and that if men were chosen between the ages of twenty and thirty, there would be no great loss, for those were the years given over to libertinism, seeking one's fortune, and travelling, and they were of little solace to parents; a characteristic touch. This method would supply an inexhaustible reservoir of good soldiers, but there must be no exception to its application, falling on rich and poor, noble and non-noble alike.

Saxe declared that drill was necessary to make the soldier "steady and skillful," but that it was far from deserving exclusive attention. He anticipated Napoleon in saying, "The principle of drill is the legs and not the arms: all the secret of maneuvers and combats is in the legs; it is to the legs that it is necessary to apply oneself. Whoever does otherwise is only a fool." [32] Thus like all great generals, he laid stress upon the principle of mobility as being of prime importance in warfare.

This leads Saxe quite naturally to his next point, the problem of marching. He condemned contemporary practice in this respect with great vigor. It was impossible to make any uniform movement because the troops did not march in cadence. Some wished the troops to march rapidly; others wished them to march slowly. But what could be done with troops which could not do either? He described a battalion on the march.

One would say that it is a badly fitted machine which breaks down every instant, and which only gets under way with infinite trouble. Does one wish to advance the head [of the column] promptly? Before the rear knows that the head accelerates, intervals appear; and in order to regain [its position] promptly, it is necessary for the rear to run at full speed; the head which follows that rear will do the same; which soon puts all in disorder, and which puts you in the necessity of never being able to march your troops rapidly, because you do not dare to accelerate the head.[33]

The remedy for this was to march in cadence, said Saxe, who pointed out all the now obvious advantages of that method of marching. Cadence had infinite consequences in battle, he declared, for it enabled you to increase or decrease the speed of your march at will. Without it, it was impossible to charge the enemy vigorously, he declared, and further, one reached the enemy with ranks open if one did not use it. It is in this connection that one of the strongest contrasts between the work of Saxe and that of Puységur becomes evident. The latter had much to say on the inconveniences of marching without cadence, but the solution of that problem eluded him, if he ever sought it. The former also castigated the existing method of marching, but far from ending with that, he proposed the solution.

Saxe next examined the method in which battalions were formed and fought. Each battalion touched its neighbors, since all the infantry was together and the cavalry likewise. This was contrary to common sense. In action, the battalions advanced slowly, for they could not do otherwise. The majors called out, "Close," and the center gave way making intervals between the battalions, a situation which compelled the general to halt and dress again. This would cost him the battle except that the enemy was as badly formed as he was. "What happens? Each side begins to fire, which is the depth of calamity. Finally one approaches; and one of the two sides ordinarily flees at fifty or sixty paces, more or less. Here is what one calls a charge." [34]

What he wished was the impossible, he said. He wanted two battalions which attack each other to march without wavering, folding, or breaking. Which would win in such a case, the one that "amuses" itself with firing, or the one that does not? Experienced people would tell him the latter, and they would be correct, for if one side fired and saw the other come at it through the smoke, it would be disconcerted. In order to fire, it was necessary to stop, but if one side stopped while the other kept coming, it would be overthrown.

The subject of fire was one of the few matters wherein Saxe was not forward-looking. He had little use for fire, which, he declared, caused more noise than damage. Those who relied upon it were always beaten. He claimed that if the War of the Spanish Succession had lasted longer, generals would have come to see the abuse of firing and would have resorted unfailingly to fighting with *armes blanches*. One can only wonder if Saxe would have written the same thing fifteen years later after seeing his whole front rank laid low by the British with a single discharge at Fontenoy and attack after attack upon them shattered, while they themselves were only repulsed by the deadly crossfire which he himself brought to bear against them.

It is difficult to understand how Saxe came to this point of view. He cited numerous examples of the ineffectiveness of fire, the best of which was one that he experienced at the battle of Belgrade in 1717. Two Austrian battalions fired a volley against attacking Turks at thirty paces. The volley and mêlée were practically simultaneous, and the two battalions were cut to pieces with only four or five men escaping. Among these was Saxe himself. He was later over the ground and counted only thirty-two Turkish dead from that point-blank volley, "which has not increased the esteem that I have for infantry fire." [35] That might well be the case, yet Saxe was also present at the battle of Malplaquet where some twenty-five to thirty thousand men were casualties in a single day. It is difficult to see how any man, let alone one so penetrating as Saxe, could go through such a day and retain any illusions concerning the noneffectiveness of fire.

Like most of the other writers of this period, Saxe had his own system of tactics.[36] Instead of being purely theoretical like some of the others, it was based upon ideas bearing a relationship to the actual conditions of warfare. He praised the Roman legion upon which his system was based and declared that, since he wrote for his own amusement, he would give full play to his imagination. He would form his infantry in legions, each of which was composed of four regiments which were in turn composed of four centuries. Each regiment would also have a half-century of light infantry and a half-century of cavalry. Each century would have ten companies with three different footings; peace, war, and full war. On the first basis, a company would have two noncommissioned officers and five men. This strength would rise to ten men on the second footing and to fifteen on the third with the noncommissioned officers remaining the same. This made it possible to increase the strength of a legion by sixteen hundred men in preparation for war without having to add any officers, commissioned or noncommissioned, who were difficult to train, or to create new units. The latter is a great advantage since new regiments have little value for several campaigns. Cavalry was always to be kept on a war footing, for only veteran men and horses were worth anything.

Saxe discussed his system on a full war basis. A century would have a strength of one hundred eighty-four officers and men. The fixed number of officers would provide uniformity in drill for all footings which was essential for uniform evolutions in wartime. He declared that he had seen troops of the same government, assembled after a long peace, which differed so much in drill and formation that one would say that they belonged to several different countries.

Saxe's regiment would have a strength of seven hundred forty-one officers and men plus seventy light infantry and seventy cavalry, making a total of eight hundred eighty-one. His legion would have a total strength of three thousand five hundred seventy-nine officers and men, two twelve-pounders and two pontoons. In addition, each century would be furnished with a weapon which Saxe invented himself and called an *amusette*. It looked like an oversized fusil mounted on wheels and equipped with carrying rails so that two men could pick it up and carry it anywhere. It fired a half-pound ball at ranges up to four thousand paces, Saxe claimed. This was nearly four times the range of German and Swedish battalion guns whose place it was designed to take. He maintained that there were a thousand uses which one could find for these weapons.

His special troops would be recruited from the rest of the

regiment. The cavalry should be chosen by preference from old soldiers. Such cavalry would never abandon its infantry, and would be used to pursue the defeated enemy or to cover one's own retreat. The light troops and their officers would be chosen from the most active and youngest men and must be trained frequently in jumping, running, and firing at a target from three hundred paces. He was opposed to grenadiers—the élite troops used for every variety of special service and consequently quickly exhausted.

The troops would be armed with breech-loading weapons of Saxe's own invention. He would also equip them with leather bucklers for forming a parapet and with plug bayonets—certainly a regressive step which shows his mistrust of fire power. The purpose of returning to the plug bayonet was to enable the officers to reserve the fire of the troops as long as they desired and so prevent them from firing when charging—a practice which Saxe vigorously opposed.

The basic formation of the troops was on four ranks. The first two would be armed with fusils which they would use, while the second two ranks would carry their fusils slung over their shoulders, and would have half-pikes of Saxe's own design. These were fourteen and a half feet in length, very light and strong, and did not whip like pikes, he claimed. They weighed only four pounds compared to seventeen. This interesting survival of prejudice was not justified by a single sound reason. In this matter, Saxe was certainly far less forward-looking than Puységur.

For one who was at this time opposed to much fire action, Saxe had some sound ideas on the subject. He admitted that there are times when one is reduced to fire action whether it is desired or not, and one has to know how to employ it. Fire must be used in enclosed or rough ground and against cavalry. The type of fire in use, fire by command, was contrary to common sense, Saxe declared. It kept the soldier waiting in a constrained position between the commands to aim and to fire. His attention could easily be distracted, greatly affecting the accuracy of the fire, and making a difference of some yards in it.

When the legion moved to attack infantry, the light troops should be in front in dispersed formation at a distance of one hundred to two hundred paces from the line. At a distance of three hundred paces from the enemy, they should commence firing at will, and continue doing so until reaching a range of fifty paces. The captain should then order a retreat and bring his men slowly back, firing as they retire, towards the main body, which should be under way at this time. The light troops were to fall into the intervals between the regiments. As they advanced, the regiments doubled ranks giving a depth of eight. The attached cavalry formed two troops of thirty men each, thirty paces behind their regiments.

What, asked Saxe, would the enemy, whom one supposes to be discountenanced by this time, be doing? They would neither be able nor dare to break their battalions to take the centuries in the flank, for the intervals would be filled by the light troops, or by crossed pikes. How could they resist, on a depth of four, an attack by fresh troops on a depth of eight after having been harassed by the fire of the light troops? They should surely be beaten, and then the light troops and the cavalry would emerge to pursue them and complete their destruction while the heavy infantry reformed ready to renew the charge if necessary.

This was the best of all formations for battle according to Saxe. Some objected that the enemy would launch his cavalry upon the skirmishers. To this he replied that they would not dare to attack for what could they do against them? Could they fire upon them? "It would be like shooting at a parcel of fleas." If the enemy adopted skirmishers in turn, they would have no place into which to withdraw, since the battalions presented a solid rampart of men.

Saxe calculated that his light troops would fire upon the enemy for seven or eight minutes, the time it took to advance four hundred fifty paces, and though they could fire six shots per minute, he calculated on a basis of only four per minute. Thus each man could fire about fifty shots during the attack (thirty would seem to be the correct number), and each enemy battalion would have received between four and five hundred well-aimed shots from troops who had practiced firing at greater ranges. Such fire, he believed, was ten times as effective as any other.

Then there was the fire of the *amusettes*. These could be drawn by two men and served by one. They were to be advanced with the light troops to the front where they could cause great damage to an enemy attempting to form after debouching from a wood or defile. They could fire twice a minute at ranges up to at least three thousand paces. There would be sixteen of them per legion, and joined together in batteries, they could easily silence any battery of hostile artillery for they were more accurate and of greater range than any artillery then in use.

Thus Saxe advocated a flexible formation with the troops advancing to the attack in units that were small enough to avoid the wavering to which the battalions were subject. The units allowed some room for maneuver. These units, the centuries, were thus able to advance rapidly, and he would have them do so without stopping to fire. Fire preparation was confined to skirmishers trained to accurate fire and unconstrained by commands. Such a formation avoided the inconveniences which the extant battalion formation possessed. It also avoided those of the heavy column advocated by Folard and his followers. In fact, it presented a third school of tactics, and one which found more widespread acceptance among experienced officers than that of Folard. Its chief weakness was found in Saxe's dim view of fire power. This last did not need to be retained, however, and one cannot but feel that Saxe must have modified his view in later life. Unlike Frederick, who shared the same prejudice for many years, he did not leave a later record to reflect such a change.

The legion, which Saxe envisaged as a permanent unit, was the forerunner of the infantry division which thirty years later was adopted permanently by the French Army. Saxe thought of it as being capable of employment in the body of the army or on separate service. If the commander-in-chief desired to occupy a certain post or have the enemy forestalled in some enterprise that he had undertaken, he had only to assign a particular legion to the task.[37] It was a large enough unit and well enough equipped to maintain itself for some time against an opposing army. Saxe put his ideas into effect in his campaigns, forming divisions of infantry with artillery which anticipated the famous Instruction of Marshal Broglie for the campaign of 1760.

Saxe turned his attention next to the problems of cavalry.[38] He insisted upon the importance of mobility and upon the ability of both men and horses to withstand fatigue. Above all the horses must not be fat. They must be made to gallop and run at full speed so as to develop their wind gradually. The practice of maneuvering slowly and only once every three months, he declared to be a mistaken kindness to them. The cavalry's maneuvers should be simple and massed, for the troops should be taught to fight together and never to disperse. When they charge, they should start with a slow trot and gradually increase their speed as they advance. They should close in boot to boot at a distance of twenty to thirty paces from the enemy. This movement should be done like lightning. They should be trained both in winter quarters and in peace quarters to gallop long distances in squadron formation without breaking, for Saxe declared it to be a fundamental point that any cavalry which could not charge two thousand paces without breaking was not fit for war. All mounted troops should be kept in condition in quarters by violent drills and exercises at least three times a week. When cavalry knows how to charge as above and is in good condition they will be fit for action and the rest will seem easy to them.

There should be two kinds of mounted troops, cavalry and dragoons. (The term cavalry is used here as in all European armies to mean heavy cavalry, i.e., cuirassiers. Dragoons were still considered as mounted infantry. They were to become more and more a medium cavalry, and to lose their characteristics as infantry.) Saxe had no use for light cavalry. The dragoons could perform any service that hussars could and many others that they could not.

The amount of cavalry must be kept small because it is very expensive, requires special attention, and must be kept at full strength in peace as well as in war. Saxe declared that forty squadrons are enough for an army of thirty to fifty thousand men. Such cavalry is for battle action. It should engage in no other duties except to supply the main guards. Like the heavy artillery, it should march with the army.

The cavalry would be armed with a triangular-bladed sword to prevent the troops from cutting instead of thrusting. The former, he declared, was a bad and ineffective method in combat. They would also carry a breach-loading carbine [39] and a fifteen-foot Polish lance. This last proposal was a radical departure, for heavy cavalry outside Poland had not used the lance for centuries, while the dragoons, who would also carry it, had never used it.

More surprising than Saxe's proposed weapons was his desire to equip cavalry with full armor instead of only with cuirass. He insisted that it was "the precious comfort" which caused armor's abandonment. "It is indolence and the relaxation of discipline which has made one abandon it [armor]: it is irksome to wear a cuirass or to trail a pike for half a century [in order to] make use of them a single day. But when one slackens on discipline, when being comfortable becomes an objective, one can predict without being inspired that one is near his ruin." [40]

Saxe had invented a suit which he claimed weighed only thirty-five pounds and was proof against all but direct hits at maximum velocity. He felt that this armor would make his cavalry invincible. Hostile cavalry would be reduced to resisting his by fire action which he rightly felt would be fatal to the former. Saxe ignored the fact that the greatly increased weight which full armor involved would so add to the fatigue of men and horses as to render them unable to charge after a long march. This was borne out even in the case of cuirassiers by the battle of Eckmühl in 1809. Moreover, it would seem an assumption not borne out by experience to think that armor would reduce enemy cavalry to doing nothing but fire. The whole idea is another example of retrograde thought in a generally forward-looking soldier.

The second type of mounted troops were dragoons. These should be twice as numerous as the cavalry, though the regiments should be of the same size. The men and horses should both be smaller than those of the cavalry, presumably for greater agility. They needed to know both cavalry and infantry drill. Their

armament should be the same as that of the cavalry, except that
they should have fowling pieces, in place of the carbines. Their
lances would serve as pikes when they were dismounted. The
rear rank should be taught to vault and skirmish, rallying in the
intervals between squadrons. The dragoons should perform all
the exterior service of the army which required mounted troops,
such as covering the camp, forming escorts, performing reconnaissances, locating the enemy, and seizing posts.

Both cavalry and dragoons should be formed in regiments composed of four centuries, like the infantry, each of one hundred

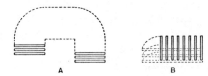

FIGURE 7   A   B

thirty men. The necessity of keeping cavalry always at full
strength and composed of veteran men and horses is not so essential for the dragoons. They may be diminished in numbers and
even dismounted, for, as long as they remain organized as infantry, they will be useful.

The only maneuvers which cavalry needed to learn were to do
rights and lefts by half-quarter-ranks and to caracol. The latter
was executed as in Figure 7A. (In both parts of Figure 7, each
unit represents a single rank of cavalry, and the whole represents
a single squadron in each case.) The former was a maneuver
which enabled the cavalry and dragoons to gain ground to the left
or right when there was not room to wheel the whole squadron.
It was performed as indicated in Figure 7B. The dragoons ought
to be especially well trained in this maneuver for it was the one
which they performed preparatory to dismounting to fight on foot.
The men at the extremities of the ranks as formed by the maneuver, sixteen in all, supervised by two noncommissioned officers,
should take charge of the led horses and lead them to a place of
security.

In action one cannot emphasize too much, said Saxe, that the
cavalry must keep together and never pursue the enemy helter-

skelter. They should consider their standards as sacred and rally to them, however the fighting goes, never mixing with the enemy. Cavalry would be invincible if it based itself upon these principles.

Saxe declared that the usefulness of cavalry detachments depended upon the nature of the theatre of operations. Large detachments seldom accomplished anything except in sudden, vigorous enterprises, such as seizing a convoy or post, or supporting infantry detachments covering the army's march. On such occasions they were very useful. Small detachments, on the other hand, were absolutely necessary and should be sent out every day. They should have a strength of fifty men and should avoid fighting, for their purpose was gathering information and taking a few prisoners. There was likely to be petty warfare between the parties of two armies. One should send out double size parties to ambush and curb those of the enemy. This would enable one to gain the upper hand and thus obtain information, make one's foraging parties secure, and generally to harass the enemy while denying these advantages to him. This kind of service was what the dragoons were for, and they were far superior to hussars because they were equally swift on the march and were steadier and firmer than the latter. Having the upper hand in such war would give the advantages mentioned and would develop capable officers. In opposition the enemy could offer only patience.

Saxe agreed with Montecuccoli that each of the two major arms needed to be supported by the other, but he vigorously condemned Folard's mixture of arms, advancing already familiar arguments against it. He provided immediate support for his infantry with the small troops of cavalry attached to his legions. To provide infantry support for the cavalry, he devised a system similar but superior to Puységur's. Each wing of cavalry would be supported by a legion posted in four squares, one regiment per square, between the two lines. These would provide a shelter behind which his cavalry, if defeated, could rally, and they would also break the force of the enemy's cavalry.[41] If his cavalry should be completely defeated, the squares would render it very difficult for the victors to attack the flanks of his infantry line.

Not only were Saxe's squares superior to Puységur's circles, but his disposition was generally so. By placing the squares between his lines instead of in front of them, he gave a free field for the action of his cavalry. This freed it from the essentially defensive character of Puységur's formation.

Saxe was no more favorably impressed with Folard's columns than he was with the latter's mixture of arms. The two men were mutual friends and held each other in high esteem,[42] so that Saxe's adverse comments upon Folard's system represent the judgment of a first-rate soldier and friendly critic. They form one of the soundest contemporary estimates of it.

He opened by saying:

Although I regard M. le Chevalier Follard [sic] highly and I find his works excellent, I cannot, nevertheless, agree with his opinions on columns. That idea seduced me at first. It is beautiful, and appears dangerous for the enemy, but the execution has cured me of it. It is necessary that I analyze it, in order to show its defects. It is a very easy matter of calculation.[43]

Saxe's main objection to Folard's column was based upon the fact that twice as much space is required between men in file as between men in rank. When Folard's column faced to its flanks to roll up the pierced enemy line, a very dangerous double interval would exist between the men in the new ranks. Saxe also denied Folard's famous principle of shock due to the pressure of rank upon rank. He further declared that the column was the heaviest formation of which he knew and that the chevalier deluded himself in thinking that it would be easy to move.

Saxe was opposed to large armies. He declared that he would never have one of more than ten legions, eight regiments of cavalry, and sixteen of dragoons, making thirty-four thousand foot and twelve thousand horse—a total of forty-six thousand men. He insisted that an able general who knew how to make use of such an army could stop one of a hundred thousand men, "for multitudes serve only to perplex and embarass." This did not mean that one could not have reserves, but the body of the army should be no larger.[44]

There is an economic size to an army, which may be said to be reached when size interferes with mobility, and Saxe's ideal army was one which fitted in his judgment the conditions of his time.[45] One might remember in this connection that Saxe himself was, by his theories and practice, pointing the way to methods which would greatly increase that economic size by leading to the divisional system. Frederick the Great was, by demonstration, to bear out Saxe's assertions concerning the effectiveness of a relatively small efficient army against larger and more cumbersome ones. Yet on the other hand, Marlborough was able to achieve mobility with armies at times considerably larger than that which Saxe would have. Saxe himself in the last campaigns of the War of the Austrian Succession led armies of up to one hundred twenty thousand men. It was, no doubt, this size which led him to set up divisions. Nevertheless, in those days of unitary armies, only a very capable general could handle so large a force. Saxe insisted that the enemy would almost always have to divide his forces, since whole provinces do not offer a single military position capable of holding an army of one hundred thousand men. Saxe would then attack one of the parts, and if he were successful, it would make his opponent timid, giving Saxe a moral superiority and ascendency. "Finally, I am persuaded that although these great armies have some advantages in superiority of numbers, they lose it in cumbersomeness, in diversity of maneuvers which are not made in the same spirit, in the lack of supplies, and in other inconveniences which are inseparable from them." [46]

In addition to his discussion of the basic parts of war, Saxe treated what he called the sublime parts, i.e., the various operations of whole armies. His discussion deals with some subjects exhaustively and with others rather briefly, but in all cases, he leaves the impression of a vigorous mind free from any trammels of custom.

Was it advantageous to begin a campaign early? Those who thought so were right, according to Saxe, if it was a question of occupying an important position. Otherwise, he thought it was better to remain in quarters as long as possible. Let the enemy undertake some sieges; he merely weakened himself in proportion. One could then issue forth in the autumn with an army in good condition at full strength and ruin him.[47] Saxe noticed that a hard campaign always reduced an army by a third at least, the cavalry especially being used up; so that by October, after having been harassed by detachments during the campaign, the enemy would not be able to offer successful resistance. He would be so badly handled, consequently, as to be much delayed in opening the next campaign, or perhaps not be able to do so at all. It would be all over in a month, and one could then return to camp in good condition, having ruined one's adversary.

This method of operations was one which went quite contrary to general opinion, as Saxe admitted. A general like Marlborough was always impatient to be in the field and liked nothing better than to forestall his opponent in this matter. Saxe's plan might be practical against a mediocre opponent, but it would be risky, if not impossible, against an able general who would hardly cooperate by leaving one tranquilly in one's cantonments. In his own practice, Saxe did not follow his theory, opening his campaign of 1744 by concentrating at the beginning of April, thus forestalling the Allies. He forestalled them again in April, 1745, to open the seige of Tournai. The campaign of 1746 was opened before winter quarters were broken up in January; that of 1747 in April or early May; that of 1748 in April.[48] In every one of these, his only major campaigns, Saxe was in the field before his opponents. If one pleads that particular conditions enabled or required him to do so, the answer is that such conditions are apt to be present on every occasion.

The essence of Saxe's doctrine concerning the various types of warfare was to take all the necessary precautions for security, to avoid being negligent at all costs, and then to do that which the enemy did not anticipate—to catch him off balance if possible. Applying this to mountain warfare,[49] he declared that one must never enter a defile without first seizing control of all the heights which dominate it, in order to prevent being surprised with disastrous results. If the enemy occupied the passes, one should feint at one of them while looking for a new one. These could always be found no matter how rugged the mountains might be or how much the local inhabitants insisted that there were none. This was because they used the passages already known and, hence, never looked for new ones. Such an unexpected advance would frequently disconcert the enemy who would become fearful and abandon everything.

Saxe proceeded to give a number of concrete situations in each of which he offered a solution.[50] In each case, his purpose was to upset the mental balance of his opponent by the opening moves and to take advantage of this to concentrate upon a weak spot or an unexpected one. As he said, the ground frequently would give one opportunities which the enemy had overlooked until it was too late and which would change a given situation, rendering the enemy's disposition ineffective. The enemy could be reduced to appearing ridiculous. He did not apply this principle to the wider sphere of the theatre of operations as Napoleon did, but it was a natural step when once it became possible.[51]

The nature of the French was to attack, according to Saxe, a point on which all these writers agreed. Their courage and élan had never been doubted; their first shock was terrible, and all one needed to know was how to renew it by skillful dispositions. That was the general's business. Certainly Saxe himself was a master of this. In the battles of Roucoux and Laufeld, his two offensive battles, he handled the attack in column formation for this very purpose of renewing continually the attacks which had been repulsed. In the latter battle, the attacks upon the villages of Laufeld and Vlytingen, the keys of the battlefield, were thrice repulsed and as many times renewed until the fourth was successful. Saxe had fresh troops at hand to make the renewed attack each time, and the capture of Laufeld decided the day in his favor.[52]

One of Saxe's ideas about opening moves to upset his adversary's balance was to make poor dispositions deliberately. When the enemy prepared to take advantage of them and had disposed himself for this purpose, one would suddenly change into good ones. Needless to say, the facilities for this change were absolutely essential, and they must be such as to enable the change to be made very quickly. Saxe declared that nothing would disconcert the enemy so much, for he would be left without the possibility of remedying his own dispositions. If he continued in his original ones, he would be beaten, and if he tried to change them in close proximity to the enemy, he would lay himself open to a fatal counterattack. Here one has a characteristic example of Saxe's batle tactics, of his "Hannibalic guile." [53]

Saxe dealt extensively with field fortifications. Concerning lines and entrenchments, he said, "I like neither the one nor the other of these works. I always think of Chinese walls when I hear lines mentioned. The good ones are those which nature has made, and good entrenchments are good dispositions and brave troops. I have rarely heard of entrenchments being attacked which have not been forced." [54] The enemy, emboldened by the certainty that an entrenched army would not quit its works, would undertake movements that he would not otherwise dare.

In attacking such works, Saxe emphasized the necessity of concealing the point of attack and gave methods for doing it. His major point on their defense, which he considered the most difficult and uncertain part of warfare, was to concentrate on the morale of the troops, by informing them of what they could expect and what was expected of them. They would not then be disconcerted by the unexpected. This is an example of Saxe's understanding of the great importance of morale in warfare.

Redoubts were Saxe's favorite type of field work and had many advantages, he maintained. In the first place, they gave one the advantage of field works without restricting one to the defensive. They made possible a defensive-offensive battle. If they were soundly located and constructed, they formed a series of mutually-supporting strong points in front of one's position. They broke up the rush of the enemy's attack and forced the enemy to reduce them before he could attack the defending army. One could then send forward troops to counterattack those of the enemy trying

to reduce the redoubts, and, if necessary, renew the attack successively with fresh brigades.[55] When the enemy was worn out with
his efforts, then one could assume the offensive and attack him in
turn with every prospect of success. Saxe described the battle of
Poltava where Peter the Great successfully made use of redoubts.
The Russians, instead of supporting them, allowed the redoubts
to defend themselves unaided, so that three of the seven were
taken. Yet the veteran troops of Charles XII were exhausted in
the struggle and could not withstand the eventual Russian counterattack. Since the Russians did not properly support the redoubts, Saxe attributes the victory to them. Saxe, himself, made
effective use of them. The Redoubt d'Eu, for instance, played an
important part in his most famous victory of Fontenoy.

Saxe then turned his attention to the general-in-chief. There
are three basic qualities which a general-in-chief should have:
courage, without which nothing else avails; *intelligence* which
should be courageous and "fertile in expedients"; and *health.*

A competent general must have an eye for the military characteristics of ground, the ability to recognize the decisive moment
which occurs in all battles, and the capacity to seize it with advantage. He must not swamp himself in details. His orders should
be short and simple, indicating his wishes clearly, telling what to
do but not how to do it.

Many generals, Saxe declared, occupy themselves on the day of
battle in the mechanics and details of handling troops, trying to
do everything and accomplishing nothing. He regarded them as
men who were out of their depth, who understood nothing, and
who were able to do only what they had done all their lives, lead
troops methodically under a commander. The reason for this was
that few men study the higher problems of war. They spent their
lives drilling troops, and thought there was nothing else to war.
Once in command of an army, they were at a loss and consequently did what they knew how to do. He said that he had seen
excellent colonels become bad generals and excellent subordinate
generals who could not lead a thousand men in independent operations, a condition not confined to Saxe's day. He declared that

a man must be born with a talent for war if he was to be more than a mediocre general. "Application corects ideas, but it does not give a soul; that is the work of nature." [56]

Following the discussion of the general's qualifications is the passage which caused Marshal Foch to condemn Saxe and to compare him very adversely with Napoleon.

I am, nevertheless, not favorable to battles, above all, at the beginning of a war; and I am convinced that an able general can wage war all his life without being obliged to fight them. Nothing so reduces the enemy to absurdity as that method; nothing advances affairs more. It is necessary to give frequent combats, and dissolve, so to speak, the enemy: after which he is obliged to hide.

I do not claim to say in that regard, that when one finds the opportunity of crushing the enemy, that one does not attack him; and that one does not profit from false steps that he may make; but I wish to say that one can make war, without putting anything to chance; and that is the peak of perfection and ability in a general. But, when one goes so far as to give battle, it is necessary to know how to profit from the victory, and above all not to be content with having gained a battlefield, as is the praiseworthy custom. [57]

Liddell Hart pointed out how Foch seized upon the opening sentence and ignored the rest of the passage about first weakening the enemy and especially the qualification contained in the second paragraph. He declared that Saxe was arguing "that a good general should not be cornered, and forced to fight at a disadvantage." He further declared that this betrays Foch's shallow historical knowledge. It would certainly seem to indicate that Foch lacked a real understanding of eighteenth-century warfare. [58] Saxe was, of course, writing at a time when it was still possible to avoid being compelled to battle, which was not the case in the nineteenth century.

The continuation of this quotation from Saxe presents an idea which was in great contrast to most ideas and practices of his day. It is a passage which could well have come from Napoleon's pen. Saxe said:

One follows religiously the words of a proverb which says that *it is necessary to make a bridge of gold for one's enemy.* [59] That is false.

On the contrary, it is necessary to push him and pursue him relentlessly and all that fine retreat . . . soon turns into a rout if it is disturbed. Ten thousand detached men will destroy an army of a hundred thousand which flees. Nothing inspires so much terror and causes so much damage, for all perishes there, and one must make great efforts to restore its condition; besides one is rid of the enemy for a good while. But many generals are not concerned to finish a war so soon.[60]

He cited the French after Ramillies where, he said, the unexpected appearance of an English squadron caused the retreating French Army to dissolve in a horrible rout. He insisted that anyone who allowed a defeated enemy to retire unmolested served his prince badly. He said that he did not mean that one should abandon himself with all his troops on the enemy, but one should assign troops for the pursuit and order them to carry it out as long as the day lasted. This was not a time for excessive caution on the part of the general in charge of the pursuit. If he acted in such a manner, it was not worth the trouble of sending him. "It is necessary that he attack, push, and pursue without ceasing." Truly this is a doctrine which expresses all that Napoleon could desire, all of the modern ideal of pursuit which has so seldom been completely realized.[61]

In conclusion, it can be said that Saxe was just as dissatisfied with maneuvering in line as was Folard. He was also mistrustful of fire action and inclined to prefer shock action for his main body. He did provide for fire preparation by the action of his light infantry, and he explicitly declared that if the heavy infantry could advance they should not fire. Thus he disagreed with Folard who would have his columns fire as they advanced. Like Folard, however, he sought a tactical formation which would obviate the necessity of maneuvering in line, but he rejected the latter's heavy columns in favor of a flexible formation of doubled battalions on a depth of eight ranks. With this formation, he would be able to avoid the difficulties of advancing in lines without falling into those of the massive columns of Folard. He was thus much closer to the eventual solution of light columns than was the latter.

Saxe recognized and clearly stressed the importance of mobility in troops, maintaining that the drill of both infantry and cavalry had that purpose. He made proposals not only for the tactical mobility of his troops in advocating the cadenced step, but also for their strategic mobility. His chief measures in this respect were various proposals for reducing the impedimenta of the army and his legionary organization.

In the foregoing discussion, it has been evident repeatedly that Saxe recognized the great importance of morale in military operations. He understood that many enterprises, which might otherwise be perfectly feasible, could be rendered impractical by deficiency of morale in the troops. On several occasions he discussed at some length the steps necessary to insure morale or at least to bolster the troops in this respect. He was the first to treat this subject clearly in his writings.

Saxe also recognized morale as no less important in commanders-in-chief than in soldiers. He had, as one of the main purposes in his large-scale operations, the idea of injuring his opponent's morale. This would be the result of throwing his opponent off balance and disconcerting him by his maneuvers. He also had, as an objective in such operations, the idea of so managing the campaign as to bring about a favorable opportunity to inflict a decisive defeat upon his adversary. He clearly indicated that once this had been achieved one should bend every effort, by vigorous pursuit, to making that defeat permanent. In short, Saxe was, with a few very striking exceptions, an extremely forward-looking man, many of whose suggestions were actually adopted, and whose theories certainly pointed the way to the military doctrines of later times. His inquisitive and empirical mind was always looking for methods to improve the many defective practices which still remained in the warfare of his day.

MESNIL-DURAND

The Baron de Mesnil-Durand (1729-99), who had served with conspicuous courage during the War of the Austrian Succession, published in 1755 one of the century's major works of military theory, the *Projet d'un ordre françois en tactique*. This book so stimulated the old controversy between the *ordre mince* and the *ordre profond* that after a few years' delay due to the Seven Years' War, it flared up into a new heat even greater than before. The reason for this revival was that Mesnil-Durand, even more than Folard, whose disciple he was, was an advocate of the *ordre profond* in its extreme form. His *plésion* was in many ways a distinct improvement upon Folard's column, but it was, in its essentials, the same heavy mass, and the methods of using it were also essentially the same. The claims made for it were, if anything, even more sweeping than Folard's. Towards his critics he took much the same attitude, namely, that only wilful blindness kept them from acknowledging the correctness of everything which he wrote.

In his Preliminary Discourse, Mesnil-Durand pleaded the case of the innovator and put aside objections to proposing a new system. He argued that experience is not necessary to judge in military matters, especially orders of battle, and cited Puységur incorrectly in support. He declared that theory alone was able to decide between the two orders, from which stemmed that independence of the actual facts of military experience so very apparent in his works. He spoke of Folard as his master and hoped to establish the superiority of the column to the battalion.

Mesnil-Durand began his work proper by discussing the basic characteristics which a military ordinance (here used to mean the tactical system set up by an ordinance) must have.[62] The first was solidity. An ordinance has as its end a body of troops which can overthrow those opposed to it and not be itself overthrown. To accomplish this, it must be strong and solid. Since the flanks of any corps are the weak points, it is necessary to have no flanks in the conventional sense in order to avoid weakness.

Solidity can best be obtained through depth, for it is a fundamental truth that troops in battle cannot be broken by other troops which are in less depth. "The depth of the files makes the strength of the infantry." [63] Depth increases the shock, furthermore, for the rear ranks sustain those in front, pushing them and preventing them from recoiling. Mesnil-Durand supported these assertions by examples such as the battle of Pharsalus, the practice of Cyrus the Great, and that of the Tlascaltans in Mexico, all except the last being drawn from ancient history.

Turning to the second of his principles, Mesnil-Durand insisted that depth is what makes flanks secure, therefore the greater the extent of the flanks, the greater their security. A file of thirty-two men makes a flank as secure as the front. Such a flank is immeasurably more secure than that of a battalion. The column is the only formation which possesses this feature. The battalion can only protect its flank by performing some maneuver which the column does not have to do. This security of the flanks gives the column its independence. It is completely independent of what happens to adjacent units while, if a battalion is broken, its neighbors are also outflanked and broken.

The third principle is speed, which is essential to a formation since it adds to the violence of the shock, encourages the soldier, saves men by shortening the time during which they are under fire while attacking, and denies the enemy time for countermoves. Since a single column is capable of rapid advance, and each column is independent of the others, a line of columns will not be less rapid. Such is not the case with the battalion, for it is very slow due to the great length of its front. Battalions in line are not independent of each other, and consequently, a line of battalions is even slower than a single battalion for the front is much longer and the problem of keeping its alinement is very difficult. This problem, of course, does not concern columns, for, being independent, they need not keep perfect alinement.

Mesnil-Durand expounded the advantages of attacking on the run which is both possible and desirable. Depth is the great factor, for the longer the files are, the easier it is to run! He would open his ranks to four feet of interval for running and close ranks without stopping, as one approached the enemy, for shock.

Having set forth the principles necessary for an ordinance and the advantages of columns in general, Mesnil-Durand turned to the specific system of columns which he had devised. He declared that Folard did not determine the dimensions of his column, but only limited it to from sixteen to thirty files. It could be from one to six battalions in strength though Folard preferred to have two smaller columns rather than one large column. Mesnil-Durand agreed with this. He called his column a *plésion*, a term

taken from the Greeks which referred to the formation of the phalanx in which it faced to all four sides to resist attack when surrounded. Mesnil-Durand improved greatly upon Folard in the
composition of his column. The *plésion* was composed of twenty-
four files of thirty-two men each which gave it a total strength of
seven hundred sixty-eight men. It was subdivided as follows (see
Figure 8): vertically into two *manches* which each had, therefore,

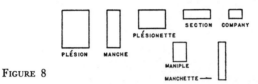

FIGURE 8

twelve files of thirty-two men; horizontally into four sections of
twenty-four files of eight men each which were grouped into two
plésionettes of two sections each, forming twenty-four files of sixteen men. Each section was further subdivided into two companies of twelve files of eight men each. To each *plésion* were added
two platoons of grenadiers, totaling ninety-six men, and one of
horse grenadiers of fifty men, which gave the *plésion* a total
strength of nine hundred eighteen men.[64] Thus where Folard
mixed small bodies of infantry with his cavalry, Mesnil-Durand
reversed the procedure. What Mesnil-Durand presented was actually the then existing battalion column with intervals suppressed, the two being the same in depth and front.

Mesnil-Durand, again like Folard, was a strong advocate of the
mixture of arms. He cited Saxe and Montecuccoli in his support
and also gave classical examples. His horse grenadiers were to be
used to harass the forces which he was attacking, as a screen to conceal his last-minute changes in disposition, and to prevent any
countermeasures. He seemed to think that on occasion the horse
grenadiers alone would be enough to throw the enemy into confusion.

Bravery and discipline are essential for any order, declared
Mesnil-Durand, but in this, as in so many other matters, his *plé-
sion* was superior. It would promote them by its very nature.
The same man would be braver in the *plésion* and would fight

better than in the battalion. One reason was that the speed of march animates the soldier, and of course, the *plésion* was much faster than the battalion. Then the bravest men would be placed in the posts of danger, first ranks and flank files, where they could inspire the more timorous. The officers, being closer to their men, could also inspire them better. Then again, weak flanks always instill fear in soldiers, but the *plésion* did not have them. Lastly, the men could not run away in the *plésion*. The rear ranks could run away but being out of danger would push on, forcing the front ranks forward. It would be possible for the flank files to flee sideways and then to the rear. That contingency was provided for by having the officers and support platoons shoot down any fugitives who left their formation. The men would, therefore, face the possibility of death at the hands of the enemy rather than the certainty of it if they fled. Still another effect of the *plésion* upon the men who composed it would be freedom from sudden panics, since they would know that they could overthrow any corps which opposed them.

Mesnil-Durand went on to deny that his ordinance needed more discipline than the battalion. The contrary was actually the case, since its formations were simpler, and it need not worry about the perfect alinement so necessary to the battalion. He went on to quote Saxe to the effect that all troops which fire in the presence of the enemy are defeated, and those which hold their fire are victorious. The *plésion* would never fire. Further, he declared, nothing is more difficult than to rally a battalion, but if, by chance, a *plésion* should be thrown into disorder and confusion, its small and numerous divisions would make it easy to rally. The great difficulty with the French in sustaining an attack was to maintain order. The *plésion* would remedy this, for the fault lay not with the nation but with the existing ordinance.[65]

The method of fighting used by the *plésion* and the course of a battle as seen by Mesnil-Durand were derived from Folard. His *plésions*, normally in a single line, would advance upon the enemy at the most rapid rate possible, running at least part of the way. See Figure 9A. They would be screened by the support platoons and the horse grenadiers, who apparently would lead the attack.

The former would do what firing was to be done, and would seek, as skirmishers, to unsettle the enemy and prepare the attack. Once the *plésions* came in contact with the enemy's line, they would rupture it immediately, for, of course, thirty-two rank files could not be resisted more than momentarily by those of three ranks. See Figure 9B. Having ruptured the hostile line in front of each *plésion,* Mesnil-Durand would then have these separate by

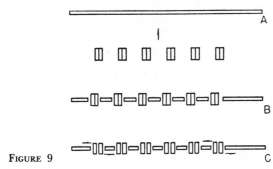

FIGURE 9

manches and proceed to roll up the enemy's line. This would appear to be similar to the representation in Figure 9C.

In the face of such an attack, nothing could save the enemy unless he could stop the rolling up of his line. Mesnil-Durand believed that he had the reply to every counter which the enemy could make. If the enemy tried to stop this process by advancing the battalions of the second line, they would have to cover three hundred paces (the normal distance between two lines), and during that time the two *manches* of each *plésion* would have covered six hundred paces so that the enemy's battalion would arrive in thin air! If a second-line battalion advanced to take a *manche* in the flank, the latter would face to the right or left, as necessary, and move instead to the flank of the battalion, as if marching on the second line. When opposite that flank, it would, by a facing, attack the battalion in its flank instead. There was another answer to such a counter. When the enemy arrived within twenty-five or thirty paces, the first sixteen files of the *manche* would continue their forward movement, that of rolling up the enemy's first line, for twelve paces while the second sixteen files stood firm.

These would then face to the right or left, as necessary, and move up abreast of the former which would make a similar facing. The result was a *fausse plésionette* of twenty-four files of sixteen men each which would pierce the presumptuous troops of the enemy, and treat them as the first line was treated. The *plésionettes*, either regular or false, had all the invincible properties of the *plésion* itself, he claimed.[66]

Mesnil-Durand, like Folard, favored a single line of battle, for he felt that, once the first line was overthrown, a battle was rarely restored by a second line. His normal order of battle consisted of a line of *plésions* with intervals between them to double their front. With a single line, it was possible to obtain the required depth without too greatly shortening the extent of the front. He would protect his flanks by placing four *plésions*, their platoons, and four squadrons on his wings. If the enemy tried to attack his flanks, these would, in turn, attack the enemy's.

Comparing the movements of a battalion and those of a *plésion*,[67] Mesnil-Durand came to the conclusion that the former could make no movements before an enemy, save to march forward. The only possible movements aside from this were the rear-march, the flank-march, change of formation, or dividing itself. Of these he gave most consideration to the flank-march. The battalion could do this in three ways. The first of these was the ordinary right- or left-face. This was theoretically possible for a battalion, but it was very likely to lead to confusion, especially under fire, for the battalion was almost certain to lengthen out. The second was by a quarter-wheel of the battalion. This had several defects. In the first place, it presented a flank to the enemy. Next, it required a long time which, coupled with the first defect, absolutely prevented its use in the presence of the enemy. Lastly, it was impractical unless one had very even ground. The third method was to break the battalion by divisions, which then made quarter-wheels. This method greatly diminished the difficulties of the second, but it required the troops to keep their distances with geometrical exactitude, otherwise, when one reformed the front, there would either be gaps in it, or not enough room for the troops.

The *plésion,* on the other hand, could perform a flank-march very easily by a right- or left-facing. In marching in this way, its files would be only twenty-four men in length. The lengthening would be very negligible in such short files as compared with those of one hundred fifty to two hundred men in the battalions. The *plésions* avoided the quarter-wheels by means of the movements by *plésionettes.* If a *plésion* was attacked in the flank while on the run to attack, the first and sixteenth ranks would halt, and the others would close up on them. Then they faced to the threatened flank and attacked the would-be attackers. Each *plésionette* would be, in effect, a little *plésion* of sixteen files and twenty-four ranks.

In this connection Mesnil-Durand described how three *plésions* could overthrow a whole army by attacking a single battalion! Once they had broken the battalion which they had attacked, they would form *plésionettes.* Those of the center *plésion* would join the outside *plésions,* one to each, and they would roll up the line in opposite directions. This was only a variation of the movement by *manches.* If either of these formations, i.e., the *plésion-ettes,* was threatened in the flank, then the nearest *plésionette* would face the threatening corps and overthrow it while the others continued to roll up the line. All the *plésionettes* could face the flank threat if necessary.[68]

It is not surprising to learn that Mesnil-Durand did not favor fire combat. He declared that "one should busy" oneself with musketry only when it was impossible to move on the enemy and, consequently, to use the bayonet. It would, of course, also be impossible for the enemy to move against him in such a case.

He insisted that the *plésion* was a good formation for fire. In such a situation it would take up whatever position it wished in order to obtain a good effect. The fire formations which Mesnil-Durand gave for this purpose were quite complicated and show clearly the difficulty of trying to develop the fire of such a massive formation. A characteristic method was called by him *faire te-naille.* In this the rear section of the *plésion* stood fast while the remainder (the first three sections) separated by *manches* to a distance equal to the front of the *plésion.* In other words, the right *manche* faced right, and the left *manche,* left, and each marched until its rear rank was even with the outer file of the section which remained in place.   They then made an eighth-wheel, and about-faced, while the platoons of grenadiers placed themselves at the outer extremities of the resulting formation.   This move is illustrated by Figure 10.   If it was desired to place artillery in the

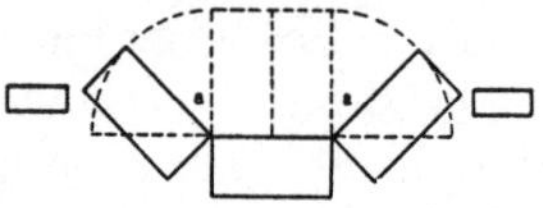

FIGURE 10

angles *aa,* the *manches* could open the required additional distance before making their conversions.   Mesnil-Durand was very emphatic about the deadly nature of the crossfire which the *plésion* would provide while firing in this formation.

The *plésion* could also fire by *manches.*   To fire in this manner the first four ranks, which formed a *tranche* or half-section, remained stationary and fired from their position.   The second *tranche* would separate by *manches,* that is, move out to right and left until clear of the *plésion* and fire.   It then would return to its original position, and the third *tranche* would go out, and so on consecutively until the grenadier platoons had fired.   The performance would then begin all over again and go on as long as necessary.[69]

There was still another matter upon which Mesnil-Durand agreed with Folard.   He thought that an army should keep a certain number of pikemen for it would generally be possible to come to shock combat in battle.   He pleaded the greater length of the pikes in justification saying that they would come into action before the hostile bayonets.   He would place them in the same manner as Folard, alternating with fusils.   The loss of fire power, he declared, was more apparent than real, because his system had only half the usual amount of cavalry, and it fought in one line instead of two with reserves.   It would have, therefore, much greater fire power when formed in line of sections despite the pikes.[70]

Mesnil-Durand favored shock combat, declaring like Saxe, that fire was not very formidable, and that it would be fatal to depend upon it. It was best to rely upon cold steel and to come to grips with the enemy. He referred to Puységur's declaration that the great trouble with coming to grips was that from one hundred sixty yards on, one lost many men from enemy fire, which caused the troops to speed the march, with resultant disorder. The *plésion* naturally was not subject to this, because it would move so fast that it would not lose many men, and it feared no disorder from marching. This method of fighting was especially suited to the French, he declared, who were a nation of great impetuosity and vivacity which were just the qualities required for combat with *armes blanches*. Another advantage of such combats was that they were less bloody and more decisive.

If a *plésion* should be surrounded, it would pick one side and charge that, breaking it in pieces and leaving the others as spectators. If one of the latter came within charging distance, the *plésion* would change face and charge it by *plésionettes* instead of the original objective. It was a matter of indifference to the *plésion* from what direction the enemy attacked it. It could defeat him as well from one side as another, front, rear, or either flank.[71]

In connection with his advocacy of shock action Mesnil-Durand denied that firearms had worked any profound change in warfare! Fusils only strike like bows and slings but with noise added. Cannon "count for almost nothing in battles."[72] They have the advantage over catapults and ballistas only in being simpler. He denied that fire was master of the battlefield and declared that he had proved that it could not prevent his *plésions* from getting at the enemy. He cited examples of the effectiveness of shock action which had been used by Folard. All but one, drawn from the campaigns of Gustavus Adolphus, came from ancient history. He declared elsewhere that cannon have little influence on battles, since they have so little time to fire. He cited, as an example, the battle of Mantinea where the Spartan catapults had little time to fire and did very little damage. After all, the catapult was a much more formidable weapon than a canon![73]

Mesnil-Durand followed Folard in mixing platoons of infantry with the cavalry in his order of battle in order to harass the enemy by its fire. They would enter the intervals between the enemy's squadrons to attack them in flank and rear. He tried to circumvent the difficulty caused by the speeds of the two arms when attacking, by having the platoons advance before the cavalry started, and having the squadrons advance at the trot until ready to charge. Even so the platoons would be exposed to the enemy cavalry for some time. It would require the greatest skill in timing, furthermore, to coordinate the two arms, each starting at a different time, moving at a different speed, and yet expected to strike the enemy at the same time.[74]

Mesnil-Durand then turned to a comparison of the two systems in pitched battles and to the use of *plésions* in the various operations of war. It is not necessary to go into detail upon these subjects. He discussed the various orders of battle, and again the *plésion* proved superior for each of them at his hands. He examined various types of operations: flank attacks on armies, ambushes, attacks on rear guards, attacks on the march, surprises of armies, passages of rivers, opposing descents on one's coasts, mountain warfare, attack and defense of entrenchments, and sorties and assaults in sieges. In all of these, he examined the requirements for the particular operation, and, not very surprisingly, these requirements are found to be possessed by the *plésion* in much greater degree than by any other formation, especially the battalion.[75]

In connection with his claims for the *plésion*, Mesnil-Durand complained of unfairness on the part of his critics. They seized upon particular faults, and ignoring its advantages, tore it to pieces, he declared. They failed to make any general defense of the battalion system at all. Of his answers to specific objections, the most important concerned the charge that his columns would suffer more than battalions from fire. He agreed that each cannon shot would do more damage, but since a *plésion* had only one-eighth the front of a battalion, it would receive only one-eighth as many shots! He apparently expected that cannon would be spread evenly over the hostile front and that they would fire straight ahead whether there were troops before them or not! In any case, he declared, the object of battles is to gain victories, not to avoid losses. His system would ensure the former. As for musketry, he denied that his order would lose as heavily as battalions, because its greatly superior speed would cut decisively the time under fire.

In concluding, Mesnil-Durand declared that Folard did not go far enough. Mesnil-Durand would use columns on all occasions and not limit them to special ones as did Folard. He would compose his formations only of columns and not mix them with battalions *à la Folard*. Since columns were equal to battalions in fire action and vastly superior in all else, the latter formation had no utility. He claimed the role of perfecter of Folard's invention in devising his own system which enabled him to see, as his master did not, all the advantages of columns.

Such was the system of Mesnil-Durand, and such were the claims he made for it. It is necessary to examine his system critically to see what its defects were and what advantages it might have had. The first thing which stands out is his contempt for fire action. He at least abandoned Folard's pretensions concerning the potency of the fire power of the column. Fire would be used only when it was impossible to get at the enemy, and in that case, the *plésion* would deploy to make use of it. In all other cases, the *plésion* would charge without firing. Fire action would be confined to the support platoons which, on occasion, would go before the *plésions* acting as a screen and unsettling the enemy by their fire. In every case, since the enemy had only his fire with which to defend himself, he would be overthrown without fail. because that fire was in no case very severe and dependence upon it was fatal. Mesnil-Durand considered that he would always be decisively superior in numbers regardless of the overall strength of the forces engaged. Each *plésion* when engaged against a battalion would number seven hundred sixty-eight against ninety-six. He counted as opposing him only those men who were exactly opposed to his front of twenty-four men. All others could be ignored apparently!

This whole scheme completely ignored the developments of two and a half centuries of warfare. Mesnil-Durand ignored the salient lesson of that period, the domination of the battlefield by fire power, with less excuse than Folard and Saxe, for he wrote after the War of the Austrian Succession in which new demonstrations were provided at French expense.

Mesnil-Durand expected his troops to rush forward through the fire of the battalions without replying. He declared that they were bound to win for depth was always victorious. Files of deeper ranks were certain to overthrow those of thinner formations. This is, in itself, a debatable point, to say the least, having been contradicted long before the invention of firearms,[76] but Mesnil-Durand presented it as incontestable, and upon it his whole system depended. If it was not true, then there was no assurance of victory even granting that the *plésion* could reach the enemy's line, an assumption which in itself was doubtful.

For Mesnil-Durand, victory depended upon a tactical system and nothing else. His *plésions* would always be victorious. He asserted this over and over again. "One has seen, for example, that the first [principle of solidity] gives the certainty of overthrowing that which one charges in front; the second [security of flanks] that of having to fight, in reality, only in that manner; the two together, consequently, that of conquering every time that one fights." [77] Again, "*Plésions* are made for this type of fighting [shock action] and are invincible." [78] And again, "But if one examines what will happen to the battalion attacked by the *plésion,* one will see that it [the former] will not resist it [the latter] a moment, will not even make it [the latter] buy the victory." [79] These are but a few samples of his repeated assertions. Superior numbers, able generalship, powerful positions, and strategic combinations counted for nothing. In fact, generalship was reduced to acquiring perfection in the technique of the system, knowing which maneuver to use in a specific situation. In his discussion he never made any allowance for the nature of the ground. His *plésions* were apparently to run to the attack even if up a steep hill or across ditches. Tactics was reduced to geometry. Actually, he reduced it to geometry and physics. It was merely the geometrical application of physical force.

In all of this, human psychology was ignored. He assumed that troops would advance through enemy fire and not reply, that they would not shrink from a danger which they could not answer, that is, that they would neither halt and attempt to fire, nor recoil. He assumed that heavy losses would merely stimulate his troops to press on to contact in order to end them. He assumed that this mass, advancing rapidly, would preserve its ranks in perfect order and not crowd up, causing interior confusion. Such confusion would be more fatal to his system than to others, because it must be ready instantly to separate by facings along any one of its various subdivisions, *manches, plésionettes,* etc. Which particular subdivision was employed depended upon circumstances which could not be forseen, hence the necessity for instant readiness to make any of several maneuvers. Mesnil-Durand did not ask himself any questions on this subject. He declared that his system improved discipline and that the rear ranks would encourage the front ones. Actual experience was to show that the contrary was the case and that the rear ranks, which were not actually engaged in conflict, needed to be encouraged, not the front ones which had their hands full.

Mesnil-Durand also adopted the mixture of arms "so recommended by all the masters of the art." Many officers, however, including no less a figure than Marshal Broglie, were opposed to the mixture of arms.[80]

The whole system stands or falls upon the question of whether or not the *plésion* can get through the defending fire. Mesnil-Durand insisted that it could because of its solidity, security of flanks, and speed. His claims for the invincibility of his order rested, in the ultimate, upon these and upon the idea that the files of greater depth will overthrow those of lesser depth. But the testimony of Dettingen, Fontenoy, Roucoux, and Laufeld, indicated that "the withering effect of the fusillade is a very real element," [81] which Mesnil-Durand did not take into account, and which one could not test in peacetime experiments.

Colin asked, how did one form a route or marching column from the *plésion?* How did one reform the *plésion* from a route column? Would it not take longer to form an order of battle with *plésions* than with lines? He declared that these were important questions which Mesnil-Durand did not answer. While this is an important and reasonable question if one is thinking of combining standard practice in marching with the system of *plé-sions* for combat, it would not appear to apply in this case for the simple reason that Mesnil-Durand did not intend to make such a combination.   He gave in his revised system three formations for the *plésion:* (1) the closed-up formation, *en phalange,* taken just before the shock, in which the *plésion* presented a solid mass; (2) a formation, *en bataille,* used in approach-marches to the battle-field, in which each section had its ranks closed but with intervals between the sections; (3) the formation with open ranks which was to be used in marching when there was no danger of being at-tacked.   The last was also to be used in charging on the run. From all this it seems clear that Mesnil-Durand intended to march in *plésions* as well as to fight in that order in his revised system. It would appear, since he did not mention the matter in his orig-inal system, that such was also his intention then, and that Colin's criticism was beside the point.

In concluding, one can say that Mesnil-Durand exhibited the exclusiveness of many of the military writers of this period in its most extreme form.   He went considerably further than Folard in insisting upon the use of heavy columns and would employ them without any other infantry formations save his support pla-toons.   He had little excuse for his stubborn refusal to face the facts of warfare as they existed and had been demonstrated in the last two great wars.   More than any other writer he held the naive idea that a tactical system could guarantee victory.   He was grad-ually compelled to abandon some of his ideas, but he held to oth-ers obstinately in spite of the preponderance of condemnation, as will be seen.   He is the supreme example of the military ideo-logue.

Within three years, Mesnil-Durand was compelled to modify some of his theories.   He published his *Suite du projet d'un ordre françois en tactique* in 1758.   He made some changes and im-provements in his system, mostly along the line of increased flexi-bility.   Each *manche* was subdivided into two *manchettes,* having a composition of six files of thirty-two men each.   Each *plésionette* was subdivided into two maniples of twelve files of sixteen men each [82] (see Figure 8). The three formations, already referred to, were added, i.e., *en phalange, en bataille,* and fully open.[83]

In addition to these changes, Mesnil-Durand also cut in half the company of grenadiers to three officers and forty-nine men. In place of the suppressed grenadiers, he substituted a company of light infantry with a strength of three officers and fifty men.[84]

Mesnil-Durand devoted considerable attention to the question of fire and fire action in his revised system, ending all pretence of making fire with his column. He did claim that his system had the ability to fight with fire when necessary, for he said, "In its [the *plésion's*] natural state, it is not very proper for musketry. I have acknowledged this and renounced the claims of Folard on this matter. But what compels it to remain in its natural state? What hinders it, when necessary, from developing itself by some maneuvers, as rapid as [they are] easy, in order to give itself a fire equal, or even superior to that of the battalion?" [85] A bit further on he set forth a principle. "One ought never, and the *plésion* will never, forget this principle, to amuse oneself with musketry, only when it is impossible to employ the *arme blanche*." [86]

He declared that if the *plésion* could not charge the enemy because of some impassible obstacle, then it could not be charged and could make its maneuvers without fear of interruption.[87] The *plésion* was superior to the battalion in all cases where it could charge, and it was not inferior in any way when it had to make fire.[88] In this connection, Mesnil-Durand declared that he would not stop to describe how the first rank disencumbered itself of pikes, as this would uselessly lengthen his *mémoire*. The only *à propos* comment is, "no doubt!"

The first system for making fire was by developing or deploying the *plésion* which was done by a line of half-sections, which would form a firing line on a depth of four ranks. (Mesnil-Durand declared in his text that the line was on three ranks' depth. He did not explain how it obtained this depth. He referred to this as being done by half-sections which would give four ranks since a section had eight ranks. This is not the only place where there are discrepancies in his text, or between text and plans.)

The leading half-section would not move. The rest of the *plésion* would face right and left by *manches* and march by the flank. As each half-section was unmasked, it would halt, face to the front, and move up to the firing line on a level with the first half-section as indicated in Figure 11. The fire was made by *demi-manches*,

15	13	11	9	7	5	3	1	2	4	6	8	10	12	14	16
							3	4							
							5	6							
							7	8							
							9	10							
							11	12							
							13	14							
							15	16							

FIGURE 11

that is, by half of one of the units shown in the figure. The center *demi-manches* of half-companies 1 and 2 would fire as soon as the facings were made. Then the two flank *demi-manches* of these half-companies would fire in their turn. By this time, the half-companies of the second half-section, numbers 3 and 4, would have come into line, and their *demi-manches* nearest the center would fire, followed by the flank ones. By the time the whole section had thus fired, the second section would be ready to commence fire, and the *demi-manches* which fired first would be ready to fire again. Each section fired by itself and in four divisions.[89] The *plésion* could also deploy by maniples, putting all four on the same line at the necessary intervals, and then deploying as above.

To make use of the above methods, the *plésions* would have, of course, come upon the field with intervals sufficient to give room for deployment. If they were closer together, so that they could not fully deploy, one could form a firing line on three ranks by drawing some platoons from the rear of the *plésion* and joining them to the support platoons to form the firing line in front of the shortened *plésion*.[90] A further method of fire was by *manchettes*, in which the *plésion* separated by *manchettes* so that there were six paces of interval between them. The fire was conducted on the principle of the *feu de chaussée* with the half-companies filing successively to the rear after firing. (In the *feu de chaussée*, the front rank fired and then filed away by the right and left faces of the column to the rear in order to form behind the last rank and reload. The second rank fired, did the same, and so on. This was the type of fire used by the British at Concord where they could not deploy on the bridge.)

Mesnil-Durand had obviously come a long way in the course of three years. He had been compelled to make very drastic concessions to fire action and to adapt his *plésion* to deployment and to systems of developing fire which were quite analogous to those in use by the battalions of his day. He still would not admit of fire action if it was possible to get at the enemy, but he had come to see that this latter was not always feasible.

He reasserted all the claims which he had made for the *plésion*. He declared that the *plésion* was immune to fire to a large degree. This point seemed to bother him, however, for he declared once more that, even if he did lose more men, the purpose of an order is to assure victory and not to prevent exposure to artillery. He did not seem to think that heavy losses would repulse his attack.

The *plésion* gains thus very notably in mobility and flexibility. It is no longer, far from it, the mass formerly proposed by Folard; but one can note that, the more progress it makes in this direction, putting intervals between the ranks and sections, the more it tends to have no further *raison d'être*. The day on which it will become light enough and flexible enough to be of practical use, it will be no more than an ordinary column scarcely condensed.[91]

Tactical Developments of the First Half of the Century

The French Army continued to be essentially as Louis XIV left it for a half-century after that monarch's death. There was some little improvement in detail, but nothing of major note was accomplished until after the War of the Austrian Succession, when the general drill books or regulations began to appear. Until then each regiment had handled such matters to suit itself. The open column of march continued to be the only one, since the armies were still confined to deploying on the flank by quarter-wheels. Training of troops was extremely elementary, being generally limited to the manual of arms and marching. The recruit, turned over to a sergeant or corporal, was given no special instruction. The most astonishing thing was that no fire training was given, either individually or collectively, in spite of the evidence, repeated emphatically during the War of the Austrian Succession, of its paramount importance. The old badly-founded idea, which Folard never tired of repeating, that the French troops were suited only for shock action and were too badly disciplined to engage in steady fire combat, led to supine acceptance of the enemy's superiority in this matter. The soldiers were allowed to fire forty rounds per year, but no effective use was made of this.[1] There was some improvement in armament though the fusil and bayonet were much inferior to those of 1789. It was only after the War of the Polish Succession that the iron ramrod, which so improved the rate of fire, was issued. The cartridge, adopted in 1744, also tended to increase the rate of fire.

There was some progress in evolutions even before the appearance of the drill books. Even the simplest, however, breaking a line to right or left into column by wheeling, came to be done easily only about 1760. The greatest difficulty was the four-yard interval between ranks. Many regiments began to close ranks for maneuvering, though not for marching, which merely added one more complication to the theory of movement. This situation continued without much change until 1754 although means of speeding deployment were sought. This, in turn, led the Ordinance of 1753 to vary the distance between ranks according to the front of the column. This distance was to be four feet in columns of sections and platoons, eight for those of *manches* and half-ranks, and twelve for those of battalions. These were with lines, the only formations recognized.[2] Regimental staff-officers were everywhere engaged in the search for more easily handled formations.

Though the column of Folard met with some acceptance, it also met with much criticism. There were many officers who agreed with him upon the advantages but who would not accept his version. They remembered the lessons of the battles of Spire and Denain, and they looked no further for a column of attack than the ordinary route column. St.-Pern, Crémilles, Chevert, and Brézé favored them.[3]

At the middle of the century, regulations or ordinances, that is to say drill books, began to be issued. Several of these appeared in rapid succession and the period of regimental autonomy in the field of tactics was over. Not all of these ordinances are preserved today; some are known only by the extensive commentaries and critiques made upon them. Commenting upon them collectively, Colin declared that they were successively less and less imperfect and that they established, with all the necessary detail, the numerous precautions which had become so familiar to the soldiers of his day. This familiarity, and the habits and traditions formed in consequence, made it possible to abridge the necessary directions which were essential in the eighteenth century. To this succession of ordinances, culminating in that of 1791, he attributed the "rare perfection" with which the volunteer battalions maneuvered at Jemappes in 1792. "It is in comparing Rossbach and Jemappes that one can appreciate the work of the tacticians and instructors of the age of Louis XVI." [4]   This is anticipating, however, for a long road remained to be covered, of which the various ordinances were the mileposts.

The first was referred by Villate to the year 1748,[5] but Colin dated the first of the series in 1750. At any rate, the Ordinance of 1753 was the first to receive general application. This regulation, drawn up by a friend of Folard, adopted a heavy, massive column similar to his, as did the Ordinance of 1754 which soon followed. The column of the former was formed as indicated by Figure 12. The battalion was divided into three *manches* and formed on four ranks. The whole battalion about-faced and then

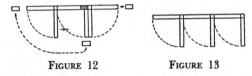

FIGURE 12   FIGURE 13

each *manche* wheeled; the first making a left quarter-wheel and the second a right quarter-wheel in such a manner as to face each other. The third *manche* likewise made a right quarter-wheel and then moved forward to place itself adjacent to the second *manche*. The whole battalion then faced to the front giving a column of twelve files and about forty ranks. Finally, the grenadier company moved to its left to place itself at the head of the column, while the picket moved to place itself at the rear. There was also a simpler but slower method by which the battalion, after about-facing, made right quarter-wheels with all three *manches* at once, closed up, and faced forward as in Figure 13. The resulting column was of the type advocated by Folard, a closed and condensed column without intervals or internal subdivisions.[6] This method of ployment was clumsy at best, and like Folard's, it required the battalion to be stationary. This ordinance would certainly not have been drawn up if Saxe had been living for he had never accepted the deep, condensed column in spite of his friendship for Folard. Saxe's disciples, who had heard and understood his observations, sought to make armies more maneuverable, less in deepening the formations than in increasing the intervals between battalions. Saxe and d'Herouville, one of these disciples, had understood the advantages of the Roman legion much better than Folard, for the last ranks do not furnish moral support for the front ranks, which are much better supported by a second force some distance to the rear.[7]

In actual practice, small columns were often used even though the ordinance did not mention them. They were formed by breaking the line by platoons which made right quarter-wheels followed by left-turns, somewhat similar to the right-by-squads long used in the American Army. See Figure 14. The grenadiers

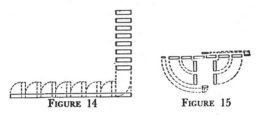

FIGURE 14   FIGURE 15

and the pickets (not shown) would place themselves in the intervals, head the attack, or cover the retreat.[8]

Various forms of hollow squares were tried out during the period, dispite Folard's vigorous denunciations, which led the Ordinance of 1754 to form a massive column of attack in this style by means of rearward quarter-wheels of the wing *manches*. This was performed in a six-platoon battalion. See Figure 15.[9]

The Chevalier de Puységur, captain in the Régiment de Vermandois, strongly criticized the column of 1753. He declared that the divisions were not distinct and that the officers could only watch and control their particular parts with difficulty. The center and rear of the column, since it marched by files, could not accurately follow the movement of the head for very long. With all liaison destroyed, it would lose much of the force of its impulsion. It was not suitable for either attack or retreat, since it was a mass incapable of any movement or execution which required promptitude and rapidity.[10]   Others declared that the column, on penetrating a trench and wishing to deploy to meet a counterattack, would have to penetrate to its full length before it could deploy.

This would frequently be impossible for any of a thousand reasons.[11]

In summing up the developments to the year 1755, it can be said that a certain number of officers had become partisans of the *ordre profond* for attacks with the bayonet and believed them more efficacious than musketry. In spite of this, the troops were still formed, generally, on the *ordre mince,* and combat by fire was still the order of the day.[12]

The battles of the War of the Austrian Succession had made the French realize how efficacious good fire could be. The French suffered very severely from the fire of the British and Hanoverians, particularly at Dettingen and Fontenoy. Nineteen officers and six hundred men of the French and Swiss Guards fell at the first British volley in the latter battle.[13] Saxe used very diverse formations in the battles of this war, lines, columns, and skirmishers.

The Ordinance of 1754, however defective its column might be (and it was without doubt even more so than that of 1753), adopted some very important improvements. First, it finally established the march in cadence to the consequent great improvement in the ease and accuracy of maneuvers. Second, it made the obvious change demanded by the great improvement in the rate of fire, namely, the reduction of the number of ranks from four to three, already adopted in the Prussian Army. This formation allowed the more effective use of firearms. Once again the improvement in the rate of fire was followed by a reduction in the depth of the order. It was not to be the last time.

One more development of infantry during the period remains —the revival of skirmishers. In the seventeenth century, such generals as Turenne made great use of skirmishers, drawing them from a picket of fifty fusiliers in each battalion as well as from the company of grenadiers, occasionally used in this manner. This had given much flexibility to their tactics. During the War of the League of Augsburg the use of skirmishers ceased and they were absent from all the great battles of the War of the Spanish Succession. Dragoons, which had also been used in this manner, had been pretty much assimilated to the cavalry. The pickets of fifty men continued, but they were not used outside of the line with the battalion. Their chief use was for petty warfare, affairs of posts, and campaign service. There were many free companies, but they were used far from the armies on independent service.[14]

From the time of the Regency, however, the use of skirmishers not only reappeared but became very extended. The pickets and grenadiers were used in advance or on the flanks of the line. They were sometimes regularly deployed and sometimes spread out to line a hedge, a farm, a mill, or the edge of a wood. Their fire greatly increased in rapidity, one or two shots per minute for each fusilier. They began to exercise an important influence on the course of battles, and were no longer at the mercy of the bayonet charge.[15]

There was increasing experimentation with them in camps of instruction, particularly those of 1727 and that of Gray in 1754. At the former the grenadiers advanced to fire and retired to the right and left of their battalions to load. The report on the latter camp declared that a doubled formation on six ranks, firing only with its pickets and grenadiers, would destroy entirely a formation on three ranks, firing with its whole line. At the Camp of Aprémont, skirmishers alone successfully defended villages. At the Camp of Plobsheim, having a brigade in support, they successfully drove enemy posts from behind hedges.[16] Saxe was a strong advocate of the use of skirmishers and employed them extensively. Those of his school naturally were in agreement, and Bombelles in his observations on the Ordinance of 1754 said that French infantry should fight with the bayonet and not with fire. He said that when they found themselves behind a trench, hedge, or brook, they should use their *feu de chasseur* (independent fire) which was very deadly when well aimed, while fire by command produced only a mediocre effect. The former was more in line with the national genius.[17] In summary, one can say that no French Army was henceforth complete without skirmishers.

Colin reported, as an example of the use of skirmishers in war, the regiment of Grassin (composed of irregular troops, eight hundred foot and four hundred horse) which was dispersed along the edge of the Wood of Berry at Fontenoy, and there, by their fire, stopped completely the flanking attack of Ingoldsby's brigade.[18]

This event is illustrative of still another development of the period. From the War of the Austrian Succession, where the French came in contact with the Austrian Army's swarms of light irregular troops, the French began to enlist similar bodies. The Regiment of Grassin was one of these. They were called legions

FIGURE 16

and were usually composed of mixed horse and foot. They supplemented the battalion skirmishers and were also used independently, as in this case, to cover the front, flanks, and communications of the army. They were the precursors of the regular light cavalry (hussar) and light infantry regiments of the army.

The reduction of the number of ranks to three alarmed not only the partisans of Folard but also those of Saxe, though the latter were mollified when the Ordinance of 1754 permitted the doubling of the ranks in all cases except fire combat. The Ordinance of 1755 continued this, and also abandoned the rearward wheels for ployment. Under this last Ordinance, columns were formed merely by placing one platoon behind another, though Folard's influence prevailed to the extent that no intervals were left between them, and two battalions were joined to make a column.[19] (See Figure 16.) The grenadiers and pickets remained on three ranks. They were supposed to form the head of the column and to fire while the column charged.

The doubled formation on six ranks was strongly criticized by Bombelles. He declared himself against keeping the grenadiers and pickets on three ranks and the rest of the battalion on six, pointing out that an accidental shot in a battalion will almost always cause the whole battalion to fire despite all that the officers can do. Bombelles thought that just as soon as the grenadiers and pickets started firing the whole battalion would join in. "Woe to the infantry which has committed that fault!" He insisted that fifty years' experience showed that the formation on three ranks made a battalion too weak and too wavering and that the formation on four ranks was best. The formation on three subjected the battalion to opening gaps more frequently while marching in line, while the fourth rank shortened the front of the battalion and sustained the first three sufficiently. The fifth and sixth ranks only caused confusion.[20]

Crémilles in 1753 wrote in the contrary sense.[21] He insisted that for fire, it was necessary to have a formation with the greatest front and the least depth possible, while for bayonet action, less extent and more depth was necessary. He felt that the formation on four ranks, then still in use, was very defective for either type of action.

About this time, 1755, there began to appear partisans of an *ordre mixte* standing between those of the *ordre mince* and *ordre profond*. Sparre declared that Folard had demonstrated sufficiently the advantage of attacking in column, but he felt that the advantage would be even greater if the columns were sustained by a deployed line.[22] The Comte de Beaujeu, in a letter of December 17, 1754, proposed alternating columns of two battalions with battalions formed on three ranks. He was opposed to the exclusive use of a deployed line in fire combat and favored rather a mixture of shock and musketry.[23]

The foregoing indicates the conflict of opinion. Some were partisans of the exclusive use of columns and shock; others, apparently fewer in numbers, were partisans of the line and fire combat only; still others were looking for a middle ground which would allow at least some of the advantages of the two extremes. It was generally admitted by those of greatest experience that French troops were too little disciplined and too badly trained to sustain fire combat against British or Prussian troops and that it was necessary to utilize their ardor by charging with the bayonet. The thin order of three ranks did not seem to give enough force or propulsion to the battalions for this. They were difficult to direct and to keep from wavering. There was adopted, consequently, a section or platoon column of battalion, or smaller, strength. Many followed Saxe, however, and were content to double ranks.[24]

So far attention has been concentrated upon the infantry. A brief word is needed upon the other arms. The cavalry showed little, if any, improvement over the infantry, tactically speaking. Maneuvers consisted practically of changing from line to column and vice versa. The small tactical unit was the squadron which might run from one hundred thirty to one hundred sixty or more men. The large tactical unit was the brigade, formed on two lines, the first continuous, the second with intervals between squadrons. The cavalry dressed so badly that in the War of the Austrian Succession when the companies were increased from twenty-five to thirty-five, it could not march in line. Notwithstanding the efforts of various officers such as Folard and Drummond de Melfort, aide-de-camp to Saxe at Fontenoy, the Ordinance of 1755 merely imposed uniform organization on the two ranks. This was the "only progress realized during half a century when already for ten years the Prussian cavalry had an almost modern regulation, which, as one knows, was drawn up by Seidlitz." In addition to this, the French cavalry was badly armed, its saber being too short and unwieldy, and though France had 37,000 cavalry, its two-squadron regiments were too weak for fighting purposes.[25]

An important reform was made during the period in the artillery. The artillery materiel of Louis XIV "was powerful and solid, but heavy and not very mobile." The minister of war of the late Regency and after, Le Blanc, had placed De Vallière at the head of the artillery. The latter, in 1732, carried through the adoption of a new system of artillery named for him. It made little or no improvement in the matter of weight over that of Louis XIV and was still very heavy and solid. The major achievement was in the reduction of the number of calibers and their standardization. The field guns were four-pounders, eight-pounders, and twelve-pounders. The siege guns were sixteen-pounders and twenty-four-pounders. They were well made but showed little or no improvement in rate of fire.

There was a younger school, led by Marshal Belle-Isle, which was impatient at the stagnation in the artillery. The marshal was guided by Belidor, great pioneer in ballistics. Belle-Isle was able to impose the adoption of regimental guns and mounted mortars. The former were much in vogue during the eighteenth century. In addition to batteries of regular field artillery, there were attached to each battalion light guns, one or two in number, which were supposed to be very effective because of their rapid rate of fire, and because, unlike the regular guns, they could accompany the infantry in its attack. The guns used for this purpose were called Swedish guns (four-pounders apparently), being very much lighter than the field guns. They were adopted in the French Army in 1740 and were supplemented or replaced in 1756 by others called Rostaing guns. Reboul claimed that they could fire eight or ten shots a minute. Many officers were opposed to them, especially among the high command and the artillerists, because they felt that the rapid rate of fire could not compensate for their dispersal along the line. Among these officers was Gribeauval, who also campaigned against the whole of Vallière's system.[26]

Down through the year 1755, the French Army could show some progress tactically although it was not very great. The infantry showed most improvement, but this was chiefly in matters of detail which had the effect of committing the Army still further to fire action at a time when many of its best minds were seeking means to reduce dependence upon it. Little improvement was made in fundamentals beyond the cadenced step. Maneuvers were still slow, deliberate, and limited to changing from open column to line and vice versa by wheeling. They in no way matched those of the Prussian army in promptitude, a handicap which played its part in more than one defeat of the Seven Years' War.

The old fire by rank had been abolished for a dozen years, and fire was now performed by section, platoon, *manche,* half-rank, or battalion. These were all the same in type, differing only in the extent of front firing at one time. There was in addition the *feu de chaussée* for use by columns. Speed of fire in the standard deployed formation reached three and four shots per minute.

The cavalry showed little improvement. It had had its moments of glory in the War of the Austrian Succession, as at Fontenoy, but also its moments of shame, as at Dettingen. In the Seven Years' War, it was to have its moments, not only of shame, but of stupidity. At the battle of Minden, for example, seventy-two squadrons calmly watched 8,000 British infantry debouch and deploy before them. They sat motionless boot to boot in three lines, receiving their attack and their fire before stirring! [27] The artillery had been improved to the extent of being standardized and made uniform in calibers and construction. The Army was still, however, essentially as Louis XIV had left it, save in one respect, for under Louis XIV, the Army was still that of the king; under Louis XV, it became that of the state.

Most of the tactical progress had come in the last two years, and the Army was by 1755 in the condition in which it was to conduct the Seven Years' War. Line, column, and skirmishers were about to be submitted to the test of war. The experimentation had been extensive within the Army, but the conflict between the thin order and the deep order seemed to have concluded in a compromise between the extremes. This apparent conclusion of controversy was delusive, however, for the appearance of Mesnil-Durand's book reopened it more bitterly than before.

DURING AND AFTER THE SEVEN YEARS' WAR

As the French Army entered the Seven Years' War, it still had very serious difficulties in maneuvering due to the lack of precise rules for deploying a column instantly. Open columns were used, and it was necessary to correct intervals and alinement before deploying. This had been improved but not eliminated by the adoption of the cadence and elbow-to-elbow files in 1754. No one even dreamed in 1755 of deploying closed columns directly. [28]

The partisans of the *ordre profond* had, by their writings, greatly stimulated the study of columns, but unfortunately, the net effect of the books of Folard and Mesnil-Durand had subordinated the question of the column to that of exclusive shock action, and this tended to confuse the problem. Excess of interest in fire had led to excess of interest in shock and a tendency towards exclusiveness which stimulated lively controversy. [29] The experienced officers generally distrusted the massive and unmaneuverable columns whether they were those in the theoretical writings or those in the Ordinances of 1753 and 1754. These men, on the basis of their writings, would never have dared to use them on the battlefield.[30] There were considerable differences of opinion on the tactical formations which should be employed and on how they should be used. The Ordinance of 1755, which was in force during the war, permitted them all; thin line, doubled line, closed column, and skirmishers.[31]

General knowledge about the French part in the Seven Years' War [32] has been largely confined to the fact that French troops were generally badly led and often beaten. There is one idea which needs to be dispelled, and that is, that, while the troops were poorly commanded, they were mediocre in all respects, especially tactics. On the contrary, this period is one of the most interesting, tactically speaking. During the war, all the ideas of the past thirty years, thin lines, mass formations, skirmishers, formations of readiness, battalion guns, and the divisional system, were tried out "with a mistrust of routine and a desire for progress which was to lead to the complete recasting of our regulations and our tactics." [33]

The French normally kept the traditional formation of two lines of deployed battalions when the ground was regular enough to permit it, as was the case at Crefeld. But in other battles, notably at Rossbach and Minden, the *ordre profond* appeared. In the former battle, the Allied army of Marshal Soubise was surprised by the Prussians under Frederick while on the march. The leading regiments were able to form in columns of attack and did so, attempting to charge and break the Prussian line. The latter's fire quickly brought these attacks to a standstill and brought French officers "to sounder ideas on the superiority of the *arme blanche*." [34] At Minden the *ordre mixte* appeared. Each infantry brigade was ordered by Marshal Contades to form its first battalion in column and its others in line. The former was not to be deployed even after the action began.

At Hastembeck, the first major battle of the war where Marshal Richelieu defeated the Duke of Cumberland, it seems certain that the grenadiers and pickets which General Chevert sent forward on the wooded heights, must have fought as skirmishers, except perhaps those grenadiers held in reserve. The brigades

were formed first in columns of battalions, but they broke by platoons to form several columns as the forest became denser. At
Klostercamp in 1760, the Auvergne brigade charged the enemy
in column while the Alsace brigade deployed to attack the village.
Several other brigades debouched in column and then deployed.
At Sundershausen in 1758, the bulk of the French were deployed
with seven companies of grenadiers scattered some two hundred
meters in front as skirmishers. The right was covered by three
more companies and the left by light troops who very effectively
turned the enemy's right.

Very much the ablest of the French leaders in the war was
Marshal Broglie (1718-1804). At the battle of Bergen in 1759,
he replaced the traditional second line by a massed reserve. This
was the first time that this had been done. He occupied the village with eight battalions and placed seven battalions in column
to sustain it. Four more regiments, also in column, were placed
still further to the rear, ready to march to the village if necessary.
The regular troops in front of the village fought in line (or as
skirmishers) and in column by turns. The sustaining troops were
brought up as needed for the fighting around Bergen and repulsed all of the enemy's attacks. Colin declares that Broglie, or
his councilors, were thus completely freed from the conventional
practices of the preceding generation and employed the various
formations according to the situation. He says that the accounts
of the battle do not mention the battalion skirmishers as they are
too concise for that. Several battalions of "Volunteers," that is
light troops, which all fought as skirmishers, held the advance of
the left and fought the enemy to a draw there.

Broglie instituted a company of chasseurs, light troops, in each
battalion of the line, intending them to fight as skirmishers. This
started a controversy for he was accused of desiring to separate
them from their battalions as was sometimes done with grenadiers. He denied this vigorously in a letter to the minister of
war. The minister, in 1762, refused to create permanent chasseur
companies in each battalion, however. The Regulation of 1764,
which was drawn up by Broglie, recommended a section of tirailleurs in front of each column of attack. The matter of chasseur

companies did not end there as other advocates for their establishment appeared.

In the Seven Years' War, the deployed line remained the basic combat formation, the one most frequently used, even by generals who were declared partisans of the *ordre profond* in time of peace. They were used, not only in open ground, but also on the edge of orchards, gardens, and along hedges. Columns were used on a variety of occasions for combats of posts and for surprises. Though they were used in combat, their most frequent use on the battlefield was as formations of readiness and as marching formations. In the broken country of Western Germany, numerous small columns which deployed and reformed completely were used. "Certainly our infantry had gained very much in flexibility and, in the hands of more capable leaders, it was able to obtain some decisive successes, in spite of the greater precision of its adversaries." [35] It is evident that French officers generally considered the *ordre profond* to be advantageous on many occasions. The mixed order also began to appear, and there were no actions without skirmishers. The latter were used spread out in front of the regular order, whether in line or column, but their most frequent use was in concentrations on the wings of the armies where they were used both offensively and defensively.

The armies which had been used throughout the modern period down to the middle of the eighteenth century were single entities. They marched in a formation which was directly analogous to that in which they fought, i.e., they could take up their order of battle by a direct maneuver from the order of march. The difficulties which had long attended even such a simple maneuver as the simultaneous wheel into line have been discussed already. The Prussian Army, during the period under consideration and especially during the Seven Years' War, reached the ultimate perfection of this traditional method of warfare. Through long years spent in meticulous drill, it had attained such rapidity and precision of performance that it could deploy from two or three open columns by simultaneous wheels in a very few moments, and thus present a well-dressed line to a surprised enemy. A master of war, such as Frederick the Great, had in his hands the most highly perfected instrument possible for this old style of warfare in which armies fought as rigid, unitary bodies. It is not surprising that the results achieved were so successful.

The French were far from attaining anything like an equality in this matter of deployment. Like other European armies, they were at a serious disadvantage when opposed to the Prussians. To compensate for this disadvantage, the French began to multiply the number of columns, in order to cut the time and distance required for deployment. This led to the establishment of the divisional system, one of the greatest landmarks in the history of warfare.

It has already been remarked that Saxe's theories on tactics foreshadowed the divisional system. It was sketched out still further by his practice in the last campaigns of the War of the Austrian Succession. This system was regularized and fixed by the famous instruction given by Marshal Broglie at the outset of the campaign of 1760. Its purpose was to compensate for the mediocrity of the French troops in drill and to speed the process of deployment.

The infantry of the army was divided into four equal divisions,[36] while each wing of cavalry also formed a division, and this organization was to last throughout the campaign. The army ordinarily marched in six columns as compared to the two or three of the old system. Great emphasis was laid upon speed of deployment and accustoming the troops to it. The generals assigned to command the divisions were ordered to take great care to maintain the distances between columns so as to have room to deploy. When warned that the enemy was near, the generals were to see to the carrying out of the following: (1) forming at least two columns of the one they led, and, if possible, forming each of these of one-half first-line troops and one-half second-line troops; (2) maintaining the intervals by sending an intelligent staff officer to ride half way between the columns to warn if they began to converge; (3) closing up the battalions and squadrons to twelve-pace intervals on approaching the ground of deployment; and (4) deploying the second line simultaneously with the first and three hundred paces behind it. Each brigade was to have a battalion of grenadiers and of chasseurs.

Each division was to be composed of not more than sixteen battalions which would form in a column of platoons at three-pace intervals between ranks and twelve paces between battalions, a column about one thousand paces long (six hundred seventy yards). By the formation ordered at deployment time, this would be cut to five hundred paces or two hundred fifty for each line. Only four battalions would deploy together according to this arrangement, and this would be done under the protection of four battalions of grenadiers and chasseurs which formed the division's advanced guard. It is to be noted that this organization aspired only to a linear combat formation in spite of Broglie's manifest preference for the *ordre profond*. It should further be noted, however, that the employment of columns was essentially the same as under the Republic and the Empire, to steer the troops easily forward to the logical ground for deployment. This use was laid down by the instruction.

A manuscript was drawn up somewhat later under Broglie's inspiration which was entitled *Observations sur l'armée française en Allemagne.*[37] It set forth the maneuvers in which the army was to be trained during winter quarters and formed a natural sequel to the instruction. It established an infantry division at a strength of sixteen battalions and eight park guns which was to be commanded by a lieutenant-general. A *maréchal-de-camp* was to command eight battalions and four guns while a brigadier commanded four battalions. A cavalry division was to be composed of twenty-four squadrons and eight guns under the command of a lieutenant-general and would be subdivided in the same way as an infantry division.

This manuscript set forth four principal maneuvers for the army: (1) to deploy the columns into lines; (2) to charge the enemy in line, or posted, with the different arms and make the victorious troops do a quarter-wheel on the enemy flank; (3) to form the general retreat of the army; and (4) to reform the army after a victory. There were also four particular maneuvers for the division: (1) to form columns of retreat by division; (2) to attack infantry outside of the line with the cavalry division; (3) to sustain a separate attack by the arm most proper to procure success to the attacking corps; and (4) to turn an enemy post by a movement to flank or rear.

The order of battle in a plain would have the infantry in the center in three sections of two divisions each (which would envisage six infantry divisions, of course, instead of the four of the instruction). Each division would have eight battalions in each line, and, in a third line, four squads of pickets ready to charge the enemy at the first disorder to prevent his rallying. The cavalry would be on the wings, having its first line full and its second with intervals, that is, it would have more of its squadrons in first line than in second. The extremity of each line was to be reinforced by a brigade of infantry in column ready to form to the flank and fire on the pursuing enemy cavalry if it defeated that of the French. The dragoons and hussars were to be divided into two halves drawn up in column in third line behind each wing of cavalry, ready to debouch on the flank of the enemy cavalry if the first charge was successful. If it was unsuccessful, then it could make a quarter-wheel on the flank of the retreat and charge the victorious enemy in its flank. The reserve was to be composed of grenadiers, carabiniers, gendarmerie, two brigades of infantry, and two of cavalry.

Each infantry divisional commander should seek to shake the enemy by the fire of his first line and then advance at the double to attack with the bayonet. The second line should also advance at the double, closed up. The four squads of pickets should then debouch and charge the enemy's second line while the infantry reformed and also moved upon it. It should be easy to overthrow because of the disorder caused by the flight of the first line. The infantry should at once quarter-wheel upon the flank of any part of the enemy line which still held. This was the conception of a standard pitched battle in a plain, the kind which seldom, if ever, occurred any more.

In summing up, the French wished to compensate for the Prussian precision and rapidity in drill by employing columns of divisions or brigades which were easy to maneuver and deploy.

They had adequate troops and regulations; all they needed was competent leaders.

At the conclusion of the Seven Years' War, the Duc de Choiseul, who was secretary of state for war, planned a general reorganization of the French Army. This was to remedy the defects which the war had disclosed and was in keeping with the general practice of armies which have signally failed in a war. For this purpose, he assembled a committee in 1762 in which Marshal Broglie naturally took a preponderant part, although he was unable to put through the establishment of the company of chasseurs per battalion which he advocated.[38] The first result was a series of ordinances, issued in late 1762 and in 1763, which carried through a considerable reorganization of the troops. The first of these was issued on December 10, 1762, and concerned the infantry. It reduced the number of companies in a battalion to eight of fusiliers and one of grenadiers. The former were to have a strength of three officers and sixty-three men, and the latter was to be of three officers and fifty-two men which would make a battalion of twenty-eight officers (counting a sub-assistant major) and five hundred fifty-six enlisted men.[39] The importance of this reform was to make identical the tactical unit, or platoon, and the administrative unit, or company. The section became a half-platoon, and the internal organization of the battalion was much simplified.

On December 21, similar ordinances were issued governing the cavalry and the dragoons.[40] The regiments of both arms were established at four squadrons, with each squadron composed of two companies. The company of cavalry was established at three officers and fifty-three men, which gave a squadron of six officers and one hundred six men. The company of dragoons was to be composed of three officers and forty-six men which formed a squadron of six officers and ninety-two men.

On the same day, further ordinances were issued governing hussars, certain special regiments, and the foreign infantry. The last merely regulated the number of battalions per regiment which varied. The composition presumably was the same as in the French infantry.   The last of these ordinances was that concerning the light troops, which appeared on March 1, 1763.   It retained five regiments or legions.   The composition of each legion was to be one company of grenadiers, eight companies of fusiliers, and eight companies of dragoons.[41]   Thus the light troops still remained mixed arms and had not yet become wholly light infantry.

Along with the reorganization of the Army, it was Choiseul's intention to bring out a new drill book based upon the experiences of the Seven Years' War.   The first result of this was the Regulation of 1764 which was drawn up, either by Broglie, or under his direction.[42]   The regulation devoted a great deal of space to precision and included many rules on discipline and drill. Many of these were borrowed from the Prussians.   The reason for this was the lack of discipline and facility in maneuver which had characterized the French troops during the Seven Years' War.   It was drawn up with great care and was far superior in all respects to previous ones.   It went into great detail on the individual drill of the soldier, attempting to make clear that precision in this was essential for prompt and orderly maneuvers.   The formation was to be on a depth of three or six men (grenadiers always on three) as had previously been the practice.   The intervals between ranks were to be one pace for closed, two paces for half-open, and four paces for full open.   The column of attack in 1764 was much the same as that of 1755, being composed of successive platoons ployed one behind the other, with the two center sections forming the leading element and the two wing sections the rear element. They were formed on a depth of six with an interval of two paces between platoons.   This marks the end of Folard's "closed and suppressed" column in French tactics.   There was also permitted a column of two battalions which had a front double that of the preceding one.   It was formed in the same way, but with the platoons by which the battalions were in contact forming the leading element and the outer wing platoons the rear one.

Great attention was given to the detail of making fire.   The various types of fire, by section, platoon, quarter-rank, half-rank, and battalion were defined with more care.   A new type, parapet fire, was added. It went back to old practices for in it two files of three men each went forward, formed on two ranks, fired, and returned to their position. Then the next two files did the same.

The Regulation of 1764 was the only one in the eighteenth century to mention skirmishers. It sought to regulate the practice of the Seven Years' War by pointing out that, while one should always charge the enemy without stopping to fire if possible, one could always detach the two wing half-sections and scatter them in front to fire on the enemy during the advance. They could retire behind the battalions by the intervals shortly before contact with the enemy.

In short, one can say that the Regulation of 1764 seems to have adopted the best ideas from those which had been expounded in the past or practiced in the recent war. The formation in line and the fight by fire remained standard, but the column of attack was not only adopted but recommended, and a strong offensive spirit characterized the combat regulations. The new column reconciled the ideas of Folard and Mesnil-Durand with a flexibility which the *plésion* of 1755 lacked. Lastly, there was finally given an official sanction to the long-standing use of skirmishers.

There was a vigorous and lively criticism of the Regulation on the ground that it was still too complicated and contained many useless maneuvers which formed an unnecessary burden for the troops, while some called for a larger proportion of skirmishers. An example was one general, probably the Prince de Montbarey, who declared that all the maneuvers he wanted were: to be able to march and to maintain intervals at all paces; to be able to ploy in all possible ways by half-sections, sections, divisions, half-battalions, and battalions; to make quarter-wheels; to be able to double and undouble the files by sections. He was much opposed to the columns of attack and retreat which he declared were never formed.[43] The Comte de Puységur (Louis Pierre de Chastenet, 1726-1807, afterwards secretary of state for war) agreed with Montbarey on all counts. "The column of attack will never be of use in war for too much time is necessary for its preparation and its formation. . . . The column of retreat has more inconvenience than the other." [44] Puységur also wished to cut down the maneuvers to a few simple ones. Otherwise he was favorable to the Regulation.

An anonymous officer wished to adopt the Prussian system of fire while marching, but Broglie rejected this as not fitted for the French temperament. The Prussians, he said, did not advance to charge the enemy with the bayonet but to obtain a more effective fire from closer range. This could not be used in the French Army for French troops halted as soon as they began to fire. If the fire of two sections of skirmishers was not enough, one could use two platoons according to the marshal. Broglie declared further that the enemy's fire was least dangerous when he was fired upon. Firing while advancing perhaps agreed with the phlegmatic spirit of the Germans, but not with the ardent Frenchmen. He said "perhaps" because Frederick did not always use it and Saxe condemned it.[45]

Following this vigorous discussion, the regulation was modified. The nearly unanimous opinion of the ablest generals carried the adoption of the formation on a depth of three as the habitual one even in the column of attack. All mention of skirmishers was suppressed though this did not mean that skirmishers were suppressed, and they continued to be used and even mentioned in some texts, official and otherwise.[46]

The result of this extensive correction was the Ordinance of 1766. This ordinance retained the detailed emphasis upon individual instruction and the manual of arms to which the first eleven titles were chiefly devoted.[47] The principles of marching were taken up in Title IX which declared that marching is one of the most essential parts of all drill. All regiments were commanded to neglect nothing in perfecting the march and must, above all, be able to march to the front with several battalions in line, and also to the flank.[48] Each regiment was to drill, and if possible several together, in marching at the double up to five hundred paces in all sorts of ground without ever increasing or diminishing their intervals and distances.[49]

Title VIII prescribed that each regiment was to be formed on three ranks whatever the occasion, though it was sometimes to be drilled in greater depth, i.e., to double ranks. The grenadiers were exempted from this for they were always to be on three ranks.[50] This meant that, for the first time, the column of attack was to be formed directly from the three-deep formation, and the preliminary requirement of doubling ranks before forming column was abandoned. This simplified the problem of ployment very considerably.

The process of forming columns of attack was covered in Title XV and was similar to that in the Regulation of 1764 except for the change just noted. Each column should be composed of one or, at most, two battalions. The regiments should regulate the number of columns which they have to form on this principle according to circumstances. The column formed of one battalion would have a front of one platoon, or company, and a depth of eight.

In forming the column the two center sections marched straight forward at the command of execution, while the sections on the right wing made a left quarter-wheel and those of the left wing made a right quarter-wheel, and both marched towards the center. On arriving at the ground from which the center sections had left, the wing sections successively made quarter-wheels in the opposite direction [51] from those previously made, which placed them directly behind the center sections in column.

The company of grenadiers did not take part in this movement. It had a separate one of its own. At the command of execution, it made an eighth-wheel to the left and marched diagonally to the center. On reaching position at the head of the column, it made a second eighth-wheel, this time to the right, and was in place. To form a column of two battalions, the same method was followed except that the units of the maneuver were platoons instead of sections, and the column, when formed, had double the front of the first column, that is, a front of a division instead of a platoon.[52] (The term division in the French infantry from this time on is confusing because it has two uses. It is used to mean the largest subdivision of the army, and it is then composed of two or more brigades. It is also used, as in the present case, to mean the largest subdivision of a battalion which is composed of two companies or platoons, which latter are synonymous.)

See Figure 17.[53]　Although the method of ploying was subsequently simplified, this remained its basic definitive form.[54]

For the first time, the column of retreat was formed by the same principle as the column of attack.　It was done inversely, starting with the wing sections.　These would march six paces to the rear, and then facing left and right respectively, would march by the flank towards each other.　When they met immediately

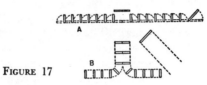

FIGURE 17

behind the center sections, they would face to the rear and march off.　As each pair of sections was cleared, it would in its turn march six paces to the rear and perform the same movements as the wing sections.　The center sections had, of course, merely to about-face and step off when their turn came.　The grenadier company followed the movement and, on reaching the ground of the center sections, it also about-faced and formed the rear of the column.[55]　The column of retreat could also be formed of two battalions.

There were two methods of deploying the column of attack. If it was a closed column, this was done by having the sections face right and left respectively and march obliquely by the flank to their position in line.　The grenadier company marched by the flank straight to its right until opposite its place in line and then alined itself to the rear.　If the column was opened to full intervals, the sections made eighth-wheels to right and left and marched straight before them until they came onto the line. They then wheeled into line on the pivot opposite the first wheel. The grenadier company made the same movements as in the first method of deployment.[56]　See Figure 18.

Beyond the method of ploying and deploying columns of attack and retreat, there were few evolutions covered in the Ordinance of 1766.　These evolutions were for the passage of defiles in the presence of the enemy, for which one used the column of attack if the passage was to be made advancing and that of retreat if one made it while retiring.[57] In addition, two methods were given for the passage of deployed lines through each other. The first was by sections, in which case, both lines doubled the sections of the platoons, one behind the other, in such a way that the first line passed through the gaps thus created in the second line. The second method was by files, in which the first line, when

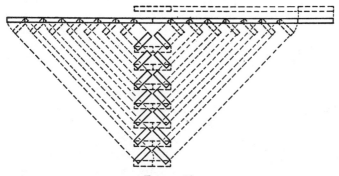

FIGURE 18

near the second, halted, faced to the right, and marched by the flank, each platoon forming a little column which wheeled to the right and marched through small gaps in the second line. These were made by doubling the end files of the platoons into the adjacent files. Once the passage was made, the lines reformed, the new second line by quarter-wheels in the opposite sense to their first, after which they faced to the front.[58]

The Ordinance of 1766 retained the various types of fire established in the Regulation of 1764, and, in addition, the *feu de chaussée* was readopted for making fire while formed in column.[59]

In summing up, it may be said that the Ordinance of 1766 was an improved version of the previous regulation and much superior to anything which had preceded it. It laid great stress upon accuracy in marching, the basis of rapid and accurate maneuvers, and upon the individual instruction of the soldier. It simplified the processes of ployment and deployment, particularly in the matter of the formation of columns of retreat which were, henceforth, formed on the same principle as the columns of attack. It reduced the number of evolutions to a very few essential ones which were also relatively simple to perform, and in all but one case required no additional instruction.

There was one question which was not settled by the Ordinance of 1766. That was the problem of marching in battle (line of deployed battalions) and of accurate deployments, i.e., methods for maintaining proper alinement during deployment. This was the subject of numerous *mémoires* to the minister during the years 1764-70, and was to lead to an aberration from the general line of French tactical development in the next decade.[60]

About the year 1766, a very considerable progress was made in tactics, for at this time there was introduced into the French Army the method by which closed columns could be deployed. (The terms ployment and deployment have been used rather loosely heretofore. They have been used in speaking of forming a column by simultaneous quarter-wheels of the units of a line, and of forming lines by simultaneous quarter-wheels of the elements of a column. The lines are always formed to the flanks of the column in this method. In the technical terms of the day, these two maneuvers were known as "breaking the line into column" and "reforming the line from column." Ployment and deployment, properly speaking, refer only to forming a column which faces in the direction which the line faced, and a line whose front is the same as the columns. The terms will be so used henceforth, and the older maneuvers will be referred to in their correct terms.) The importance of being able to form an order of battle ahead of the line of march, directly from marching columns, by a short and rapid maneuver cannot be overestimated. It would henceforth be possible to delay deployment much longer and, consequently, to execute it closer to the enemy. This would enable one to maneuver in column, a tactical development of exceedingly great possibilities. The necessity of maneuvering in line, and of long approach marches in order of battle, was obviated by this method. The circumventing of these slow and difficult movements was the true objective of the tactical quest since the end of the War of the Spanish Succession which had been misdirected by Folard's digression into the controversy of shock versus fire. This method did not require any wheelings, nor any of the square movements which had hitherto been employed. It was introduced into the French Army by the Comte de Guibert. Documents indicate that it was known and practiced in most of the regiments around 1769.[61] The resulting columns were called *colonnes de Guibert* or *colonnes à la Guibert*. They were officially adopted in the Instruction of 1769 for Light Troops.

These columns were apparently first proposed to the minister of war in a *Projet d'instruction sur les deploiements de l'infanterie*. It was written after 1764, and probably after 1766. Colin declares, and the present author agrees, that it was written, without any doubt, by Guibert, who reproduces a great part of it in the *Essai général*, of which it may be taken as a first draft.

Guibert

The most important and influential of all the military writers of eighteenth-century France was the Comte de Guibert (1743-90). With the possible exception of Saxe, he was also the most interesting. His importance lay in the fact that he devised the system of tactics which—after a period of vigorous controversy, followed by eclipse—became the basis of the Ordinance of 1791. This, in turn, was the basis of French tactics for over forty years, nearly four times as long as any of the other drill books under discussion was used. When the long tactical controversy in France was settled, it was the ideas of Guibert which were adopted. This is not all, however, for Guibert had caught the vision of a new system of grand tactics which the armies made possible by the divisional system could employ. The new mobile warfare which he sketched was one of the major sources of Napoleon's inspiration. Guibert can claim an important part in the new warfare which the Wars of the French Revolution ushered in and which Napoleon perfected. It is because of this dual influence—on the science of war on the one hand and on the art of war on the other—that Guibert can fairly claim the place of greatest importance among the writers under consideration. His influence was the greater because he did not confine himself to the infantry as so many writers did, nor to infantry with a lesser attention to cavalry as did the rest. Not only did he deal in detail with artillery, but he proceeded to emphasize over and over again the necessity of coordinating all three arms, using the properties of each to attain one's objective. In this respect, too, it does not seem too much to assume his influence on that master of the coördination of arms, Napoleon.

Guibert was only twenty-nine years old when he published his great work, *Essai général de tactique,* in 1772. He had had much less actual experience in warfare than some of the writers already discussed, but he was fortunate in his father, a very distinguished soldier, although too little known. The elder Guibert was the source of many of the ideas which his son advanced, as the latter acknowledged. He had served with distinction in the War of the Austrian Succession and in the Seven Years' War he had become what we would call chief of staff to Marshal Broglie, taking an important part in the formation of the latter's famous instruction.[1] After the war, he was employed under Choiseul, minister of war, in working on drill regulations. All the evidence indicates that the Instruction of 1769 for Light Troops was chiefly his work.[2] While on the staff of the Army of the Lower Rhine, he was accompanied by his youthful son. Here the latter served during the last campaigns of the Seven Years' War. Young Guibert served with much distinction in the Corsican War, winning the approbation of Marshal de Vaux, his commander. This completed his active service, for he was balked in his desire to serve overseas in the American Revolutionary War, and died before the outbreak of the Wars of the French Revolution.

Guibert's training in the business of war began as a small boy when his father gave him his first lessons in tactics. These lessons consisted first of talks, followed by diagrams, and finally by demonstrations on the ground. When the young Guibert understood the elements of tactics, his father made a number of movable figured plans which could represent various conformations of terrain and demonstrated with small wooden blocks the mechanism of armies, illustrated by representations of battles especially of the War of the Austrian Succession then in progress.

Following these basic lessons, the two would go out on reconnaisances where the young Guibert developed his judgment and recognition of the military features of topography. Then they took up their war game, the two forming armies and maneuvering against each other on the pasteboard plans. The son was encouraged to make objections and use his imagination. Then the two would discuss the reasons for what they had done, with the elder Guibert encouraging questions and even disagreement. Guibert remarked that his father made the study so interesting that they frequently spent the whole night at it. One can only remark that this was, in its limited field, as progressive an approach to education as can well be imagined. Few French officers in that day could have had so thorough a theoretical education as Guibert. One sees the foundation of the close bond that always existed between Guibert and his father.[3]

Guibert was something more than a soldier. There is only one term that describes him: he was a military *philosophe*. He was filled with a great enthusiasm and was always intensely ambitious, desiring fame not only as a soldier but also as a writer and literary figure. He was, further, something of a publicist; and, whereas most of the works already discussed were largely confined to the profession, the *Essai général* was widely read and discussed. The *salons* had an added topic of conversation, the relative merits of the *ordre mince* and the *ordre profond*.[4] The great éclat made by such a young man created enemies for him which seems, in part, to explain why his career was so largely one of frustration,[5] and why he leaves the impression of a potential genius who never quite fulfilled his promise.[6]

THE PRELIMINARY DISCOURSE

The *Essai général de tactique* opens with a Preliminary Discourse in which the *philosophe* in Guibert speaks, comparing the states of Europe in his day with Rome, and with an ideal state. He admired the Rome of the Republic based, he said, upon a fixed plan of aggrandizement which had, as its foundations, patriotism and virtue; the Rome which never laid down its arms until its honor was satisfied. He admired its military constitution, based upon its political constitution; the education of its youth; its great men who filled all the employments of the state.[7] He vigorously deplored the lack of these qualities in the states of his day, and he condemned their governments as weak, inefficient, extravagant, irresponsible, and oppressive. Nor were the military constitutions any better, for what happened when the debt-ridden countries of Europe went to war? They struggled with each other for years until they were exhausted, and then they made peace, transferring a colony or province here or there, with the cause of the trouble frequently not settled. What possibilities might there be for a people who constituted themselves as he felt the Romans had in their great days! Such a people could conquer all their neighbors "like the north wind bending reeds," but this would not happen for there was no people in Europe powerful enough, or new enough, to do it. One was as corrupt as another. There had been such a people at the beginning of the century, the Russians, with a sovereign capable of accomplishing all this, but Peter introduced not only the arts, but also the vices, of Europe. "He neglected the fruits for the flowers." Europe might have been overwhelmed by a new flood of barbarians from the North, but Peter failed to seize the opportunity and Russia became like the rest of the states.[8]

Existing states could be partly reformed. Although any thoroughgoing revolution such as that suggested was impossible, it would be possible for a state to accomplish something and be in a position to fight decisive wars. Such a state should strengthen itself at home rather than seek to extend itself abroad. It should even contract itself if overextended. It should perfect its administration, increase the public power, improve the laws, in a word, carry through a partial reform. He believed that France was best constituted and situated to do this, for it had the resources and natural boundaries on nearly every side. It "can be powerful enough to fear nothing and desire nothing." [9] The purpose which he had in writing this work was to set forth a plan for this regeneration.

The trouble with the governments of the day was that each minister was concerned only with his own department, was frequently a jealous rival or even enemy of his fellow ministers. There was, therefore, no cohesion and cooperation in administration, no attempt to provide a balance of benefits to all the activities which government supervised. For instance, commerce might be encouraged while agriculture was neglected or vice versa. The army might be lavished with support while the navy rotted. It was necessary to have a "general system" which coordinated administration, determined general policy, and executed it.

Guibert had the belief, common to the *philosophes,* that a government based upon a sound constitution could guarantee the prosperity, virtue, and happiness of its people. With this accomplished within, foreign policy would have as its objective to make the state respected abroad. "Only a state which grows powerful on its interior resources deserves to be respected abroad!" [10] All the evils which existed were due to the weakness of government. He painted a rosy picture of a country which, having perfected the science of government, applied these principles and became truly powerful. Such a state would have a stable and uniform foreign policy; it need not fear its neighbors, because it wished nothing from them. A brave citizens' army would stand guard on its frontiers while an abundant and virtuous people prospered within. It would neither have to be jealous of the wealth and conquests of foreign powers, nor overextend and weaken itself with colonial possessions the commerce of which would only support luxury and vice at home. It would have no need for mercantilist restrictions upon foreign commerce. It need not keep its military and naval strength secret, for with its citizens' army it would have nothing to fear from the mercenary armies of other countries. "What a difference the motives and prejudices would produce in the courage of the two sides!" If such a state was forced to make war, it would employ its full power. "Terrible in its anger, it would carry flame and iron home to its enemy." All people would tremble before it, and it would not lay down its arms until its honor had been fully satisfied. It would not enter alliances, but would act as an arbiter, pointing to itself as an example for others to follow. Finally, such a state would have a simple administration easy to manage.[11]

This is indeed a comforting picture; it is the "heavenly city" of the *philosophes* in a clear and brief compass. And it could all be brought about merely by finding the true principles of the science of government! Guibert's peroration was eloquent. "Oh my country! This vision will perhaps not always be a fantastic dream. You can make it real; you can become that fortunate state." [12] Some day, he said, perhaps a prince will come who will carry through the necessary revolution, and when he has completed it, turn over the machinery of government to the people, keeping for himself "the honors of the crown, the right to propose wise laws, the power of executing them when you [the people] will have ratified them; the absolute authority, the dictatorship in all crises which threaten the state." [13]

Here is a curious idea which shows a great ignorance of human psychology. What is required for such a program is not a man but a demigod. It clearly bears out a recent judgment that Guibert, and the *philosophes* generally, did not understand that revolutionary thinking must be followed by revolutionary action [14] if the program which is the result of the former is to be realized. Guibert seems a curious mixture; now carried away by his ideal, believing it possible to accomplish; now daunted by the obstacles and feeling that it could only come if some superman arose to achieve it.

Guibert gave a rapid review of military history from its real beginnings (under the Persians, he said) to the present. He presented the standard idea of the military renaissance, that the knowledge of the military art developed to reach its peak under Alexander and the Romans and was lost after the fall of Rome. Then it began to emerge from darkness under Maurice of Nassau and Gustavus Adolphus and reached a new peak under Turenne and Montecuccoli, a period when great generals "commanded small armies and did great things." The invention of powder did not improve the military art, it merely furnished a new method of destruction and finished chivalry. It even retarded the development of tactics. The seventeenth century showed some progress, especially in siege warfare under Vauban and Coehorn, but it also produced some bad developments, especially in the great increase in the size of armies and the very excessive amount of artillery. Armies became much more difficult to lead. Condé, Luxembourg, Eugene, Catinat, Vendome, and Villars [15] could do so, but Villeroi, Marsin, and Cumberland along with many others were overwhelmed by them.

No further progress was made in this period; only mediocre generals remained. The essential cause, the failure to study military science, was ignored, for no good work existed on the subject. Puységur had some meat among many husks, but only with Frederick did real progress resume. He invented the art "of dividing an army, of simplifying marches, of deploying troops, of handling a hundred thousand men as easily as ten thousand." This reflects the great admiration in which Guibert, in common with other *philosophes,* held the great king. He was the representative of their ideas, the man who was capable of bringing to pass the realization of their ideals, and for Guibert he was the man who had accomplished a considerable part of the warfare he desired to bring into being. In this conception, Guibert, dazzled by Frederick's achievements, misinterpreted the role of the Prussian king. Frederick was not an innovator of the new warfare which was to come into being, and in the development of which Guibert, himself, had an important part. Frederick was not the inventor of the art of dividing armies, for his armies still remained essentially of the unitary type. Actually the first ideas and practice of the divisional system belonged to Saxe, and the development of the practice on a permanent basis seems due to Broglie, or perhaps to Guibert's own father. It is true that on the field of battle, Frederick occasionally separated his armies in action, especially in the great turning movement at the battle of Torgau, but in operations his armies still remained unitary.[16]

Guibert declared that in this period, mid-eighteenth century, came the great schism of military science over the questions of whether firearms had changed tactics, and whether one should reject the ancient order because of the effect and range of artillery. Folard advocated columns almost exclusively, "and such was then the ignorance, that he had many partisans. . . . One saw the moment that all infantry would take up the pike again and form itself in phalanx." [17] From the practice of Charles XII came some gleam of light, and then came Frederick. He created almost a new system of tactics. He was nearly always successful when he was able to maneuver, and almost equally unsuccessful when he could not. Of all wars, the Seven Years' War was the most instructive. "There were performed actions worthy of the greatest captains, and faults at which Marsin would have blushed." Among the developments of the war were the very great increase in the amount of artillery, the Russians once having nearly six hundred guns, and the similar increase of light troops to an excessive proportion to line troops.

Guibert formulated the true objectives of military science as follows: The science of war should be perfected and simplified. This would make the armies smaller and easier to maneuver. The size of armies should be regulated by the topography and type of war which they are going to undertake. Officers should serve in all arms so as to know the details of each, if and when they become generals. With armies easier to move and lead, one would abandon routine movements for rapid operations, making great expeditions, forced marches, engaging and winning battles by maneuver. Positions and the defensive would be less frequent and less important. "Finally all the branches of military science would form a bundle of rays; and it is this conjuncture of light which, brought together in the mind of a single man would constitute him a *General*, that is to say, capable of commanding armies." [18]

INFANTRY

Having sketched the background and expounded the purpose of his book in the Preliminary Discourse, Guibert began his major task. For him, tactics is more than the science of handling troops. He said:

In the eyes of most soldiers, tactics is only a branch of war; in mine, it is the basis of that science, it is that science itself, since it instructs in organizing the troops, in moving them, in making them fight. It is the resource of small armies, and of numerous armies, since it alone can supplement numbers and handle multitudes. It embraces, finally, the knowledge of men, of armies, of ground, of circumstances, since these are all the collected information which ought to determine their movements.[19]

There are two parts to tactics, said Guibert. Elementary tactics include all the details of forming, instructing, and drilling the basic units of the troops. "This is what has been agitating our minds and will do so for a long time." Grand tactics is the science of generals, including all the "great parts" of war, such as movements of armies, orders of march and of battle, fortification, and employment of artillery. "It is all in a word, since it is the art of employing troops, and all other parts are only secondary things which, without it, would have no object, or would produce only embarrassment."

There had been a few partial works on this subject, he said, but it had never been fully treated. Puységur had a few good suggestions. Saxe had nothing to offer in spite of his ability. "He knows the ignorance of his age; he says it in his work." The honor of furthering grand tactics belonged to Frederick who had demonstrated that an army could be numerous and yet disciplined, that one hundred thousand men could be subjected to calculations as simple and accurate as ten thousand, and that when one had learned how to move a battalion, one could move a large army by a combination of the basic principles.

Tactics divided in two parts, and developed as I conceive that it can be, is simple and sublime. It becomes the science of all times, of all places, and of all arms; that is to say, that, if ever by some revolution not now foreseeable in the nature of our armies, one wished to adopt the *ordre profond,* it would be necessary to change neither maneuvers nor constitution to arrive at it. It is, in a word, the result of all that which the military ages before ours have thought good, and that which ours have been able to add.[20]

This is, then, Guibert's concept of tactics. He did not claim to be its originator, far from it, for the ideas were partly those of Frederick and partly those of his own father. He made these latter his own. He claimed the role of expositor and commentator.

Infantry, Guibert held, is the most important of the arms. Consequently, infantry tactics was the first with which Guibert dealt. He opened with a discussion of the education and training of the soldier. This included three parts: bodily exercise, drill and use of arms, and actual field maneuvers as nearly like war as possible. The entire youth of the country should be trained in the first.

Guibert condemned the time wasted in useless maneuvers and the perfection of ridiculous details. He would reduce the manual of arms to four movements. Instead of drill, he would spend the time in fire training and in fencing with the bayonet—a practice unknown in that day. Thus in this basic and elementary matter,

Guibert insisted on simplicity and essentials. The soldier was to be taught only what was useful to him in his profession, and there were to be no useless complexities attached to any of these matters. This passion for reducing all to the fewest and simplest items possible is found throughout his work from the lowest to the highest parts of warfare.

Contemporary infantry had the advantage over all that of the past, because there was only one kind, uniformly armed with a weapon superior to all earlier weapons, the fusil and bayonet. Infantry was both a fire and a shock arm, and its ordinance should be designed for both. He asked which function of infantry was primary and which secondary, and consequently, what would be the primary and secondary orders. To answer this question, he laid down a very sound principle which showed his grasp of the realities of combat, a grasp much more sound than that of most writers of his time. Before one could come in contact with the enemy, one must reach him without being destroyed or disordered by his fire, Guibert declared. To do this, one must gain fire superiority over him. The fire order, which means the thin order, is therefore the primary one. Moreover, the large amount of artillery and the wide use of field works made shock action between infantry very rare. This also indicated the fire order as primary. If one could come to grips with the enemy without resorting to fire action, one should do so, but even for this he thought the thin order best.

This distinction between the "primary and habitual order" and the secondary order was unfortunate for it perpetuated the quarrel between the partisans of the *ordre mince* and those of the *ordre profond* which had no real basis after Guibert's work.[21] He represented the common ground towards which the less extreme partisans of both schools had been tending and upon which they were at last to unite. When Mesnil-Durand returned to the lists, his very much modified new system led to the final and most bitter controversy between the two schools. The chief issue at point for Mesnil-Durand was whether the "habitual and primary order" should be for shock or for fire. The distinction is essentially unimportant, for troops needed to be able to fight in both ways and therefore needed a tactical system which would allow them to do so. This unfortunate dispute delayed for a number of years the final agreement.

Guibert condemned, as completely false, Folard's idea that the force of shock was increased by the depth of the order. The laws of physics did not apply, he said, because the formation was not a contiguous mass but rather was full of intervals. The shock was furnished only by the first rank. All that the rest could do was to crowd up and add to the confusion.

The order should be on a depth of three ranks for all these reasons. Three ranks, moreover, could easily fire their fusils while the bayonets of the second and third ranks projected in front of the first, thereby supporting it. Where four or six ranks were used the extra ranks could neither fire nor support the first with their bayonets. *Depth of order should be determined by the kind of arms which the troops had and the protection they could afford the front rank.*[22] Here for the first time, there was a clear recognition of the fact that the tactics of troops must conform to their armament and be determined by it. It was not to be determined by an unproven idea or by any other secondary consideration.

Guibert would permit forming in depth if the nature of the ground made it necessary or desirable to reduce the front of the formation, but not for Folard's faulty reason. To do so would provide a successive renewal of effort which was often necessary for success and would give confidence to one's own troops while intimidating the enemy's. The résumé of the doctrine is, "The primitive, fundamental, and habitual ordinance of infantry will be on three ranks of depth; the momentary and accidental ordinance will be in column." [23]

How can one move a battalion whose front is extended at the expense of its depth? This question had agitated many minds. Guibert's answer was to divide the battalion into parts. A battalion needed to be able to advance in this formation at a uniform step without wavering. He felt that a battalion should have a front of from one hundred forty files to not more than one hundred eighty. This would give a battalion of from four hundred twenty to five hundred forty men which, it will be noticed, was considerably smaller than any advocated by previous writers. A larger battalion would be too extended and subject to wavering. A smaller one could not sustain many losses without becoming too weak. His battalion would have three divisions, each of which would be subdivided into three companies. Three battalions would form a regiment, and three grand divisions an army. In this matter as in so many others, Guibert ran counter to practice and to the theories of previous writers, all uniting to support square numbers with two, four, etc., forming the basis of their tactics. Guibert declared that he used three because it subdivided naturally into left, center, and right, and three divisions of a battalion and an army. The fourth part, used in the French Army, was embarrassing since it would not fit into this division. He would not, unlike some writers, propose a new unit divorced from reality, for he thought that the battalion, with some slight changes, was the best possible unit, combining as it did, the properties of "fire, shock, simplicity, rapidity, solidarity [cohesion], and even, when one wishes it, that of depth."

Guibert declared that, while battalions must keep themselves well alined internally, it was not necessary that a whole line do so. In fact this was useless since troops seldom came to grips, another evidence of his desire to free tactics from useless complications. In contrast to the matter of alinement, Guibert insisted that troops must be able to maintain accurately their direction of march. A battalion must be able to march straight forward without wavering, opening its files, or closing on its intervals. He went into great detail on how to train troops to march correctly, how to keep internal alinement, and how to maintain direction of march. Once troops were trained in drill hall and parade ground how to do these things, they should be taken out into uneven country and taught how to pass obstacles, seize heights, or prevent their being seized. Here is another feature of his insistence upon rigorous and thorough training of the troops. There were no frills, but the troops must be as thoroughly trained for the actualities of warfare as it was possible to make them.

The ordinary step which he would increase from sixty to eighty per minute was the principle and parade step. The double, or true military step, was for maneuvering and charging, while the triple, the exact rate of which could not be fixed, was for use in emergencies such as forestalling the enemy at some essential position, gaining a flank, or charging before the enemy had a chance to form. Music was desirable, or even essential, for keeping the march regulated and encouraging the men. As for route-marches, the men should be allowed to take their natural pace. The higher officers must learn to judge the time required for infantry to cover a given distance over various road conditions and types of terrain. This can only be done in practice marches over all kinds of roads and country.[24]

Of all parts of tactics, the most faulty training was probably to be found in firing, said Guibert. It was "the most complicated, the least thought out, and the least related to actual warfare." Guibert declared that contemporary firearms were far superior to any weapon which the ancients had. He further declared that, though musketry could be reduced to theory, he doubted that there were ten officers who had done so. The whole business was left to chance, and the soldier was left to aim as he would with no training in principles of accuracy. No two fusils had identical ranges, but the general horizontal range was about four hundred yards, though the effective range was hardly more than one hundred seventy-five yards.

All the emphasis had, heretofore, been placed upon speed of fire, following the Prussian example which was much admired, he said. Though the Prussian battalions had the greatest rate of fire, they were also the least accurate. Their first discharge, loaded outside the action, was usually effective, but after that the soldier did not ram the charge home. This cut the range by as much as 75 percent. Moreover, the men did not aim, they merely raised their guns and fired. All other armies imitated the Prussian fire which had been introduced into the French Army via its German regiments.

Guibert followed Saxe in the latter's strong condemnation of the uselessness of "burning powder at the birds." This devotion to speed of fire at the expense of accuracy, "as if noise killed," hardly made it astonishing that there were battles in which five hundred thousand shots were fired and two thousand men were killed.[25] To get away from this, Guibert would give the troops a thorough training in fire principles and, in so far as possible, fire action. They should first be taught, with blank discharges, to fire alone, then in file in all three ranks, then in several files, and lastly by half-companies and companies. The same method should then be used in training them to fire with ball, all preceded, of course, by the teaching of loading and firing by the manual of arms.

Guibert would absolutely forbid the men in the front rank firing from the kneeling position, saying, "I see nothing so ridiculous and unmilitary as that genuflexion." The men in the front rank should remain standing and fire straight before them; those of the second rank should crowd up on their file leaders and fire over their right shoulders; those of the rear rank should fire over the left shoulders of the file leaders. He had seen this method used in battle. The men should be taught the principles of aiming without its theory, learning to aim directly at, above, or low on the target according to range and circumstances. He would also train them to fire obliquely to right or left, which could be done as easily as firing ahead. This method was very valuable when the enemy attacked in column, or otherwise on an inferior front, and one wished to cross one's fire on him. Those not attacked could help defend those who were. Contrary to accepted opinion, this could be done in the open as well as behind entrenchments, but the troops must be trained for it.

Guibert admitted only stationary fire. The *feu de charge* of the Prussians, he condemned, even if Frederick did use it. One could either advance on the enemy in battle, or one could not. In the latter case, one was reduced to a stationary fire action, but in the former case, it was necessary to advance upon the enemy without stopping and without firing.[26] He declared that fire delivered while advancing was not nearly as effective as that of the enemy. It caused one's troops to lose the assurance which a bold and vigorous movement gave. The latter caused the enemy, who saw one advance in spite of his fire, to waver. There was no situation in which troops should fire while advancing.[27] The Prussian *feu de charge* was contrary to all military views and impracticable in war. The only answer is that the Prussians *did* use it.

For fractional fire, such as firing by platoons, he had only one rule. It was that one part should not fire until its neighbor had finished loading, in order that the fire be as continuous and equal on the whole front as possible. The battalions should be trained to fire by ranks and at will as well. Fractional fire was best used in entrenchments. Fire by rank was best for repulsing cavalry or defending an abattis or post which the enemy was attempting to storm. The most proper type of fire for a musketry combat in the open, however, was voluntary fire. This, like Saxe, he regarded as most deadly. The troops also liked it best. They must learn to keep silent while performing it, and to cease fire on signal. This was formerly thought to be impossible, but Guibert saw it done at Filingshausen.[28]

There is a strong contrast between the attitude of Guibert and that of many other writers on fire and fire action. Many of them, including Saxe, regarded fire as highly ineffective, and hence, to be suppressed as much as possible in favor of shock action. Guibert admitted that fire was ineffective, but he pointed out the reason for its ineffectiveness, inadequate training and faulty methods. He then set about establishing methods for improving fire and giving it more efficiency. This was Guibert's characteristic attitude towards all parts of military science. He desired to obtain the most effective results and concentrated his attention to that end.

Dealing next with the problem of evolutions, Guibert demonstrated these same characteristics. Some held that evolutions were useless, he declared; others would multiply them infinitely, holding that, if nothing more, they served to exercise the troops. Guibert insisted that it was necessary to have some evolutions, for otherwise the troops would form an inchoate mass which would have to remain in whatever formation they were placed (as troops did before it was possible for infantry to perform evolutions and maneuver). On the other hand, he maintained that they must be simple, easy to perform, few in number, and have a practical use in war. They needed to be capable of rapid execution, for troops were disunited and weak while in the midst of them. He made the eminently sensible observation, "All evolutions which do not have all these properties together ought to be rejected as vicious, superfluous, and even dangerous. For in a profession where there are many necessary things to learn, one is occupied with those which are useless only at their expense." [29] Evolutions should remain fixed and invariable unless replaced by superior ones at the government's order. All evolutions were impossible under fire unless the troops were well disciplined and inured to warfare. If they were so, they might undertake evolutions, provided that they could not be attacked before completing them, or that they were protected by sufficient covering troops. No evolution was dangerous in and of itself, but it did not follow that one might use any combination indifferently. "Simplicity and speed" were the essentials. Guibert felt that only four evolutions were needed: doubling ranks, wheeling, forming column, and putting oneself in order of battle.[30]

In considering the first of these evolutions, Guibert took up the problem of infantry resisting cavalry. When infantry was expecting an attack by cavalry in a plain in which it had no points of support for its flanks, he admitted to the one exception in his general condemnation of the *ordre profond*. Here the first of his evolutions would be required. He would have his troops double ranks, not by inserting one rank between others as was usually done, but by one of the two following methods. All the right (or left if desired) half-companies of the battalion would march three double paces forward, and the others would double behind them, the battalion then closing the intervals thus created. If the cavalry were too close to permit this method, then he would do the same by half-battalion. The grenadier and chasseur companies would in any case do their doubling separately. The reasons why Guibert permitted the deep order in this case were: (1) there was only cavalry opposed, hence there was no fire to sustain; (2) by diminishing the front, there was less purchase for the cavalry if it was numerous; (3) since he supposed the infantry in a plain with no support for its flanks, the cavalry would try to envelop him if it maneuvered well, and he must have a formation which could face in all directions; and (4) the greater depth gave the formation more solidity and consistency, and incidentally, it also gave more confidence to the men.

Cavalry should learn never to attack infantry which was ready to receive it any more than it would attack fortifications. Its proper functions were to cover the flanks of infantry and sustain it, to form detachments and make raids, and to fall on the enemy's infantry when disordered either by success or defeat. It would also attack any infantry which it caught unprepared to receive it.[31]

Wheelings, the second evolution, Guibert discussed only briefly, declaring that they were so familiar as not to need a lengthy exposition. He did propose a change which he credited to a Sardinian officer and which made a great improvement in these evolutions. It was shortly adopted in the French Army by the Instruction of 1769 for Light Troops. It had been the custom to use a fixed pivot and not to permit one rank to begin its wheel until the one ahead had completed its turn. Thus the second rank arrived at the point of turning before the first had completed its wheel, causing a congestion there. The first rank marching on, while the second wheeled, increased the interval and, consequently, lengthened the column at every turn. This inconvenience could be remedied, said Guibert, by having the pivot advance progressively about four paces which allowed the second and third ranks to begin wheeling as soon as they arrived at the pivot point. Thus, by this simple device, which Guibert was quick to recognize as having merit, a long-standing inconvenience was rectified.

The real innovation of Guibert, however, lay in his formation of columns by ployment, the third of his evolutions, and the complementary formation of lines by deployment, which was the fourth evolution. Declaring that these had never been treated by any work, he went into great detail. Ployment could be executed to the right, the left, or the center. To form the column on the right,[32] the first company did not move, the grenadier company faced left and all others faced right. At the command to march, the grenadier company filed off obliquely at the double to form in front of the first company and all the others filed off obliquely at the double to the right and rear behind the first company, as in Figure 19. (To see the difference from a column formed by breaking the line see Figure 14, bottom part of figure.) This method could be carried out on any one of the fusilier companies, not merely on the right, left, and center ones, and as a result, it was extremely flexible. The quickest ployment was that on the center company, that is the fifth fusilier company, and it should be used whenever possible as it speeded up ployment.[33]

FIGURE 19

The advantages of Guibert's method have already been discussed to some extent. Forming a line directly from the columns without any turns or "processional movements" was an enormous advantage. It was certainly the greatest single tactical advance of the century and was still being used in company columns in the French Army at the beginning of the present century. Colin, who was a great admirer of Guibert, has this to say concerning it. "We, who practice this operation daily, could only find it very natural to us, and it astonishes us that it had not been adopted sooner. It is necessary to go back to that period, in order to comprehend the independence of mind and the high intelligence of the man who made that very simple maneuver replace all at once the successive wheelings and the complicated movements by which one ployed the battalion in column." [34] This is high praise from one of the ablest military historians and critics of the twentieth century, but it is followed by even higher. "If one includes the whole of these proposals on the elementary movements of infantry, one establishes undeniably that there is there a true revolution: from the position of the soldier to the movements of the battalion, nothing is regulated according to former prejudices or geometrical formulae, all is personal, dictated by the most practical, the most unpretentious mind, attached only to realities, and only to those which have a real importance." [35]

Guibert then took up the employment of columns. There had long been a controversy over the use of columns for attack, and Guibert had, of necessity, to discuss when one should employ them. He gave certain special cases in which one should use columns for attack: if the enemy was behind entrenchments or some other post which restricted one to the necessity of attacking salients while not presenting oneself on the faces; if one could only debouch on the enemy by a road, and one was compelled to assemble the troops so as to arrive by this single passage; if one wished to sortie from entrenchments or other closed works on an enemy whose attack one had repulsed.

In using columns in this way, Guibert reasserted his contention that they would not increase the shock of the attack. They are used when circumstances prevent one from attacking on a larger front. Guibert described an attack by columns in open warfare, opposing the claims of Folard and Mesnil-Durand that closed, dense columns would assure order and give better discipline.

Here is how all attacks in column take shape. One gets under way; one approaches the enemy; one cries to the soldiers "Close up, close up!" The mechanical and sheep-like instinct which causes every man to crowd upon his neighbor, because he thinks to put himself out of reach of danger by it, has already caused only too much execution of this command. The soldiers are then crowded, the ranks are soon mingled, nearly to the front rank and to the exterior files, which maintain some freedom of movement. The column forms no more than a tumultuous mass, incapable of maneuver. If the head and flanks of that column are struck by a lively fire, if it does not overcome the obstacles which it encounters at the first effort, the officers can no longer make themselves heard, there are no more intervals between divisions, the soldier dazed begins to fire in the air, the mass whirls, disperses, and can only rally at a very great distance. . . . I ask all veteran officers if this is not the picture of the bulk of the attacks which they have seen made in column.[36]

This description was based upon his own experience, and apparently upon Feuquières's description of the battle of Neerwinden. It is an exact account of those battles which took place in the Peninsula, thirty-five years later, in which the French repeat-

edly misjudged the ground of deployment and found themselves
in combat with the British while still in column. Oman quoted
at second hand a passage from Marshal Bugeaud, who served as a
battalion commander in the Peninsular War, a passage which
seems remarkable when placed in juxtaposition with the preceding quotation. It follows in part.

The usual matter of fact cannonade would commence the operation, then hurriedly, without reconnoitering the ground, we marched
against the enemy "taking the bull by the horns" as men say.

As soon as we got about 1,000 metres from the English line, the
men would begin to get reckless and excited. They exchanged ideas
with each other, the march began to get somewhat precipitate. Meanwhile the English silent and impassive, with ported arms loomed like
a long red wall—an imposing attitude which impressed novices a good
deal. Soon the distance diminishes; cries of *"Vive l'Empereur"*, *"En
avant"*, *"A la baionette"* broke from the mass. Some men hoisted their
shakos on the top of their muskets. The march turned into a run.
The ranks began to get mixed up. The men's agitation became a
tumult; some discharged their weapons without halting and without
aim. And all the while the red line in front, silent and motionless,
though we had gotten within 300 metres seemed unaffected by the
gathering storm.

The contrast was striking; more than one among us began to think
that when the enemy's long reserved fire *did* begin it might be in-
convenient presently. Our ardour began to cool. The moral influence of apparently unshakable calm is irresistable, in action against
disorder which strives to make up by noise what it lacks in firmness.
It used to sit heavy on our hearts. Then, at the time of most painful
expectancy, the English muskets would come down, they were "making ready." An undefinable impression nailed to the spot a good
many of our men, who would halt and open a desultory fire. Then
came that of the enemy, volleyed with precision and deadly effect,
crashing upon us like thunder. Decimated, we turned half around,
staggering under the blow and trying to regain our balance, when
the long pent up silence of the enemy was broken by cheers. Then
came a second volley and perhaps a third, and with the third they
were down upon us, pressing us into a disorderly retreat.[37]

These quotations answer all the claims of the partisans of the
ordre profond on the subject of the irresistible shock of the formation in depth, on how their speed was such that they could not

be halted by fire or suffer much from its effects, and how the thinner an order becomes the more fragile it is. The British were formed on only two ranks in the engagements described above.

Guibert repeated the advantages which a column has in the particular attacks where he allows its use.[38] These arguments left him open to his critics, because the reasons which he advanced for the special cases in question were favorable to the column in all circumstances.[39]

Attack columns should not have a front greater than a division (two companies), says Guibert, nor be formed of more than two battalions. A greater front was useless since it did not strengthen the effort, and it was not a question of fire. A greater depth was also useless, for if two battalions were unable to succeed then ten would not. Instead of a long column, he would have several columns with several companies of chasseurs scattered in between as skirmishers, who would advance to draw the enemy's fire and unsettle him with their own. They would also link up the attacks which would advance at the double until about two hundred paces from the enemy when they would increase to a moderate triple and break into a run at thirty paces, sweeping into the enemy's lines. There must be officers at the head to keep the men from running away with themselves and others on the flanks to maintain the intervals. If the attack succeeded, it was essential to deploy at once to receive the counterattack, the chasseurs seizing every vantage point to harass it. Guibert declared that this method of attack was especially good for the French, because it took advantage of their impetuosity. If their ardor was not thoroughly controlled, however, this type of attack would fall afoul of their indiscipline and ignorance. Here Guibert put his finger on the weakness of column attacks so clearly shown in the Bugeaud quotation, one which would indicate that this method should be avoided whenever possible. Guibert certainly weakened his position against his opponents in this section.

There were four occasions when it was advantageous to maneuver in columns, Guibert declared. The first was where one had to withdraw in the face of cavalry. If attacked, the column would close up, face to the four sides, call in the skirmishers which were covering the march and, when the attack had been repulsed, march on. If there were several columns, Guibert would arrange them so that the head of each was just even with the rear of its neighbor to right or left. He would not hesitate to cross any plain in this formation no matter how numerous the cavalry present. This disposition confirmed his opinion that battalions in column or line were animated fortifications considered relative to musketry. The whole basis of the defensive order lay merely "in knowing how by simple and rapid movements to dispose them in a way to augment and assure the effect of their fire." [40]

The second occasion for maneuvering in column was in the moves preparatory to deploying in order of battle. One could reinforce one sector at the expense of another, refuse one part of the order or feint at one point of the enemy's order to distract his attention from the point of attack.

The third occasion was when, having deployed, it was found necessary to move troops from one point to another or otherwise change one's order of battle. Guibert pointed out that the tactics in use up to thirty years before in all armies, and still used by some, were so cumbersome that an order of battle took hours to arrange. The arrangement had to be done at a great distance from the enemy, and once taken, only a bold general dared change it. With his new tactics, the movements were so expeditious, so adaptable to all kinds of ground, that deployment would be delayed until much nearer the enemy. This concealed the objective of the attack much longer and gave the opposing general less time to parry it.

The fourth occasion was for countermaneuvering, i.e., making maneuvers which were caused by those of the enemy and were designed either to counterbalance them or to reduce their effect. Actually, the last three occasions could be grouped together. The resulting movements are called battle maneuvers. One should maneuver in column on the battlefield, either in preparation for fire action, or after the action had begun. It was Guibert's method of ployment and deployment which made it possible to do this without serious danger.

Guibert would form his columns of maneuver by divisions,

composed of as many battalions as desirable. The rule to remember was that, if one had too many weak columns, they could hinder one in debouching, and if they were too large, then they would be slow and difficult to handle. All columns must march at the double, or even triple, when maneuvering. The intervals between their units would depend upon the direction in which they were to form in battle. If ahead, one used closed columns, if to the flank, open columns. It was essential that troops know how to keep accurately their intervals and direction of march. They need to be trained to do this through actual exercises.

Troops could form columns of march in either of two ways. If they wished to march forward from their position, they would ploy into column. If they wished to march on a prolongation of the flank, they would break into column. There would be times when these rules must be modified. Sometimes one would wish to march forward, but the nature of the ground would not permit ployment. It would be necessary in such a situation to break into column and, when past the end of the obstruction, take up the line of march by wheeling. Sometimes the road would not be wide enough to contain the standard platoon column, and one would have to form by subdivisions of the platoon. The rule was that the front of the column should be wide enough to prevent a disproportionate length, and yet not so wide as to necessitate frequent doublings on the way.

Guibert concluded his discussion of columns by saying that he had reduced all the different kinds of columns—those of march, maneuver, and attack—to a single one, designed for all these purposes. He had simplified its formation to so great an extent that every soldier could not but see the incontestable advantages of the change. He went on to point out that the troops then had five or six methods of getting under way to march, "all slow and processional." They had different columns for different purposes. These columns were so complicated as to be impractical in war. Finally, he had given the principles on when and how to use columns. "No military work has given any; which is not to say, nevertheless, that much has not been written on the ordinance of the column." [41]

Just as there were two methods of forming columns, so there were two for forming lines from them. They might be made by reforming the column in line by wheeling, or by deploying the column in line. The choice was determined by the direction of the front on which one wished to form, and it was necessary to keep in mind the method which one intended to use since the spacing of the units in column was different for each. The first method was so well known, Guibert said, that he spent no time upon it.

The most masterly of all evolutions, the simplest in conception and execution, the most susceptible to combinations, was, according to Guibert, the deployment of columns. He said that it was invented by the King of Prussia and had spread to all European Armies. It was the evolution which reversed ployment, and was carried out in exactly the same way by reverse movements. It could, like ployment, be based upon any of the fusilier divisions of the column. Division columns were always used for deployment, however, because one needed the most shallow column possible in order to speed deployment. A platoon column would be too deep, but, on the other hand, a column of half-battalions would have a front so extended as to give rise to confusion when deploying which must be done at the double or triple. The deployment was made to right, left, or both, depending upon which division was that of alinement. Since the division of alinement was already in place, it would remain motionless if the deployment was made standing or would move forward at the regular step if deployment was made advancing. Which of these two methods was used depended upon circumstances, as for instance, if one deployed on the last division to occupy a position at the column's rear, then one would deploy standing. This was easier and more accurate, but deploying advancing gave the advantage of gaining ground while evolving. It was necessary for the staff officers to supervise the deployment so as to correct any mistakes of judgment of the division commanders before they could cause confusion. Guibert set forth the rule that any deployment should put the divisions in line in the same order they occupied in column, that is, the first division should be to the right or left of the second division according to whether the deployment was to right or left. There is a great variety of possibilities of deployment in this evolution which renders it very flexible. Thus for instance, one may deploy three divisions to the left of the first division or to the right of it. (The leading élite company always deploys to the right; the rear one to the left.) One may deploy two divisions to the left of the second and one to the right, or two to the right and one to the left, and so on through all the possible combinations.

In connection with deployments in the various directions, Guibert vigorously attacked the strong prejudice which existed against inverting the order of units within a battalion or regiment. Normally, the order of divisions of fusiliers for example would be one to four from right to left with the grenadiers always on the right and the chasseurs on the left. Prejudice insisted that this order must always result upon the completion of deployment. Guibert, on the other hand, might ploy to the left and then deploy to the right if necessary, which would cause the former left to become the right. He answered the objection that this would destroy all order in the units by saying that it would not. At the beginning of the day, the battalion would form in its normal order, but if it became necessary to deploy with a resulting reversal of that order, it would be senseless to go through complicated maneuvers to avoid inversion. Why should a battalion which wished to march on a road on its left flank, ploy on the right and then march back to the road instead of ploying to its left in the first place? He condemned Puységur's complicated tactics for this reason.

The great advantage which Guibert claimed for his tactics was its adaptability to the situations of war. He condemned the "makers of systems" who lost out by their exclusiveness. That was the trouble with Folard who said, "Take the order which I propose . . . it is suitable for everything, it is the sole good one, the absolutely good one, the good one *par excellence.*" Guibert did not intend to follow this example, and therefore he examined certain situations in which his method did not exactly apply. He gave as an example the case of a column of march which wished to form a line at the exit of a defile from which it could not entirely debouch. In such a case, the elements of a column would face right or left, as the situation demanded, as they emerged from the defile, would move out to the ground which they were to occupy and face to the front. In this and various other situations, it was possible to devise means of forming lines, passing defiles, and so on, when his normal formations did not apply.

The tactics of Guibert had great flexibility in comparison with those which were previously in use, as he was at pains to point out. He gave two methods by which one might deceive his opponent as to the strength of one's columns and the point of attack. A column to be deployed might be kept opened to full intervals as if intending to reform in line, then be suddenly closed up and deployed when ready. On the other hand, a column which one intended to reform might be kept closed up. Then when the rear of the column reached the ground on which it was to reform, it would halt and each division would halt in turn when it had opened the necessary interval between it and the one behind it. This enabled one to keep the direction of attack concealed as long as possible, for there was a difference of up to ninety degrees in the fronts produced by the two methods.

The movements which deployed a single battalion applied with the same ease to a column of several battalions. One merely determined which division of which battalion would be that of alinement, and then deployed to both right and left without considering inversion since speed was essential. If the line upon which one intended to deploy was oblique to the front of the column, the division of alinement had to be placed upon it before the deployment began. If one was deploying several columns which marched together, one had to make sure that the intervals between them were great enough to give room for deployment. Light artillery (battalion guns) should be so placed as not to hinder deployment, and so as to come into the intervals between battalions by its own deployment. If one was deploying several columns together, as would be the case in an army, then one must arrange convenient signals for the purpose.

Guibert sought to convince those who doubted the advantages of his tactics, by taking two battalions in column and forming one

in line by the old method and the other by his.   The first battalion in column of platoons had a depth of seventy-four paces, for
each platoon occupied five paces and the intervals were three paces
$(10 \times 5 = 50 + [8 \times 3] = 74)$.   To form in line, the first must keep
this depth, but the second formed a column of divisions by doubling its front which shortened its depth to twenty-eight paces, for
each of the six divisions had three ranks, each occupying one pace,
and five intervals of two paces each $(18 \times 1 = 18 + [5 \times 2] = 28)$.
There were three methods by which the first column could form
a line ahead.   It could form a line on its flank by simultaneous
quarter-wheels, and then form the line ahead by a quarter-wheel of
the whole battalion.   It could move by a processional march in
column turning on to the line it wished to occupy and then forming the line by simultaneous quarter-wheels.   Or lastly, each platoon could make an eighth-wheel and march forward until its
flank was on the line when by another eighth-wheel in the opposite direction it would be in line.   See Figure 18.   Compared with
this, the simple deployment of the second battalion would be from
four to six times as rapid.[42]

In summing up Guibert's infantry tactics, one can say that he
recognized the preponderant role of fire power in action.   He
would normally fight in a line on three ranks.   In combats of posts
he would permit fighting in small columns of divisions with intervals, the columns linked together by skirmishers.   In this he did
not differ from the partisans of the *ordre profond,* if the question
was not one of the kind of column, for he would not admit closed
and massive ones.   He wished his troops trained as soundly as possible in the principles of firing and in all that they would be called
upon to do in actual warfare.   He wished his troops capable of maneuvering, and he would maneuver as long as he was able to, de-
laying his formation in order of battle to the last possible moment,
which his method of tactics allowed him to do.   He reduced the
number of evolutions to the bare essentials, allowing only the four
above mentioned, and yet he achieved a maximum flexibility with
these.   He was not alarmed by the prospect of wavering lines
though he did not hesitate to march on the enemy without firing

if he could get at him. Guibert's doctrine on combat was based essentially upon French practices in the Seven Years' War. This doctrine was: the preponderance of fire, thin order for combat in open country, small columns for combats of posts, skirmishers for covering attacks.[43] Guibert, by his tactics, permitted taking much greater advantage of these methods. His system of march-maneuvers, in the same way, allowed full advantage to be taken of the wartime practice of multiplying the number of columns in order to speed the formation of the order of battle. Guibert had, then, the role of applying and perfecting the lessons learned in the war. There is no clearer case of this in history.

THE OTHER ARMS

Guibert declared that he was not going into as much detail concerning cavalry as he did with infantry. The tactics of the two arms were, or should be, closely related, which did not mean that there were not interior differences, but that their movements should produce the same results when completed. All candidates for high command should know the maneuvers of both arms.

Cavalry had its advantages, he declared. Its role was to make raids and rapid expeditions for reconnaissance. It formed the advanced guards. It was the arm which frequently decided battles, completed successes gained by the infantry, and protected infantry which had been dispersed and defeated. Yet cavalry was only the secondary arm in a well-regulated army and should not be too numerous, for it was quality not quantity which counted. An excess of cavalry served no good purpose, he maintained, and it was a heavy burden in peacetime, since it all had to be maintained through the peace. Guibert agreed with Saxe and Puységur that cavalry raised, either in whole or in part, at the outbreak of a war was ineffective. What was necessary was that

a general, a man of genius, be struck by the resources which the new movements, more rapid and more refined, will offer; that from that cause, he dares to take the field with an excellent and not very numerous cavalry; that, his cavalry once based upon his projects and the strength of his infantry, he sees the enemy increase his, not only without being tempted to imitate him, but even with the conviction that the superiority which his adversary believes to have procured, only weakens him, because beyond certain proportions numbers produce only embarrassment and slowness.[44]

The only proper method of fighting for cavalry was shock. Fire action was not proper for cavalry combat as any one could judge who had seen it, though occasionally, when no infantry was available, cavalry had to dismount and hold an important defile which it had seized. As a consequence, it needed to be armed with carbine and pistol. Since shock was its only method of mounted combat, the problem was to increase it as much as possible. This meant increasing the speed of the charge, because the amount of shock was dependent upon the rate of speed. This did not mean the greatest possible speed which each individual mounted man could obtain from his horse. It meant the maximum speed which a coordinated troop could maintain.

Guibert declared that it had long been falsely believed in France that speed and order were incompatible. The result had been that French cavalry charged in headlong dashes which had no order and had to succeed at the first attempt, since there was no way of rallying them, nor could they exploit a success if they obtained it. Many old officers upheld this method, citing Fleurus (1690) and Leuze (1691) as victories which it had gained, to which Guibert retorted that Crécy, Poitiers, Agincourt, Ramillies, and Höchstädt (Blenheim) were examples of battles lost by "our chivalrous ignorance." This was at least an oversimplification on Guibert's part. He declared that no nation had suffered so many shameful defeats and gained so few decisive successes as the French.

Speed being necessary for cavalry, nothing was so erroneous as the old custom of arming it from head to foot in defensive armor. "One does not see in history, without pity for the blindness of that time, the gendarmerie, covered with iron, going to the charge at a walk or trot; unable to move if the rain had softened the ground, and perishing then under its useless armor and under the blows of the archers or of a lighter cavalry." [45] This was certainly a much more realistic view of the matter than that taken by Saxe.

He went further, for he said that light rapid cavalry was the best kind, and one ought to abolish the term "heavy cavalry." The only difference should be in the size of men and horses, the largest of these forming the *cavalry*, that is, those mounted troops who always fought in squadron and in line, chiefly on the battlefield itself. The dragoons and hussars, who must move rapidly, disperse, and carry on the war of detail, should be made up of smaller men and horses. He would even abolish the use of the breastplate or cuirass and all defensive arms which were musket proof. Here Guibert went contrary to all the previous writers who dealt with cavalry. His reasoning was that cavalry should not attack infantry prepared to receive it, while, in attacking unready infantry, it would not have to endure an effective fire. He did not think that the number of casualties avoided by defensive arms compensated for wearing a cuirass during a whole campaign, often uselessly, and for the fatigue on men and horses. How different from Saxe's attitude on pikes, namely, that they should be carried for fifty years because there might be a day when one needed them.

To protect cavalry from sabers, Guibert would use the same method as for infantry. They should wear helmets and three chains attached to the shoulders of their uniform jackets on leather epaulets. He would also prohibit the use of lances since they were too heavy and awkward for fighting. They also prevented maneuvering and simultaneous shock. The only cavalry using it in his day was the Polish, the poorest in all Europe. The best arm for cavalry was the short two-edged sword. The troops must be taught to use the point which was much deadlier than the edge.

In the attack speed was important, but it must be regulated speed. If one charged from six hundred paces, one should not move as rapidly as from two hundred, or one would tire the horses before they reached the objective. He suggested proceeding at a slow trot for two hundred paces, taking a rapid trot for the second two hundred, then taking up a gallop, and finally giving the horses their heads at fifty paces. He declared that he saw last year (1771?), for the first time, twelve hundred French cavalry charging in single line. This proved that ordered cavalry charges were possible. It also proved their superiority over the old impetuous French charges as well as over the ordered but slow charges of the Germans. No infantry could resist such charges, he said, without some defensive barrier capable of rapid erection.[46]

Cavalry should fight on two ranks. The second was not for increasing the shock, but rather for reinforcing the first when it broke up into mêlée. The front of a squadron ought to be proportionate to its depth for, if it was too small, the squadron would have no consistency and its shock no effect. A large squadron would be unwieldy. Guibert advocated smaller squadrons, therefore, just as he did smaller battalions, again running counter to other writers. Instead of squadrons of one hundred fifty to one hundred sixty men, he would have them of only eighty. If two of the latter size met one of the former, they would have the advantage of being more easily handled, could outflank and reach the rear of the larger squadron. They would be able to act in two directions while the latter could act only in one. The latter would always believe itself outnumbered. Moreover, when two squadrons met in shock, the victor never overthrew the whole front, but only the center or a wing. Two small squadrons which could maneuver on the flank with success would be better, therefore, for attacking the enemy. The internal organization should be based on odd numbers as in a battalion. Each squadron would be composed of one company of three divisions plus one élite division, each of twenty men. The élite division of the cavalry would be called carbiniers, and that of the dragoons, grenadiers. Each regiment would have nine squadrons grouped in three brigades.[47]

A long time was required to train a good cavalryman. Guibert did not mean by this a good riding master with all the finesse of an excellent horseman. A good cavalryman is a brave man on horseback, daunted by nothing, who loves and cares for his horse, knows all the duties of campaigning, and is not surprised by anything. Guibert found much to criticize in the existing training of cavalry. He condemned the continual feeding of untrained men and horses into regiments which kept them at low effectiveness. It was all wrong to make riding-school equitation the basis of cavalry training. One needed the simplest utilitarian training which would give the men the necessary knowledge and put them into the squadrons in the shortest possible time. He declared that half of the cavalry did not ride as it should. He wanted cavalrymen, not fancy riders. It was necessary to determine the best method of training and apply it outdoors on ground chosen to give the men experience with the conditions of warfare.[48]

Given men trained and ready to act in squadrons, one had the first analogy which Guibert said should exist between cavalry and infantry in the matter of tactics. Cavalry tactics had fewer movements than that of infantry, since it made use of shock action only. These movements were: forming columns, forming lines, marching in line, and certain special movements indicated by circumstances. Cavalry, like infantry, needed to be able to form a column to the front or flank. It could perform the latter by breaking into column by two, four, or eight files, or by half-companies, which would be determined by the ground. It would, of course, have to maintain its intervals to form line again. It could perform the former by breaking in column forward, or it could ploy in column like the infantry.[49] For instance, if a squadron wished to ploy to the right on the head of the column, at the first command the right company would move forward three paces, the others would "dislocate" and make ready to move by the flank, by drawing back the right flank about four paces in such a way that the right of the first rank was on the ground where the rear rank was. The two men of the right file could thus turn their horses and file off at a gallop diagonally, which they would do at the command of execution. Each file would follow successively by right-faces, forming again by left-faces as they arrived on the proper ground.[50] The intervals for marching should be two paces between ranks and four between companies. The intervals for maneuvering should be half of that. Ploying was primarily for forming maneuver columns, for the camp usually did not allow enough room to form marching columns by that method. In forming columns, one needed, as with the infantry, to remember whether one intended to form line to flank or front and to maintain the proper intervals accordingly. What was said about inversion also applied to cavalry.

The formation in line was the most important evolution for cavalry; "in it consists truly almost all the science and instruction of cavalry, for cavalry has strength and ability to act only in so far as it is in battle [line]. In all other orders, it is feeble and defenseless." [51] It was, above all, in this evolution that the analogy between cavalry and infantry held true as cavalry formed line in the same way that infantry did, with certain minor differences due to its physical composition. The deployment was performed as in infantry, except that, due to the length of the horse, the men had to make their horses give way so that the head of each was even with the boot of the man next to his left (assuming a left deployment). They were then in a position to make successive left-faces and file off diagonally at a gallop to the correct point on the proposed line, marked by the leader of the division. They then reformed by right-faces.[52]

The decisive moment for the cavalry was the charge. Guibert declared that cavalry charges succeeded more frequently by frightening and dispersing the enemy than by spilling blood. All charges normally should be made in line, but he admitted one or two situations where they might be made in column. These were: (1) attacking surrounded infantry, especially a flank or some angle unprotected by fire; (2) charging inferior cavalry so posted that its wings could not be enveloped. The same principles applied to these as to infantry attacks in column.

Aside from these situations, all charges should be made in line, because the great advantage of superior cavalry lay in its ability to extend its forces and embrace the flanks of the enemy's disposition. The art of inferior cavalry lay in preventing this, which might be done by drawing back the wings, or having some reserve squadrons placed there ready to take in reverse those of the enemy which sought to envelop its line.

Guibert attacked the method of cavalry combat of his day, because it did not seek to take advantage of the ground, nor to maneuver and countermaneuver on the wings, nor to support itself with infantry when inferior. The lines advanced and charged. More often than not they did not join because one side or the other fled before it was attacked. If it did not flee completely, it merely rallied to make another feeble charge. An able general would not chance all to a single charge with his cavalry deployed in simple lines. If he was superior in numbers, he would have some squadrons on the extremities of his wings, ready to envelop the enemy. If he was inferior, they would take in the flank those who attempted to envelop him. In the latter case, he would draw back his wings, or better still, rest them on some secure support. He would keep his second line, which could not remedy the failures of the first and was more apt to be disrupted by these failures, in hand for offensive-defensive maneuvers to counteract those of the enemy and to complete any victory the first line might gain. Victory would rest with the side which maneuvered best, had reserves, and made the most intelligent use of them. Perhaps some day a general would appear who would not be afraid to diminish the excessive amount of cavalry, and compensate, by able and rapid maneuvers, for overall inferiority so as to gain local superiority at the decisive point. He might, with eighty squadrons against a hundred, know how by maneuver to bring sixty squadrons against fifty and overthrow them before reinforcements could arrive. This was exactly what Marlborough did at Ramillies.

This call for a warfare of mobility and maneuverability is the essence of Guibert's doctrine of grand tactics and, on a larger scale, of strategy. It was here applied to the problems of cavalry to cut down the excessive amount, as Guibert saw it, which so complicated the problems of supply. It could also be applied to the larger scale of the theatre of operations, and Guibert sketched these possibilities later on. The ablest generals of the past had practiced it in so far as it was possible with their imperfect instruments. Now, just as an instrument which could take full advantage of a war of mobility was being forged, the doctrine of such a war began to be stated explicitly.

The government should assemble large bodies of cavalry frequently, said Guibert, to give them practice in combat movements on a large scale. They especially needed to be trained in marching in line, both for approaching and charging. They needed to be able to keep their alinement as perfectly as possible by means of the equality of speed and movement of all squadrons. This did not mean an alinement absolutely precise, but one of sufficient degree to enable all parts of the line to contact the enemy at about the same time. They also needed to be able to keep their direction, marching perpendicularly to the front without wavering, opening, closing, or losing ground to one or the other flank. Cavalry also needed to be frequently exercised in large bodies in conjunction with the other arms, for the essence of war is a just combination of all arms and little use had been made of cavalry in this respect, heretofore.[53]

Thus Guibert called for a cavalry trained in the actual needs of campaigning and freed from all the frills of showmanship. It was to be mobile and maneuverable in order to take full advantage of its special properties. To that end, it should be relieved of all useless encumbrances. Not many in that day would agree to his abolition of the cuirass for cavalry proper, and perhaps he went too far in that respect, but his motive in making cavalry as mobile as possible was sound. He seems far superior to Saxe in this regard. His cavalry should know its possibilities but also its limitations. It should know how to cooperate with the other arms to obtain a victory, in the gaining of which all arms were needed. This, he felt sure, would cut down the amount of cavalry needed, thus simplifying the problems of the commander and, incidentally, the cost of the Army to the State. All of this is sound doctrine, certainly representative of the best ideas of the day. It fits into the general pattern of the military establishment which Guibert desired to see, and for which he foresaw great possibilities and achievements.

Light troops were composed of both mounted and dismounted men. They differed from those of ancient times in that they were armed and equipped the same as the line troops, Guibert said, but had no place in the line of battle. They were used for petty warfare, the war of detail. Light troops, except for dragoons, were unknown until near the end of the previous century, the first hussar regiment having been raised by Luxembourg in 1692. In his latter days, Louis XIV employed free companies with the dragoons and hussars. Saxe raised uhlans. The importance of light troops really dated from the War of the Austrian Succession, however, when Maria Theresa was compelled to rely upon troops drawn from her eastern dominions, many of whom fought as irregulars. The Seven Years' War saw further increases in their numbers, as most other countries imitated the Austrians, until there were many in France who maintained that light troops were the most important and so must be increased and made superior in numbers and quality to those of possible enemies. This was a strange perversion, said Guibert, to make light troops the school of war. They might produce good advance guard chiefs but no Turenne or Luxembourg. He thought that it would be possible to work out a less complicated system for armies to protect their communications. Could not line troops do a large part of this service? [54]

It would be possible to reduce the number of light troops if armies were not so large and loaded with so much baggage, artillery, and similar encumbrances. They would then occupy less extended positions, move faster, have less fear of surprise, and would not have to make many detachments. Instead, one-fifth of the army was composed of light troops who fulfilled no decisive purpose, since they could not prevent the enemy's advance without support, nor did they take any part in battle if the two armies engaged.

Having made these "ifs," Guibert declared that it was, however, impossible to abandon this system of warfare, which required large numbers of light troops, within the existing order of states in Europe. This conclusion would seem to be dubious, especially in view of the fact that he sketched means for doing just this. He recapitulated briefly the necessary qualities of a people, qualities which he had already discussed in his Preliminary Discourse. This led him to a well-known quotation.

What will hinder one day a general, a man of genius, commanding fifty thousand men against an army of the same strength, from turning aside from the accepted routine, from not having in this fifty thousand men, ten thousand light troops, or from so constituting them that they could perform line service at need, and hold a place in the combat dispositions? . . . What will hinder him in almost all circumstances from refraining from splintering his army, from making fewer detachments, fewer reserves, fewer movements of detail than one makes today, from maneuvering more with his whole mass? What would the enemy do, astonished at this new kind of war? Will he parcel his army out, will he separate his army, will he have there a pawn here another, will he seek to make one uneasy, to threaten, to conceal a march? The first will remain always closed up, always united, if he can, in range or in sight of him, always in readiness to attack the bulk of his army or the parts which he has detached, always in force and secure from surprise, because he will be assembled and disposed for combat, while his adversary will always be obliged to be fearful, always to wear himself out in fatigues, because he will be dispersed and vulnerable at several points.[55]

Taken by itself, out of context, this quotation is practically a sketch of the methods used by General Bonaparte in the Italian campaign of 1796. Those basic elements of keeping one's troops in hand, of maneuvering with them, are the ones that he used so effectively against Beaulieu, while the picture Guibert presented of the opponent parceled out in detachments, trying to cover everything and covering nothing is, on the other hand, an accurate representation of the latter's operations. There seems no doubt that the young Bonaparte, reading this passage, must have had his imagination kindled.

Just what Guibert himself visualized is not quite so clear from what he adds to this. He first said that he would develop these ideas further in greater detail. There is no question but that, in so far as a war of mobility is concerned, his vision was clear, for that theme runs through his whole work. He continued by saying that these ideas had been confirmed by Frederick's campaigns. "No general has ever known as he knew how to maneuver armies as numerous and to make with them movements as great and as decisive; no one has splintered his armies less, and no one is less a partisan of reserves and detached corps. He has said it in his writings; he has proved it in his campaigns." [56]

It is somewhat difficult to decide whether Guibert was looking back to Frederick's campaigns or forward to Napoleon's. The campaigns of both had the common element of mobility, but what is not clear is whether Guibert had in mind the rigid unitary army of Frederick or a divisional army like Napoleon's. By keeping his army together did he mean merely keeping its parts within a mutually supporting distance? On the whole, considering the tendencies then existing in the French Army, the balance very definitely favors the conclusion that it was the war of the future that Guibert visualized. This conclusion is also supported by Guibert's later discussions of the subject in connection with his examination of grand tactics.

Guibert went on to remark that Frederick had few light troops in the usual sense of the term, a few battalions of enemy deserters. For advanced guards and important detachments, he used battalions of grenadiers or infantry of the line. He had many dragoons, but these performed all kinds of service. He had eighty squadrons of hussars, but they were the best troops in his army, fighting in line in battle, composed of Prussians and not of foreigners raised by chance. They were, for all intents and purposes, regular troops.

It was possible, declared Guibert, to create a system in which there was less necessity to employ great bodies of light troops. It was even more possible to employ line troops to perform their duties. There were no great differences between the two, both being armed and equipped alike and subject to the same discipline. He said that he would use the same system as Marshal Broglie, who formed special battalions of grenadiers [57] to serve outside the line in 1760. He regenerated the dragoons and used them both for the war of detail and with the army. The results justified the method, said Guibert, for the campaign was successful for a change. Employing line troops in the petty war, he suffered fewer checks and inflicted more on the enemy.

Guibert declared that he had shown that light troops could be greatly reduced. This was especially true of their infantry which was absolutely useless and should be replaced by infantry of the line. But if one retained them, how should they be constituted? Certainly not in bodies of from two to three thousand men as was then the custom, for it was difficult to find officers capable of handling such large bodies which were moreover, less mobile and, consequently, less aggressive. He went on to condemn the spirit of particularism which arose in bodies more or less permanently detached from the army. He would prefer instead forces of from one thousand to twelve hundred strong, two-thirds mounted. Their purpose was to make raids, scout, and harass the enemy; be here today and there tomorrow. If they had too much infantry, they could not do this very well without leaving them. Such bodies as above could take their foot up behind if necessary. The horse needed to know how to fight dismounted as well as mounted, and in battle as well as in detail. They should be picked troops and never doubtful ones, for the security of the army was confided to them.

As for the other arms, so for this one, Guibert had sound ideas on their training. They needed to exercise in swimming, running, and all that would increase their agility and strength. They must, like all arms, have peacetime drills as nearly like war conditions as possible. Their officers needed to know how to make patrols, reconnaissances, and reports; how to establish both foot and mounted posts, to entrench them, and to cover them by pushing vedettes and patrols in all directions. They needed to be shown how to prepare surprises, seize or attack a post, defend or attack a village, and many other features of petty war. They needed to know how to orient themselves in a country, to recognize its military features, which required considerable training, to judge distances, to estimate the strength of forces by their dispositions and maneuvers. They needed to be trained to know the different tricks of art or ground by which troops were made to appear more or less numerous than was actually the case and to compensate for them. Above all, and on this Guibert was most emphatic, they must learn to make their reports accurate and truthful, not exaggerating the number of troops they had seen and fought. They must understand the necessity for accuracy and the serious consequences which neglect of it could entail. He attacked this abuse because it existed in all the light troops of Europe, the arm where truth and accuracy were most needed.

Guibert closed his essay on light troops with the following characteristic passage. "I have written this little piece before being placed in a body of light troops. Serving there now is no reason for changing the opinion nor suppressing it. Shame on the writer, and above all, the military writer, who sells his opinion to circumstances or to fortune!" [58]

Before dealing with Guibert's essay on artillery, it is necessary to review the major reform of French artillery accomplished during the very fruitful ministry of the Duc de Choiseul (1761-71).

The reform which Vallière carried through as inspector general of artillery under the Regency has already been discussed. It will be remembered that this had concerned chiefly the standardization of the materiel, reduction to a few uniform calibers, and so on. It had not changed the form of the materiel itself, which remained of the same massive construction as under Louis XIV. Vallière retained this materiel as long as he lived, and so did his son who succeeded him as inspector general of artillery. They both resisted all idea of change. This massive artillery could serve in the days when infantry was largely immobile and unable to maneuver. As soon as progress began to be made on these matters, however, a school of younger artillery officers arose. They wished to follow the developments of the Prussian and Austrian artillery in obtaining a materiel which was mobile, could maneuver and change position on the battlefield, in short, could render full support to the mobile infantry then appearing. This school found powerful support in Marshal Belle-Isle who became secretary of state for war in 1758. He was guided, as has been noted, by the able artillerist, Bernard Forest de Bélidor (1693-1761), whom Reboul terms the great pioneer of ballistics, long before he became minister. Their collaboration had resulted in the adoption of battalion guns.

Bélidor conducted research at the artillery school of La Fère which proved that the charge of powder could be reduced without reducing the range of the guns. This led to the reduction of the charge from one-half to one-third of the weight of the projectile.[59] This reduction in charge meant that it was possible to reduce markedly the massiveness of the gun, but here the opposition of the younger Vallière prevented the necessary reform. The consequence was that French artillery, usually in the forefront of Europe, was decidedly inferior to its opponents during the Seven

Years' War. Reboul went so far as to say that this inferiority was a chief cause of the French defeat in that war.[60]

Choiseul attacked the problem of the artillery among the many with which he dealt. To do the work in this department, he chose, in 1763, a very able artillery officer, named Gribeauval (1715-89), who had long campaigned against the system of Vallière. Gribeauval had been on a mission to the Prussian Army and had served with the Austrian Army during the Seven Years' War, which gave him a background for his work. He continued in charge as long as Choiseul was in office and became inspector general of artillery upon Vallière's death. Dismissed by Choiseul's successor, he was brought back by St. Germain in 1775 and given a free hand by him and his successor.

Gribeauval brought in a completely new system of guns which were first adopted in 1764. The new materiel was much superior in carriages, in the method of mounting guns, and methods of harnessing and drawing them which rendered the new materiel lighter and more mobile. The guns had improved elevating screws and sights which increased the range and accuracy. The diameter of the balls was increased slightly so as to decrease the windage (the space between the interior of the gunbarrel and the projectile) which, in turn, increased range and accuracy. Most important of all, he reduced the length of the guns and designed them in much lighter construction; for, since heavy charges were no longer used, the guns no longer needed such thick barrels and chamber walls. The weight of the four-pounders was reduced from thirteen hundred pounds to six hundred with proportional reductions in the heavier calibers.[61] The calibers remained as they were under Vallière: four-, eight-, and twelve-pounder field guns; sixteen- and twenty-four-pounder siege guns. There was also an eight-inch howitzer and a ten-inch mortar. Although the length of the gun was reduced, the other improvements, such as the reduction of the windage, prevented any marked reduction of ranges. The rate of fire was much increased. French artillery regained its old superiority, and Gribeauval's system remained in use until 1827, except for the brief reaction to all of Choiseul's reforms which took place under his successor from 1771 to 1774.

The question of tactical doctrine for the employment of the new artillery now came to the fore. The need for a mobile artillery had led some officers to think about the problem, and several had already hit upon the essential idea of coordinating the artillery with the other arms. One of the reasons why Vallière had opposed change, according to Villate, was that he was a technician rather than a tactician. Supply and munitions were more important to him than supporting an attack. "He took the means for the end." [62] Nevertheless, ideas were beginning to form. Villate quoted the then inspector general of artillery, Destouches, who declared in 1720 that all arms should act together on the battlefield, that artillery should fire against other artillery, if opposed only by guns, on the assumption that the troops were behind it and might be hit by the balls after the first bound. When one found troops opposite ready to maneuver favorably, Destouches continued, one must ignore the hostile batteries, no matter how much one suffers, to concentrate one's fire on the troops. Further, the artillery should follow the movements of the troops in so far as possible.[63] This is the core of the doctrine preached by the artillery officers after the adoption of the new system.

This was the situation when Guibert published the *Essai général*. It was the first of the great military works to deal with artillery, which, in itself, is revealing as the previous writers apparently did not feel that its influence upon tactics was great enough to concern them. Guibert's work was the first, moreover, to appear after the adoption of Gribeauval's reforms.

Guibert described artillery as the third arm of the army. More properly speaking, he said, it was an accessory of the army, since, unlike the other two, it could not fight alone. The science of artillery was far ahead of anything the ancients had, but it was still far from perfect. This was especially true of ballistics, both interior and exterior, which had many problems not likely to be solved for a long time to come.[64] The government could stimulate research in this field, and it should follow the principle of rejecting nothing without testing nor accepting anything without proof.

Some officers claimed that artillery had no effect, that it should

have no place in tactical combinations, being more of an encumbrance than an assistance, more noisy than deadly. Others,
chiefly artillerists, maintained *"artillery is the soul of armies; that
the superiority of the artillery ought to decide the victory."* [65]
Guibert wished to know what was the sound middle position between these two extremes. He declared that the purpose of artillery was to support and sustain troops, to take reverses and prolongations of lines which they occupied, to buttress the parts of
the line that were weak because of the number or quality of the
troops which held them or because of the nature of the ground.
It should keep the enemy off; hold him in check; hinder him from
debouching. Artillery was a useful accessory for the man of genius. Its tactics should be analogous to those of the troops, since
the commander needed to know what to expect from its various
dispositions in order to combine artillery in his general disposition.

There were many things which made a gun inaccurate and its
range uncertain. If one pointed a single gun at a single small target, one might not get a hit in less than a hundred shots, but that
was not the way to use artillery. It needed to be combined, with
many guns firing on a large area occupied by masses of troops.
The "great objective, the decisive objective . . . ought to be to
cover, to cross the fire on the ground which the enemy occupies,
and that by which the enemy wishes to advance. Artillery thus
placed, thus served, does very much damage, and [creates] still
more terror." [66] The more accustomed to war the men become,
the better ordered and the more able to maneuver, the less effect
artillery fire would have. They would learn from experience to
know what artillery could and could not do and what to do when
they came under its fire, taking advantage of all the cover the
ground afforded when advancing to the attack and throwing out
skirmishers to harass it. "The first law of war is not to expose the
soldier when it is not necessary; to expose him, thereafter, without
regard when necessity demands it."

Guibert examined the relative merits of the new artillery as
compared to the old. He declared that the opinion of neutral
artillery officers, those not violent partisans in the controversy

which raged for and against the new system, was that in the balance an improvement was made. They commended the lightening of the guns to give them maneuverability. They felt that any loss in range was at such distances that guns were so inaccurate as to make the loss more apparent than real. They felt that, while there was perhaps some loss in accuracy, it was so small as to make no serious difference. They did not like the abandonment of sixteen-pounders as field guns, because one sometimes met obstacles in the field that lighter guns could not demolish. They also thought there was too large a proportion of four-pounders and not enough emphasis on howitzers.

Guibert denounced the excessive amount of artillery employed by armies of his day. In this he was not himself speaking, he said, but only expounding accepted ideas. This excessive amount of artillery was a practice which, he declared, came from the Turks and the Russians, going back to Ivan the Great and Basil III who used as many as three hundred guns against the Tartars. In the last war, the Russians used as many as six hundred guns in one campaign. The Austrians copied this practice from the Russians and had become less given to great maneuvers as a result. While the Prussians had also followed, Frederick never allowed artillery to encumber his maneuvers, and most of it was kept in reserve in his arsenals to replace his losses. At Rossbach, he had only twelve guns in battery, according to Guibert, and forty in park. Lissa (Leuthen) was not won by his artillery. "A general rule: when one turns his enemy, when one attacks him by maneuvers, when one engages one's strong part against his weak part, it is not with artillery that one decides the success; since to begin then an artillery combat would give the enemy time to realize his situation, to reinforce [the threatened point], and consequently to lose all the fruit of the maneuver one has made." [67] This same influence had spread to the French Army since 1762, he declared, and the new system contemplated it, thus losing the great advantage gained by its maneuverability through the excessive number of guns. Consequently, this artillery did not bring any advantage, but slowed down warfare, subordinating it to problems of supply.

Guibert favored not more than one hundred fifty guns for an

army of a hundred battalions. He would have fewer four-pounders and more eight-, twelve-, and sixteen-pounders. He would have at least twenty howitzers. To compensate for his inferiority of one hundred fifty guns to four hundred, he would have adequate reserves in his depots from which to draw. With fewer guns, he would have more skillful gunners, more expert officers. He would seek to compensate by rapidity of movement and more skillful dispositions for his inferiority in numbers. This leads Guibert to his dominant theme, mobility.

He [the general] will create for it [artillery] tactics of deployment and ruses, by which he will know how to oppose equality and superiority in the parts of his order of battle which ought to be attacking or attacked, at the same time that he refuses and places out of range of the enemy, the part of his order that he strips of artillery. The operations of his campaign will be calculated according to the constitution of his army in that respect, and according to that of the enemy. He will make *vis-à-vis* him a war of movement, he will harass him by forced marches, to which the enemy will be compelled to oppose countermarches which will be slow and destructive for the prodigious train ... which he will drag behind, or else which will oblige [him] to leave behind the greater part of this encumbrance. Then one will be armed equally, and will have the perfection and superiority between them. Finally, if he is obliged to attack the enemy or receive his attack, he will not believe himself beaten because he will have fewer cannon to oppose to him [the enemy]. His batteries better disposed, better emplaced, better served, of heavier calibers, with prolongations more ably taken, will still give him the advantage. For what battles have been lost because the conquered army lacked artillery? I see everywhere that few guns have acted, and that many have remained in inaction, either for lack of emplacement, or inability to reach the target, or inability to move rapidly to the point of attack. ... Diminish the quantity of artillery, and make the perfection of the art to consist in firing a large part of a small number of pieces, to form the best possible artillery, rather than to procure the most numerous.[68]

It must be said that Guibert here ran counter to the trend of the future which was towards greater quantities of artillery until it became practically the dominant arm in the First World War. Yet his purpose was sound. He feared that the great increase of artillery would nullify all his hopes for a warfare of mobility and

maneuver. It must be said that for the short run his fears were
not wholly justified; the most mobile warfare lay in the immediate
future. Yet its ablest practitioner, himself an artillery officer,
sought a much larger proportion of artillery than Guibert would
admit. There are those who would say that in the longer run
Guibert was right and the First World War bore him out. In any
case, here as elsewhere, it was the war of mobility which was his
first concern.

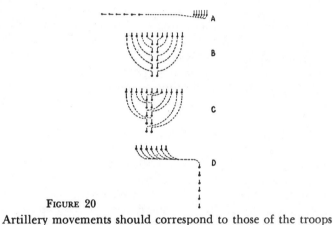

FIGURE 20

Artillery movements should correspond to those of the troops
and be regulated by them. They should be rapid and simple.
Artillery could put itself into column by flank or front just as the
troops could. In the first case, each gun or wagon merely made
successive right wheels and was in file. In the second case, each
gun or wagon broke into column either to front or rear; or it
could be done by two, three, or four vehicles, depending upon the
front one wished to give the column. As in the case of troops, if
the march was to the front, one needed to keep the depth of the
column as small as possible in order to deploy as quickly as one
could. For this purpose, one should double the guns at least to a
front of two, on approaching the area of deployment. This was
less important for a flank march, for one formed the line by successive wheels. See Figure 20A. Deployment should be made
from a double column, at least, either by single guns (Figure 20B)

or by pairs (Figure 20C). It should not be made by processional marches as was done in the Seven Years' War (Figure 20D).[69]

Guibert declared that he had used his own ideas on the evolutions of artillery because these evolutions were related to those of the troops, but in the matter of serving it, he drew his ideas from artillery officers since that was a professional topic. Serving the artillery included, for Guibert, not merely the loading, pointing, and firing of guns, but also the calculating of their effect, their emplacement, and direction so as to do the greatest possible damage to the enemy and afford the greatest possible protection for one's own troops. Because of the close affinity of troops with artillery, the artillery commander needed to know something of the former's tactics, at least enough to understand the results of their evolutions and the injury or support which troops in a given situation could receive from artillery emplaced in a given manner. The reverse was also true, for those who commanded troops, either infantry or cavalry, also commanded artillery, and they needed to know, consequently, what to expect from it. Otherwise they would not be able to employ it wisely.

The best position for artillery was that which would enable it to obtain the most deadly effect upon the enemy. It did not obtain this effect in firing straight ahead upon the *ordre mince*. The position for batteries should enable them to cut the enemy's lines obliquely. Batteries should be placed at an angle to the enemy's lines, and the closer they approach the more acute that angle should be. Guibert set forth as a general rule that one should not place batteries opposite the targets if it was possible to obtain an effective oblique fire upon them. Further, if one wished to fire upon several points at the same time, as was usually the case in a line of battle, then one should emplace one's batteries so that the shots of one struck opposite another, in other words, so that the batteries afforded mutual protection to each other.

Batteries should not only protect each other; they should be strong. Therefore, one should not scatter one's guns singly over the whole front. Instead they should be concentrated in strong batteries. The first method merely irritated the enemy and produced no decisive effects. "The purpose of artillery . . . ought not to be to kill some men along the whole of the enemy's front: it ought to be to overthrow or destroy the parts of the front, either about the points from which he can attack most advantageously, or about the points where he can be attacked with the most advantage." [70] Villate remarked correctly that here was forseen the great batteries such as Drouot and Sénarmont were later to organize. He added that he believed that these principles would not be disavowed by modern artillery schools (those of the French in the middle 1930's).[71] He remarked, not so aptly, that this was written by an infantryman, for Guibert stated explicitly that he got his ideas from artillery officers. Guibert did not mean to say by the above passage that one should concentrate too many guns in one battery, for that would only give the enemy a better target. Rather one should have them in several batteries not very far from each other and able to fire on the same target. Nor should all batteries be placed on the same line, for if the enemy could obtain prolongations on them, he would be able to enfilade them all at once. The guns should be spaced sufficiently for ease of serving and to reduce the enemy's target.

In placing batteries, Guibert declared that it was a great error to believe that it was advantageous to place them on a high elevation. An elevation of fifteen or twenty feet was advantageous for a range of six hundred fifty yards, for it helped to gain favorable reverses. A higher elevation resulted in plunging fire which was much less deadly than grazing fire, for the balls buried themselves in the earth instead of bounding along and plowing through formations. It was also necessary, in placing batteries, not to establish them where there were obstacles to subsequent movements, such as ravines or marshes. One should not place them before one's own troops or on a low elevation behind them, as this merely offered the enemy two targets for each shot. In a defensive position, the heavy guns should be put in battery at the principal points where one wished to fend off the enemy, while the light guns should be held ready to move rapidly to reinforce threatened points, or to counter enemy dispositions.

Artillery could and should be used in conjunction with cavalry, according to Guibert. It was especially good for reinforcing an inferior wing. Howitzers could be used here with great effect as they were very deadly against charging cavalry. The loss of the guns added only a little more to the disaster if the cavalry was beaten, while it could render success more decisive.

Artillery must be mobile and able to change its positions when necessary during the course of battle, either to maintain its prolongations, or to concentrate on some decisive point. It needed to seek accuracy above all else, especially at long range. This was more important than speed of fire. As one shortened the range, which made accuracy greater, one could increase the rate of fire. Artillery should never be used in counterbattery action, except when there were no troops to fire upon. *The true targets of the artillery were the enemy's troops and the works which covered them.* Its purpose was not merely to cancel out the enemy's artillery but to cooperate with the troops in winning a decisive success.

One should know when to use balls and when cartridges. The latter were often used at long ranges when the former should be. There was an underestimation of the effect of solid shot, which, by ricochet, would often reach the second line when it missed the first. It overthrew obstacles, and unnerved new troops by its noise and appalling wounds. Artillery should rid itself of its old prejudice against them.

Finally, one should not too lightly abandon one's guns, neither should one pay an enormous price to retain them. Troops should attach a point of honor to not losing their guns because this would give confidence to the gunners. If the latter knew that the troops would protect them, one would get more effective service from them. The artillery should also be accustomed to take risks when necessary, and the gunners should not abandon their guns prematurely when the enemy got close, because the last discharge was the most terrible and deadly of all. But if, in spite of this, the enemy came on, the gunners should not defend the guns for their only task was to operate them. If the guns were to be retaken, the troops should do it. The general must decide if the cost of retaking them was greater than the value of so doing.

Guibert declared again that his knowledge was based upon

the *mémoires* of artillery officers.[72] "Everywhere my purpose is the same, and it is the light of others, more often than my opinions, that I seek to spread." In many cases this is either too modest or too circumspect.

Once again in the matter of artillery, Guibert concentrated upon essentials. He wished to have an artillery trained in all that it needed to know, maneuverable and mobile, able by simple basic evolutions to accompany troops and support them in all their efforts. Since artillery was a technical arm, he devoted a good deal of space to outlining a sound doctrine for its employment. Considering the limitations of the materiel which was available in that day, it would seem that his doctrine was sound, and that few would find fault with its essential features.

GRAND TACTICS

Guibert declared that grand tactics, a term to which he gave currency, was the science of generals and that a general was one who needed to know all the science and art of war. He should be familiar with all the arms, and know how to lead them, either separately or in combination. "What words, those of *general* and *army!* And if one thinks at all deeply, what an immensity of ideas, it presents to the imagination!" [73]

Just as the purpose of elementary tactics was to enable one to move and maneuver a regiment, so that of grand tactics had as its purpose the moving of armies under all conditions. Guibert believed that he could demonstrate its principles just as he had those of elementary tactics. That was the task which he undertook, the real goal of his work.

The whole goal which lay behind his writing on grand tactics, as on elementary tactics, was mobility, the creation of mobile warfare. In dealing with the latter subject, Guibert was at great pains to establish a machine which was mobile, whose basic parts had all the properties necessary to enable them to move rapidly and easily. Two essential qualities were necessary to accomplish this end, and those qualities Guibert was able to give to the French Army far beyond anything that it had had before. They were simplicity and flexibility. The former word inevitably appears repeatedly in any description of Guibert's tactics because of his passion for reducing all to bare essentials. But in cutting out many useless evolutions and substituting his system of ployment and deployment, he had achieved, not only simplicity, but also flexibility. An army based upon his tactics could not only perform all the maneuvers that armies previously could at a rate far faster than they; it could also perform others that previous armies could not. Guibert's purpose in grand tactics was to provide the doctrine to enable a capable general to take advantage of the mobility which he had made possible for armies. It is obvious that mobility is of no use unless one knows how to employ it. The possibilities which mobility and its by-product, maneuverability, give to an army was the theme of the second part of the *Essai général*. One must be able to march in such a way as to have the possibility of maneuvering when coming in contact with the enemy, and one must be able to maneuver so as to fight with advantage.

Marching, for Guibert, included all the movements of an army and, as such, was the most important part of military science. It was the basis of success for an army and the resource of able generals. For Guibert agreed with Saxe before him, and Napoleon after, that marching is the key to both. Liddell Hart feels [74] that Guibert's insistence upon a faster rate of march in his elementary tactics was a key to the subsequent successes of the French, that it made possible their ability to maneuver at a faster rate than their opponents. At any rate, Guibert recognized and clearly stated that mobility was the resource of the able general, immobility of the inferior. Marches were better organized and executed by the former, and that was the source of their mobility.

They become more frequent in that the man of genius can rarely remain in inaction; his mind perceives more objectives, embraces more combinations; and consequently, where the mediocre general sees only his position to defend, or the impossibility of acting, there presents itself to the imagination of the first an advantageous movement which he executes.[75]

To achieve this desired mobility, it was necessary to break armies up into divisions, following the pattern of Broglie. These divisions must be combined in their marches so as to be able to

support each other in battle. Guibert, confusing Frederick's temporary divisions in marching with the permanent divisions which
the French had been developing, thought that Frederick had used
this method. It was the use to which these divisions were subsequently put that Guibert foresaw and developed, though he did
not foresee such a wide dispersal as was actually made. In fact,
the unskillful generals of the early campaigns of the Wars of the
French Revolution made an altogether excessive dispersal of divisions and a rather, or even quite, uncoordinated use of them in
battle. Guibert would not have been guilty of this fault, for
while he saw that conditions of the country might cause the divisions to be separated from one another on the march, he expected
that they would remain within supporting distance and, above all,
that they would be employed in a common effort on the battlefield.

The main purposes of divisions for Guibert was to enable an
army to march with ease and to maneuver with facility in preparation for battle. Like Saxe, Guibert was opposed to very large
armies because he felt that they only caused embarrassment. An
army such as Guibert foresaw should be divided into three or, at
most, four divisions of infantry and two of cavalry. The infantry
divisions should be of not less than twelve nor more than twenty-
four battalions. Since each division formed a column, one which
was composed of more than twenty-four battalions would be difficult to maneuver. One would lose a principal part of the advantages of the divisional system in that case. Guibert felt that, if
the divisions were of less than twelve battalions, they became too
numerous, and it was difficult, or even impossible, to provide
enough roads for them. This problem was, of course, reduced
when the divisions were spread out over a much wider front than
he envisioned.

Guibert conceived of a standard order of march whose fundamental principle was equality of all its parts—facilitating the reinforcing or thinning of any part of the line which might be necessary. However, he recognized that the nature of the ground would
prevent a slavish following of any particular pattern. Moreover,
and this was extremely important, he divorced the order of battle

and the order of march from their rigid conformity to each other. An essential purpose of maneuvering in columns was to enable one to form whatever order of battle circumstances indicated from one's order of march, so as not be confined to a single one imposed by that order of march.[76]

Turning to the handling of artillery in such marches, Guibert believed that it should be grouped into divisions corresponding in number to those of the troops and assigned to them. There should be an additional reserve division, composed of heavy guns and howitzers. Lastly, there should be a small division of from two to not more than six heavy guns assigned to the advance guard. Its purpose was to batter down any posts which might hold up the latter, and to make the signals necessary in deployment. All divisions of artillery assigned to divisions of troops should be of equal size and composed of all calibers of guns. Each should be further divided into sub-divisions composed of six guns of the same caliber, i.e., batteries.

Artillery normally should march at the rear of the column to which it was attached. When it came to maneuvering, the artillery should be so disposed as to be able to enter the order of battle at any point desired and yet hinder the troops and slow the march as little as possible. When a frontal march was made with the purpose of engaging the enemy, the columns should be headed by one or two batteries of heavy artillery, preceded only by a battalion of grenadiers, and carrying only what ammunition it could on its limbers. This would make it possible to cover one's deployment with the fire of these batteries. If there were regimental guns (and Guibert did not approve of them, considering them more of an encumbrance than an aid), they would, of course, accompany the troops to which they were assigned.[77] Thus Guibert clearly envisaged the close coordination of artillery and troops which he expounded as essential in his elementary tactics.

The term, "order of battle," meant two things to Guibert. He distinguished between the stereotyped order in two lines with infantry in the center and cavalry on the wings, which he called the primary and fundamental order, and all orders derived from it—

the ones an army actually employed in battle. The latter were
the fighting orders which resulted from the maneuvering that one
employed as a preliminary to the actual engagement. The army
advanced on the enemy in five or, at most, six columns (one for
each division). Arrived within reach of the enemy, the general,
who marched with the advance guard, would look over the situation, the dispositions of the enemy, and the nature of the ground,
determining his own order of battle as a consequence.

Normally the advance guard would be followed in close proximity by the columns of the army, for "it would be desirable that,
just as the lightning has already struck when one sees the flash, so
when the enemy sees the head of the army appear, the whole of it
should be there, allowing him no time to counteract the dispositions that it takes." [78] Sometimes one had an advance guard several leagues to the front which was advantageous for certain operations, but this was the exception.

He [the general] reinforces or weakens such and such columns as he
deems proper for that purpose [forming his battle order], advances
one, holds back another, directs that one towards one point, this one
towards another, gives the signal for the order of battle to be taken.
Instantly all his troops, who are accustomed to the execution of grand
maneuvers, who have methods of rapid deployment, put themselves in
battle [deploy], and the attack commences before the enemy has had
the time to discern where one wishes to strike him, or if he has dis-
cerned it, before he has had the necessary time to change his disposition in order to parry it. What cannot the general do, having his
columns behind him, in his hands so to speak, ready to take whatever
dispositions he indicates! Arrived in sight of the enemy, and finding
him not to be in a disadvantageous situation, he maneuvers opposite
him, he seeks to deceive him, he makes use of all the resources of
ground and of tactics in order to delude him concerning his project,
he feints an offensive movement on his left in order to form his real
attack on his right; there he presents columns open at full intervals,
here he presents them at closed intervals. He does so much, in a word,
that if the enemy is not as able as he, he swallows the bait, abandons
or occupies a post that lays himself open, or else weakens himself at a
point, either in leaving too few troops there, or in leaving too few of
the arm proper for its defense there, or in leaving the poorest troops
of his army there, and then that fault is seized upon, the able and

maneuverable general directs all his efforts upon that weakened part. If the enemy lays himself open, however, neither by his position nor by his disposition, then the general has committed nothing; he withdraws, takes a position and awaits a more favorable opportunity.[79]

Here in this single passage is summed up the entire doctrine and practice of maneuver in columns. Here is stated clearly all the advantages which that method gave. All the disadvantages of maneuvering in line, which French officers had been seeking to avoid throughout the century, disappear. This, it will be remembered, was the real tactical problem. The quest for a solution had been given a wrong direction by Folard, who had ignored the whole period of preliminary maneuver, or else confused it with combat. A vigorous controversy had started, consequently, which when nearly dead had been revived by Mesnil-Durand. Having died down again, it was about to be given another and still more virulent revival when Mesnil-Durand published his second system, including a direct attack upon Guibert's methods. It will be remembered that what Folard and Mesnil-Durand had done, especially the former, was to ignore the facts of actual combat concerning the dominance of fire. The latter was brought to make some further concessions in his revised system. He was to go still further in his second system, as will presently be seen.

The method of maneuvering in column which Guibert sketched in the above quotation was made possible by the elementary tactics described earlier in this chapter, tactics which were gradually adopted in the French Army through his efforts. They were the basis of French tactics throughout the Revolutionary and Napoleonic Wars. In this field, Guibert's influence was concrete and definite. The less skillful generals of the earlier campaigns of the Revolution were not capable of realizing their full significance, or at least of employing them completely. It was left to Napoleon to draw the full benefit from them and make use of all the resources which they made available. In this respect, though Guibert drew much inspiration from Frederick, and though he regarded himself, apparently, as developing further the practice of the Great King, he was really more Napoleonic than Frederician. This is also true of his strategic concepts.

Orders of battle were classified by Guibert in two basic types, the parallel and the oblique. These do not mean, necessarily, an exactly parallel or oblique line in relation to the enemy. A parallel order of battle was one in which action was joined along the entire front, accounting to Guibert. It was no longer used, he said, because there was great difficulty in bringing the huge contemporary armies together along the totality of their fronts. Moreover, armies needed to be approximately equal for such battles, otherwise the inferior was bound to be enveloped by the superior. Battles of this type have a great advantage or disadvantage, depending upon the point of view. They are more "terrible, decisive, and bloody" and involve the total destruction of the defeated army, while battles such as were actually fought between able generals "can never have great results." [80] Such battles were fought in the oblique order, which was the most masterly and the most susceptible to tactical combinations. By the oblique order, Guibert meant not necessarily a line of geometrical precision, but rather an order in which one attacked the enemy at one or more points with a portion of one's order of battle, including one's élite troops, while refusing the remainder, keeping it out of range of attack by the enemy. There were thus two oblique orders, the true oblique, *oblique de principe,* and the *oblique de circonstance* in which the army was not disposed obliquely to the enemy's, but as a result of the nature of the ground or its own able movements, it could attack the enemy at one or several points while being safe in its refused parts.[81] Thus the oblique order meant far more for Guibert than its name alone implies. Liddell Hart says [82] that Guibert's presence at the battle of Bergen where he saw Broglie's skillful dispositions no doubt helped him to make this distinction. It should be remembered that Broglie used columns for maneuver at Bergen.

Guibert was, at the time he wrote the *Essai général,* closer to Frederick than to Napoleon concerning some aspects of his conception of battle. This is not to say that he had not gone beyond Frederick to a considerable degree, as in his conception of battlefield maneuver, described above. But once the maneuvers had ceased, and the actual order of battle was taken, he still thought in terms of the rigid, unitary, and concentrated line of battle. That is to say that his divisions on deploying formed a single striking force rather than a series of separate, but coordinated, ones as in a Napoleonic battle. Guibert's ideas did not cease to grow with the writing of his first major military work, however, and he was to develop them beyond this point.

In closing his discussion of battle orders, Guibert expounded some rules for deployment which the French were to neglect to their cost in the Peninsular War. One must deploy the troops at a distance from the enemy so well chosen that one could attack without loss of time. No exact rules could be given as to what that distance should be. It would depend upon the enemy's character, whether he was aggressive and able in maneuver, the quantity and quality of his artillery, and whether there was cavalry, infantry, or both opposed. There was, however, one general rule which must be observed in deploying. One must deploy as close to the enemy as possible, *without coming under a fire which was deadly enough to cause disorder among the troops while they were deploying.*[83] Neglect of this rule in the Peninsula led to the results described by Bugeaud in the quotation already given. Distance of deployment also should depend upon whether there was cover behind which one could deploy close to the enemy's line, or whether one must deploy in the open, which meant that it must be done at a considerable distance from the enemy.

Guibert felt that an army employing his tactics would, through its mobility and maneuverability, be able to compensate for the superior numbers which would be opposed to it. It should also be freed from excessive amounts of what, he said, the ancients so aptly called *impedimenta*. In the matter of the relative merits of numbers versus maneuverability, Guibert showed most clearly the influence of Frederick. He had in mind such battles as Rossbach, Leuthen (Lissa), and Zorndorf where the Prussian gained great victories over decisively superior numbers through the greater mobility of his troops. This gives further evidence of the Frederician concept of battle which was still dominant in his thinking. He did not, yet at least, understand the full implications of the divisional system in the strategic as opposed to the tactical sense. That is to say, he did not yet understand that the division had a strength sufficient to withstand superior numbers for such a length of time as to enable one to disperse them over a relatively wide area and still retain them within mutually supporting distance of each other. This gave to large armies the mobility which once had been confined to small ones.

An army such as Guibert conceived would have less cavalry, fewer light troops, and less artillery. Its infantry would be better armed, better disciplined, more aggressive and maneuverable, more self-sufficient, like the Roman legionaries. Its cavalry would make up for its smaller numbers by its speed and ability to maneuver. The light troops would be able to serve in the line, and the line troops would be able to perform detached service. (Incidentally, the light infantry and cavalry of the Republican and Imperial armies fulfilled the prescription laid down by Guibert in this respect, being used in battle as well as in petty war.) Its artillery would be less numerous, composed of useful calibers only—that is to say, of heavier guns to produce real results. It would be better constituted, better drawn, better emplaced, and better served in action. The tactics of all arms would be simple and analogous one to another, so that they could all be readily fitted into the general's combinations. Such an army would not be weighed down with excessive baggage, would live on the country, freeing operations from the dictation of subsistence and considerations of supplies. "Finally such armies, commanded by great men, would renew the prodigious works formerly [accomplished] by small armies against ignorant multitudes; there would still be great conquests and revolutions in empires." [84]

Just as in the case of elementary tactics, so in grand tactics, Guibert was not content merely to set forth the theory and practice. It was necessary to train the troops for the kind of war which he envisaged, and since it would take a revolution to bring about the kind of army sketched above, it was necessary to train existing troops so that they would be disciplined and instructed. Just as he insisted upon the most realistic training possible for the small units, so he insisted upon the same practice for large armies. This led him to a discussion of training camps. They

had been held since the time of Louis XIV, but they had been occasions of festivity and parade, Guibert said. Following the example of Frederick II, there had been more serious ones since the
end of the War of the Austrian Succession, but he did not believe
that anything useful was learned. When one suggested that they
should be employed usefully, he was told that there was not time
for it or that "general officers are not made in order to come to
school."

Such camps, for the instruction of troops and for officers of
both high and low grade, Guibert advocated. He would form
camps every year of three months' duration far from the capital
and other large cities. This was a point upon which he was insistent. He felt that the influence of the cities, especially Paris,
militated against the camp's purpose by the corrupting influence
they exerted upon the officers. These camps should be places of
serious business. In them he would assemble an army of the second order, 50,000 strong. An army of the first order would be
from 60,000 to not above 70,000, which was the largest he would
permit, feeling that even an able general could not handle a
larger force in the manner he conceived. For the army he proposed to assemble in camp, the composition would be eighty battalions of not more than four hundred fifty men each, or 36,000
infantry; eighty squadrons of cavalry and dragoons (in his maneuvers, the dragoons form an extra eight squadrons) of not over one
hundred twenty men each, or 9,600 cavalry; two thousand light
troops, nearly all mounted, and one hundred fifty guns. In war,
the proportion of cavalry would depend upon the theatre of operations. It would be reduced if the army were to fight in mountainous country, and the infantry would be increased proportion-
ately. The artillery would be composed of six sixteen-pounders,
thirty twelve-pounders, fifty eight-pounders, only forty four-
pounders, and twenty-four howitzers. There would be no regimental guns. In actual operations, he would have artillery re-
placement depots for both guns and horses near the theatre of
operations. An army of the first order would have the same proportions.

Such an army would form three infantry divisions of twenty-four battalions each, twelve for the first line and twelve for the second. Each division would be commanded by a lieutenant-general, with another as second in command, and three *maréchaux-de-camp* who would each command two of the brigades of four battalions each into which the divisions were divided. The remaining eight battalions would form two flank brigades which would be used to support the wings of cavalry, as the name implied, or as a sort of reserve to be employed as the occasion indicated. The cavalry would form two divisions of forty squadrons each, subdivided into five brigades of eight squadrons each, commanded by a lieutenant-general with four *maréchaux-de-camp* under him. The light troops would be attached to the advanced guard and, in battle, would guard the army's flanks and menace those of the enemy. The artillery would be formed in three divisions of thirty-six guns each, one for each infantry division, with a fourth division in reserve and a battery of six guns attached to the advanced guard. An army of the first order would have an additional infantry division and, presumably, an additional artillery division, but no more cavalry.

Such was the army which Guibert advocated. It would not have the great hoards of general officers which had been French practice since the days of Louis XIV. It would have thirty-six including some spares for detached duty compared to the thirty per division which was not unknown. The staff would not be composed of creatures of generals or ministers as they then were, but from the *maréchal-général des logis* (chief of staff) down, they would be chosen for their knowledge and ability in their special tasks. The higher ones should be trained in grand tactics.[85]

The advanced guard would be composed of light troops, dragoons, and several battalions of grenadiers drawn from the élite companies of the battalions.[86] He proposed the use of grenadiers for there were an infinite number of occasions when one needed an élite and reliable force. He would also use grenadiers when he wished to make a secret reinforcement of the part of his order which was going to attack. By drawing the grenadier companies from the refused order, one could obtain such a reinforcement, for the enemy, counting the full number of battalions there, would be unable to discern the fact that these companies had been withdrawn.

Guibert proposed a number of maneuvers for the specific training of his army after it had been assembled in camp. In these maneuvers, both troops and officers would become familiar with the problems of forming orders of battle. After having carried through these formal maneuvers, which were apparently to be made on selected ground which presented no problems, the army should go on to more advanced maneuvers in country which required adaptation of the standard formations to the requirements of terrain and to the countermaneuvers which the enemy might make. He gave several examples of what these could be like, in the course of which he also demonstrated the maneuvers in column which he had previously advocated. Thus Guibert would proceed by progressive stages to train the troops and officers in grand tactics and to fit them for war as nearly as it was possible to do.[87]

Maneuver in battle was not limited to the offensive army, however. It would be an imperfect science which dealt with only one side of war and left the defensive with no resources against those it placed in the hands of the offensive. An able general, who found it necessary to receive battle, would not take up his position and supinely await attack. He would oppose maneuver to maneuver, ingenuity to ingenuity, and perhaps induce his opponent to commit some error. In a word, he would not limit himself to a mere passive defensive, and might even assume the offensive if opportunity permitted. He would not try to occupy in force all the points at which he could be attacked, for the troops not attacked would be useless to him. He would merely occupy them with the heads of his columns, holding the bulk of his troops to the rear, committing them only when the enemy had definitely committed himself to the attack of some point.

What will the enemy general do meanwhile? He sees the heads of the troops in the principle points of the disposition that he wishes to attack, and instead of an army in battle and disposed to allow itself to be reached and beaten, that army divided into columns of which he can judge neither the depth nor the purpose. Will he maneuver? That army maneuvers also. Will he seek to deceive it? It guards itself against him; it seeks to delude him in his turn. Will he decide to attack a point, and assemble his forces in order to carry it? The forces of that army unite to defend it. Between two such armies, victory will belong finally to whomsoever surpasses in genius and celerity of movement.[88]

In this way, which is strongly prophetic of Napoleon's defensive manner, one achieved the same flexibility for the defensive as for the offensive. The troops needed to be familiarized with this in order to free them from the general opinion that an army about to be attacked should dispose itself as quickly as it could to receive it.

Guibert recognized the importance of topography and insisted upon its close relation to tactics. It should not dominate operations, however, and reduce them to a mere war of positions, as was long the case. Reconnaissance and the choosing of good positions was important, but it was only a part of the science of tactics. Therefore, Guibert insisted that all staff officers, who should be men of the highest intelligence, activity, and wisdom, with a sound judgment of terrain, needed to be tacticians and know how to handle and dispose troops of all arms as well as to choose positions. They should be trained in staff schools on a plan somewhat similar to that by which his father taught him. The staff schools should be located in the major garrisons, where the officers would have troops with which they could apply in practice what they had learned in theory.

With staff officers so trained, and thus become tacticians, the generals also being tacticians, of course, there would be much less passion for taking up positions. Armies would maneuver more, would act in the mass, and would not spread out in small detachments, as in the pernicious cordon system. They would win battles by maneuver. When confronted by an opponent in position, they would seek to turn him. If it could not be done close at hand, then it should be attempted at a distance. They would seek to gain the position's rear. Guibert said that people think that, because they have never heard of an army being attacked in the rear, it cannot be done. Actually nothing is more possible.

Let us suppose on the one side, an army overloaded with encumbrances, unskillful in maneuver, such as ours actually are; and on the other side, an army well constituted, maneuverable, commanded by a general who has thought over the resources of tactics. The one will seek positions, will place all his confidence in them; will move slowly and with difficulty, will be shackled by his methods of subsistence, will believe himself lost if he does not always have his magazines exactly behind him. The other will be active and easily handled, capable of bold movements, of rapid forced marches. It will be always on the offensive, will almost, never enclose itself in positions, and will be contemptuous of those which one opposes to it. Will the enemy believe himself stopped by one of these supposedly impregnable positions? He will know how to conceal a movement from him [the defensive general], or even without concealing it, move in full view on his flank or behind him. In order to execute this maneuver, he will carry eight days' provisions with him, if necessary, and cut himself off from his magazines. What will the enemy do, astonished at this new kind of warfare? Will he wait, while an army able to move itself, to pounce rapidly on the weak part of a disposition, to pass in a moment from the order of march to the order of combat, finds itself in readiness to attack the flank or rear of his position? That inaction will be fatal to him. Will he change position? Then he will lose the advantage of the ground on which he had relied, and he will be compelled to accept battle where he can. Perhaps his clumsy and slow movement will compromise him. He will be embarrassed by his baggage and his means of subsistence; he will be afraid of being cut off from his magazines, with which he will not know how to dispense, because he will have formed the habit of being subjected to them, and because his troops, more numerous than those of the other army, will be, apart from that, less moderate and less patient. . . . I say that a general, who relieves himself in that respect, of established prejudices, will embarrass his enemy, will astonish him, will leave him no place to rest, will force him to fight or to retreat continuously before him. But for such a general, an army differently constituted from ours would be necessary; an army which, having been trained and organized by him, would be prepared for the completely new kind of operations which he would execute with it.[89]

Here, in what is probably the most quoted passage of his work, Guibert again depicted, in his vivid language, the mobile warfare which it was his purpose and hope to forward. Here again he painted a word picture of Bonaparte's campaign of 1796. The mobile army striking now here now there, but never where expected, which he here portrayed, could well be the Army of Italy in its advance from Savona to Mantua. The army rely-

ing upon positions could as well be that of Beaulieu in cordon
along the Ticino, suddenly discovering its enemy crossing the Po
at Piacenza, far in its rear, to conquer without a battle the whole
Milanese which it supposed it was defending.   This maneuver of
placing the whole army astride the enemy's communications was
the most deadly strategic weapon in Napoleon's arsenal.[90]   That
it was balked in the case cited was due entirely to the unavoid-
able delay in crossing the Po.   There is no doubt that Bonaparte,
who specifically included Guibert's work among the books which
he took with him to Italy, must have meditated over this passage
and the means of implementing it.   It is here that the strategic
influence, alluded to at the beginning of the chapter, is most
clearly evident though it also appears in many of the passages
which have been quoted.

It will be noted that Guibert pointed out the necessity, at the
close of the passage, for an army differently constituted from
those then existing.   It was especially in regard to supply that he
pointed out this need, and to the problem of the subsistence of
armies he turned in his final chapter.   It would be impossible to
carry out the rapid maneuvers he wished to institute, if one were
tied down to a rigid supply system based upon an inflexible line
of magazines.   This system, he declared, was the result of the
practice of turning over the supplying of armies to private con-
tractors.   Since officers no longer had anything to do with supply,
they did not study it and were ignorant of the entire problem.
Guibert doubted that there were ten officers in France familiar
with the works on the subject.   This, he felt, was the reason why
generals, instead of being master of their supplies, found supplies
and suppliers master of their operations.   It is the reason why
Parîs-Duvernay (half of that team of brothers which was so potent
an influence in the reign of Louis XV, and which was specifically
referred to by Guibert) could dictate operations during the Seven
Years' War, vetoing operations in cooperation with the Austrians
towards Saxony, and insisting upon operations towards Hanover,
where it would be easy, and no doubt profitable, to subsist the
army.

Such interference was anathema to Guibert.   He insisted

vigorously that officers should take over the duties of supply and that private enterprise be excluded. The amount of baggage and number of magazines should be reduced to reduce the handicap to the army. A more efficient use of the resources of the country should be made, and he believed would be, if the general himself, or a suitable officer, had charge of them. Armies in enemy territory should live off the country at the enemy's expense, if it was rich enough, with magazines for supplementary use only. As in other matters, Guibert was not dogmatic on this, for the method of supply must be adjusted to the resources of the country. But with the army subsisting in whole or in part upon the country, then operations would be freed from the shackles which had, theretofore, bound them, especially in the Seven Years' War.

It is necessary that the enemy see me marching, when he believes me chained by calculations of subsistence; it is necessary that this new kind of war astonish him, leave him neither time nor place to rest, and make him see at his own expense, that constant truth, that there is almost no position tenable before a well constituted army, moderate, patient, and maneuverable. The moment of crisis passed, my movement having accomplished its object, then subsistence returns to the usual system of order and precision.[91]

In other words, when necessary, the army should be able to go on short rations for the sake of rapid movement. In this as in so much else, Guibert's influence was great, for this was the system of supply that was developed and used in the great wars which followed.

This was the concluding theme of the *Essai général,* and it is significant that it looked towards the implementing of the dominant theme of mobile warfare. It is necessary, however, to go back to another subject with which Guibert dealt, namely fortifications. He insisted that the science of fortifications, like all the other parts of military science, was linked to tactics, that the tactician must know fortifications and the engineer, tactics. The former was acknowledged, but not the latter, for engineers had disdained all knowledge of tactics since the days of Vauban. This mutual knowledge was especially needed for field works. In default of such knowledge, one was apt to multiply the works without considering the great numbers required to defend them, nor that the troops enclosed in them lose all advantage of maneuver.

Like all other writers, Guibert condemned the extensive lines which were used to defend a large area. He was contemptuous of that "absurdity which recalls that famous and useless wall which the ignorant Chinese have built six thousand leagues from us." The use of such lines was succeeded by powerfully entrenched positions (such as Saxe knew so well how to employ). This was an improvement over lines, said Guibert, but it was always fatal to generals who knew nothing else. Today, he said, one was coming to a truer sense of the role of field works, but it was necessary to go further and convince oneself "that the sublime defensive consists, not in always seeking positions and receiving battle, but in making the enemy continually fear the offensive; and for that, maneuvering, forcing him to do the same, and watching for the moment where some faults divide him, slow him up, lay him open, in order to operate immediately on him offensively." [92] Again and again Guibert reverted to his constant theme, the resources which mobile warfare offered as opposed to static warfare. He pounded it home, as here, in advocating an offensive-defense.

Guibert declared that entrenched positions, even when they consisted only of redoubts or fortified batteries and villages, reduced one to the passive defensive. The enemy ran no decisive risk in attacking them, for if he failed, it was merely a repulse. It was extremely rare that one was pursued, if he had taken precautions, while victory was complete if he succeeded, as witness Höchstädt (Blenheim).

The defensive founded upon entrenched positions was contrary to all the great views of war. The battles of great generals were nearly all offensive, or if they were defensive, they were almost never fought behind entrenchments. Guibert went further than Saxe in this matter, for Saxe, it will be remembered, advocated redoubts which he would use for a sort of counterattacking defensive. While Guibert was correct upon the evils of mere passive defense, there was merit in Saxe's conception, as Guibert would probably admit for certain occasions.

He did not mean to say that there was no room for field works. They were useful in those rare positions where the enemy, in order to accomplish his objective, had to attack one in front. Such was Broglie's position at Bergen. But the works must be so designed as not to prevent one from taking the offensive, if the enemy's attack dispositions presented the opportunity. They were also useful for detached posts whose purpose was to delay the enemy's advance, for they added greatly to the powers of resistance and supplemented the inferior numbers of the defenders.

Guibert was also opposed to the great multiplication of fortresses based upon the imitation of Vauban and Coehorn, which seemed to desire to make every city a fortress. This policy of fortification without plan, needlessly multiplied the number of fortresses, many of which filled no strategic role, while others, second or third rate, were too small to be useful. In peace they were a heavy and needless drain upon the financial resources of the country, while in war such fortresses absorbed many troops that could be more usefully employed in other ways. Guibert also objected, as one can well imagine, to the tedious and inconclusive methods of warfare to which they had led.

Fortresses had their place. They should be relatively large and few in numbers. Guibert would have one or more in each frontier province. They should be located so as to close the debouches into the country when these were few. Belfort would be an example of what Guibert had in mind here. When the frontier was open, they should be at commanding points such as the confluence of rivers. In addition to their defensive role, fortresses served as major depots on which one could base one's offensive operations into neighboring countries. They also could be used to receive the debris of a defeated army, serving as a refuge for rallying and reorganizing. Fortresses needed to be large defensively in order to make their siege a major operation for the enemy. Offensively, they also needed to be large in order to serve as an adequate major depot for the army. Only a large fortress could receive a defeated army, moreover. There should be a policy on fortresses. All that did not fulfill these objects needed to be demilitarized. When the frontiers changed, one should not hesitate to demolish those which were no longer useful.

Behind the fortresses, Guibert would have four major arsenals in France for the manufacture of all the materials of war. They should be well away from the frontiers which was the weakness of Douai and Strasbourg.[93]

One cannot read Guibert along with the other authors of the century without being struck by the contrast. In spite of his vivid and vehement style, in spite of the strength of his opinions, he was free from the spirit of system which marred some of the other writers. One has the feeling of reading something which pertains to the actual conditions of warfare, and not something which was conceived in the study by someone who either did not know warfare, or should have known better. Here is a mind which has grasped the essentials and potentials of warfare as practiced in his day and has reduced that science to basic principles and methods. In his wider ideas, there is something useful for the present, that is the whole doctrine of mobile warfare. Only Saxe approached him in this, and Saxe never intended to set forth a complete work on war as Guibert did. Puységur had the same practical approach, but in a more limited way, and, of course, in a system of warfare which has no practical meaning for our day.[94]

Guibert's influence was far greater than that of any of the others, not only because of the possible and actual application of his ideas, but also, because through his personality and ability as a publicist, he was able to spread them. His work was promptly translated into all major languages and even into Persian. In the realm of elementary tactics, his methods and formations gradually won their way against extremists from both sides of the controversy between the *ordre mince* and the *ordre profond* until they came to occupy a lasting place in the French Army. Guibert thus played a major role in bringing about the kind of army he wished for. His ideas on the employment of such an army formed perhaps the largest single influence in the formation of the strategic concepts of the military master which he seems to have foreseen, or at least ardently desired.   In this, he is only rivaled by Bourcet.

It is only natural that the deeds of Napoleon should have obscured, in fact nearly obliterated, the ideas and works of him who was his chief inspirer.   Then came the military interpreters of Napoleon, Jomini and Clausewitz, and that obscurity was complete.   Though a few writers have appreciated his worth, he has not received just attention.   Guibert deserves to rank with the two named above as a major military writer, not of one period only, but of all time.

It will be necessary to return to him again in connection with the final conflict between the two orders and their partisans, which brought forth his second major work.   At that time, certain criticisms of him will be examined and discussed.

V

Bourcet

The books written on military theory in eighteenth-century France deal with two lines of development which were reflected in the actual changes within the French Army. There was, first, the unspectacular, but exceedingly important, developments in petty tactics which, by 1770, had led to a battalion having very great flexibility as compared with the battalion of 1715. There was, in addition, a development in grand tactics of fundamental importance, the divisional system. This system grew out of the inadequacy of French tactics when opposed to the Prussians and the great difficulty in handling unitary armies of the size which was usual by mid-century.

The great debate which occupied the bulk of the pages of French theoretical works was concerned with the development of petty tactics, but even more important were the works which set forth a new doctrine for the employment of divisions. Guibert played a dominant role in both of these developments, hence his salient importance.

Pierre de Bourcet (1700-1780) played at least as important a role in the latter. Considered by some to be the greatest of chiefs of staff (he was a staff officer all his life because, being of the lower nobility, independent command was closed to him), he served in all France's wars from that of the Spanish Succession through the Corsican War. Both by his practice and his writings, he demonstrated the art of employing divisions. It was the writings of Bourcet and Guibert together which supplied the basis for Napoleonic warfare.

In his last three wars, Bourcet was the principal adviser of a number of generals. Says Spencer Wilkinson, "On every occasion when an important decision had to be made Bourcet would write a memorandum in which he analyzed the situation and set forth in detail, with full explanations and reasons, the course which seemed to him best.   In very many cases his suggestions were adopted and were usually justified by success, and when they were rejected the results were seldom fortunate." [1]

The principal ideas and practices of Bourcet can be gained by studying the campaigns in which he served as adviser and the memorials which he drew up for them.   These ideas are also to be found in his work, *Principes de la guerre de montagnes,* which he composed while director of the staff school at Grenoble (1764-71) for the use of his students.   This work was not published, being apparently regarded as a confidential document, but was circulated in manuscript form among the officers of the French Army.   A copy was sent to the Ministry of War in 1775.   It was privately printed, though not published, by the Ministry in 1888.

The title is, to some extent, a misnomer, for though the *Principes* emphasizes mountain warfare and draws its examples primarily from the Alpine frontier of France, which Bourcet knew so well, it is, nevertheless, much wider in scope.   The principles and practices expounded in this work are applicable generally to warfare and were so applied by Napoleon in the great wars which followed.

Bourcet made a fundamental distinction between two sorts of war, offensive and defensive.   The former always required a great superiority of troops.   When a general is appointed to the command of an army which is preparing for the offensive, his first task, according to Bourcet, is to designate the point of assembly for the army and to draw up his plan of campaign.   His decisions will be based upon the instructions which he received from his government and his knowledge of the frontier upon which he is to operate.

The assembly may take place either before or behind the frontier fortresses.   In the latter case, the troops will be assembled by routine marches determined by the date for commencing operations.

Several alternatives are open to the commander as his army assembles depending upon the circumstances of the situation.   If the objectives of one's operations are close to the point of assembly, one can establish posts and proceed to the first operation without any other preliminaries. If such is not the case, one has to make one or more marches to reach the first position. These marches will be made either by one or by several *débouchés*.

The distribution of the troops in assembling is determined by these latter alternatives. Bourcet was insistent upon the necessity of keeping one's intentions concealed as long as possible in order that the enemy might not know how to prepare his defense in advance. The early distribution of the troops should be governed in so far as possible by this consideration. If there are several *débouchés*, one chooses a position in the middle of the overall interval between them and divides the army into several camps, one for each of the *débouchés*. The number of troops in these camps will be determined by the facilities of each *débouché* and the operations which will be required of the division concerned. On the other hand, if there is only one *débouché*, and the theatre of operation is extensive enough to permit, then one forms three camps, those of the wings being a day's march from the central camp. The whole front will then cover some twenty-five to thirty miles. The hostile general is left in uncertainty as to just where the first blow will fall and what objective his opponent has in mind, for all points in front of the army are threatened at the same time, and the army can reach any of them in approximately the same amount of time.[2] This disposition of troops is essential in mountain warfare, for if the enemy holds in strength the defiles by which one wishes to advance, it becomes practically impossible to make that advance. It is also true for all warfare, that one needs to delude the enemy as to the point one intends to strike.

In preparing his opening operations the general must take into account all the possible moves and dispositions of the enemy. He must also consider whether the enemy has only begun to move his troops up to the threatened portion of his frontier, or whether the hostile assembly has been completed. When the latter is the case, it is much easier to foresee those dispositions which the enemy can make. In the former case, it becomes necessary for the offensive general to pin down the defensive army and deny to it the possibilty of assembling elsewhere than on the pro-

jected line of advance of the offensive army unless it exposes its
frontier to rupture. If in spite of all the offensive general's precautions, the defense is able to accomplish this result, i.e., to assemble on the flank of the proposed advance and still protect his
frontier, the former must be prepared to alter his plan so as to
meet the new situation. "It is upon these first dispositions which
are made on both sides that the plans of offensive or defensive depend, and as the offensive general will have had to make all the
possible suppositions on the obstacles which one can oppose to
his first operations, it is necessary to consider that the defensive
[general] will have taken the same precautions on his side and
that he will be prepared for all events." [3]

The first operations are generally successful, says Bourcet, but
the second ones depend upon the reaction of the defense, for, as
the defensive general was hampered at first by ignorance as to
where the blow would be struck, so the offensive general, once he
is committed to a line of action, is hampered by ignorance of the
reaction which the defense will make. No matter how thoroughly he may have considered the possibilities, it is highly un-
likely that he will have thought of everything that the defense
might do. The latter's reaction may quite possibly upset all his
calculations and compel him to measures quite different from
those which he had intended.[4]

Bourcet points out that, while it is essential to hold the army
united in plains (which was still largely true in his day), in the
mountains, however, it is possible to divide one's forces into several parts. He favors therefore the division of the army into a
number of columns if it is at all possible. Advancing in this
manner, spread out over a large front, it becomes possible to conceal one's objective more easily from the enemy and perhaps to
mislead him as to one's intention. Then in proportion as one approaches the enemy, the columns *are reunited on the decisive
point.* This point and even the very words occur again and again
in Napoleon's correspondence. This movement in several columns enables one to arrive in strength. It is indispensable that
there be crossroads so that the columns can communicate with
one another and, if necessary, support each other. A column can

be overwhelmed by superior force if such intercommunication is lacking without any aid being able to reach it. These intercommunicating roads are also required, Bourcet declares, by the maxim of always marching in order of battle. It is much more difficult to do this in a mountainous country than in level country. Experienced and capable staff officers are required, and they must make a most careful survey in order to provide the necessary communications and positions for assembly.

Since it is not possible to assemble the army at all points in mountains as one can in plains, there are a number of precautions to be taken. The nature of the roads must be taken into account. If each column can be accompanied by its own artillery and wagon train, then no serious problem arises. If only one column has a road which permits this, however, then the assembly of the army can only be made upon that column, and the others must have their march secured by detachments.

The general must be kept informed by his aides of the level of the columns which may be facilitated along with the general communication between columns by the occupation of the heights separating the valleys. Bourcet thinks that it would be dangerous for one column to pass a cross *débouché* before the neighboring columns have reached it in adjacent valleys. So essential does he consider the simultaneous arrival of troops on a given position, that if there are serious differences in the length of the various routes, he wishes the troops to make proportional halts to assure that they arrive at the same time. If the enemy can interfere with the march, all these precautions become more essential. If the march of one or more of the columns is obstructed, either by nature or by the enemy, so as to delay it for some days, the whole advance needs to be held up until the obstruction is overcome.[5]

Bourcet deals at great length with plans of campaign. Such plans must be regulated upon the topography of the theatre of operation, the size and composition of one's army, the extent of one's resources, and the obstacles and opposition which have to be overcome.[6]

Such plans may be either offensive or defensive. In the

former case, Bourcet remarks that the frontier will always be extensive enough no matter how one regards it, to be divided into two parts. One of these will be more favorable to the objectives which one has in mind, while the other will always be available for diversions. There follows what Liddell Hart calls Bourcet's cardinal principle:

It will then be necessary that the plan of campaign include the two parts, and that it *ought to have several branches.*[7] One ought to base the examination of the operations upon the obstacles, more or less great, which one has to overcome on the inconveniences or advantages which will result from their success in each branch, and, after having made the most plausible objections, to determine the branch which can lead to the greatest advantages, in employing diversions and all that can most successfully delude one's enemy and convince him that one has decided upon some other choice.[8]

If all of the diversions, countermarches, and other ruses fail to hide one's true objective, then one must proceed to a second and perhaps a third branch of the plan without allowing the enemy time to consider the available alternatives. It is this examination of operations relative to each which determines the army's place of assembly. This last should be located in such a manner as to allow having a reserve so placed as to be able to reinforce either the main body of the army or the diversionary force. The great advantage of mountains, Bourcet repeats, is that it permits this division of troops with safety, by reason of the natural obstacles which the country presents.[9]

An essential part of Bourcet's strategic concept is the role of diversions. He declares:

Nothing is, without contradiction, more advantageous in war than diversions, but it is necessary that they be well thought out, prepared in advance, and the more distant [ones] are the best, likewise the nearer ones are also [advantageous] in a plan of operations of several branches.

It is an always assured means of profiting from superiority, of which it is necessary to make use when the inferior power determines upon an active defense.[10]

It is necessary for the plan of campaign that those parts of the frontier which are useful for main operations be distinguished carefully from those which are useful only for diversions or are not useful at all. This should not prevent one from collecting supplies, munitions, and materiel, including transport, at all cities located at the forks of principal *débouchés* along the entire extent of the frontier. The most important depots should be located in the fortresses which are nearest the center of the frontier or those which have good communications with all parts thereof. In this connection, Bourcet points out that such preparations as collection of supplies and repair of communications carried on far from one's objective are frequently the most effective and most essential type of diversions. Such preparations often do more than anything else to convince an opponent that one's plans are other than those actually intended. Bourcet advocates that magazines be kept full at all times, if possible, in order to avoid alerting an opponent, but if this is not possible, then, except where delusion is an object, supplies should be drawn secretly and from the interior to fill them.

All these preliminaries—drawing up of plans, collection of supplies, repairing of communications—having been completed, it is necessary to assemble the army, as soon as possible, in such a manner that it can "respond to the different branches which the plan embraces." Thus the major direction of the troops will be concealed from the enemy who will be noting every available move and indication as to one's objective. One must, therefore, conceal from his subordinates the objective of the orders which they have to execute, and one should add orders designed to confuse the enemy and add to his uncertainty. To this end Bourcet insists upon the necessity of feints. Troops and artillery should be pushed in a direction designed to distract the opposing general from the true objective and to draw him away from it. The necessary supply arrangements in support of this feint should also be made in order to give it the semblance of reality. "The disposition of supplies and the opening of the marches will be to no purpose, but it is necessary to spare nothing when it is a question of deceiving one's enemy." If the ruse has trapped him into a false move, then the troops and artillery can be brought back by a countermarch to assure the success of the first operations. The commander-in-chief should take only his chief of staff into his confidence concerning the feint which should succeed in its purpose in that case.[11]

Bourcet deals also with defensive plans of campaign. Such plans must take into account every point on a frontier which may be the objective of a hostile enterprise. While offensive plans demand a distribution of troops, defensive plans require a wise combination of the available forces which can be employed at each point. This requirement will determine whether the troops will be divided into several divisions assigned to the various threatened points or will be kept together in a single body.

The first of these alternatives means a passive defense. It requires fortresses or similar obstacles to supplement the troops on the points where they are stationed; otherwise they will be so weak that they cannot successfully resist the enemy. The second alternative leads to an active defense—always preferable to the passive since the latter cannot prevent the enemy from piercing the frontier at some point. There are several requirements for an active defense. First, the position must be taken up near the center of the frontier's extent so as to be able to profit to the greatest degree from any enemy mistake. Second, supplies must be freely available from the rear. Third, the position must have obstacles which cover its wings and front so that it cannot be turned nor attacked in front except with too great disadvantages. Fourth, the surrounding country needs to be defended by fortresses or at the very least the position itself should be under protection of a fortress. Lastly, wood and water must be so located that the supply cannot be cut off by the enemy.

The defensive general must always attempt to divine his opponent's plans. If the offensive general succeeds in his undertaking in spite of all the defensive general's efforts, then the latter must be prepared for all eventualities. He must have selected several positions for the purpose of meeting these eventualities. Otherwise he may find himself driven into a fortress.

To form a defensive plan is always more difficult than an offensive one, because many of the factors can only be conjectured until the opposition discloses its hand by its opening moves. Frequently the defensive general is unable to avail himself of the defensive advantages of a frontier because of a particular situation in which he finds himself. He may find himself forestalled at the essential positions—always the greatest inconvenience in defensive operations that can be imagined.[12]

In defensive warfare, the general, after having thought over the possible enemy undertakings which need be feared and made the required disposition of his troops, must take necessary precautions. These precautions take the form, essentially, of destroying everything advantageous to the enemy which lies in front of one's positions—roads, bridges, mills, ovens, etc.—and burning all supplies which cannot be carted away. At the same time, one must repair all the communications which lead to the rear. In sum, the essential is to raise every possible obstacle to the enemy's progress. Bourcet had mountain warfare principally in mind, of course, where the campaigning season is limited and where time is perhaps even more essential than elsewhere.[13]

Bourcet points out a number of advantages which the offense has over the defense. The essence of these is that the offensive has the inestimable advantage of the initiative which allows it to threaten or even to attack numerous points, leaving the enemy in doubt as to the true objective and unable to do more than take preparatory measures for defense. If the defense, threatened along his entire front, attempts to cover the whole of it, he weakens himself at all points. Whatever the defensive general's precautions for reinforcing the point of true attack, the reinforcements cannot arrive in time if the offense has effectively concealed his plan and early movements. This is true no matter how good are the reports received from spies or deserters, because of the time necessary to receive warning, send out orders, and move even the nearest troops. The offensive general can know positively the number of troops he will have to oppose while the defense cannot know this.[14]

Bourcet concluded that since communications across mountains are not to be relied upon beyond the end of September, troops must retire across the mountains unless they have secured themselves in safety beyond them. All plans of campaigns for mountain warfare should limit themselves to (1) main operations which can be concluded by the end of September and which would be favorable to a second campaign, (2) taking full advantage of the campaigning season from June to September, (3) providing a sufficient force, distinct from the combat troops, for guarding communications if one enters winter quarters beyond the mountains, (4) having the ability to assemble in a few days in one's quarters in event of an enemy offensive, and (5) making adequate canvass of possible enemy moves in determining the place of assembly from no matter what direction the enemy might advance.[15]

Bourcet advanced a new and sound doctrine, both theoretically in his book and practically in the many campaigns which he directed. Combined with the ideas of Guibert (which they, in effect, extended from the tactical to the strategic level), they provided the doctrine of employment for an army organized on the divisional basis, a doctrine which Napoleon brought to full development. Bourcet's influence upon Napoleon was very great. The latter often quoted the need for alternatives in a plan of campaign sometimes almost in Bourcet's very words. The careful examination of all possibilities open to the enemy and the means of meeting each of them which was so characteristic of Napoleon's thinking also reflects Bourcet's doctrine on plans of campaign. It is permissible to think that Bourcet provided at least one of the sources of the offensive spirit which dominated Napoleon the general. Finally, Napoleon's great defensive campaign of 1814 reflects Bourcet's defensive theories.

Joly de Maizeroy

A new entrant appeared in the lists with the publication in 1766 by Joly de Maizeroy (1719-80) of the *Cours de tactique, théorique, practique, et historique.* Maizeroy, then a lieutenant-colonel, was a profound student of military history, who had served with distinction under Saxe in Bohemia and Flanders and in the Seven Years' War. With the single exception of Folard, no author showed so much the influence of classical history.

Maizeroy certainly represented a retrograde movement when compared with Guibert for though Maizeroy's work was published first, Guibert's ideas were already beginning to have a practical influence at the end of the sixties. Villate calls Maizeroy an extreme partisan of the column, which is, to say the least, inexact. He was a partisan of the *ordre profond,* but not by any means of its extreme forms. He was very critical of Folard's ideas at many points while expressing a general respect for him. He did not approve of the exclusiveness of Mesnil-Durand's original system, preferring the revised form. He was much closer to Saxe and his intermediary position than to any of the other "makers of systems." This does not mean that he was content merely to follow Saxe, however, for though he quoted him frequently with evident approval on many subjects, he rejected the tactical system of Saxe, and proposed one of his own.

Maizeroy left a record of his reaction to Guibert's work, for in the Preface of his *La Tactique discutée,* he had this to say:

I intended to finish my preface here, when a new book entitled *Essai Général de Tactique,* whose author wishes to remain anonymous, having fallen into my hands, its title and its reputation have made me read it with avidity. I have been struck by the force and energy of the style; I have admired the depth of the reflexions and the extent of the views that it contains, but I have seen with sadness that a military genius, who announces himself with so much brilliance, should be attached to the system least agreeable to his nation; that in pretending to fight that which he calls prejudice in others, he remains himself enslaved to the most dangerous of all . . . and that in seeking to destroy contrary opinions without reservation, he wishes to seat his own imperiously on their debris.[1]

And a little further on:

It is a question then of combating this new enemy, who comes to the aid of error and wishes to reduce it to principles; who claims that every other system but his is complicated and *far from the possibilities of circumstances;* that all which deviates from his opinions is *a residue of ignorance and of old prejudices;* that there exists no *dogmatic work which can instruct; that one has treated one or two branches of war, but that no one has perceived the others, nor the indispensable connection which they have between them;* who disdains the sources of our knowledge and of our enlightenment [ancient tactics]; who raises a vast brilliant edifice, regular in appearance, but which has no foundations; who overthrows the first laws of tactics, in saying that *he wishes to destroy nothing, but that he wishes to turn to account that which exists;* who finally, for all these reasons, believes to have written with more usefulness than all the other tacticians have done. If this adversary appeared less formidable to me, if his book were not filled with excellent things, which merit for it a just claim to the general esteem, even admiration, I would have kept silent, and would have contented myself with thanking him, as I do here, for that which he has said in a note, gratifying on my account. I am flattered at having, as he declares, contributed to excite his emulation; but I would be still more so, and I would merit much more from the nation, if I should succeed in convincing him that he is saddled with a bad cause.[2]

The above passage reveals Maizeroy as a vigorous controversialist, and illustrates also the powerful reaction which Guibert stimulated. It indicates something of the vigor of the controversy involved in the last conflict between the two orders. It was Colin's contention that Maizeroy appeared to be a partisan of the *ordre mince* in so far as purely infantry combat was concerned. While such a contention might be based upon Maizeroy's original work, it cannot be reconciled with the above quotation nor with Maizeroy's supplementary works.[3] He was a partisan of the order in depth and primarily of shock action though not of the column for all situations. He thus represents an intermediate position in the controversy.

Maizeroy was among those writers who rejected the idea that the invention of firearms should have resulted in any major changes in tactics or tactical formations. He said:

Although the invention of powder and the new arms has occasioned various changes in the mechanism of war, it is certain that it ought to have influenced the principles of tactics only very little and those of strategy not at all. It is the contrary opinion which, for about a century, has made bad maxims prevail, and has caused us to deviate from the true road. It is that which has made [us] extend the battalions at the expense of their depth, which has made [us] form thin and wavering lines without solidity and without action. It is that which has multiplied excessively the guns, and made [us] seek in the extreme speed of their shots, a support for the feebleness of the ordinance. It is that finally, as well as flabbiness, which has made [us] quit defensive arms, and lose sight of all the means which sustained bravery in giving them more audacity.[4]

He admitted that the fusil with bayonet was a superior weapon to *pilum* or javelin, but infantry still needed an ordinance which was solid, a depth of eight or not less than six ranks. It needed to be well trained in obtaining the full advantage of its arms. He then went on to condemn those who wished to return to the pike as not having fully examined the effect of firearms, thus showing that he was not contemptuous of fire as some previous writers were.

One of Maizeroy's characteristic traits was his great preoccupation with the combat of infantry against cavalry. Colin declared[5] that it was this preoccupation which led Maizeroy to his normal formation on a depth of six or preferably eight. This does not seem to be the whole story, for he repeatedly inveighed against the wavering and fluctuation of the long thin battalions and the great difficulty with which they moved. It would follow, therefore, that this concerned him at least as much in his advocacy of formations in depth.

It is difficult to know exactly what was Maizeroy's opinion of the effects of fire. There is his statement above that those who wish to resume pikes have not sufficiently understood the effects of fire. On the other hand, he stated elsewhere that the dis-

charges of defending infantry on his attacking forces would be ineffective because of the defenders' demoralization.[6]   He also referred to fire as useless and frequently dangerous when one relies
upon it improperly [7] without explaining what he meant by improperly.   Fire was, however, indispensable against cavalry,
where bayonets alone or even pikes alone were insufficient and
would succumb eventually.   Fire alone was also insufficient in
that case, but fire coupled with the bayonet was very formidable.
enabling infantry not only to resist cavalry, but to act offensively
against it like the Roman legionaires.

It was Maizeroy's contention that an ordinance for infantry
must be based upon sound principles.   The fundamental one was
that an ordinance must combine mobility with solidity to the extent that neither hindered the other.   Such an ordinance must be
suitable for both offensive and defensive action.   All its subdivisions must be able to separate and reunite with both speed and
precision.   The result would enable a general to calculate all his
movements accurately in dimensions of space and time required.
"It would join activity to precision, and far from trembling at the
sight of an army more numerous than his, he would know how to
move the strong part against the weak, and render himself superior in the points where he attacks." [8] Here Maizeroy set forth
a principle which was one of Guibert's major points of emphasis,
but unlike Guibert, he did not indicate the method of implemen-
tation.   He did assert that the success of all a general's enterprises
depended upon the formation of troops on such principles.

Maizeroy declared that he was almost ashamed to present as a
problem the necessity of depth for infantry destined to fight in a
plain.   The contrary practice was a violation of common sense
and was never in question until the eighteenth century.   Those
who had questioned it insisted that the invention of gunpowder
affected a total revolution in warfare.   They regarded warfare as
a trade, a matter of routine, and not a science.   A study of both
ancient and modern military systems indicated as a basic principle that the ancients ranged themselves in a manner which had
strength both for attack and resistance.   This principle was the

basis of the science of tactics. "The sole order proper for the offensive is that which unites solidity and speed. Speed is supplied it by the small extent of its front, solidity by the number of its ranks and by its arms." [9]

What does one mean when one speaks of a charge by infantry? Your line of infantry approaches that of the enemy to a distance of two hundred or at most one hundred paces. You fire at him. He fires at you. You advance if he recoils. You recoil if he advances. This is not a charge. It is the maneuver of two poltroons who are afraid of each other and dare not risk crossing arms.

Maizeroy declared that the notion of shock had been lost, and soldiers of his day had only very confused ideas concerning it. Some considered it a sort of physical contact resulting from the simultaneous impulsion of all the ranks; others denied this absolutely, saying that the shock was confined to the first rank only, with the following ranks contributing no force whatever. Both are wrong, declared Maizeroy. A body of men in ranks and files could not be considered as a contiguous body, and hence, the simultaneous impulsion of shock could not exist because of the spaces between the men. Thus far he was in accord with Guibert in condemning Folard's famous principle. There was shock, however, to which more than the first rank contributed. Here Maizeroy parted company with Guibert. It was produced by the concurrence of several forces at the point of contact. This doctrine was backed up by one of Maizeroy's ingenious physical principles and calculations. The shock was produced by the file leader first and successively by those who followed him in file. The shock of each man in file was successively less because it had to be transmitted through those ahead. This shock was composed of speed and weight. It diminished for each rank according to the square of the number of the preceding rank! Thus the shock produced by the eighth rank was only one forty-ninth that of the first. Beyond this rank the added shock was hardly sensible, and that was why he limited his order to a depth of eight. This was not to be construed as meaning that there were not occasions where it would be useful to double ranks, or even to form columns of from sixteen files on a depth of twenty-four up to not more than twenty-four by thirty-two.[10]

Besides this physical impulsion which really existed up to sixteen ranks and sensibly up to eight, there was a moral impulsion which really existed up to eight ranks and sensibly up to six. This was due to the fact that the mass following behind the first ranks presented an insurmountable obstacle to their flight, and even the most faint-hearted had to go on and fight, while the enemy in a thinner, and consequently weaker, order would be terrified at seeing this depth which seemed irresistible and would be beaten even before he was approached.

Both of these impulsions are debatable to say the least. In the first, there is an example of the influence of physical science which was referred to in the Introduction. In the second, Maizeroy, who had earlier accused Guibert of "giving ideas without proofs, without calculations," himself asserted such an idea. It is no excuse to plead that this concept was commonly held by all writers of the school of the *ordre profond*. What is more surprising, Maizeroy himself had given historical proof of the erroneous nature of the idea in an earlier volume where he declared that the Greek order was based much more upon Folard's principle of shock and that the Greeks could not deny that they were sometimes disillusioned in this. For he declared that only the men in the front ranks contributed to the effort. If they failed and recoiled in disorder, *this disorder communicated itself at once to the rest*, and there was no way for the rear ranks to reinforce or replace the front ones.[11] One needs only to ask why that insurmountable barrier to the flight of the first ranks did not apply to the Greeks as well as to the moderns. One might also ask why the Greek front ranks did not have to go on and fight. He would respond that, in the case of the Greeks, the front ranks would be opposed to a similar order in depth. Nevertheless that does not dispose of the problem. This is another of the inconsistencies which makes it difficult to know Maizeroy's ideas on some points.

What was the foundation upon which a tactical system should

be based? "It is not the arms which should regulate the form of the ordinance. It is necessary to begin by establishing this upon good principles, and join to it afterwards the best arms possible." [12] He declared that he would prefer to fight with his system armed with swords and javelins rather than with three-deep battalions furnished with the most potent arms obtainable. With good arms one could supplement the lack of a greater depth. "Thus eight ranks, perhaps even six well armed, could defeat sixteen, badly armed." In that case, why could not a well-armed three-deep battalion defeat his system armed with swords and javelins?

Numbers, or rather a number, formed the basis of a tactical system. One must choose a number in order to compose such a system, a number upon which one regulated all divisions and movements. Upon the soundness of the choice depended "the harmony of the different parts of a body of troops, the accuracy and simplicity of maneuvers, the speed and safety of operations." Maizeroy spoke of the Roman system based upon ten and also of the Greek system. The latter desired a number capable of division to unity and multiplication to infinity, always providing even roots and products. The progression 2, 4, 8, 16, etc., was the only one which satisfied this requirement. It was adopted by the Greeks and also by Maizeroy who maintained that all that pertained to tactics should be simple and capable of being increased or reduced without changing its basic form. A system based upon odd numbers was imperfect because it was unequally composed according to Maizeroy.[13]

This Pythagorean [14] concept of tactics is difficult to maintain. There is no reason why the progression 3, 9, 27, etc., cannot as well be the basis of a system as that which Maizeroy adopts, unless one accepts some mysterious properties for numbers. It will be remembered that Guibert preferred odd numbers of units for sound reasons. More important, however, is the fact that Maizeroy was in great error in thinking that geometry was the fundamental basis of tactics. The evidence of history, ancient as well as modern, is conclusive that the formations of troops should be and has been based upon the weapons with which they were armed and secondarily upon the tasks assigned. It is clear that, no matter how able an historian Maizeroy was, he was unable to interpret the evidence of history correctly when it ran counter to his theories.

Maizeroy called his basic unit the cohort, adopting the later Roman system of tactics as his model. The cohort was composed of eight maniples of eighty men each and was normally drawn up on a depth of eight men which would give a front of eighty men and a strength of six hundred forty for the cohort. For fire combat, he would reduce the depth to four men. If he desired to

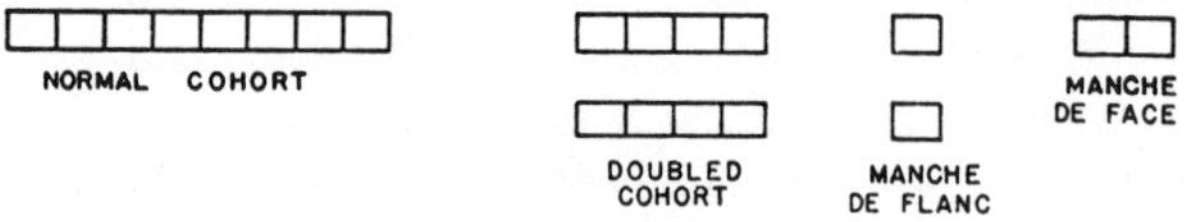

FIGURE 21

have a smaller front, say for crossing rough ground even faster, then he formed a doubled cohort, placing one division of four maniples behind the other, keeping twelve paces of interval between divisions until the moment of shock. Two such doubled cohorts, one behind the other, formed a doubled phalanx. This formation was for use when one was on a depth of more than four.[15] See Figure 21. It would be even better, ideally, to reduce the cohort by sixteen files so that each maniple would have a strength of sixty-four men who would then form a perfect square in formation. The front of sixty-four men which the cohort would form is also a perfect square and is the most proper one of all for precision of movements.[16] Again this Pythagorean *mysticisme* of numbers!

To each cohort, Maizeroy would join one hundred twenty light troops and a company of sixty-four grenadiers.[17] The light armed troops needed to be trained to fight alone or with the heavy infantry. They needed to know how to run, jump, climb rocks, swim, and support cavalry either by being posted on the latter's wings or by platoons between squadrons. They needed to know how to load and fire while marching or even running.

They should be formed on three or even two ranks in order to be able to fire easily. There were a few cases where it would be best for them to fire together, but generally, they should fire at will, than which there was nothing deadlier. The influence of Saxe is here quite evident.[18]

Somewhat further on, Maizeroy returned to the subject of light troops. Skirmishing was not their major function as far as he was concerned. Maizeroy differed from Saxe in this respect. The chief purpose was to protect the flanks of his cohorts and gain those of the enemy. They were to be held opposite the intervals and to go out from them when needed. These intervals, which were regarded by many generals as an inconvenience, were, according to Maizeroy, indispensable since without them the march of a line was always heavy and irregular. Since they offered openings for the enemy to gain one's flanks and rear, one needed to have troops near at hand to close them.[19] He would thus appear to expect to launch his cohorts on his foe without benefit of any fire power at all. Moreover, the reference to marching in line offers more evidence that he did not differentiate between maneuver and combat. He did not seem to grasp the idea of maneuvering in column and then deploying for action.

Maizeroy declared here that he would form his regiment of four cohorts. He changed his mind later, however, declaring that he would prefer each regiment to be composed of five cohorts, with a sixth in depot composed of old officers and men employed in training recruits instead of being sent to the Invalides. In order of battle, the regiment would normally present three cohorts in the first line and two in the second. Each regiment would also have a squadron of one hundred twenty light cavalry attached.[20]

Maizeroy would dispose his cohorts, simple or doubled, in the checker formation of the Romans with intervals of forty paces between them in line.[21] He maintained that this formation would invariably defeat troops arrayed in conventional manner. Their rate of march was such that they would suffer not more than three

musketry discharges before closing. Artillery would be somewhat more formidable.

For Maizeroy, it is the formation employed which guarantees
the victory. He declared:

It is certain that everywhere that one will employ it, it will force its
way through the enemy line. The victorious cohort will divide itself
by *manches* [see Figure 21], which will hurl themselves to right and
left in order to attack the enemy in flank and rear. While it will be
executing that, the second cohort which follows the first, will march
forward through the breach. It will charge the second line battalion
which will have advanced opposite it. It will also have marched well,
and the light armed will have completed the destruction.[22]

It is apparent that Maizeroy is just as confident of his formation as any of the other "makers of systems." There is certainly
more justification for him than for any of the others, save possibly
Saxe. The cohort had a flexibility that was lacking in the closed
and massed column and in the *plésion*. Its chief weakness was in
its waste of much of its fire power. Maizeroy proposed to use
only four ranks for fire action, but he was not clear as to when
and under what conditions he would employ that formation. He
certainly would not fire while advancing to the attack which
would be done in a deep order. Maizeroy recognized the moral
advantages of the offensive and wished to attack at all costs. He
rejected fire while the troops were advancing. He was not clear
as to just what form combat should take in all respects. Colin,
who would seem to have studied him somewhat less thoroughly
than he had the other writers, declared that Maizeroy would have
a fire preparation before attacking. This is not entirely clear,
however, for most of his discussion of attack concerned shock.
He did not specify, for instance, from how distant a point he
would launch his attack, either in discussing his cohorts, or later
on in his extensive discussion of the ineffectiveness of artillery
against them. Thus he declared that his cohorts would suffer two
or three discharges of musketry at most while advancing. It
would take well-trained infantry not over a minute to deliver
them. The cohorts could not cross effective musketry range in
that time no matter how fast they marched.

Colin said that Maizeroy never declared himself hostile to the linear order for the combat of infantry "if it is not because of the difficulties which the march in battle presents for a long thin line." [23] On the contrary, he said, Maizeroy pointed out the defects of the column in one or two passages. This is all true, but it is also true that he expressed vigorous condemnation of the linear formation for the reason which Colin excepts from his general statement. Nowhere did he envisage such a combat unless one calls his formation in simple cohorts a linear formation, which Maizeroy most certainly did not. Combat for him was a matter of shock, and his idea of rupturing and rolling up the enemy line was very similar to that of Folard and Mesnil-Durand. Moreover, even while condemning Folard's column, he pointed out that "it is the antipode of that of the battalions, whose feebleness is incontestable, and cannot be disavowed by good sense." Somewhat further on, he said, "The use of the column is certainly preferable to that of long, thin battalions which have neither force nor consistency; obstinacy and ignorance alone can contest it." [24] One looks in vain to find support in Maizeroy for the *ordre mince*, unless it be for fire action when there is no possibility of coming into contact, and even on this he was not clear.

Maizeroy's own contemporaries advanced the same criticism against his system as against the other variations of the *ordre profond*, namely, that in increasing the depth, one decreased the extent of the order. His answer was also similar to that of the others subjected to this criticism. He concluded, "My tactics are consequently very practicable, and my principles have nothing contrary to modern usage. In following them, one can face superior forces, and no longer count the number of one's enemies with timid regard. One can supplement one's weakness by one's dispositions, and astonish one's adversary by bold maneuvers that one has not dared to risk till now." [25]

In summing up Maizeroy's infantry tactics, one can say that he called for a flexible order of units of battalion strength, but formed on a depth of not less than eight ranks (he would admit six if necessity demanded) for offensive action, to which he would couple small bodies of light troops and grenadiers for support. He envisaged offensive action in almost all cases, and he expected to go forward at his enemy without firing until just before the clash when his men would pour in a point-blank volley and close with the bayonet. The type of action he described is a shock action with the place which fire occupies being extremely vague. Following Folard and Mesnil-Durand, he hardly distinguished between maneuver and combat, having the same formation for both. He spoke occasionally of bold maneuvers to confuse the enemy, but with little or no amplification. He seemed to rely primarily upon his formation for success as the previous two did entirely. He represented a distinct improvement over them, but was by no means Guibert's equal. He was, however, in the middle ground, and despite occasional vigor of language condemning the *ordre mince,* he was far from being a partisan of the extreme forms of the rival order.

Maizeroy had little of permanent value to contribute in regard to the other arms. His views on cavalry were almost identical with those of Guibert save that he presented a defensive disposition, a form of action which Guibert would not permit for cavalry. He originally favored small squadrons in terms almost identical with Guibert's. "Two units which maneuver separately, ought to defeat an equal, or even superior, number assembled in a single troop." Later he increased the size up to one hundred twenty men.

In regard to artillery, Maizeroy had little to say on its tactical employment. His ideas were similar to Guibert's and probably show the latter's influence. His chapter was largely devoted to ballistics and a curious conception of the nature of air. He was opposed, in balance, to the changes which Gribeauval had initiated.

Maizeroy's discussion of grand tactics fell far short of Guibert's. It did not contain much that had meaning for the future. He laid down certain general principles concerning marching which are principles of the past not the future.

The science of marches is one of the parts of the art of war which demands the most attention and knowledge. One can regard it as the basis of all operations, since one arrives by it at that which one wishes to accomplish. . . . They [orders of march] vary according to circumstances. Nevertheless, they are all related to a general rule, which is to march in the order most nearly approaching that in which one wishes to fight, and in a manner that one can be in battle promptly and without confusion if the enemy appears during the march.[26]

This is essentially similar to the ideas and practices which had long existed on the subject and contains nothing new. He declared that columns need to be multiplied when making a march to the front in order to deploy as rapidly as possible. This principle had long been followed in practice.

Maizeroy was agreed with Guibert that the oblique order of battle was the supreme manifestation of the tactical art, "comprehending the greatest perfection of tactics." It was the resource of small armies enabling them to engage and to defeat large ones.[27] It is, however, not entirely clear just what he intended as the preliminaries of action. He spoke without amplification in at least two places, already noted, of maneuvers on the battlefield for the purpose of deceiving one's opponent. When he discussed the approach to the battlefield, all talk of maneuvers disappeared. He had no desire for preliminary maneuvers before engaging. If one wished to reinforce one part of his order for the purpose of taking up an oblique order of battle, this would apparently need to be done before the approach march began. In summing up his discussion of approach marches, he went so far as to say: "In concluding this chapter, I will say summarily that the order of battle ought to be designed in the same way as the order of march; that the battalions and squadrons should be ranged in such a manner that they will form the front of the line in the direction which they wish to be by very simple movements, *that one be not obliged to transport troops from one place to another, even when the enemy will be in a different disposition from that in which one expects to find him,* the only reserves ought to be destined for unforeseen exigencies." [28] This passage would seem to indicate that Maizeroy wished his army to be in its order of combat when it developed from its order of march without any changes whatever. If that is the case, he does not expect any period of maneuver before battle, but wishes to take up his order of battle at once and proceed to action. Such a concept, which Folard and Mesnil-Durand advocate, seems very difficult to accept in the more practical and realistic Maizeroy. At any rate, this is another point upon which he is inferior to Guibert.

In summing up, it can be said that Maizeroy represented a moderate element among the partisans of the *ordre profond* which did not fall into many of the errors of the more extreme advocates of that order. It can be said that, as Guibert stood further toward the center than the extreme advocates of the *ordre mince* of the Pirch school, so Maizeroy held the same relative position in relation to Mesnil-Durand in the controversy between the two orders. His work contained a great many sound ideas, and his system was more practical and realistic than any of the others, save that of Saxe, which was very similar. He did fall into the error of excessive reliance upon shock action and did not distinguish enough between preliminary maneuver and actual combat. In this latter, he was much inferior to Guibert. It was difficult to tell just what his views were on many points because he said one thing in one place and modified it in another. At any rate, he belonged rather to the old school of warfare than to the new for which Guibert acted as prophet.

Pirch

That Prussian tactics became influential in France after the Seven
Years' War is not surprising. The great triumphs of Frederick
the Great presented a brilliant contrast to the many disasters of
the French Army. Many French officers, visiting Prussia, were interested spectators at Prussian reviews and drills. They sought to
find there the reasons for Frederick's victories. Preoccupied with
tactics as they were, it is hardly surprising that these French observers believed that Prussian tactics held the secret of Prussian
success.

It cannot be denied that by the accession of Frederick II Prussian troops had achieved a high degree of perfection in the execution of their maneuvers. This was the result of constant drill and
an iron discipline which enforced rigid conformity with the
abundant minutiae of Prussian regulations.

It is not so true that the maneuvers themselves were so excellent or that they were good models to follow.[1] The organization
of Prussian troops was less logical than that of the French even
before the reforms of Choiseul. The Prussian battalion contained six companies for administration, yet these formed eight
for tactical purposes. The only formations in use until 1743
were the deployed line, the open column, the square, and filing
the column by simple or double files for the passage of narrow
defiles.[2] The rate of march was very deliberate, even the double
being only seventy-five or eighty paces per minute.

Some changes, however, were being made. After the War of
the Austrian Succession, Frederick began to experiment with
closed columns and the means for deploying them ahead. For
this purpose, he first used half quarter-wheels, and then in 1752,
he substituted deployment by square movements (*en tiroir*) executed on the center platoon, preferably while slowly advancing.
Finally in 1754, Frederick began to use deployment by flank

marches obliquely to the proposed line which Guibert subsequently introduced into the French Army. These and other maneuvers were apparently intended to make troops more flexible rather than to increase the number of war maneuvers.[3]

It is by the precision of its movements, and not by their variety, that the Prussian infantry has been an instrument of exceptional value in the hands of a general as able as Frederick. The foreign officers, and in particular the French, deluded themselves without doubt in seeking in the Potsdam evolutions the secret of Prussian victories; but it is certain, on the other hand, that the error was healthy for us, for it is the adoption and practice of the new formations and maneuvers which have procured for the armies of Louis XVI the tactics with which the generals of the Revolutionary and Imperial periods were to conquer.[4]

French observers, including Guibert, felt these new maneuvers to be the essential part of Prussian tactics. They were not used by Frederick in combat, however. They were peacetime experiments made apparently for use in war if circumstances required. Frederick preferred to arrive on the battlefield in such a manner that he could form his battle line by the simultaneous quarter-wheels of two long open columns, one for each line. This he was able to accomplish in almost all of his battles, and such was the precision and perfection of drill of his troops that they could outmaneuver their opponents and form line far more rapidly than the latter could. Frederick's victories were due, therefore, to his own ability, to the mobility and maneuverability of his troops, and to their discipline rather than to the excellence of their maneuvers. The Prussians had brought the old-style unitary army to the peak of its possibilities.

Prussian influence upon the French Army took two directions. The first was the revolution effected by Guibert. He seized upon the experiments of Frederick's peacetime camps and, applying the tactics there outlined to the French divisional system, initiated the tactical revolution which eventually triumphed in the French Army. The method of deployment was Frederick's; the rest was Guibert's.

The second form of Prussian influence was in the direction of imitation rather than adaptation. It consisted of attempts to transfer Prussian methods of drill and of discipline to the French Army with the purpose of achieving the same precision. Out of these, under the influence of a Baron de Pirch, there emerged a major aberration from the main line of development of French tactics.

Pirch was a Prussian officer who had entered the French service. He became an officer in the Corsican Legion in which Guibert also served. A *mémoire* of his criticizing the Instruction of 1769 for light infantry attracted considerable attention and led to his being charged with drawing up some infantry ordinances. In 1773, just as Guibert's *Essai général* was beginning to attract attention, Pirch submitted to the Prince de Monteynard, minister of war, an elaboration of the ideas of his earlier effort, called *Mémoire raisonné sur les parties les plus essentielles de la tactique*. It commanded an enthusiastic reception, and one would gather from the comments that the French Army learned for the first time that one "point of view" was not enough to ensure proper alinement and direction and that three-quarters of a century's debate had not indicated the simplest rules for maintaining direction.[5]

Pirch emphasized the great importance of selecting and maintaining points of view, which is to say landmarks, and made them the basis of his tactics. He defined them as follows:

Points of view are exterior and distinctive objects chosen and determined by the general-in-chief to furnish the direction for the various movements that he wishes to have his army execute and to ensure the accuracy, the facility and the precision of them. This definition makes known the importance of the practice of points of view, since it is on them that are founded the accuracy, the facility, and the maneuvers of an army. In fact, it is by them alone that a general can give to his army the exact position which he wishes it to take. It is by means of these points of view that he obtains a military alinement, that he simplifies and accelerates the formation in order of battle, an important advantage which often contributes to the favorable outcome of a day and which determines it almost infallibly when those who avail themselves of them have to do with a less maneuverable enemy who ignores or does not use these essential and elementary principles.[6]

Pirch went into great detail on the selection and maintenance of points of view, and he repeatedly stressed the great need of precision in this matter which, in turn, provided the necessary precision in maneuvers. "Reason proclaims and experience has confirmed," he wrote, "that a maneuver cannot be precise if one has not begun by establishing the exterior marks in an invariable manner." [7] From this followed the excessive formalism of Pirch's tactics, for that formalism, which reigned in the Prussian Army, was necessary to the achievement of the precision which Pirch desired. The vogue which he attained resulted from the belief of French officers that here lay the secret of Prussian success.

Pirch elaborated a whole system of tactics and applied points of view to it. In fact, he made points of view dominate all tactics. "He made a specialty of them; which at least was very clever for putting himself in fashion." [8] His system was not a doctrinaire one such as those of the supporters of the *ordre profond*. It was essentially the one in use with the restrictions necessitated by his points of view. These restrictions tended to cut down the flexibility of the troops which Guibert's columns were just beginning to provide. His *mémoire* abounded with details in all aspects of tactics, especially in those designed to procure accuracy and precision of alinement. This applied particularly to the interior alinement of battalions, for even Pirch recognized that a whole line of battle could not maintain a perfect alinement.

It is, however, physically impossible that several battalions together, or an army corps marching in battle, be absolutely alined in a straight line. It is necessary then to devote oneself to observing a *military alinement,* and in such a case, a general would be wrong to neglect important dispositions in order to obtain a purely imaginary precision which often produces a contrary effect.[9]

Pirch laid special emphasis upon taking the greatest precautions to direct each platoon exactly upon its point of view when a column executed its final change of direction for forming the line of battle. This would give them the proper direction.

The method of deployment used by Pirch to achieve this line of battle was called by him "deployment on the center at the level of the head." If the column were composed of twelve platoons, the first six would deploy by square movements (à tiroir), the sixth platoon moving straight ahead until it occupied the ground originally occupied by the first, while the first five moved by their right flanks until opposite their place in line and then moved forward onto the line of deployment. The last six platoons moved obliquely by their left flanks, and when they were opposite their place in line, they made a half quarter-wheel to the left which placed them in position. Pirch declared this to be the most rapid form of deployment. It differed from Guibert's central deployment, first, in that it was made by platoons instead of divisions, and second, in the fact that the leading elements used square movements instead of oblique movements to the rear. The square movements did not require the head of the column to cross the line of deployment. The advantage of speed would appear to favor Guibert because of the lesser depth of a column of divisions.

The ideas of Pirch on tactics were promptly adopted by the French Army. On June 11, 1774, an Instruction for Infantry was issued which was essentially Pirch's *Mémoire*, reproducing it almost textually. The preamble declared that the king wished "to establish the greatest uniformity in the evolutions, commands, means of detail, and schools of instruction" and also "that the particular drill of each regiment be directed on the principles applicable to all the circumstances in which a considerable body of infantry can find itself in war." [10] These were the essential points of Pirch's ideas. Pirch had not treated all the possible evolutions in his *Mémoire*, however, and a principal weakness of the Instruction of 1774 was the gaps in its coverage.[11]

A new Instruction for Infantry was issued May 30, 1775. It made only slight changes in the preceding one. It was chiefly notable for prescribing fire drill for troops. They were to fire at targets at ranges from a hundred to two hundred twenty yards and to perform the various commands of firing. This was the very modest beginning of fire instruction. Since only a very small amount of ammunition was allotted for this purpose, the value of such training was slight.[12]

Opinion was nearly unanimous in support of Pirch's principles, and it was felt that he had propounded the solution to a problem which had been long and unsuccessfully studied. His principles were felt to have made possible the speed and perfection in deployment and marching in line which the Prussians possessed.

The generals were nearly all enthusiastic for Pirch's principles. The Prince de Montbarey was charged with experimenting with the Instruction of 1774. Montbarey declared that the unanimous opinion of the inspectors for the new system was based "upon the importance of the subjects which they [Pirch and La Chapelle] discussed, upon the simplicity of the means that they proposed, on the solidity of the bases upon which they erected their structure much more than on the servile imitation of a foreign power."[13] The inspectors' approbation was motivated "by the clarity of the principles of points of view adapted to our tactics."[14] The more he had examined them, declared Montbarey, the more he was convinced of his first favorable reaction. "The principle of points of view is of so great a utility, in my opinion, that I believe that one cannot too strongly demand their employment, and that it ought to be a principle that no troop should move without its commander indicating to it its points of view before and behind."[15]

The enthusiasm was not quite unanimous. Among the chorus of approval a few examples of adverse criticism survive. An anonymous officer of the Régiment de Chartres claimed that there was nothing in Pirch's principles which the best regiments had not practiced for a long time. With more justification, the same officer declared that Guibert's maneuvers were superior.[16]

Lieutenant-General de Nicolaî tried out the new maneuvers and declared them to be too formal. He wanted simpler and more rapid maneuvers at least for regiments.[17] Brigadier Comte de Clarac declared that one could easily take points of view without being preoccupied with keeping them all through maneuvers.

No army of any size, the latter declared, would maneuver as a single body, but rather each major part (division) would maneuver on its own.[18]

With a few discordant voices such as these, the French Army adopted the principles of points of view, and Pirch took over Guibert's position of tactical guide. To a considerable degree the search for flexibility and speed gave way to the attempt to achieve precision and accuracy. This is the aberration from the main line of French tactical development which resulted from Prussian influence. Its prophet, as is clearly evident above, was Pirch and not Guibert. This aberration was confirmed by the issuing of the Ordinance of 1776.

Just as in the case of Choiseul's reforms, when the preliminary instructions and criticisms had been followed by an ordinance settling the forms of drill and maneuver, so the instructions of 1774 and 1775 were followed by the Ordinance of June 1, 1776. The Ordinance of 1776 was in effect the last drill regulation of the Old Regime, for the Instruction of 1788 was never put into effect. There were a number of differences from the Instruction of 1775 which took the form of considerable non-Prussian elements. In so far as evolutions were concerned, however, it was strictly in conformity with Pirch's principles. This disposes of the claim of various nineteenth-century writers that it was the work of Guibert. No contemporary document confirms such an assumption, and since the ordinance departs extensively from the ideas of the *Essai général*, it is hardly possible to accept the idea of Guibert collaborating in a work which conformed to Pirch's principles.[19]

In the Ordinance of 1776, the principle of points of view was no longer isolated. The ordinance also differed from its predecessors in the order of its chapters.[20] The first seven titles dealt with the details of individual instruction and the drill of small units. Title VIII was concerned with the question of forming column from line. It prescribed that the formation should always be done by breaking the line into a column of full intervals either to right or left. If a closed column was desired, this would then be formed by closing up to the desired interval. This maneuver should be done by platoons preferably, but it could be done by divisions sometimes, and by sections if necessary.[21]   Once formed, the column could be moved in any desired direction by changes of direction.   The various possibilities were covered by the ordinance.[22]   The ordinance differed with Guibert in prohibiting inversions and in not permitting the ployment of lines into column.

The various ways of forming lines of battle from columns were dealt with in Title X.   It was in the second article of this title that the long digression on points of view, or points of direction as the ordinance called them, occurred.

The points of direction should be distant and distinct objects, chosen by the commander-in-chief in order to determine the direction which he wishes to give to his line, in such a manner that in all movements the new position ought not to be determined by chance, but by the will of the commander-in-chief, who, choosing about the ground which the eye can encompass, two points, one on his right, the other on his left, will thus give to the line or to the column, the direction most conformable to his plans.

These objects should be as isolated as possible, and prominent enough to be distinctly perceived, such as a tree, a steeple, a house, a mill, or in default of them, some mounted officers [should be] placed on the points of direction and in the intermediate points, because of the number of troops and of obstacles which could hinder their being perceived.[23]

This is followed by details on the use of points of view in changes of direction and by articles dealing with the reforming of columns in line.   Here there were four possibilities.   A column could be led by either its right or left wing and could arrive either before or behind its line of battle.   Each of these four possibilities is dealt with.   In the first of the four, the column turned to the right along the line of battle, and when it had completed the turn, it formed line by a simultaneous left quarter-wheel. In the second case, where the column arrived in front of its line of battle, it would turn to the left and form by a simultaneous left quarter-wheel.   The third and fourth cases would be the inverse of the first and second respectively.[24]

In cases where a column did not arrive at the extreme left of its position, the ordinance also applied a special maneuver of Pirch's called the *wourff-manoeuvre*. In such a situation, some platoons or battalions would still be in column when the head had reached the right extremity of the line. The platoons remaining in column would each file to the left diagonally by a flank march and wheel into position on reaching the line. If there were whole battalions still in column, they would go out from the column, march to the left of their respective positions, and turn to the right along them just as the head of the column had done.[25]

The ordinance prohibited direct ployment into closed columns but not the direct deployment of such columns. The method used was that of Pirch. It also dealt with the deployment of a column which was too deep for the ground of its deployment. The method in this case was to form first a line of battalion columns and then to deploy each column separately.[26] In all the methods of forming lines from columns, the method of employing points of direction for each problem was discussed.

Title XI dealt with marches in battle and with the passage of obstacles and defiles. No new principles were advanced. There was a new principle, however, in Title XII dealing with the passage of two lines. If, for any reason, the first line had to withdraw behind the second, the first made flank marches through gaps formed in the second by ploying the battalions of the second line in columns of divisions. The platoons of each battalion would march by the flank and by the shortest route behind the two central platoons, which held position, thus forming a column of divisions. If it was necessary to have larger gaps in the second line, then columns of platoons could be formed by doubling the outer sections of each division behind the inner ones.[27]

Title XIII dealt with changes of front and had numerous and very complicated rules concerning the various possibilities which occurred in these circumstances.[28]

Title XIV dealt with fire. Fire by platoons and divisions was suppressed as well as the *feu de chaussée*. The first type of fire described was fire by files. Here the fire began with the first

file on the right of each platoon and progressed by files to the left.
Thereafter each file promptly reloaded and fired without the men
regulating themselves upon the others either in their own or
neighboring files. In other words, it became fire at will. Speed
and accuracy were declared to be essential.[29]

The other type of fire permitted was volley fire by half-battalions and battalions, ahead and to the rear, advancing and retreating. The line about-faced to fire to the rear. The advancing fire was performed when advancing upon a discomfited
enemy, if it were judged desirable. The fire while retreating was
for use when retiring in good order and too closely pursued by an
enemy. It was, of course, preceded by an about-face.[30]

Criticisms of the Ordinance of 1776 are neither as authorita-
tive nor as numerous as for those preceding it. One anonymous
mémoire does express general approval. The author declared
that the three consecutive ordinances had extended the knowledge of moving armies very much, but he feared that generals
would have difficulty assimilating the delicate new maneuvers.
He called strongly for improvement in the discipline and training of troops, which was the great defect of the French Army.
He felt that the ordinance had suppressed some useful movements while retaining others which were not. The regularity of
movements of conversion he condemned as needlessly complicated, and the use of columns against cavalry he held impracticable for war. He strongly advocated the reintroduction of the
charge in column which would enable generals to use either the
ordre profond or the *ordre mince* and thereby terminate the long
dispute. Finally, he approved the introduction of the fire at will
(by files) and desired to have the men trained in it.[31]

It would seem, then, that the Ordinance of 1776 was open to
two general criticisms. First was the excessive formalism resulting from the strict adherence to Pirch's principles and leading to
over-complicated maneuvers. This was true of Pirch's system of
deployment as compared with Guibert's. No good reason existed
for compelling the platoons ahead of the platoon of deployment
to use the slower square movements. The reason given, that the

column need not cross the line of deployment, could usually be met by placing the line of deployment some paces to the rear. The column could then deploy with its head no nearer to the enemy.

The second general criticism was the excessive reliance upon the *ordre mince*. Pirch's triumph meant the triumph of the partisans of that order and exacerbated the dispute between the advocates of the two orders. It was not until 1791 that a new ordinance representing the middle position of Guibert was adopted. It permitted both orders without going to the extremes of either. All in all, it must be said that the adoption of Pirch's tactics represented a deflection from the general line of French tactical development.

VIII

Mesnil-Durand's New System

The decade of the seventies marked the culmination of the controversy between the two orders. The contention was ostensibly still between the *ordre profond* and the *ordre mince,* but the partisans of the former were making large concessions to those of the latter with the professed desire of bringing about a compromise.

The signal for the outbreak occurred when Mesnil-Durand "reentered the lists" after an absence of twenty years. He published his new system in *Fragments de tactique, ou six mémoires* in 1774, to which three additional *mémoires* were later added. Colin declared that Mesnil-Durand had gained wisdom through age and experience, had recognized the impossibility of winning acceptance for his *plésion,* and so accommodated himself to the spirit of the day.[1] This may be so, but it was a limited amount of wisdom for he retained in a large degree the exclusive spirit of system. It is difficult to see how he improved upon the existing system, let alone the proposals of Guibert. His new system was full of useless complications which could be justified only by principles which he deduced and which others would not concede. He had been forced by twenty years' experience to make concessions to the facts of fire combat, but they were reluctant concessions which did not go very far in the case of artillery.

Mesnil-Durand declared that he was going to accept battalions as they were, that it was his purpose to give them as many of the advantages of columns as possible, and that he proposed to perfect the actual system by freeing it, in so far as he was able, from the reasons which caused him to reject it. He declared that he would so identify the two methods that the supporters of the *ordre mince* would feel that he had changed nothing with as much reason as he would feel that they had adopted his system.

Mesnil-Durand commented upon Guibert and his work. He called him a man of "distinguished talents," and he agreed with

Maizeroy that one could say "neither enough good, nor enough evil" about the *Essai général.* He paid honor to Guibert as a person, as a capable soldier, and as an able writer and thinker who had, however, taken up a bad cause. He would like to convert him. He declared that he knew that he would be accused of writing out of jealousy of a rival writer who had made a great success. His only motive, however, was to reply to a criticism of his principles, since he believed them to be correct and most desirable for adoption. "I think that with some excellent principles, some noble ideas, he has mingled some trifles and some errors. I think finally that against those who are not of his opinion, he has more affirmed than proved, and that he has understood and judged the ancients, the great generals of past ages, and the *makers of systems,* a little too lightly." [2] He felt that the part of Guibert's work which dealt with tactics was very inferior to his abilities, but that in the other parts of military service, "one finds them in all their brilliance." He commended him very highly for his fiery love of country; he was "charmed" with that frankness which he found in Guibert even though he had suffered more from it than anyone else. He took up his counterreply without ill humor.[8] To this counterreply he devoted his Sixth *Mémoire,* which comprises half of the original part of the work.

Mesnil-Durand's first concern was with the problem of fire preparation. His solution to the problem was the use of skirmishers. He condemned Choiseul's abolition of Broglie's chasseur companies. He agreed with Saxe that troops which charged must not fire. To the objection that one could not reach the enemy without the assistance of fire, he asserted that the answer was simple. It was to have another line which fired but did not charge. The fire of these skirmishers, while much less in volume, would be more accurate and they would offer a difficult target. Under cover of the screen which they provided, the battalions would arrive on an enemy shaken by fire.

In Mesnil-Durand's first system, which had appeared before *Mes rêveries* was published, the screen for the main troops was very inadequately described. His full account of the use of such a screen of skirmishers in his second work demonstrated first that

Mesnil-Durand, in spite of his words to the contrary, had some misgivings now about reaching the enemy without any fire support at all. It demonstrated further that he found his inspiration in Saxe, who had supplied an answer to the problem, the answer which he adopted.

In his Second *Mémoire,* Mesnil-Durand set forth the exposition of his new tactics. He could not escape from the "spirit of system." The question of maintaining the *ordre profond* against the *ordre mince* was displaced by that of sustaining the central column against the standard company or divisional columns then in use. Since this column was the normal formation and the essential part of the system, its employment led to "a series of awkward dispositions which would be bound to be rendered inapplicable in the field every time that losses and detachments occurred to break the harmony of the system." [4]

Mesnil-Durand insisted that ployments and deployments must always be by the center and that the various units of troops must be arranged with that in view. This led to "somewhat childish" complications. Mesnil-Durand used the standard battalion of that day—consisting of eight companies of fusiliers, one of grenadiers, and one of chasseurs. Within a battalion all even companies were to the left of center and all odd companies to the right. The first section (half-company) of the even companies would be on the right while the first section of the odd companies would be on the left. This was to enable them to be nearest the center.[5] See Figure 22A.

In a regiment composed of two battalions, the first battalion would always be on the right. (There is an error here apparently except when the regiment is alone or in the center of the line. To follow Mesnil-Durand's system through, the same conditions would have to apply as for a regiment of four battalions, namely, that the order of the battalion in the regiment would depend upon the regiments' place in line.) The grenadier companies would be placed on the right flank of the first battalion and the left flank of the second. The chasseur companies would be placed on the flanks opposite to those of the grenadiers. In a regiment composed of four battalions, being alone or at the center of a division having an odd number of brigades, the battalions would be placed numerically like the companies, that is, from the center, odd battalions on the right, even battalions on the left. If such a regiment was in line and not in the center, the battalions would be placed by the left if it was on the right side of the line, but by the right if it was on the left side. In such a regiment, the élite companies would be placed as if it were two

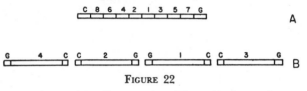

FIGURE 22

regiments of two battalions each. Thus, if the regiment was alone or at the center of a division, the chasseur companies of the first and third battalions would be between them, and the same for those of the second and fourth battalions. The grenadier companies would be on the opposite flanks of their respective battalions. Figure 22B represents a regiment drawn up in this way. In all other cases, Mesnil-Durand said that "it is not the odd and the even, but the first and the last, which in this manner make the two pairs." This would seem to mean that, for the other situations, when the regiment was part of the right or left wing of the division, the numbers of the battalion would be ignored so as to place the élite companies in the same manner as in the situation illustrated.[6]

The companies were also platoons which meant in French practice that they were both tactical and administrative units. The battalion broke into open column of march and reformed in line just as any other battalion by simultaneous quarter-wheels. It was in ploying and deploying that complications resumed for this was always done by the center. In all cases of ployment, each battalion ployed on its own account by the center. A battalion fully deployed was on a depth of three ranks as in the formation shown in Figure 22A. The position of the élite companies would, of course, depend upon the battalion's position in the line, but this would make no difference in method of deployment. To ploy it first doubled by companies to a depth of six, as in Figure 23A. It then proceeded to ploy as indicated by Figures 23B, C, and D. The élite companies, as the figures indicate, had their own movements accomplished apparently by oblique marches. In the column they formed the first section, chasseurs ahead of grenadiers. They were destined to form the screen.

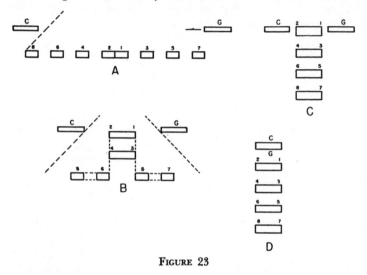

FIGURE 23

Their movements were designed to cover the ployment, as they always masked the extremities of the battalion until ployment was complete.

The battalions of a regiment would march likewise by the center in numerical order. The brigades of a division also marched by the center, each brigade following without mixing itself with the others so that the whole division marched as if it were only a regiment. Thus, if the division contained an odd number of brigades, the center brigade would lead off, followed by the first right brigade which marched to the left, then by the first left brigade which marched to the right, then by the second right brigade and so on. If the number of brigades was even, the right center brigade would lead off, followed by the left center, the second right, and so on. To put a line of battalions in col-

umn for marching each battalion in column marched by right or
left to the center of the line.[7]

Whatever front a battalion column had, it must form on a
front of company extent to deploy.   In other words, it had to be
formed of two companies on a depth of six joined together in order to deploy, the same formation which resulted directly from
ployment.   To deploy, the column closed its intervals to two

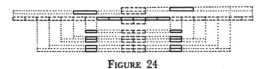

FIGURE 24

paces.   On arriving on the ground of deployment, the battalion
stopped with the leading three ranks of the first fusilier section of
the column on the ground they would occupy at the completion
of deployment.   The odd companies of the remainder of the column faced to the right, the even companies to the left.   The two
vertical halves of the column, save the first half-companies (three
ranks) of the first section, moved off to right and left respectively.
As each half-company arrived opposite the ground which it was to
occupy, it halted, faced to the front, and moved up into line.
The chasseurs and grenadiers moved separately to their respective
positions masking each half-company as it completed its deployment.   This was, therefore, a deployment *à tiroir*.   See Figure 24.
If a battalion arrived on the right of the ground it was to occupy
on deploying, it had to march to the center before doing so.   It
might divest itself of its grenadier company and its odd fusilier
companies in measure as they arrived opposite their ground.   If
it arrived on the left of its position, it did the same with the chasseur and even fusilier companies.   A regiment or large force must
be in a column of double front called *jumelle* in order to deploy.
In such a column, the odd battalions were on the right and even
ones on the left and they moved diagonally into position opposite
their ground and deployed as above.   A *jumelle* column was
formed by a regiment of four battalions as follows.   The odd battalions (it being in a simple column of four battalions) moved
fifteen paces to the right and the even battalions the same to the

left.   The latter then moved forward and alined themselves with the odd battalions which closed up to normal interval.   They thus formed two parallel columns with a small "street" of five or six paces between them.   To deploy, each battalion moved out, odd ones to the right, even ones to the left, and when opposite their ground, deployed as above.   A division of twelve battalions

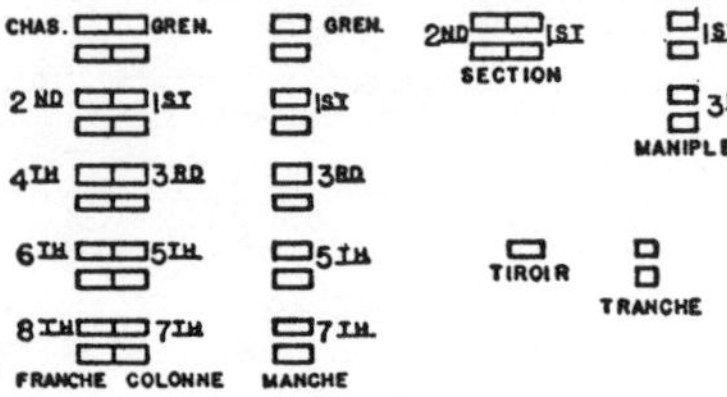

FIGURE 25

would do the same.   If the division deployed on two lines, the fourth battalions in each part of the column would go only as far as the first ones and deploy behind them.[8]

Such was Mesnil-Durand's new system of elementary tactics. It bristled with difficulties, not the least of which was its terminology which would have required a nearly complete revision of existing tactical terms.   Figure 25 [9] illustrates the rest of the terms. If the front of a *franche colonne* was reduced to that of a single company, then it became a *mi-colonne*; if to a half-company, it became a *quart-colonne*.   Two *franche colonnes* joined together gave a *jumelle colonne* with the two parts forming right and left *jumelles*.

Mesnil-Durand proposed this method of deployment because it was shorter, and hence quicker.   He made a great point of its being better covered than any other, because the central half-companies were in position to fire from the start of deployment while others came rapidly into action as they successively came into line.   The accepted method by half quarter-conversions (Figure 18) was not ready for action until deployment was completed.   It was necessary, he insisted, for a battalion to ploy by the center if it wished to deploy by it.   He declared that the head was the post of honor not the flanks.   He insisted that there must be only one method of deployment, and that all others must be surpressed.[10]   The column of attack must be of one battalion only unless the battalions were very weak, and it was to keep its intervals until just before the shock, when it closed up.[11]   One must use the column for charging and the line for firing, he declared.

The objections to Mesnil-Durand's new system are many and serious.   It is true that the central deployment, taken by itself, was shorter, and consequently quicker.   But the phrase, "taken by itself," is a very important qualification.   If one arrived on the center of one's position, central deployment was quicker.   If one arrived at the right or left extremities of the position, then it became necessary to move in a processional march along the front before deploying.   This march might well consume all, and more than all, the time saved by such a deployment.   This meant that one must know, if he arrived by the left, the exact left extremity of the position for the column divested its companies or battalions, as the case required, as it moved along the position.   This was so serious a difficulty that Mesnil-Durand devoted a whole chapter to proving that it was not as serious as it appeared.[12]

It was not necessary, as Mesnil-Durand insisted, that a column wishing to deploy by the center must ploy by it also, as Guibert had already shown.   This was the point that led to all that complex arrangement of units which created such serious difficulty in arranging troops and which would be thrown completely out of balance by any alteration.   If the general needed to detach a brigade for some special mission while the column was in route, the whole "structure collapses." [13]   One has only to recall the simplicity and flexibility of Guibert's tactics, their ability to ploy or deploy on any unit of line or column whatsoever, and to compare it with the complexity and rigidity of Mesnil-Durand's, to wonder how there could ever be any question concerning preference.

Mesnil-Durand's new column of attack, that resulting directly from ployment, was his old *plésion* of 1755 with only slight differences.   These differences consisted primarily of better differentiated subdivisions for he had come to see the need of intervals within the column.   It was also somewhat shortened since it was based upon a line of a depth of three instead of four.   It had the same dimensions as the columns of attack of various ordinances from 1755 to 1766.   In other words, he had gradually modified his column to that which existed, but he destroyed all the good effects of his concessions by insisting upon his complex method of ployment and deployment. This added a new and unnecessary set of complications and resulted in continuing the controversy between the two orders after there was little or nothing left to contend about.

As for the system of central deployment being better covered, it would seem that if one followed the rule of not deploying so close to the enemy that he could interrupt the process before it was completed, this matter would not be so important. It certainly was not worth all the complications which the system involved.

Mesnil-Durand tried to establish a basis justifying his system of tactics by stating a series of twenty-eight tactical principles. Some of these principles were excellent, but many were "strongly tainted" with the spirit of system. The striking fact concerning them is that those which were sound were those which were generally held by able soldiers while those which were peculiar to Mesnil-Durand were just those most "strongly tainted." In some cases, moreover, principles which were sound in the abstract were carried by him to such extremes as to destroy their validity. Thus he said that there should never be more than one maneuver for a single objective, and one should form and deploy columns in *exactly* the same manner. The first part of this principle was sound, but the latter part required identical methods no matter what variations in situation existed. This led to the complicated system of tactics already described. He accused Guibert of violating this principle by having six methods of ploying and six of deploying, counting each variation as a separate method.

While Mesnil-Durand's tactical system exhibited great complications, his ideas on order of march were surprisingly excellent. He felt that the principle that the order of march should correspond to the order of battle needed modification because it was not always possible to foresee the latter. He felt that there should be a fundamental order of march just as there should be a fundamental order of battle. The former should lead directly to the latter, and when one proposed to take up a different order of battle, the order of march should be designed for it. The fundamental order of march should lead not only to the basic order of battle but to any desired modification thereof. It should be possible to form any desired order of battle almost as easily from the fundamental order of march as from an order specifically designed for a particular battle formation. In other words, if the order of battle could be foreseen, Mesnil-Durand would dispose his troops for it before the march began, but if this was not possible, he would take up his fundamental order of march which would enable him to assume any battle dispositions which the situation required. This is perfectly sound and would find no disagreement even from Guibert. Mesnil-Durand was much in advance of Maizeroy on this question.

He closed by saying that an army of sixty-four battalions marching in four columns could deploy in two lines of three ranks each in seven and one-half minutes "at a moderate double step." All deployments without exception must be made from a *jumelle* (double) column.[14]

Mesnil-Durand recognized four orders of battle: the parallel, the oblique, the perpendicular, and the separated. In a parallel order the forces were spread evenly along the whole front and were enaged along its whole extent. Mesnil-Durand disliked the parallel order because of the difficulty of marching in it. Furthermore, if the enemy did not imitate the equality of distribution, every part of such an order would be inferior to the forces which the enemy could concentrate upon any point. The flanks were very weak, and an attack there would readily lead to defeat. "One has to equal the enemy's front which means that one's own front will be dangerously weak if he is inferior in numbers." On the other hand, if a general was superior in numbers, he would frequently be compelled to shorten front and would thus be unable to employ all his troops! The question arises as to why one could not have a longer front than the enemy or concentrate su-

perior forces on some part of it. Lastly, Mesnil-Durand objected
to this order, because the combat along the whole front was difficult if not impossible for a general to control.

Two principles govern the use of the parallel order. It
should never be employed unless the flanks were well supported
in such a way as not to lose their support. This order ought
never to be lengthened in the accepted manner unless the whole
front was covered by an obstacle which prevented the enemy
from reaching it, otherwise the order should be shortened and
reinforced.[15]

The oblique order, said Mesnil-Durand, was that which reinforced one part of an army, with which alone one expected to attack, so as to give superiority in that part, while the other parts,
more or less withdrawn from contact (depending upon the degree
of obliquity), were refused. An attack could be made by either
wing or the center, but Mesnil-Durand preferred the latter since
the flanks were frequently unassailable. Battles won on the wings,
moreover, were not decisive enough, for it was a "little thing" to
turn the enemy, but when one ruptured his center and separated
his army, its destruction was the infallible result. The oblique
order formed by the center was, he claimed, the only true, essential, universal one; the only one which always gave the means of
attacking the enemy, regardless of whether or not one outflanked
him.

The principles for the oblique order were: (1) superiority of
number at the point of attack so overwhelming as to decide the
combat in the first charge; (2) concealment of maneuvers until
the last feasible moment and the speediest possible execution; (3)
reliance upon a vigorous charge, not fire action, for victory; (4)
concentration of all the strength of the attacking elements in one
line; (5) attack upon the center unless one could charge the flank
at the same time one attacked the front.

Mesnil-Durand continued that the attack should always be
parallel even when one extended one's line to outflank the
enemy. The flank attack should be made by cavalry, separate
from the oblique attack, although regulated upon it. While the
line should be oblique in its whole, it should *never* be so in its

component parts, but should *always* be composed of parallel echelons, successively withdrawn. Mesnil-Durand thus ruled out a
line which was actually oblique to the enemy. He would deploy
in a parallel order first and then advance the echelons successively. With deployment at three hundred thirty-six *toises* (seven
hundred seventeen yards), Mesnil-Durand said that the bayonet
contact would come in eight or nine minutes if the troops moved
at forty *toises* (eighty-five yards) per minute. If the deployment
was at two hundred *toises* and the troops moved at sixty *toises* per
minute, it would be only three or four minutes. Since the first
charge would overthrow the enemy, it would follow that a major
battle should be decided in fifteen or twenty minutes! The artillery should advance "briskly" and "thunder on all the enemy batteries." [16] He thus confined the artillery to counterbattery action. The purpose was to silence the enemy's batteries so they
could not harm his charging columns, though he professed not to
fear any damage which the hostile guns could do.

Mesnil-Durand condemned the Prussian oblique order because it presented only a line of battalions. It could not, he said,
provide any superiority of numbers over the attacked part of the
enemy's line nor any reason to claim victory. The only way to
gain superiority of numbers was to form a second, and perhaps a
third, line in order to give successive efforts. The delayed effect
of these lines would prevent gaining the victory at the first blow.
Unless the enemy could be taken in the flank, the Prussian oblique could not accomplish anything. This Prussian order did
not hide its objective from the enemy; it did *not* move so swiftly
that the enemy could not parry it; it did *not* assure brief battles.
Whenever the Prussians had met resistance, they had had a long
fight. He cited, as proof that the order could be parried, Daun's
doing so at Kollin and the French at Crefeld. Mesnil-Durand
agreed that Frederick had brought modern tactics to their highest
perfection, but not that he had brought tactics to their highest
perfection. [17]

The third order was one of which Mesnil-Durand was very
proud, and of which he claimed sole parentage, declaring that it
could not be found in ancient or modern history nor in Holy

Scripture. This order, which he called the perpendicular, was essentially the oblique order, as he defined it, carried to extremes, the refused troops arranged directly behind the attacking force instead of echeloned out to the flanks. This order was in the form of a rectangle with the short side presented to the enemy, a side which Mesnil-Durand persistently refused to call a flank although that term has always been used to refer to the shorter dimension of the order of battle. He admitted that the perpendicular order would be more outflanked than the oblique order, but declared that if the enemy presented themselves on the flank, it could immediately form, by a simple facing, a front stronger than the foe's. It would very rarely employ the whole army which could be formed in parallel and out of range. Formed at two hundred eighty-eight *toises* (six hundred fifteen yards) with the troops covering forty *toises* per minute, it would reach the enemy in seven minutes from the first step of deployment.[18]

What Mesnil-Durand was actually proposing was to form an order of battle in which he presented a flank to the enemy, however much he might deny it. It was his idea to use this like a spear and thrust it clear through the enemy's order of battle. Then apparently by making face to the sides, he would be in order of battle, perpendicular to the enemy's order and completely astride it with defeat the only possible outcome for the ruptured hostile army. This infallible victory rested upon two assumptions. The first was that the attacking portion of the army could march at a rate of eighty-five yards a minute for seven minutes under fire, and without any disorder whatever appearing in its massive formation. The second was that its relatively short "front" would pierce the enemy's line with its first rush, and not only his first but his second, and third if there was one. Still without confusion, it had then to be ready to make its facing and roll up the enemy, if he was stubborn enough to need further demonstration of his defeat. A large portion of Mesnil-Durand's troops, furthermore, would not be employed at all. This was really only an application of his and Folard's principle of the column on the scale of an order of battle, for his perpendicular order of battle was in reality only a giant *plésion*. The counter to it is obvious. By a series of attacks upon its sides, which Mesnil-Durand called flanks, one would compel it to face in that direction which would in turn compel it to halt. A concentration of artillery should inflict enormous damage upon it while it was thus halted. The fourth of his orders of battle, the separated, was merely one in which several attacks were made together in the perpendicular order.[19] The basis for it and the difficulties were the same.

Mesnil-Durand's orders of battle illustrate very well a point which is evident to the reader of his works throughout their entirety. They contain a mixture of sound ideas and vicious details which has the unfortunate characteristic that the sound ideas were already generally known before he wrote while the vicious details form his personal contributions. His own hand contributed only complications and unsound formations wherever it appeared. It was not necessary to revive Folard's columns in 1755 because officers generally accepted the column formation for attacks on posts, while Guibert had already expounded a method of maneuver in closed columns before the *Fragments* appeared and without the needless complexity that Mesnil-Durand imposed. Another vain pretension of the latter was that the advocates of the *ordre mince* were convinced of the excellence of his system and were trying to steal part of it without acknowledgment. The more Mesnil-Durand made his system conform to that in use, the more he seemed to think his opponents were conforming to his.

Another contradiction in Mesnil-Durand's system was his statement that if one should prefer closed columns to lines and open columns at all, it was because of the ease with which they could be moved and directed, yet those of Mesnil-Durand could be moved only with extreme difficulty. He imposed defects which denied to them the very qualities which he attributed to them.[20]

Mesnil-Durand devoted half of the original *Fragments de tactique* to an examination of the *Essai général* relative to the subjects which he had discussed. The examination was devoted in large part to a discussion of basic principles. Since he was convinced that depth was an indispensable necessity for charging and breaking the enemy's lines, he naturally denied, as he had throughout all his writings, that a battalion could charge with the bayonet while formed in three ranks. He further denied the necessity for any fire preparation for an attack with the bayonet. Since Guibert had just as strongly affirmed that a battalion could charge in that way and that fire preparation was necessary before advancing to the attack, there was little agreement between them. Where Guibert had declared that only one ordinance was needed since there was only one kind of infantry, Mesnil-Durand insisted that since infantry fought in two ways, it needed two ordinances. Mesnil-Durand sustained his arguments only by assertion and the deductive method without citing any concerte facts or examples to support his position.[21] He confined himself, actually, to re-assertion of old arguments.

Mesnil-Durand cited the passage from Guibert (see page 124) describing attacks in column. He claimed that what Guibert said about troops crowding together was proof that Guibert admitted his argument on pressure! He maintained that his principles would dissipate the inconveniences Guibert described. One had only to reduce the column to a *plésion* front and one battalion strength, refrain from exposing it to such a vigorous fire, and maintain the intervals between elements until the moment of shock. Mesnil-Durand did not explain how these highly desirable objectives were to be achieved. Finally one should never think of firing when charging, which would stop the firing in the air! [22]

Mesnil-Durand cited Guibert's statement concerning dispositions of method and of circumstance, the former of which Guibert declared could be found only in camps and tactician's dreams. Mesnil-Durand insisted that dispositions of method were quite proper to win battles because they must have the same properties as the latter and were essentially alike. Thus he asserted the prime importance of particular orders taken without regard to the peculiarities of a given situation. The properties of the order itself would therefore be what was important and not the adaptation of a type of order to a given set of circumstances.

This was another basic difference between the two men. Mesnil-Durand placed his faith in a particular order, a particular formation, and its "intrinsic force" which if always used would always win, apparently without regard to the variations of circumstance, the quality of the enemy, or any measures he might take. Guibert placed his faith in a method of action capable of great variation to fit the situation and the moves of the enemy, and in the capacity of the general to make intelligent use of the resources thus placed at his disposal.[23] It is not difficult to choose between the two.

Mesnil-Durand gave Guibert credit for having by his influence done much to eliminate the system of deployment by quarter-wheels and to substitute the "Prussian System" by flank marches. He agreed with Guibert that it was the only way to deploy, but he persisted in maintaining that Guibert had a dozen methods of ploying and deploying while he himself had only one for each.[24] This was, of course, nonsense. The method of deploying which Guibert advocated was the same in all cases. He merely refused to say that it must always be done on a particular element of the column. He wished it to be done on whichever one was most convenient in a given situation. When Mesnil-Durand took the opposite position, he was far from simplifying matters as he claimed, but rather complicated them by denying flexibility to his tactics. There would be many more cases when a column could not arrive on the exact center of its position than there would be when it could. The time gained in the more rapid deployment by the center was at least partially lost in the necessary movements preliminary to deployment.

The discussion of deployment led Mesnil-Durand naturally to orders of battle and grand tactics. Mesnil-Durand did not agree with Guibert that there were only two orders of battle for this would obviously deny his own two cherished inventions. He would not recognize Guibert's "oblique of circumstance," any attack by a portion of the troops while the others were refused, as an oblique at all and insisted that the attack must be geometrically oblique to be classified as such.

Mesnil-Durand condemned Guibert for not laying down a

definite distance from the enemy at which one should deploy and for not giving a definite degree of obliquity to his echelons of attack. Guibert declared that the former depended upon circumstances such as the quantity, quality, and accuracy of the hostile artillery, conditions of terrain, and so forth, while a number of conditions such as the maneuverability of the opposing troops governed the latter. Mesnil-Durand said that since artillery was not effective beyond four hundred twenty-five yards (which was an assumption contrary to the preponderance of evidence) one could deploy at that distance while the echelons should be between two hundred twenty and two hundred sixty yards apart.[25] Here again is the contrast of the inflexible with the flexible.

Mesnil-Durand discussed with disapproval Guibert's system of march-maneuvers at very considerable length. Mesnil-Durand felt that they revealed their objective much too soon by their preliminary maneuvers, that they were too complicated to execute, especially as the enemy would not always select a position with a three-quarter league plain before it. He seemed to feel that Guibert's maneuvers were quite impossible on broken ground, yet he was the great proponent of the facility of columns in movement. His own columns moved straight forward and the condition of the ground played no part in his movements. He did not believe that Guibert's method of deception would be successful. He approved of Guibert's concentration of artillery on the attacking part of his front, but he did not approve of its firing chiefly on the enemy's troops. He thought it better to silence the enemy's batteries. This difference of opinion stemmed, of course, from their difference of purpose. Guibert wished to gain fire superiority so that he could advance to the attack and used his artillery to facilitate and prepare the attack by unsettling and disordering the enemy's troops. Mesnil-Durand wished to rush at the enemy without any preliminaries confident that the speed of his attack would carry him across the intervening ground and that once the bayonets crossed success was a matter of but a few moments. He recognized that artillery was the chief threat to his formations during the advance, however much he attempted to minimize it.

Consequently, he wished to use his artillery in an attempt to disrupt that of the enemy and thus reduce the hazard to his attack. With only solid shot available, it would appear impossible to silence hostile batteries without at least a lengthy duel, certainly not in the few minutes that Mesnil-Durand allowed for his attacks.[26]

The "Prussian oblique" was further condemned by Mesnil-Durand as having no other object nor advantage than outflanking the enemy. It had no means nor way of reinforcing itself on the point attacked! Its entire success depended upon cavalry. Mesnil-Durand, of course, would make a direct frontal attack upon the enemy's position preferably upon the center of it. He took no thought that his wings might be crushed while he was attempting to rupture the center, which would leave him in a parlous state, because he was confident that the battle would be all over before the enemy could make a move to counteract his thrust.

Mesnil-Durand insisted that the flanks of Guibert's echelons were so exposed that the slightest attack or demonstration would force them to face front diagonally, thus effectively halting the "hammer." Despite all his denials, his own orders were not exempt from this fault.

Finally Mesnil-Durand condemned the great length of time which it took the "Prussian oblique" to achieve its objective, citing Guibert's statement that Frederick maneuvered for four or five hours at Leuthen and then crushed the Austrians in half an hour. Half an hour, he exclaimed, his own attack would succeed in four minutes! Since his advance took from three to nine minutes depending upon distance of deployment, the whole battle from beginning of deployment until assurance of victory would last at most thirteen minutes and possibly as little as seven minutes! Truly a highly desirable state of affairs!

He concluded by asking Guibert to compare principles without prejudice and see if his own were not better. He owed a great obligation to Guibert's work for it had shown him how right his own ideas were and confirmed him in them. He would willingly have acknowledged Guibert's being right if such had been the situation, but since the contrary was the case and Guibert was not right, he should acknowledge Mesnil-Durand as right.[27]

To the original six *mémoires*, Mesnil-Durand added another three before his book was published. Among other matters he undertook to show that artillery was not so deadly as to prevent the use of the *ordre profond*, and that while Gribeauval's artillery was, in some respects, an improvement over Vallière's, the improvement was not great enough to invalidate his principles.[28] He was answering, apparently, a work, *L'artillerie nouvelle*, whose author, Tronson du Coudray (1738-77), seems to have attacked some of Mesnil-Durand's ideas. At any rate, Mesnil-Durand entered the lists against Coudray and added a new controversy to that in which he was already involved with Guibert, a controversy which raged with much heat for some time.[29] Tronson du Coudray implied, or Mesnil-Durand thought he did, that the latter claimed artillery had no effect. Mesnil-Durand denied vigorously that he ever said any such thing. He claimed only that artillery would have so little time to play upon his columns that it could not stop their assured success. Thus all his arguments rested upon a postulate that no one was disposed to grant him, namely, that his columns could cross six hundred fifty yards in six minutes, and from that premise it was easy to prove that artillery and musketry would not have time to inflict enough losses to stop them.

Mesnil-Durand asserted that the claims for the effectiveness of artillery were much greater than was the actuality. Three or four rounds per minute were the most possible for cannon. Even this could not be counted upon in battle with a rapidly moving target and cannoneers distracted by danger. With these reasons, he justified his maximum effective range of two hundred *toises*.[30] A good cannoneer could hit a target in three shots, he declared, but his columns moved so fast that every shot was a first shot and the accuracy was consequently greatly reduced. Moreover, his skirmishers by their fire would unsettle the gunners and by killing many, slow the service of the guns markedly, while at the same time they screened the columns so that they would be imperfectly seen, and therefore poor targets. His columns would, consequently, suffer little from artillery.[81]

He continued by arguing that the new eight-pounders were not as maneuverable as the old fours, nor the new twelve-pounders as much so as the old eights. The two heavier calibers would not have time to maneuver against the French Order which would have only the fours to fear. This is most certainly specious reasoning because the older guns were so heavy as to be hardly moveable once emplaced, and the whole reform was designed to lighten them so that they would be maneuverable. It was not a question of relative maneuverability, but of whether the guns could be maneuvered at all. Mesnil-Durand went on to say that a four-pound shot could kill only three or four men in file, which would not be admitted by artillery men.[32] The advantage of the new artillery over the old was not as great as that of the French Order over the Prussian, and consequently, if the old artillery was not effective against the Prussian Order then the new was even less so against his.[33]

One of Mesnil-Durand's basic arguments on this question was that since a column had a very much smaller front than a deployed battalion, it would receive a much smaller proportion of shots, one for every eight on the latter according to him. For this argument to have validity, artillery would have to fire indiscriminately against the whole extent of the opposing line whether it was occupied by troops or not, that is, to fire on the intervals between the columns equally with the columns themselves. Now this may have been the practice when guns were distributed singly or in pairs along the whole extent of the line and there were no intervals in the opposing lines. It would certainly not be the case with artillery concentrated in batteries to defend those parts of the line which could be attacked, as artillery men proposed for the new guns. Mesnil-Durand's argument failed right there, while another argument, which was that, if the guns were concentrated in batteries, his columns would attack at points where there were no batteries, failed because of his ignoring conditions of terrain in all his orders of battle. A position has certain key parts, possession of which must be gained to dispossess the defenders. This means that these key parts must be attacked and this is just where the batteries would be concentrated. Moreover with the quantity of artillery even then employed, no part of the line would be completely denuded.

Mesnil-Durand, upon the basis of these arguments, rejected the idea that artillery alone could win battles, which he claimed was implied by those who said that it would defeat his columns. His system was not antagonistic to artillery; on the contrary, the latter could be used very well with it,

affording it the means of always being superior in the place where the combat is decided, leaving it more ground and freedom for its emplacements and movements—giving it more ease in availing itself of its teams—giving also more facility for maneuvers by man-handling, of which the duration and distance would be much shortened—finally putting it in a state to act in front of the line without really masking it, and always sustained in such a manner as to fear nothing. Apparently for the artillery itself, our French Tactics would be much better than Prussian Tactics.[34]

Thus Mesnil-Durand tried to disarm and win over his critics in the artillery corps.

The specious arguments with which Mesnil-Durand disposed of artillery were all assumptions which rested upon no facts or experience. He wished to ignore technical developments of which the new light field artillery, adopted by all major European armies by this time, was one. His system was based upon the premise that tactics was a matter of geometry only, and that weapons had no effect upon it, that what was once sound tactically remained so forever. This is really his basic assumption, one which is completely false, and consequently, his entire system built upon that assumption is also faulty.

Lastly, Mesnil-Durand presented an ordinance, or drill book, which gave the actual drill and maneuvers for his system. Some changes were made in it to conform his system to changes made in the French infantry at this time. The companies were reduced from eight to four while the platoons remained at eight. They thus became only half-companies instead of being identical with companies. The platoons became the basis of the sections of the column which meant that each section was composed of half of two different companies and each company was divided between two sections. This would prove very troublesome in diminishing the front of the column.

One of the most surprising things is that Mesnil-Durand followed part of the ideas of Pirch. He said:

Points of view and their use are a small problem of practical geometry, very happily applied by the Prussians to the direction of the marches of columns and lines. If they have not given the *ordre mince et allongé* by this excellent means an ease and swiftness [in maneuver] of which it is not susceptible, at least they have been able to give it very much more than one would have believed it capable of receiving. By whatever manner and in whatever order one maneuvers, one ought not then to neglect this means which, as soon as one pays a little attention, will have nothing difficult or embarrassing.

But it is necessary not to forget that, if the *ordre mince* cannot dispense with a perfect alinement, without which it uncovers its feeble flanks; if it is indispensible to it that each battalion observe its direction exactly without deviating too much to right or left, which opens dangerous gaps in some parts of the line, confounds the battalions in some others, and makes them rupture, it is not the same with a line of columns, which has no reason to embarrass itself, beyond a certain point, either with perfection of alinement, or with exact equality of intervals. That line of columns ought then to make use of points of view in its own way, that is to say, with much vivacity, very little scrupulousness, not making a major matter of attaining a minute perfection of which it has no need, and having always for the principal object not losing time which it knows how to employ better. In a word, points of view will be good for it, because they will serve it in alining itself and directing itself more easily and better; because perfection, more or less necessary, is always good when it costs nothing; but it would become very bad for it if, in running after that perfection, it makes it lose the speed which belongs to it, and which is supremely important to it.[35]

This passage is one of the most judicious things which Mesnil-Durand ever wrote. It contains all that is excellent in the *ordre profond* which survived all the systems and their complications,

showing the facility which columns had for movement on the battlefield under all conditions.   However this, like most or all the
sound parts of his writings, was not original with him for Guibert
and others had preceded him in pointing this out.[36]   Mesnil-
Durand himself missed the point that the advantage of columns
was for maneuver not for combat.

In summary, there is little need to comment on Mesnil-
Durand's system or arguments.   In spite of his own self-confi-
dence, he suffers badly in comparison with his chief rival, Guibert, while the arguments he used against Coudray are entirely
unconvincing and without any factual corroboration whatever.
He tried to gain the support of national prejudice for his system
by calling it the French Order, and labeling the opposed system,
the Prussian Order, as if the Prussians alone made use of the
ordre mince, and as if the advocates of the tactics employed by
French armies for a century and long before Prussia became a
prominent power were mere foreign imitators.   There was such a
group in France, composed of Pirch and his followers, but it was
most unjust to include within it all the supporters of the *ordre
mince.   Mesnil-Durand contributed nothing of value to French
tactics which was his own,* save by keeping alive the fire of controversy which caused the French Army to test thoroughly the extreme forms of the *ordre profond* and reject them.   This was
valuable in itself, but it probably delayed the final consolidation
of French tactical progress by many years.   Fortunately, the next
major war was delayed long enough for this to be accomplished.

IX

The Camp of Vaussieux

The new tactical system of Mesnil-Durand took on major importance when Marshal Broglie and several generals declared themselves to be its partisans. Since Broglie was France's first soldier, his support added much prestige to the system. Mesnil-Durand's proposals were, therefore, tested in trials undertaken by two regiments (four battalions) of the garrison of Metz in 1775. From various sources concerning the tests, it would seem that the results were inconclusive, that they showed that Mesnil-Durand's maneuvers could be executed, but did not indicate that they were preferable to those already in use.[1]

More extensive tests were made following the entry of France into the American Revolutionary War early in 1778. At Vaussieux in Normandy, between Bayeux and Courcelles-sur-Mer, an army was assembled where it could not only defend the province but also threaten an invasion of Great Britain if the French fleet proved successful. Altogether, forty-four battalions of infantry, six regiments of dragoons, and a large train of artillery were collected under the command of Marshal Broglie, while another partisan of the *ordre profond,* the Marquis de Lambert, was *maréchal-général des logis* (quartermaster-general). Mesnil-Durand was one of his assistants. The Comte de Guibert Père was major-general (chief of staff) while the younger Guibert and the Chevalier de Broglie were among his assistants. A number of the most famous generals of France were subordinate generals. De Vault, Chabot, Lückner, and Gribeauval were among the nine lieutenant-generals. Rochambeau, La Tour du Pin, Conflans, Durfort, and Wimpfen were among the eighteen *maréchaux de camp.* Chastellux was one of six brigadiers attached to headquarters.[2]

As the troops were established in the camp, they began to drill in accordance with the new system of Mesnil-Durand, preparatory to the trials.   First they drilled by battalions, then by regiments, brigades, and divisions.[3]   Three weeks were consumed in this manner; then finally on September 9, they were ready to exercise as a whole.

For the first maneuver on the 9th, Broglie did not desire to begin with war movements but with general evolutions of the columns. Thirty-two battalions were assembled in four divisions, each consisting of two brigades of four battalions each.   The first movement consisted of forming a line of battalion columns with intervals equal to half the front of a deployed battalion.   Next this line was to march straight forward until halted.   Then the line of battalions formed in a double column of brigades and marched forward.   Following this the battalions formed in double columns of divisions.[4]

Mesnil-Durand bitterly protested these movements in a commentary which he wrote on this first maneuver. In regard to the passage from double column of brigades to double column of divisions, he declared,

I would never have proposed that folly. The first thing to do in such a case was to put the army in its habitual order of march. But, according to the regulation for field service, and the organization established by the marshal himself, the division is the main part, or rather the whole, of which the column should be formed. . . . It was necessary then to form first double columns by division to present in all its simplicity this mainspring of our machine. . . . In order to pass from the first to the second, it required a wretched little movement, tucking up one *jumelle* of each brigade, and which if one makes the slightest mistake there, as is very easy, and as already happened, changes the order of some battalions.[5]

This protest shows more clearly than all the criticisms of the partisans of the *ordre mince* the weakness of Mesnil-Durand's system.[6] The difficulty can best be shown by a diagram in which the numbers represent the battalions from right to left in a deployed line.   In a double column of brigades, a division would have the arrangement below:

7	6	3	2
8	5	4	1

In a double column of divisions, the arrangement would be:

5	4
6	3
7	2
8	1

The complications involved in passing from the one to the other are obvious.

After having formed in a double column of divisions, the next movement was to form a single column of divisions and to march on in that formation. Then all the battalions of the first division changed front to the right and marched as if to attack an enemy who was supposed to have appeared on the right flank of that division. The other divisions made the same movement and followed the first, maintaining only half the interval which had previously separated them. Then, it being supposed that the enemy had taken position behind an obstacle which required fire action to dislodge him, the next movement was to halt the left battalions of each regiment in the line while the right battalions marched fifty paces forward and deployed for fire action.[7]

Mesnil-Durand was disheartened by this maneuver for he did not approve of undoubling the column before changing front to attack. His complaint was that only one line was presented to the enemy instead of two, and that one was half again as long as the two would be. This increased the number of hostile battalions to be engaged.[8] This would certainly seem to indicate that even Broglie would not accept Mesnil-Durand completely. It was evident from the day's maneuver that the latter's system could be used successfully only if the army did not maneuver, but always operated directly from the double columns of divisions.[9]

After having repulsed the supposed enemy, the troops resumed their formation in column and returned to camp in double column, repulsing a supposed enemy pursuit by making an about-face and deploying.[10]

Wimpfen observed concerning this first maneuver:

Nothing of all that which had been prescribed had been well and exactly executed. Moreover, the ground had been badly estimated;

joined to which there had been many errors in the commands, and that day presented no matter for instruction. It added, on the contrary, to the prejudice which one already had against these new maneuvers.[11]

September 10 was devoted to correcting the errors of the 9th by means of a repetition of the maneuvers of detail. The whole of the first day's maneuver was repeated on the 11th. Wimpfen declared that the repetition was much smoother and more accurate. However, he went on, "one was confirmed, nevertheless, in the opinion that one had in the defects and dangers of these maneuvers; but, whatever demonstrations of them that one could give to the marshal, he protested so vigorously, that it was not possible to convert him. He defended the maneuvers with all the obstinacy of which he is capable, without opposing any satisfactory reason to the objections which were made to him." [12]

The second maneuver took place on September 12. One brigade, that of Bassigny, which had retained the maneuvers of the ordinance maneuvered against that of Aunis, trained in the new ones. Rochambeau (brother-in-law of Marshal Broglie) commanded the former, and, according to Wimpfen, won all the applause. The latter declared:

A facility of execution, an ease, was seen which it was impossible to hope for from the order which M. Dumesnil-Durand wished to introduce, and one could not conceal from oneself that these maneuvers, that the troops regretted, were within the range of intelligence of each officer and even of each soldier, who easily perceived their end, and that they presented the double advantage of *l'ordre mince* and *l'ordre profond*. Finally, it was also seen by all that which happened in that trial that terrain was entirely subordinated to them, that they merited the greatest confidence and could procure the greatest success.

The marshal, far from yielding to the evidence of that demonstration, only becoming angry with it, had a lively discussion with M. de Rocheambeau who said to him with courage and firmness: "The love of my country, the interest which I take in the glory of the king's arms, and even in your own, will always move me to make the greatest efforts to extract you from the error in which some seek to involve you, and which is so much more appalling since you are destined by the will and the regard of the sovereign, the voice of the nation, and the commendation of the military to command our armies. My affection is known to you, and my opinion cannot be suspect to you."

At the same moment, M. de Conflans said loudly, "If these new ideas can make some proselytes, the old ones ought to make some martyrs." All the general officers present, seeing that all which occurred did not produce any effect upon the marshal, but, on the contrary, only increased his anger, drew away from him in order to avoid being questioned, so that he went away alone, followed only by his aides-de-camp; and from that day, he did not attempt a second trial.[13]

The third maneuver was carried out on September 14.[14] Because of the experiences of the first two maneuvers, apparently, a battalion of alinement was designated for every movement. Broglie had apparently recognized this to be necessary to avoid confusion in maneuvering. Wimpfen remarked, "Until this day, it had not been dreamed that, in order to move any line whatsoever without difficulty and with accuracy, a determined point of alinement was necessary. One was forced to return to that method, which the author of the so-called French Order could not recognize." [15]

The schedule of the maneuvers called for a march in line and a change of front of the whole line. Next the left battalions of each regiment were halted while those on the right advanced a hundred paces, whereupon the whole force advanced in checker formation. The chasseurs were then advanced a hundred paces in front of this formation and spread out to act as a skirmishing screen. Next the battalions resumed a single line, fixed bayonets, and executed a charge. In pursuing the enemy, it was supposed that the line came to an obstacle which required it to resort to fire action. The right battalions were advanced and deployed for fire. When they had exhausted their ammunition, they were withdrawn and replaced by the left battalions which took their turn in firing. Then the whole line was formed in column of retreat. The enemy was supposed to present itself on the right flank of the line. There followed various ruptures of the column of retreat and changes of front for the purpose of refusing the threatened wing. Finally the troops were reformed in double columns of brigades and returned to camp.[16]

Broglie professed himself well satisfied with this third maneuver, writing that it was impossible to wish for more accuracy in maneuver than that exhibited.[17]   Wimpfen hardly agreed with him.

The Comte d'Egmont, and under him the Baron de Lückner, lieutenant-generals, had been given the infantry brigades of Aquitaine and Aunis and six squadrons of dragoons to represent the enemy army, in order to impress the advantage of that new method of fighting better; but these generals, master of their dispositions, having always opposed genuinely military movements to the prescribed movements, had by this demonstrated their defect, that there did not exist in the principles of Dumesnil-Durand any means of taking advantage of ground because they are of a nature never to command it.   There resulted therefrom a necessary change in the general disposition and a contradiction of orders, nothing of which could be executed, which led to inconceivable confusion and disorder.   It is certain that in reality, the entire destruction of the army would have been the result. When the impossibility was seen of disentangling this chaos, which presented the most deplorable spectacle of an army truly in rout, the marshal found no other remedy but to order the troops back to camp.

It must be added, moreover, that the terrain had been badly estimated; that in various circumstances, it did not allow the operation of the desired number of troops; that there was one [circumstance], among others, in which one found oneself forced suddenly into a position with hedges, bushes, ditches, and similar obstacles at one's rear, which one had not been able to investigate nor to occupy because the organization of the columns of Dumesnil-Durand did not permit, without deranging their order, the detaching of small troops to investigate or occupy these obstacles, particularly since the grenadiers and chasseurs, which could have been used, were already elsewhere.   Baron de Lückner, who had observed that difficulty perfectly, profited thereby to throw his own men there and to support them with artillery.   These columns attacked in the rear in terrain where the bayonet became useless, and where fire alone was necessary, could oppose it only in making a change of front to the rear, which is a long and complicated movement, in order afterwards to form in deployed order; but even that maneuver became impossible because of the time that it required, and still more because the necessary space did not exist.   In all cases, disorder, confusion, and rout would then have been the result.

Suppose now that, in the Order of 1776, one found oneself in a position absolutely similar.   One would extricate himself from it immediately by an about face of all the columns and deploying them on the last platoons, which in the same instant could protect the movement by their fire, and be themselves sustained the instant afterwards by the platoons which formed promptly and successively beside them; for the reason that terrain is entirely subordinated to the former maneuvers.[18]

The fourth maneuver was executed on the 15th.[19] Wimpfen declared that Broglie was very discontented with the results of the previous day (contrary to the marshal's own report) and consequently assembled all the generals, giving careful instructions as to what he wished executed. He also prescribed to General de Chabot, who commanded the troops representing the enemy, exactly what movements he was to make.

The movements of the experimental force were very similar to those of the preceding day. Broglie profited from the difficulties of the 14th by occupying the hedges and brush patches with chasseurs who repulsed those of the enemy. The last movement found the enemy occupying a line of heights on the flank of the first line of the experimental force. The line changed direction, marched on the heights, and charged the enemy with the bayonet, driving him from the position. The charging troops were covered by the fire of their chasseurs. The enemy covered his retreat with cavalry which charged some of the columns to give time for the infantry to retire and was then also withdrawn.[20]

Again Wimpfen made extensive comments:

The marshal had given the command of the opposed corps to Lieutenant-General the Comte de Chabot and prescribed to him all that he should do in order to avoid the difficulty and confusion of the day before and in order not to be constrained by terrain. At the same time, the first disposition was changed and the line of infantry was ordered to close on the center at half interval. . . . The dragoons had been disposed on the wings of the army to protect the flanks. Each soldier was provided with six cartridges, and the company of chasseurs had ten.

Everything planned was regularly and exactly executed, because suitable terrain had been chosen and because, through the dispositions given the troops representing the enemy, the necessity of varying the first formation had been carefully avoided. A perfectly executed change of front to the right by the whole army was made this day, and a march was made in that order, changing direction with the objective of dislodging the enemy from a height supported by two villages which protected its flanks. The advantage and the effect of columns was believed proved thereby, but the result was precisely the contrary.

The most ignorant of the spectators, the women even, felt that, if it had been possible to attack thus that height without first mastering the two villages with the precaution of holding the columns outside of cannon range until then, they would have been reduced to powder by a fire from front and flank to which they could have opposed nothing but that of their grenadiers and chasseurs.

But, even supposing that the enemy flanks had not been as well protected and supported, the time that would have been necessary for these columns, marching at the most rapid maneuver pace, to arrive at the range for charging with the bayonet, and calculating the ground that they had to cover only from the point where artillery could do execution, each gun would easily have been able to fire 50 shots, and there would have followed likewise a total destruction of these formidable columns, which probably would have sought their safety in flight. But a particular observation that was made was that, when some squadrons were sent to charge the columns, they [the columns] were not in a position to oppose them with fire and would have been cut to pieces, if by the agreed upon disposition, the dragoons had not had orders to withdraw after having tried several shots. Nevertheless the partisans of this new order wished to draw advantage from it [the cavalry demonstration] and to prove that no cavalry could attack these columns or resist them; but they persuaded no one, because even the demonstration proved the contrary.[21]

The fifth maneuver took place on September 17. This time freedom of maneuver was restored to the troops representing the enemy who were again commanded by Egmont and Lückner. The only difference from the preceding maneuvers was that the grenadiers and chasseurs of Broglie's army were formed into separate battalions in Mesnil-Durand's formation, two guarding each flank of the line.

Broglie expressed complete satisfaction with the result, declaring that the troops maneuvered with all the necessary accuracy.[22] Wimpfen, however, disagreed completely.

The enemy having first threatened to turn the army by its right, it was sought to render their efforts useless by a change of direction to the right; but, whether this was only a feint on their [the enemy's] part, or this movement forced them to change the project, it was suddenly discovered that they returned in force on the left. It was the more difficult to judge them correctly because it was never possible to see where the strength of their infantry lay because of the art and the ability with which General Lückner found means to hide it. To reach a general engagement would then have been impossible.

Then, at all events, the direction was changed to the left in order to extend on the left and, at six o'clock in the evening, one was in range of the village of Creully, which appeared occupied in force. The artillery was advanced in order to cannonade it and, under its protection, all the columns of the army [advanced] in order to attack it; but the enemy, with the same ability with which they had maneuvered all day, were already succeeding in withdrawing their troops and artillery and, having turned the army by its left, they made dispositions for forming their attack at that point, which could become so much more embarrassing because, in marching to the village, the columns were so confused that the battalions never would have been able to deploy without a very long preparatory movement, and for which, probably, they would not have been given the time.[23]

A sixth maneuver was held on September 21. It resulted in complete confusion. Wimpfen's comments on this maneuver were more caustic than usual.

Always the same cause has produced the same effects. The order according to the principles of M. Dumesnil-Durand, constantly providing obstacles which compel deviation from them or else the impossibility of acting, nothing could be executed in the proper order. Then, at any moment, other orders badly given, and even more badly delivered, by ignorant aides-de-camp, or staff officers also completely ignorant, produced difficulty, uncertainty, and confusion to such a degree that after having wandered in a great plain for three hours, sometimes in line, sometimes in oblique order, the marshal, wearied of war, sent the troops to their camp by the shortest route. There were some regiments, nevertheless, which returned there only at nine o'clock in the evening.[24]

The seventh and eighth maneuvers were held on September 24 and 28. They represented a return to the first maneuvers in which no enemy force countermaneuvered. Since they were executed in a plain, terrain did not affect them, and they were completed without the difficulties which had marked the preceding ones.[25]

Wimpfen completed his account of the maneuvers at Vaussieux

by making some general observations which condemned Broglie
very harshly.

In reflecting carefully upon all that which was done at the camp of
Bayeux, the details of which have just been read, the talents that
fame and public opinion ascribed to Marshal de Broglie are not apparent, and one will not find there the lesson which he appeared to
have had as an aim, since no military insight can be perceived. Far
from having accomplished the slightest good, he has produced a real
evil by the false ideas which he has given to young people who have
never made war and above all by the disparagement of the general
in the minds of the officer and of the soldier. The marshal added to
this exceedingly by his ill temper, to such an extent that everyone
withdrew from him. He has, moreover, proved incidentally, in
various circumstances, that he understood nothing of the mechanism
of the maneuvers; the least disorder troubled him, and he found with
difficulty the remedy. It is also certain that his obstinacy in uphold-
ing a new [system of] tactics, recognized as vicious, and condemned as
such by the entire army, might have contributed to it. He always
laid the blame on the general officers, the superior officers of the corps,
and on the troops, when the whole evil had its source in these new
maneuvers themselves. Whatever objections were made to him, he
persisted in his opinions. In his public or private conversations, and
in all discussions, he showed little understanding and little dignity,
which added greatly to his disparagement, and his enemies ought to
draw a great advantage from this camp.[26]

No less severe was Wimpfen's treatment of Mesnil-Durand:

At the end of this camp, there appeared a new work with which M.
Dumesnil-Durand has bored the military public, in order to defend
his principles condemned by the trials which were made there. He
attacked our Ordinance of 1776, but like a man who has never made
war, who on no occasion has been in the situation of bringing four
men to musket shot, all that which he says to weaken its advantages
serves only to put it in a better light. He would have certain arguments and combinations prevail over the evidence of the demonstration. He imputes the fault of its failure to the general officers, to the
superior officers of the corps, and even to the troops. This is a down-
right libel. His tone is arrogant and merits being reprimanded, but it
is necessary to have much time to waste in order to take the trouble.
Moreover, what claim has an upstart, an ignorant and obscure soldier
to arrogate to himself the right to establish his own system, condemned
by the whole nation, as the French order? It seems to me that this
imposing designation can be admitted only when sanctioned by law.

It is an insolence on his part to call the Ordinance of 1776 the Prussian Order. It is not Frederick who has issued that ordinance; it is Louis XVI. It is not a foreigner who has drawn it up, but distinguished officers of the nation to whom the sovereign has given the right and the power. It is the true French Order. This right, acquired by law, can only be denied by a law. These impudent undertakings, these insults to authority are today certain of impunity; they would have been severely repressed when the administration was in firmer hands.[27]

Marshal Broglie's own opinion on the results of the Camp of Vaussieux, as reflected in his report, differed strongly with Wimpfen's.

The trial made at Metz, by the order of Marshal du Muy, of the maneuvers of M. du Mesnil-Durand, persuaded me that they were preferable to those that have, each year, been given to the infantry. I was convinced of it during the continuance of the camp by the facility which they gave me of moving thirty-two battalions together, without preparatory instruction, without having reconnoitered the country, without knowing what the corps which represented the enemy intended to do, and commanded by general officers to whom that order of tactics was entirely unknown.[28]

Broglie went on to claim that the veteran generals such as Chabot, Lückner, and Saint-Victor agreed with him on the perfect analogy of maneuvers from company to army, on the security and independence of the troops in column formation, on the celerity of movement of these formations, and the simplicity which reduced all movements to simple facings. "I am then confirmed more and more in the belief that nothing could be more advantageous to the king's service than to adopt this order." [29] He declared that he had had to overcome strong prejudice in coming to his opinion. "I will not hide from the king that this system has found some opponents. I have reason to believe that several have not enough perceived its advantages, since most are engaged in taking up some true or pretended defects in the wording of the instruction and in the organization of the columns, defects that I have corrected or which did not exist, but which, when they were real, detracted nothing from the excellence of the system and required only a day to be rectified." [30] Such people, he felt, would be easily persuaded to the new order.

The Camp of Vaussieux was of capital importance in the development of French tactics, hence the detailed account of it just given. It crystallized the opinion of the great majority of French officers for a middle ground between the extreme positions of Pirch and Mesnil-Durand. This was true whether its supporters inclined to the *ordre profond* as did Castries and Puységur or to the *ordre mince* as did Guibert.

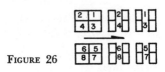

The great defects of Mesnil-Durand's system were plainly demonstrated by the maneuvers at Vaussieux and were recognized by most of the officers present. Wimpfen's account clearly shows that the theoretical objections actually appeared in practice. Every maneuver in which an enemy corps was used ended with the discomfiture of Broglie's force. Mesnil-Durand and his partisans refused, of course, to concede anything, but his very protests merely accentuated those defects. His insistence that the army should move only in double columns of divisions would make maneuver impossible, for the army would have to move directly to a line of columns and launch its attack straight ahead. There was no effective method for meeting a flank attack, save by a change of front of the whole line as Broglie demonstrated, for Mesnil-Durand's *tranchez manoeuvre* (see Figure 26) merely produced a mass as deep as before which could not deploy.

Even more disastrous would have been an attack upon the rear of one of Mesnil-Durand's double columns of divisions. Wimpfen gave a very exact account of what happened when Lückner's skirmishers did just that. Since Mesnil-Durand's column was composed of platoons on doubled files of six men, it could not aboutface and deploy as could the column of the ordinance. Moreover, a rearward deployment would be a "heresy" in Mesnil-Durand's system, for the wing platoons would be at the head of the column, thus violating the universal central deployment. It required a countermarch composed of two successive wheelings to place

Mesnil-Durand's column in a position to deploy to the rear. This was a very complicated maneuver, and Wimpfen was certainly right in saying that the column would be decimated and destroyed before having made front to the rear.[31]

The conclusion which most people drew from these demonstrations was that, while the system of central ployment could be used for a column of battalion strength, it could *not* be used for larger units. Even for battalions, the columns were clumsy in comparison with the ordinary route columns of the ordinance.

The mystery which all of this leaves is the persistence of Marshal Broglie in adhering to Mesnil-Durand's system. Almost all officers agreed that the serious defects of the system made it impossible to use with safety in actual operations. Yet Broglie not only continued his support; he recommended its adoption to the king.

How could such a veteran soldier fail to recognize the obvious defects of Mesnil-Durand's system? Colin answers this question by saying that Broglie seems not to have paid attention to these elementary matters, but was rather thinking in terms of the grand maneuvers of a whole army. He declared that from this point of view Mesnil-Durand's system presented some advantages over the evolutions in line of the ordinance, *if* it was always a question of marching in double columns of divisions and deploying in line to the front. He said that the marshal judged it much easier to handle an army in closed columns, which was the essential object of his Instruction of 1760, than in open columns or in deployed lines.[32]

While this explanation undoubtedly contains some elements of truth, it is not wholly convincing. First, it would have the marshal ignore all the serious defects in the order with which he himself had so much difficulty, despite the modifications which he had made in that system. These defects vitiated completely the advantage of operating in closed columns except under the very limited circumstances indicated above. Second, it would seem to indicate that the marshal considered the employment of closed columns an exclusive property of Mesnil-Durand's system, when for more than ten years Guibert's columns had been known in the French Army, and for more than half of that time had received wide publicity in the *Essai général*. Both Guibert and his father had been closely associated with Broglie who certainly knew that there were alternative forms of closed columns. If Broglie stubbornly continued to support Mesnil-Durand's system, he must have had other reasons. Could it be that wounded *amour-propre* had something to do with his attitude? Certainly Wimpfen's account, biased as it was, would suggest this possibility.

The middle ground upon which most officers were tending to unite was best expressed by two *mémoires,* each written by a partisan of the *ordre profond.* The first was from the pen of the Marquis de Castries who, in the same year of 1778, had commanded a camp at Paramé where maneuvers similar to those at Vaussieux were conducted, although with fewer troops. His report is dated September 30.

Castries declared that his observations were his response to an order for an opinion issued by Marshal Broglie. He preferred the columns of the Ordinance of 1776 to those of Mesnil-Durand because they could make front ahead, to the rear, or to either flank. The march columns could also form columns of attack or retreat. They had, with slight changes, all the properties needed for an order in depth according to Castries. Mesnil-Durand's columns, on the other hand, could only develop to the front. If they were compelled to form a line to the flank, they could only do so after a preliminary change of front, followed by a development of a line of battalion columns and finally by the deployment of the latter. Castries declared, therefore, that one could not hesitate in choosing the established formation over the proposed one.[33]

Castries summed up his observations in a series of twelve points. He declared that the essentials of good tactics were simplicity and easy adaptability to all terrain and that anything contrary to this should be rejected. The central formation (Mesnil-Durand's) had the greatest inconvenience because of the perpetual changes of battalions from right to left *manches* which were required with variations in the composition of the columns. The formations from right to left, or vice versa, of the ordinance had

the greatest simplicity.[34] "The exclusive central movements in
all that relates to marching or maneuvering is an awkward device
which hinders the objective which one wishes to obtain, and the
property of good tactics being the ability to accommodate to all
ground and to all circumstances, this [system] ought to be disap-
proved because it is contrary to [these principles]." [35] Further,
"the depth of this order added to the requirement of always employing square movements, lengthens the movements, requires a
terrain difficult to find, so as not to depart from the established
principle, and deprives one of the ability to overcome obstacles
by subordinating evolutions to terrain in place of mastering it." [36]
Castries continued that since the ordinance formation, being less
deep, required fewer movements in composing an order of battle,
then, if the system of columns was to be accepted, "it is preferable
to adopt the march column of the ordinance *which gives all the
conditions that can be desired in an order in depth.*" [37]

He declared that even if one adopted the tactical principles of
Mesnil-Durand, the means provided by the ordinance seemed preferable to Mesnil-Durand's for reaching the same ends.[38] He also
declared "that it would be desirable to find a middle ground between these two extremes, the column and the deployed order,
for camping, marching, and for forming ordinary orders of battle." [39] This is clearly an indication of the desire to find a compromise between the contending extremes. Here an advocate of
the *ordre profond* finds even the Ordinance of 1776 satisfactory
if it is amended to permit the use of columns for all purposes and
not merely for route marching.

The second *mémoire* was composed by the Comte de Puységur,
a distinguished soldier who was also a declared partisan of the
ordre profond. He expressed opinions almost identical with
those of Castries. "The best tactics are those of which the maneuvers adapt themselves with promptness and ease to all circumstances and to all ground. Those which have just been tested do
not appear to me to have these properties." [40] Like Castries,
Puységur pointed out the difficulties which the depth of Mesnil-
Durand's double column of divisions would entail, the difficulty
of finding ground extensive enough in depth to permit their use.
"I think, therefore, that that disposition by the center has some

advantages in an open country, that it has some great disadvantages in difficult country, and I do not believe it possible to employ it in mountain warfare." [41]   After numerous criticisms of details of Mesnil-Durand's proposed system, Puységur continued:

I venture to add that in adopting, whether for attacking, whether for marching in line, the most frequent use of columns, one would find in the actual ordinance, the means of forming them in all possible manners, even that by the center of the battalions, and not changing the principles of that ordinance, one would preserve infinitely more simplicity and security in the methods, more precision in maneuvers, more convenience for marches in difficult country, more ease for developing whatever the terrain may be, and one would avoid the great disadvantage of a complete change in the instruction of troops.[42]

The two *mémoires* which have been quoted are representative of others which agreed on rejecting the extreme form of the *ordre profond* which Mesnil-Durand had advanced and favored the expansion of the Ordinance of 1776 to include the use of a moderate form of that order based upon the march columns of the ordinance.   Guibert, a partisan of the *ordre mince* for combat, also expounded the same general point of view in his second major work, about to be published.   The only difference left between the moderates among the partisans of the two orders was whether the columns could actually be used to push home an attack covered only by skirmish fire.   No peacetime maneuvers could answer that question.

The experiences of the French in the American Revolutionary War probably had a corroborative effect upon the tactical doctrine which was winning acceptance in the last years of the Old Régime.   That they added anything new is doubtful.   The use of skirmishers and the advantage of individual fire in accuracy and effectiveness had long had their advocates in the French Army. These were the aspects which American experience would chiefly emphasize.   In this connection, it is interesting to note that the only remarks which the younger Rochambeau makes regarding the American Army concern the excellence of American drilling on the occasion of the honorary review for the French Army when the latter returned North from Virginia.

The Défense of Guibert

The return of Mesnil-Durand to the field of contest stimulated the controversy between the advocates of the two orders to new intensity, especially after he received the support of Marshal Broglie. This powerful support led, as we have seen, to an actual trial of Mesnil-Durand's tactics in the maneuvers held at Vaussieux in 1778. Both Mesnil-Durand and Guibert were present. These maneuvers led to the rejection of the system by general agreement, with the notable exception of Broglie.

As a consequence of these maneuvers, Guibert published his second major work, *Défense du systême de guerre moderne*,[1] in 1779. This is frankly a controversial work in which he attacked and refuted the tactical system of Mesnil-Durand. With some extensions, he reasserted his own tactical ideas which he had expounded in the *Essai général* and declared his purpose of vindicating the existing system of warfare as the highest perfection of the art yet attained.

Throughout his comments, Guibert continually criticized the needless complexities which Mesnil-Durand's system entailed. Recalling his own insistence upon simplicity, it is not surprising that he put his finger upon this weakness. His remarks had on occasion an acerbity of tone which quite matched that of Mesnil-Durand.

Guibert declared that the prevailing opinion after the trials was that while Mesnil-Durand's column had a deceptive appearance of perfection and simplicity, in reality it was "awkward, complicated, cumbersome, prone to disorder and indiscipline, subject to a thousand inconveniences in practice, and to sum up, in truth a product of the study."[2] It was the opinion, further, that Mesnil-Durand's exclusive central ployment and deployment subjected his columns to inconveniences in marching and assuming combat positions rapidly under many conditions which were usual, rather than exceptional, in warfare. Far from being simpler, his maneuvers were more complicated than those he wished to replace. Guibert claimed, moreover, that it was the general opinion that Mesnil-Durand's attempts to perfect his original system so as to accomplish the results of what he dubbed the Prussian Order, had only the result of making it difficult to decide whether the original or "improved" system was worse.[3] He summed up Mesnil-Durand's work generally by saying, "This is the manner that M. de M........ D........ employs almost everywhere. He always substitutes the complicated for the simple, and he calls that perfecting it." [4]

In regard to Mesnil-Durand's plan to march on the enemy on all occasions, Guibert remarked that while exceptional troops can sometimes take chances which would otherwise be foolhardy, a hard and fast rule would lead to many hopeless attacks. He insisted that a bayonet charge was a delicate operation decisive for the assailant as well as the defender. There was nothing left if it failed.[5]

It was possible to attack in line, Guibert insisted, and one should do so when to march on the enemy directly was not possible. One would occupy his attention by fire action while one turned his position or attacked him decisively at another point. Sometimes one would try to dislodge his opponent by fire action itself, or at least, attempt to shake and weaken him to such an extent that one could then take advantage of his disorder to close with him.

Guibert also advocated here the *ordre mixte,* a combination of deployed battalions with others in column, afterward the favorite order of Napoleon and usually prescribed by him when he intervened in tactical questions, as at the Tagliamento in 1797. Guibert suggested that the deployed battalions could attack the face of the line and gain fire superiority over it while the columns assaulted the salients. He also suggested using a first line of columns for assailing a post, supported by a second line of deployed battalions to consolidate the ground won and receive the counterattack. Thus one might avoid the weakness of columns, their proneness to disorder, which he had discussed previously. Some-

times the lines might be reversed. Once again Guibert's desire
for flexibility in formations and tactics is apparent. There was
no one and only system for him. The different formations had
varying properties, and he wished to employ those that best fitted
the circumstances of any given situation. Columns were proper,
according to him, when one must attack a narrow part of the hostile front such as a particular post, for sorties, or for completing
the defeat of an enemy in disorder after a repulse. Deployed battalions were proper for embracing a flank and in the various combinations of the *ordre mixte.* One attacked in line to take advantage of disorder resulting from fire action, for the delay of ploying might result in loss of the advantage gained.[6]

Guibert was rightfully indignant when Mesnil-Durand charged
that the supporters of the *ordre mince* adopted columns in order
to avoid being beaten in their own order, and implied that they
wished to adopt his system without giving him credit for it. Did
Mesnil-Durand think he had invented columns? he asked. Did
he think one had to acknowledge to him that columns were advantageous for attack? Did not the King of Prussia move 100,000
men without having read his books? Did not Broglie demonstrate the advantage of mixed orders at Bergen? He himself had,
moreover, shown that the columns of the Ordinance were very
different from those of Mesnil-Durand. He declared that if the
latter thought he had changed his views, he had only to read the
pertinent chapters of the *Essai général.* He had not changed anything which he said there in ten years time, which was more than
Mesnil-Durand could say of his earlier writings. "M. de M........
D........ has varied a little more in his." [7]

In contemporary warfare, Guibert maintained, cavalry and infantry were not rivals but mutually supporting parts of a team,
each with its own functions, but each needing the other. Infantry conducted sieges and fought in all kinds of country. It
could operate alone and was the principal arm. Without cavalry,
however, it was subject to being harassed continually, to loss of
supplies, and was not certain of success. It could do nothing
rapidly. Cavalry frequently decided or restored battles, executed

pursuits and raids, formed advanced guards. Without infantry, it could be halted by the smallest post; it could not be safe at night; it could do nothing decisive. Since cavalry had acquired speed and discipline, it was much more effective. One's great blows should be struck by cavalry. The mere fact that it was expensive did not justify abandoning or even reducing it.[8] Guibert agreed with Saxe and other writers that cavalry must be maintained during peace at near full strength. He disagreed in permitting perhaps a one-fifth reduction where most of the others insisted on none. The reasons were the same, the small value of raw cavalry.[9]

Mesnil-Durand's great mistake in regard to cavalry, Guibert declared, was to chain it to his infantry. This greatly limited its effectiveness for it confined to a defensive role an arm whose essence was offensive action. Any disposition which denied an arm its proper sphere of activity was obviously defective, while with cavalry withdrawn on the wings as Mesnil-Durand would have it, the support of the infantry was also denied it. The argument that cavalry so disposed was out of range of fire lost most of its force, said Guibert, for cavalry was not supposed to endure the enemy fire idly, but to attack him. The disposition was justified only if the cavalry had infantry in its front which it did not wish to attack and under whose fire it did not wish to remain.

It is apparent that Mesnil-Durand had faced the same problem in his use of cavalry that he did with infantry. His first position, which was to make warfare a matter of infantry action only, was impossible. He was compelled by the facts of warfare to modify his position, not once, but twice. Each modification was in the direction of the actual system employed. These modifications were reluctant, however, and he would not go all the way. The result was a method still inferior to the system in use and one which could not win acceptance.

Guibert declared that this is the weakness of what he called "tactics of the study." It sees only ideal conditions. One places cavalry on the wings. Aha! Here is the explanation of lost battles! One attacks in full cry! This is, however, merely a paper disposition, Guibert insisted, which is by no means uniformly used. If one goes out in the field, one finds much variation. "You will see that all changes, all varies, all combines, all modifies itself according to place and circumstances." [10] It was the observation of this great variation, impressed upon Guibert when only a youth, which explains his own constant insistence upon simplicity and flexibility in tactics.

In regard to artillery, Guibert declared, that while artillerymen tended to exaggerate the effectiveness of artillery, Mesnil-Durand minimized it to an even greater degree. Moreover, one needed to keep in mind that artillery also had a moral effect through the noise, the havoc, and the terrible wounds which it inflicted. It frightened as many as it killed. Since a column put ment into a compact mass, the demoralizing effect would communicate itself through a battalion much more rapidly than in a deployed formation, while the officers, commissioned and noncommissioned, were not as well placed to control it. [11]

Guibert pointed out that Mesnil-Durand's columns advanced with an interval equal to the front of half a deployed battalion between each pair, and that demonstration was made of the difficulty, even in peace maneuvers, for these columns to maintain their intervals. Add the effect of heavy artillery fire and the intervals would be even more difficult to observe, while the instinct of troops to seek each other's support would tend still more to close them. If such a chaotic mass should succeed in breaking into the enemy's position, it could not maneuver; consequently, it would be liable to envelopment and destruction by a counterattack. Guibert insisted that this was borne out by the actual trials made at Vaussieux. [12]

As to the proposed alliance which Mesnil-Durand offered to the artillerymen by claiming that his system offered artillery the best opportunities for action, Guibert became really scornful. Artillery was fully effective only when posted, he declared. When it was constantly marching and changing position, its effectiveness was decidedly reduced. In modern battles, one sought to outflank or turn the enemy's positions, to extinguish the opposing fire by a more effective one and not to attack positions head on in the face of a powerful artillery. One attacked only after gaining the advantage. Frequently it was necessary to dislodge one's foe from a succession of such positions. The role of the artillery was to second these movements and prepare the way for the attack. Mesnil-Durand's method was to arrive on the field and rush upon the enemy immediately in a headlong charge. When he claimed that his system offered artillery (1) the opportunity always to be superior at the decisive point, (2) leaving it more ground and freedom for emplacements and movements, and (3) enabling it always to operate in front of the line (which will cover the distance of artillery range in three minutes) without masking it, and yet so well supported as to have nothing to fear, Guibert said in effect that he was no doubt stupid but he did not see how it was done.[13]

Among the advantages which Mesnil-Durand claimed for his system was that his ability to put more troops on the same extent of ground enabled him to shorten his orders of battle and, consequently, to employ shorter positions. Guibert declared that this was a misconception of the role of positions which have certain basic requirements. They must include room for the army to camp within them, ability for the army to supply itself, ability to defend itself if surprised and attacked, ability to cover the points it was supposed to defend, and, finally, facility for debouching without difficulty to undertake any necessary march. These, not the deployed order, dictated extended positions, Guibert contended. He did not mean that short positions were not advantageous, for they were easier to defend than lengthy ones, but they must fulfill all these requirements. A position might be unassailable, but if it did not cover what it was supposed to defend, this advantage would be to no avail for the enemy need not attack it to reach his goal.

There were also other reasons for extended positions. If one was on the defensive, it was necessary to hold all the debouches by which the enemy might encircle one's flank or move on the points one wished to cover. If one was on the offensive, one must hold all those by which it was possible to advance on the enemy. The strength of a position was unavailing if the enemy could ignore

it and carry out either of the enterprises mentioned above. It
was also useless to hold one debouch on the enemy if he held all
the rest and could assemble all his forces before that by which
one proposed to advance.

The whole art sometimes is in knowing how to place oneself in the
center of an extended line of defense with the idea and the well
thought out possibility of falling on the enemy's flanks if he seeks to
penetrate it. . . . The whole art is also to extend one's forces, without exposing them, to embrace the enemy without becoming disunited, to link one's operations or attacks, to take the enemy in the
flank without exposing one's own, finally to deliver a check without
receiving one . . . . But this also demands a general of comprehensive
mind, profound thought, and rapid judgment.[14]

It will be remembered that in the discussion of the *Essai général* it was pointed out that Guibert's thought was not completed
in that work. It continued to expand as the above quotation
shows. In the earlier work, Guibert was still thinking in terms of
a largely unitary army. His system of march-maneuvers was tactical only, designed for use on the battlefield. The above passage
and the foregoing statements indicate that he had come to see the
full possibilities of the divisional organization, for what he is advocating here is the extension of his march-maneuvers to the
theatre of operations. He had come to realize that one can spread
his divisions on a wider front than heretofore. He said that
Frederick had perfected this type of warfare, and in truth, he had
demonstrated it, in part at least, at Torgau, his last great battle.

In this method which Guibert now advocated, it is to be noted
that he added the qualification that the operations and attacks
must be linked up. The earlier generals of the Revolution failed
to do this. They had not assimilated this idea, consequently the
divisional organization led to the cordon system of war, in which
generals frequently tried to cover everything by spreading out
their divisions over a wide area, sometimes whole provinces.
They engaged in the wider, more flexible operations which the
divisional system permitted, but they did not have the ability to
coordinate them. The result was that each division tended to
operate by itself and some of the battles of 1793 and 1794 were
really groups of nearly independent combats by separate divisions

each operating on its own.   Even in many battles properly so-
called, such as Wattignies in 1793 and Neresheim in 1796, there
was little coordination of the divisions for Jourdan and Moreau,
as well as Hoche and most of the Austrians, lacked the skill to
combine their operations effectively.[15]   It was only with the appearance of Bonaparte that this admonition of Guibert's was observed and from his first independent operation, leading to his
victory of Montenotte in 1796, this was his favorite method of action.   What Guibert is here advocating is Napoleon's method of
operation, the essential of Napoleonic strategy nearly twenty years
before Napoleon.

The latter had read and comprehended the ideas of Guibert
and Bourcet.   He saw the balance between dispersion and concentration, and understood how to bring all his forces to bear
upon the decisive point.   When this method was opposed to the
cordon system, the results could not fail to be successful.   The
contrast is strikingly clear in the dispositions of Beaulieu and of
Bonaparte for their respective offensives in April of 1796.

The turning movements advocated by these two writers were
a constant feature of Napoleonic operations.   As Colin remarks,
April 12, 1796, marks an epochal day in the history of war, for on
that day, General Bonaparte won his first battle, that of Montenotte.   It was a small affair compared to later Napoleonic
battles, and Napoleon attached so little importance to it that he
didn't even direct it in person.   Its importance lies in the fact
that all the elements of the Napoleonic battle are to be found in
this first one.   He took full advantage of the divisional organization to maneuver extensively and prepare a surprise, but the
divisions were not allowed to act independently upon their own
initiative and spread out over a wide area, for although they were
given room enough at first to make their evolutions easily, they
were directed by a single will which converged them upon a
single point.   Thus D'Argenteau was fixed in front by Laharpe's
attack and taken in front and rear by Massena, the two combined
having overwhelming superiority in numbers over him.   This
coordination was imposed upon the whole army for the remaining divisions were assembled and able to come to the support of

these two if the enemy suddenly showed much greater strength. The Austrian dispositions scattered their divisions so that not a single one was able to come to D'Argenteau's aid.

Each French division operated in the same limited area converging upon the same point, but each had its own movement, Laharpe from Montelegino, Massena from Altare. This is a clear example of the principles of concentration of forces and distribution of forces which Guibert and Bourcet had advocated. It enabled Bonaparte to obey his firm conviction that "it is by turning the enemy, by attacking his flank, that battles are won." Napoleon never failed to turn the enemy's flank if he could. He was not always able to bring it off, and there were many cases when he tried to do so only to be frustrated because the enemy retreated as in the case of General Kutusoff on the Danube in 1805.[16]

Guibert insisted that Mesnil-Durand's requirement of always operating by the center was contrary to the actualities of warfare, for it presented serious tactical difficulties and contradicted the usual requirements of operations. At Vaussieux, for instance, every time the army marched it had to close up the battalions on the center of the regiments, these latter on the center of the brigades, and the last, in turn, on the centers of the the the divisions. A good hour was thus consumed in "pawing the ground" by the time the *jumelle* columns were formed. In contrast, the ordinance permitted the army to form and move off "without preliminary maneuvers, without embarrassment, without difficulty." It would be a league on its way before Mesnil-Durand's army could even start. Once on its way, the least defile would compel the latter to maneuver and bring whole columns to a halt.[17] Guibert declared that "never has one seen so much unwieldiness, confusion, and false movement" as in the application of Mesnil-Durand's system at Vaussieux.[18]

Moreover, far from closing up your front and always attacking by the center, the actual practice of war was to extend your front so that the enemy could not pass by your flanks and move on your rear country, the points you wished to cover. Guibert declared that it was also frequently necessary to extend oneself so as to outflank the enemy or turn him out of his position. Broglie himself demonstrated this in his operations of the last war (Seven Years' War), and again at the camp of Vaussieux.[19] As Guibert said in another place, "In an attack, that which procures the greatest and most decisive advantage is assuredly to turn, outflank, and hug the enemy. There is no well-designed and successful attack but such as outflanks that of the enemy, and consequently is produced on a wider front than his." [20]

If an army while advancing had unexpectedly to take an order of battle which was not analogous to its order of march, the necessary changes would be made while the march continued. The combinations would be made "in directing [the columns] on such or such a point, in reinforcing some by others, in employing above all for this latter purpose, first the advanced guard and then those parts of the columns designed to form the second line or the reserves." [21]   All the art of army movements should be in the general's head, Guibert maintained. He could achieve everything by knowing how to move columns of march, but he must keep his army in hand to accomplish this. This did not mean that he placed himself at the head or in the midst of his army giving all orders personally, as Mesnil-Durand would seem to believe from his discussion, but rather that he marched with the advanced guard at a distance of from a half to a whole league from the army in order to reconnoiter the ground and the enemy. This would enable him to issue orders for directing the columns from firsthand knowledge of the situation. The general-in-chief would thus direct his army according to circumstances, moving it into new positions if the hostile movements required, and the divisional generals must give immediate obedience to such orders, moving on the indicated points. The Ordinance provided simple methods for doing this, as Rochambeau decisively demonstrated at Vaussieux.[22]

Thus Guibert summed up clearly his whole method of march-maneuvers, discussed in the *Essai général*, and his concept of the commander's tactical role. It was based upon the practice of Frederick and was the method which Napoleon followed. The

latter was insistent that his lieutenants should march at the head
of their forces so that they would be on the scene immediately to
deal with any situation which developed.[23] Guibert had summed
up in two brief passages the essence of Napoleon's strategical concept and his concept of a general's tactical role. The importance
of the latter has been demonstrated many times. When a general
is in a position where he can observe the enemy directly it is
possible to take advantage of many slips on the part of his opponent, witness Frederick at Rossbach and Lannes at Friedland.
In the days of slow communication, this required the general to
act as Guibert outlined.

Turning next to Mesnil-Durand's orders of battle, Guibert
dealt with them extensively. In regard to the parallel order, he
asked, how could one answer a man who thought that one was
reduced to opposing an inferior army with equal numbers in
modern tactics? Could not one act on the flanks? One's opponent either would or would not be posted. If he were not, one
moved enough troops on his front to attack or contain him and
enveloped him with the rest. "The army should be so disposed
that if one wishes, one may direct a part against the enemy's flank
while one directs the remainder against his front." [24] If the
enemy was posted, one turned his position. It might be necessary
to do this at a distance, but one most certainly would not attack
him merely with equal forces.

While admitting the great results that would follow if one
succeeded in splitting an army by a central oblique attack,
Guibert pointed out that it was very dangerous, for such an attack
was easily countered. In making it, one committed oneself ir-
revocably. Failure involved just as complete a disaster for oneself as victory would for the enemy. Having pierced the first line,
one would run afoul of the second and the reserves which would
be apt to hold up the attack and allow the wings to envelop one's
own forces. The farther one advanced the more difficult one's
retreat would become. The risk of total rout would be very
great.[25]

Guibert was quite willing to leave the doubtful glory of having invented the perpendicular order of battle to Mesnil-Durand.

As it was presented at the maneuvers of Vaussieux, the order consisted of a parallelogram whose shortest side, six battalions in
length, was presented to the enemy. The perpendicular order was
in reality only the standard order of battle with a flanking brigade
(four battalions) filling the gap between the two lines. Mesnil-
Durand, as Guibert pointed out, merely saved the enemy the
trouble of outflanking him by presenting his flank to the enemy
and, moreover, right in the center of his line where the enemy
could best envelop and overwhelm it.[26]

Guibert was bitterly opposed to what he called the French
practice of making war by detachments, contrasting it with
Frederick's practice of concentration. He stated the case very
strongly for keeping one's army concentrated and operating in
the mass, a practice so characteristic of Napoleon. One is entitled
to speculate on whether this was the influence which led the latter
to this practice which was quite at variance with even his contemporary generals of the Revolutionary armies. Speaking of the
reasons against numerous and permanent detachments, Guibert
said:

Are you superior to the enemy? It is rarely necessary to divide your
forces; for you set yourself back, by this parcelling, on a level with
him, you expose the corps which you detach to being beaten and to
losing in detail the advantages that you had in remaining together.
Are you inferior to the enemy?. You ought with greater reason to
make war without dividing your forces; for in dividing your forces in
this manner, you reduce yourself to being on the defensive everywhere,
anxious everywhere, exposed everywhere to checks and coups-de-main.
Are you on the definite offensive in a major operation within range
of the enemy? All the more reason to remain united: it is even
necessary to recall all your detached corps and light troops. In effect,
if you wish to attack, why betray yourself, make it known, uncover
yourself at any point? It would be desirable that when the enemy
sees the first troops arrive, all the army should be in support and
leave no time to parry the blow that it is about to deliver. If you are
on the defensive; if you fear being attacked, is there a better disposition than that of being assembled and ready to resist where the enemy
wishes to make an effort? [27]

In refuting Mesnil-Durand, Guibert was stimulated to some of
his soundest and most advanced statements on tactics and strategy.

This was true of his remarks on the manner of conducting a combat. Guibert condemned his rival's entire method, declaring that for Mesnil-Durand "to fight or to conquer is always synonymous." He took no account of positions, dispositions, nor the maneuvers of the enemy. "He does not march, *he runs, he flies; if he attacks, he bursts in, he overthrows, he scatters.*" [28] Inferiority of numbers mattered not at all; the victory would be more glorious. "Obstacles will not stop him any more; *provided that the enemy be approachable on the ninety-nine hundredth part of his front, that is enough for him. That is where he charges to pierce it.*" [29] He had little respect for artillery. He thought maneuvers for outflanking and turning the enemy were useless and was not fearful of their being employed against him. He preferred to attack by the center in all circumstances as a consequence. His orders of battle and his dispositions were taken and changed "with such speed, that the eye can hardly follow them." It made no difference to him whether there were one, two, or four lines. All would be treated in the same way.

Modern tactics were not so swift, said Guibert. One had to prepare and combine dispositions which must be done out of range of heavy artillery fire. The great object was to outflank and turn the enemy. All the art of a good offensive disposition was to gain this advantage, and of a defensive disposition was to avoid having the enemy do it to you.

When one attacks, it is not solely a question of assembling a large number of troops in a small space, as M. de M. . . D. . . seems to believe, and of taking a disposition which permits containing them in that space. It is a question of employing all one's forces in the most advantageous and decisive manner.[30]

This could best be done by enveloping your enemy. "It is a question of having the fewest useless troops possible." [31] It did not follow, however, that one should concentrate as large a number of troops as possible in a small space, for in such a situation a check results in their closing up, with chaos ensuing.

To gain a battle under existing conditions, Guibert insisted, demanded driving the enemy from successive positions by outflanking or turning each in turn which required one to occupy as extensive a position as one's opponent. It was not sufficient to make an irruption into the enemy's line of battle and to pierce it. One needed to maintain enough order, cohesion, and room so that one could maintain oneself. Once the enemy had been driven from a position, one had to begin to consolidate it and to find flank supports, unless the enemy was completely routed, in order to resist his counterattack successfully. "A battle can be regarded as a continuous series of dislodgements and dispositions, by means of which the attacker passes without ceasing from one parallel to another, always embracing the enemy more and more, pushing him off from his field of battle, and making him abandon it." [32]

Engaging in battle was not a question of running, flying, bursting in, nor was it a question of speeding up the process, and "of destroying the enemy's army in less time than one would need to read half of one of these chapters." [33] Rather system was necessary, caution, even slowness sometimes. Teamwork and discipline were always required. The enemy's position must be reconnoitered and the deployment based upon it, while even if the attack was successful, the enemy might take up a new position which would require a new reconnaissance, a new disposition, and perhaps even a whole new order of battle. A tremendous variety of circumstances must be taken into account in war which well might slow up or delay an attack. This was frequently true of combined attacks, either by the two wings of troops on the same field of battle or of two bodies of troops separated at some distance from each other. One could not fight and win battles in six or seven minutes as Mesnil-Durand would have it. It was necessary to do this with his system in order to avoid keeping the troops for long under an artillery fire which would destroy them.[34]

In this discussion, Guibert set forth a fundamentally sound method of combat command which his opponents tended to lose sight of. It was not only sound for his own day, but with some allowance for tactical changes, it remains true today. This is not to say that he originated it, for it was the method of capable generals before as well as since his day. It demonstrates very well, however, his freedom from that "spirit of system" with which he so correctly taxed his opponent. It demonstrates also his thorough grasp of the problems of both military science and the military art.

Guibert closed his work with a long examination of the system of warfare existing in his day in relation to politics and administration. This was, in effect, a defense of that system from its detractors, chiefly the *philosophes* whose ideas he had once espoused. He admitted there would be contradictions in this chapter with what he said in the Preliminary Discourse of the *Essai général de tactique,* but he was ten years younger then and "the fumes of philosophy inflamed his head and blinded his judgement." [35]

He declared that it was useless to rail against war as the *philosophes* did, because, as long as human nature remained what it was, wars would continue. "To declaim against war in verse and prose . . . is to beat the air in vain." [36] The result would be to weaken the warlike spirit of the nation until one delivered it weakened and badly armed into the hands of a warlike nation which might not have the same level of civilzation, but which was nevertheless wiser. The most philosophical monarchs such as Frederick and Catherine made war, the former having just done so in his old age. The English included many philosophers, but their commercial interests came first, as was being demonstrated in their conflict with their American brothers. Some dreamers had proposed that if war could not be abolished, then the rulers should keep only small armies proportionate to their resources. This was a vain dream, Guibert insisted, because you could never get the nations to agree upon the standard of measurement.

Since all such proposals for limitation of arms and abolition of war were chimerical, he turned to a discussion of methods of making war. There were two of these. One might raise troops upon the outbreak of war choosing the most vigorous, most ardent, and noblest, and undertaking it with these largely untrained men, or one might keep large bodies of highly trained troops under arms at all times. The former was used only by the Poles and Turks, and the uselessness of such troops had been demonstrated in recent wars. Without permanent trained armies, a state could enjoy neither safety nor consideration of its interests by other powers.

Such armies had on occasion served as instruments of tyranny, Guibert continued, but the mere absence of such armies was not a guarantee against tyranny. As a matter of fact, though they were the firm support of legitimate authority, they might actually act as a check upon tyranny. He admitted that if a nation had lost its liberty and right of self-government, it was almost impossible to recover it from a sovereign with a powerful army. Most nations could not, however, enjoy such liberty even if they had it, but would soon fall into anarchy and clamor for a return of authority. England was not an example in opposition to this argument, for she was an exception because of her natural situation. The monarchical government is, by the large, the best suited to the situation of Europe.[37]

Such was Guibert's argument in support of standing armies. He answered the question of whether one could successfully substitute a militia system for a standing army with an emphatic "no." Because of the great strides made by military science, a militia army, even with great superiority in numbers, would still be decidedly inferior to a professional one. The *philosophes* had pointed to the Americans as a people who had maintained their liberties in spite of armies. The successful resistance of the Americans, which might be ephemeral, incidentally, did not change his opinions. He believed that the British army had a qualitative superiority over that of Washington and he believed further that Burgoyne's army had the same over that of Gates which defeated and captured it. The British failure had come, he believed, as a result of their own mistakes, lack of plans, and division of forces. Even if the war did not end as he believed it should, this would not disprove his thesis. This was a war very different from those of Europe, in which the English were fighting some thousands of miles from their homeland base, which caused great difficulty in supply due to the uncertainty and slowness of convoys. Add to this the nature of the country with its great rivers, lakes, and forests, which presented greater difficulties than European topography, also the difficulty of penetrating a country when one drew his supplies from the coast, and one balanced the superior qualities of the troops which would otherwise favor the British.[38]   Guibert certainly underrated the accomplishments of the Americans to some extent, but it would seem that, by and large, his judgment that the blunders of the British combined with the enormity of their task in comparison with their resources had much to do with their failure was accurate.   He was in error in saying that citizen armies could never stand against professional ones, but there were more examples supporting him than refuting him.   Citizen armies, moreover, generally need training which cannot always be obtained.   Guibert was right in regarding raw troops as a very unreliable support for a state.   That was his chief contention.

He defended the "modern system" of war on the grounds that it was more humane and that it imposed much less hardship on the peoples of Europe than was formerly the case.   The "modern system," because of the nature of its arms and the difficulty of moving huge armies, had become defensive to a large degree. This tendency was reinforced by the advantages which positions give defending troops over those which attacked.   Thus the offensive had come to be the most difficult part of war to undertake.   This was proven by the fact that mediocre generals largely relied upon the defensive, and only able generals assumed the offensive.   This could be an abuse, but the results were "certainly advantageous to the peace of nations and the safety of empires." Thus the more the equality of discipline, instruction, and ability of generals reached a balance, the less frequently would nations resort to war, and when they did, the resulting wars would be less decisive and have less possibility of conquest.   There would be fewer temptations for ambitious rulers and fewer revolutions of empires.[39]   This would seem to have been written, at least in part, under the influence of the indecisive War of the Bavarian Succession then just coming to a close.   It is the concluding idea of the *Défense*.

A writer [40] who has recently discussed the work of Guibert insists that in the *Défense* the latter recants the ideas which he had advocated in the *Essai général*. This is only partially true. In the earlier work Guibert had been moved by admiration for Republican Rome and had been filled with the *philosophes'* enthusiasm for reform and with their rather naive belief that the true principles of government, once discovered by human reason, would bring prosperity and power to the state. He was much impressed by the idea of the citizen army which had been so successful in the days of the early Roman Republic, an idea which was popular with the *philosophes* in general. The new army which Guibert proposed would ideally be such an army though that was not essential. The body of the work was concerned, however, with expounding a method of elementary tactics for each arm and with a system of grand tactics for the use of armies. The former had already been adopted by the French Army. The latter went beyond any practice which had been previously employed.

This system was called in question by Mesnil-Durand in his *Fragments*. Guibert ignored that work for some years until the system there expounded found a powerful advocate in Marshal Broglie and was actually tested in the Camp of Vaussieux. It was this which led him to write his second work. In this work he did *not* retract any of his military ideas. He attacked specifically the system of Mesnil-Durand at many points. It is not correct to say that this was merely a continuation of the old debate over the merits of line and column in the combat tactics of infantry, for Guibert admitted the important role of columns in an action. The debate was rather over the clumsy columns and exclusive system of deployment advocated by Mesnil-Durand as compared with the flexible system, embodied in the existing ordinance, which stemmed largely from Guibert himself, dating back to his early *Project d'instruction*. It also involved the role of columns on the battlefield, for Mesnil-Durand made no distinction between formations for maneuver and the actual fighting formation. It was for the latter that Guibert, in conformity with practice before and after his time, advocated the line. Even in combat he advocated the column under certain conditions.

Far from retracting his military ideas, he reiterated them, often in identical language, and more than once he stated that he stood by what he had written before. In some respects, he even went beyond what he had written before. This system of mobile warfare went beyond anything previously employed and was not fully realized until Napoleon.

It is true that Guibert turned his back upon the *philosophique* ideas that he had held in his earlier days. This he emphatically stated in the final chapter of the *Défense*. Even in this chapter, however, he did not fully endorse the existing system of warfare. He condemned the excessive amounts of light troops and artillery, the excessive reliance upon fortresses, the complicated supply system, and the spirit of rivalry in the various arms and services, just as he had in the *Essai général*. These he called abuses and errors which awaited some great man who could remove these complications from the "modern system" of warfare and reduce each part of tactics to its just proportions in a complete science of war. While awaiting this simplification, "it is this mixture of enlightenment and abuses, of knowledge and error, which crushing men of mediocre mind, and exacting more ability, makes great generals so rare today." [41] The points where he condemned the existing system were those where he had proposed remedies.

Guibert's reputation as a prophet suffers from his turning his back upon the idea of the citizen army, as his critic declares, but it would seem safe to maintain that the large numbers of professional troops which were brigaded with the citizen forces during the Wars of the Revolution did much to mitigate the weaknesses which Guibert imputes to such troops and which have so frequently been borne out in practice. It should also be remembered that the Volunteers of 1791 had nearly a year's training before the war broke out. They were far superior to the Volunteers of 1792, who did not have that advantage. Even a citizen army must be trained to be effective.

Guibert's real influence lay in the military ideas which he propounded. These ideas were embodied in the Ordinance of 1791 in so far as they concerned elementary tactics. They were the basis for the best practice in the great wars which followed. Whatever may be the inconsistencies in Guibert's works, he did *not* retract these ideas.[42]

It may be noted in closing that Mesnil-Durand had the last word in publishing a *Collection de diverses pièces et mémoires nécessaires pour achever d'instruire la grande affaire de tactique et donner les derniers éclairissements sur l'ordre français proposé* in 1780.   According to Colin this collection adds nothing to his ideas.   It does contain some *Rémarques* on Guibert's *Défense* which reproach, and justly so according to Colin, the latter for not having read his works with enough care, and for having disfigured his words in citing them.   Colin's comment is, "Perhaps Guibert had not been entirely of good faith; perhaps also he had not the necessary patience to assimilate the prodigiously undigested work of his adversary." [43]

The Controversy Continues

In 1777, between the publication of Mesnil-Durand's *Fragments de tactique* and Guibert's *Défense du systême de guerre moderne,* Joly de Maizeroy also reappeared in print with his *Théorie de la guerre* modifying his original system. The new work was brought out, so he said, because of the frequent variations in tactics, the differences of opinion on that subject, and was designed to set forth a theory capable of serving as a guide and also capable of a sound application from elementary to grand maneuvers.

He introduced his subject with a long discourse in order to demonstrate (1) that the ancients, "who excelled in the science of arms," began by establishing fixed and invariable principles; (2) that for the past century and more there had not been any such principles in France; (3) that instead the country had either followed a bad routine or been swept away by foreign example in these matters; (4) that it was necessary to establish such principles; and (5) that it was necessary to set up a tribunal to maintain them, once established, and preserve them from dangerous innovations. The principles which he advocated were, he declared, based upon a study of those employed throughout the past from the earliest times down to those of Turenne.[1] He maintained that if his principles were adopted a general could only blame himself for any failure. Such failure would be due to the general's own ignorance, imprudence, or rashness.

A body of national military principles should be drawn up by a tribunal composed of men of high character. "It is necessary that to sagacity of mind, to a well-informed and reflective experience, they join the purest zeal for the well-being of the state and the glory of the nation; that with enough penetration to grasp the vast extent of a military system, and to see the relationship of all its branches, they be always ready to sacrifice vanity to the evidence of reason."[2] Once drawn up, it was essential that such a body of principles be safeguarded against ill-considered innovation. For this purpose, it was desirable to have a council of war composed of men devoted to the welfare and service of the state. Such a council charged with the custody of the military institutions would permit changes only after thorough deliberation and by majority vote.

This sustained and vigorous advocacy of a stable body of military principles was prompted by the series of innovations during the twenty years previous to his writing, beginning with the reforms of Choiseul. These latter had been generally beneficial. However, after his fall, a rapid succession of ministers had made a series of changes which were not always well thought out or useful. Many of the other writers besides Maizeroy had remarked unfavorably about this penchant for innovation.

Maizeroy opened his main discussion by defining tactics and, what is rare among authors of his day, strategy.

To tactics belongs the art of drilling the troops, of marshaling them, and of making them move; the art of attack and defense in all circumstances and in all positions, that which comprehends several parts based upon geometry. Strategy is something more elevated. In order to form its projects, it combines time, places, means, various interests, and considers all that which I have said previously to be the province of dialectic, that is to say, of the most sublime faculty of the mind, of the reason. The one reduces easily to firm rules, because it is entirely geometrical like fortification; the other appears very much less susceptible of it, because it is related to an infinity of circumstances, physical, political, and moral, which are never the same and which pertain entirely to genius. Nevertheless, there are certain general rules which one can pose with safety and regard as an invariable base.[3]

Maizeroy referred to the bitter controversy between the advocates of the *ordre profond* and the *ordre mince*. He declared that of all unprejudiced officers who saw the tests of Mesnil-Durand's system at Metz,[4] those of any experience agreed that Mesnil-Durand's maneuvers were much simpler, more accurate, and sounder than those of the provisional instruction.

He had decided reluctantly, however, since the prejudice

against the *ordre profond* was so great, to put aside his system of cohorts and establish another more analogous to the dominant opinions and to custom. He had determined to do this because it was possible to draw some elementary maneuvers from his modified system which, if not so perfect as those of his original one, were at least founded upon the same principles and on views more nearly correct militarily than those of existing regulations. A further reason which had led him to this modification was that, since many officers, including several charged with educating young officers for the military profession, desired a system of elementary tactics applied to grand maneuvers, he had felt it more desirable to apply an ordinance in use rather than one regarded as systematic, that is to say, doctrinaire. Perhaps in the future, when officers became convinced of the soundness of his principles, they would decide to separate the impurities from them and adopt them in their unadulterated form. For these reasons, he expounded a theory, which was not the best possible, but was the best reconcilable to the bad maxims from which people apparently did not desire to depart. It included all the parts of warfare from the smallest to the greatest, and was intended to be used (at least in part) as a textbook.[5]

From the foregoing, it is quite apparent that Maizeroy, like Mesnil-Durand, was led to modify his original system by the realization that it could not win acceptance. While he was not as doctrinaire as the latter, he insisted that those whom he acknowledged to be the majority of officers in the army were prejudiced, or else interested parties in the existing *status quo*. Maizeroy's new book is one more evidence that partisans of the *ordre profond* were being compelled, however reluctantly, to give up their position and move towards that of men who, like Guibert, were not extreme partisans of either system.

Maizeroy started the exposition of his new system by a long discussion of the problem of the habitual order. Like Mesnil-Durand, he felt that since infantry acted in two ways, it should have two orders. He assumed as a matter of course that it had been sufficiently demonstrated that the *ordre profond* was the only one capable of confident employment for the offensive.

While long a supporter of that order, he declared that he did not exclude the *ordre mince,* nor did he confine himself to a particular form of the *ordre profond.* Sometimes a column of say sixteen files of thirty-two men was preferable; at others a *cohorte doublée* of say thirty-two files of sixteen men. Thus by refusing to argue the point, Maizeroy established the *ordre profond* as the offensive order. Since firearms were the primary defensive weapons, however, he maintained that the *ordre mince* should be the defensive order.

Which of these should be the habitual order? Maizeroy answered this question by saying, neither. He advanced many reasons which may be summed up by saying that both orders should be rejected as the habitual order because both were improper for both kinds of fighting. The habitual order should be one which could be used for both. He chose his old favorite, the order on six ranks (or eight if the authorities ever became disabused, as they eventually would, of the error made in suppressing the fourth rank). This was essentially the doubled order which Saxe as well as Maizeroy had advocated as an alternative to column and line. Maizeroy argued many advantages for this order among which was its intermediate character between the offensive and defensive orders.[6]

The result of his long discussion seems to be simply that no one formation could be exclusive. Troops should be formed in the formation which was best suited for the purpose at hand. This was essentially the position of Guibert, and all the discussion about which should be the habitual order was largely futile. The onus for it must rest with Guibert who by introducing the term "habitual order" tended to obscure the large degree of agreement between most of the partisans of the two orders, always excepting such opinionated men as Mesnil-Durand. The chief disagreement between Maizeroy and Guibert would seem to be that the latter would deny that the *ordre mince* was improper for the attack or that all attacks should be conducted by the *ordre profond.*

Maizeroy dealt next with petty tactics. There was little that was new in the chapters devoted to this subject. He did, however, have a number of criticisms of Pirch's principles in connection with the subject of the march of a battalion or regiment in line of battle. The purpose of such a march was to move forward as rapidly as possible onto a proposed line and to arrive there in good order. To accomplish this required uniformity of step and alinement and accuracy of direction, said Maizeroy. The execution of such a march depended upon the principles used.

One should never march a battalion in three ranks, but since this was done, Maizeroy said that he would set up the best possible maxims for it. The wing captains should take up a position three paces in front of the center of their inner section, while the commandant should be three paces in front of the flag file, which was the center file of the battalion. The purpose of this was to enable these officers to be better seen for alining purposes. Maizeroy next turned to the impossibility of a battalion advancing in three ranks without wavering—"truly an idle dream." He maintained that a perfect alinement was not necessary. It was sufficient if the various parts of the battalion kept their order and uniformity and acted together. If a troop was to march straight before it, there was a limit to the possible extent of its front which if exceeded led to the outside or guide files gradually diverging with the accompanying result of opening gaps. This limit was not two hundred fifty files, nor two hundred, nor even one hundred eighty, for the wings were too far away to aline on the center. The Ordinance of 1766 tried to meet this by having the men turn their heads towards the center, but it was physically impossible for men to march any distance straight ahead when they were doing eyes-right or left.

Maizeroy also criticized choosing three points of alinement as worth nothing, because the wing captains looking alternately at their point of direction and their commandant would lose first one and then the other. Further, to choose at a distance three points precisely placed on an extent equal to the battalion's front would be extremely difficult, especially in combat when it was, moreover, a question not of one but of many battalions. Consequently, he felt it to be much better to double on six ranks which would provide only ninety-six files, a front small enough so that the outside files could keep alined on the center.[7]   Although Maizeroy started out to give the principles for marching in three ranks, he seems rather to end by proving that it was impossible.

Maizeroy dealt next with evolutions.   Closed columns of action might be formed in an emergency on six ranks, breaking by quarter-ranks, i.e., quarter-battalions, to right or left and closing up the divisions. This should only be done when one wished to charge an enemy who suddenly appeared on one's flank.   A column was formed on the same front as the line by having the two center companies move forward while the wing companies faced towards the center and marched by the flank to place themselves behind those of the center.   An interval of four paces should be maintained between the divisions to facilitate marching and to prevent disorder in one company from communicating itself to another.

When on three ranks, a column should be formed only by the center, for this disposition presupposed a passive situation in which only fire combat would be used.   One would only change to move to another position, which being done with safety, should be done by the center alone.   The center half-sections would move straight forward while all the others half quarter-wheeled to the rear and then moved straight ahead to place themselves in columns behind the lead element.   The result was exactly the same as if it had been done from the six ranks.[8]

It is quite apparent from the foregoing that while Maizeroy's ployments and deployments are free from the complexities of Mesnil-Durand's second system, they are lacking in the flexibility which characterizes those of Guibert.   This is primarily due to his insisting upon the central deployment.

An alternative to the column, of which it was merely a modification, was his doubled cohort or phalanx.   Each formation evolved readily and without difficulty.   The direction from which attack was most to be feared determined which formation should be used.   The phalanx could be formed from a battalion on six ranks by having the four center companies march directly forward while the wing companies faced to the center and marched to place themselves behind those of the center.   If one then

wished to form a column from the phalanx, the two center companies of the first division would march forward while the wing
companies faced to the center and marched to place themselves
behind the former. The second division would do the same as
soon as it had room. To form a phalanx from a column the
second and fourth *tranches* (a division of the column) separated
by *demi-tranches* and moved out from the column by flank
marches. As soon as they were unmasked, they faced forward
and moved up on the outside of the first and third *tranches*. The
phalanx then closed up. Both the phalanx and the column could
separate by *manches* and charge by the flanks. If they had
enemies both in front and flank, then the rear *demi-manches*
could charge by the flank while the leading ones charged ahead.[9]

Following his discussion of evolutions, Maizeroy turned to the
subject of fire. He opened by declaring that for sixty years no
one objected to having the first rank kneel to fire, but since "the
fury of banging away" had seized minds, a whole series of plans
for firing with all ranks upright had been proposed. Maizeroy
said that he had examined all of them, and he found none which
were practicable for combat. He could not see why it was so
dangerous for the first rank to kneel. He did not believe that the
objections to having the second and third ranks switching fusils
when the latter could not fire were valid, and therefore favored
this.

When a line marched in battle, either advancing or retreating,
it should fire either by battalion or half-battalion with the first
rank kneeling on one knee. One should limit this process strictly
for, if there were no obstacles, it was necessary to charge rapidly
in doubled battalions, columns, or phalanxes. Firing should be
confined in such cases to the chasseurs who fire at will. "This is a
fundamental maxim from which it is necessary never to
deviate." [10]

Regulated fire might be used when a line or part of the line
remained on the defensive. It might also be used when it seemed
à propos to deploy a first line of battalions while the second line
was held in column. The first line would advance, firing and re-
loading, or stop when within musket range to engage in a fire

action. In either case at a given moment, intervals should be opened and the columns of the second line should suddenly pass through them and hurl themselves on the enemy. The latter, thinking that he had only a fire action on his hands, would be completely unprepared for such a development.

When deployed battalions fire while advancing or retreating, they should fire by half rather than whole battalions. Maizeroy advocated the use of the *feu d'échiquier* in such circumstances, and would have his battalions divide at the flag (center) file for the purpose. The right half-battalions would advance ten paces, fire, and reload. The left ones would then advance twenty paces, fire, and reload, and so on alternately. The same process would be followed in retreat except that the troops would have to about-face at the beginning and end of each march.

Maizeroy criticized all *feu de chaussée* which he had seen executed, for it assumed that the enemy could not reach the flanks. This was true only on a causeway through inundated country or a marsh. Thus the men who had fired and were filing to the rear along the sides of the column masked the flanks. If the enemy arrived unexpectedly on a flank, frightful confusion would result. To obviate this difficulty, Maizeroy would open a passage down the center of the column for the men to file through.

The last method of fire which Maizeroy discussed was that of infantry attacked by cavalry. When the battalion was on six ranks, the first two ranks should kneel and fire, which allowed the next two to deliver a second volley over their heads. He declared that to delay firing upon cavalry until it was only thirty paces away was an error, for if it was not stopped by the volleys, it was on the battalion before the men could rise. One must fire at a distance of sixty or even eighty paces. If the two volleys did not stop the cavalry, the first two ranks having reloaded and risen could fire a third volley at close range. For a battalion on three ranks the method was the same.[11]

Maizeroy's principles for fire were in most part sound enough except for the kneeling of the first rank which was pretty generally condemned by opinion in his time, as he admitted in his opening discussion. Opinion seemed to agree that it was difficult to get men to stand up, once they had knelt. Guibert was, of course, vehement in his opposition to it. Another point on which Maizeroy disagreed with Guibert was in his acceptance of the *feu d'échiquier*, in which he would seem to be correct in finding it useful on occasion. Its employment would run counter to his principle of never advancing deployed. He did make an exception to that rule in permitting a line of deployed battalions to screen the advance of a line of columns until close to the enemy's line. It was presumably in this situation that he would employ the *feu d'échiquier*.

The methods of fire concluded Maizeroy's discussion of the elementary tactics of infantry, and he then turned to the cavalry. Basically the ideas advocated here were those which he had set forth in his earlier works, but there were differences of detail. Maizeroy maintained his old position that one of the gravest defects of cavalry was excessive size of squadrons which made them too long. This in turn made the maintenance of order and alinement too difficult, slowed up the movements, and made the wheelings too extended. He was strongly convinced that the front of the squadron should not be over fifty men. This was the second time that he had extended the limit for his first limit was twenty-five and his second thirty-six or forty. The reason which he gave for this extension was that, while true perfection was below fifty, he fixed the front at this figure because of prejudice and general custom. Once again, therefore, he yielded to a prevailing opinion which was at variance with his own.

Maizeroy discussed the maneuvers of cavalry at some length. To deploy a regiment of cavalry in line ahead from a column of companies open at full intervals, one determined the company of alinement. All the companies ahead of this one made successive quarter-wheels to the right on reaching the designated line, moved out the required distance, and then wheeled into line. Those which were behind the company of alinement made half quarter-wheels to the left and moved to place themselves successively in line. (See Figure 27.)

In order to conceal their strength, the columns were usually closed up to four or six paces in the same manner as infantry columns. Deployment from such a column was made as in the infantry except that, instead of flank movements, cavalry performed its marches *tête à botte,* so-called because the men turned their horses to the sides until the heads of the horses in even files

FIGURE 27

were even with the boots of the men in odd files. If the right led the column, then all divisions ahead of the one marking the aline-ment would turn to the right and move out from the column. When the division of alinement was unmasked it moved straight ahead to the line. Those which followed moved to the left as they were unmasked and did the same. (See Figure 28.) If a closed column arrived at either extremity of its position, it could put itself in battle by successive quarter-wheels, made to the right if it arrived on the left of its position and to the left if it arrived on the right. It must take full intervals in the former case so as to form line by simultaneous quarter-wheels to the left. This was not necessary in the latter case, however, as each division made a right quarter-wheel into line as soon as it had cleared those already in position.

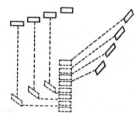

FIGURE 28

Maizeroy described the use of the chasseurs. Their main purpose was to act as skirmishes in front of an advancing cavalry line or to cover the retreat of a cavalry column. In the former case they operated fifty to a hundred paces in front of the line while it was advancing at a walk. When the pace was accelerated they withdrew through the line and rallied thirty paces behind it. They came out and pursued the enemy if the charge was successful. If the cavalry was in full line, the chasseurs must be posted on the flanks instead of behind the intervals. Maizeroy did not like that formation, however, because it was subject to opening and crowding and because it was not as flexible as a line with intervals. This was not to say that the line should have intervals equal to the front of the squadrons. He merely desired them to be of twenty paces in order to permit the platoons of chasseurs to pass through them.

Maizeroy condemned as contrary to the principles of war, the charge of a line of cavalry at full speed for a thousand paces or more. He declared that it ruined the horses to no purpose. The charge should begin with a trot and should not take the gallop at a distance greater than three hundred paces form the enemy. Otherwise, on reaching the enemy the horses would be so tired and out of breath as to lose a part of the vigor necessary for shock. A line which moved at full speed for a long distance would lose its alinement. Cavalry should not be exercised at a run in larger units than a squadron. The purpose of such drills should be merely to move squadrons rapidly from one place to another. In this matter, Maizeroy disagreed with Saxe, who insisted that a squadron which could not charge two thousand paces in formation was not fit for war.

There should be no difference in organization between the dragoons and the cavalry. In addition to learning all the service of the cavalry, they should also learn that of the chasseurs. Each squadron should perform this latter service in turn when the regiment was serving mounted. The dragoons, of course, had also to learn infantry drill, including ployment and deployment, in order to perform dismounted service. The dragoon column was actually only a phalanx (in Maizeroy's meaning of the term) having a depth of sixteen men on a front of twenty-four. The dragoons were to learn this formation, according to Maizeroy, so that they would be able to get out of a bad situation while serving on foot, or even to charge in column should occasion demand.

The only difference between hussars and dragoons was that the former should be trained as a pure light cavalry, that is, without the infantry drill.[12]

Having set forth a system of elementary tactics which he felt to be a satisfactory compromise between his system and the one in use, Maizeroy turned to grand tactics. He accepted the divisional system which had become thoroughly established in the French Army by the 1770's. In all the movements of grand tactics up to the point of contact, he adopted the ideas of Guibert. He adopted Guibert's system of march-maneuvers and described the whole period of preliminary maneuvers, including the role of the general, in much the same terms as did the latter. This was a major break from Maizeroy's earlier works in which he still held to the idea of the army marching in the order in which it intended to fight. Up to the moment of final deployment, therefore, Maizeroy's ideas had been modified in the direction of major improvement.

From that moment, however, Maizeroy and Guibert parted company, which is hardly surprising for disciples of the *odre profond* and the *ordre mince*. Maizeroy's combat tactics conformed closely to those of Mesnil-Durand. He held the oblique order to be "the height of perfection of grand maneuvers when it is well directed."[13] Like Mesnil-Durand he felt that the Prussian oblique was unsatisfactory. It necessitated outflanking the enemy and was dependent upon cavalry for success. His own method had neither defect, being capable of success independently of the results of the mounted action. It differed from Mesnil-Durand's only in that Maizeroy favored phalanxes instead of columns. He would use it for central attacks just as the former advocated. He made the same immoderate claims for the results for "the enemy, unable to resist that impulsion, will indubitably be pierced in his center without having any remedy for his misfortunes,"[14] and further on, "the best position is not sheltered from being forced." Maizeroy also advocated a formation very similar to Mesnil-Durand's perpendicular order, which, like the latter, would give inevitable victory.[15]

The same objections apply to these formations as to those of

Mesnil-Durand. Maizeroy represented a less extreme position than his fellow advocate of the *ordre profond*. He was still enamored of the rush forward without firing to assail the opposition, even though Frederick had come to see, as a result of the hard experience of battle, that this was not possible before gaining fire superiority.

Like Saxe and Mesnil-Durand, Maizeroy relied very heavily upon his screen of chasseurs, acting as skirmishers, to protect his line of columns or phalanxes from hostile fire. The chief target of the chasseurs should be the cannoneers of the enemy. This was also in agreement with Mesnil-Durand's ideas. Both of these men recognized the danger which artillery posed for their massed formations. The chasseurs were an attempt to neutralize this danger. They were intended to silence or greatly reduce the fire of artillery by picking off the gun crews. Maizeroy insisted, moreover, that no advantage would be gained by killing some men along the enemy's front. This idea also follows from the acceptance of the inevitable victory which a formation in depth would gain over a thin line.

The final subject with which Maizeroy dealt in this work was strategy or military dialectic. He said that it was not possible to lay down any rules for strategy, but if one had the necessary basic knowledge of fortification and tactics joined with the quality of *coup d'oeil*, that is, ability to judge a given extent of ground or military situation and recognize quickly its military possibilities, then one could profit from a study of past campaigns to learn the principles of strategy. He was convinced that a man who had this knowledge and capacity could learn more in six months of study than in ten campaigns with the ordinary routine.

Maizeroy set forth the basic principles of strategy as follows:

The fundamental maxims of dialectic are: not to do what the enemy appears to desire; to recognize his major interest so as not to be fooled by feints; to hold oneself always in readiness to thwart him in his enterprises without being dominated by this; to keep for oneself a general freedom of movements, whether for the foreseen plans, or those to which circumstances can give birth; to engage one's adversary in his daring undertakings, or his critical situations without compromising oneself; to be always the master of engaging, in choosing one's time and ground; and finally not to put oneself in danger of being forced to it with disadvantage.[16]

A general who had the capacity of the *coup d'oeil*, who knew the country perfectly, and who knew the resources which it provided both to himself and his opponent, could regulate his conduct and general plans accordingly.

Each [of the opponents] can have several plans at the same time. One applies oneself to thwart the enemy in his, to arrive oneself at a goal which reduces him to desist from his projects, and to dare to undertake nothing without running the greatest risks. Thus from event to event, one can reason the plan of a campaign and foresee the outcome of it. It is a question of not losing sight of the major interest of the enemy, of not deviating from the principal objective, of keeping an eye on the other's most important points, of being sure of one's communications, and of not leaving them open, of being always in a position to forestall the enemy no matter what direction he takes, of taking care to keep oneself out of range, and on the contrary to seize the occasion of breaking him without too much risk.[17]

Maizeroy then proceeded to give accounts of several campaigns for the purpose of illustrating these principles as they had been dealt with by various masters of war. The campaigns which he selected for this purpose were Turenne's campaign of 1675, Villars's campaign of 1705, Turenne's of 1652 and 1653, and Henry IV's of 1590.[18]

This is one of the relatively few attempts to deal with strategy which appeared in the writings of the eighteenth century. The advice is sound though it seems somewhat elementary. This is frequently the case with discussions of this subject. Since one can lay down only general rules, which are often in the form of maxims, they seem to be obvious. It remains, of course, for the ingenuity of the generals concerned to apply these basic propositions to the great variety of situations with which they may be faced.

This is the concluding portion of Maizeroy's work. He had attempted to do in it what Guibert did in his *Essai général de tactique*. The chief faults of Maizeroy's work are due to the fact that Maizeroy could not get completely away from the spirit of system, from the doctrinaire point of view, even though he was by no means as seriously afflicted with it as was his colleague, Mesnil-Durand.   Few capable officers would any longer admit the *ordre profond* as suitable for general combat, yet Maizeroy continued to insist upon it and upon the inevitable victories which it would gain over formations in less depth. Aside from these flaws, the *Théorie de la guerre* is a good handbook of the military art of the time.

Another author who was involved in the controversy between the two orders was Leroy de Bosroger. He was an advocate of the *ordre profond* who declared that there was much agreement between himself and Joly de Maizeroy for whom he had much praise. He dealt with the employment and role of columns in his *The Elementary Principles of Tactics*. He had his own variations of the column using principles of formation which were quite different from those of the authors previously discussed.

Bosroger declared that the column had been a bone of contention ever since the days of Folard. Both sides had been wrong in their procedures. The advocates of the *ordre mince* dwelt too much on the column's defects from which no order was totally exempt. Those of the *ordre profond* laid it open the more to attack by their useless arguments in its defense. "Thus, by adhering too closely to trifles, useful systems are decried, and a good cause is often lost by wrong proceedings." [19] It was Bosroger's purpose, so he declared, to lay aside prejudice and examine the methods of forming columns, showing their defects and advantages without exaggerating either.

Like Maizeroy, Bosroger made a distinction between column and phalanx, the latter having less depth than front. The advantages of the former were to be found in impetuosity and violence of shock. The latter had a great advantage in its resisting powers, forming the most effective defense in an open plain. Since any column may act as a phalanx (though the reverse is not true), "the shock of the one and the resistance of the other decides the question and confirms the superiority of the column over all orders known." [20] Thus Bosroger declared himself as a thorough partisan of the *ordre profond*. He did not accept, however, the validity of Folard's principle of shock, i.e., mass times velocity. He maintained that the impulsion of shock was moral, coming "from the human heart, for danger discourages a man and slows his action." [21] On the other hand, a man would act with more "ardour and courage" when aid was at hand. "He acts upon the offensive or defensive more cheerfully when followed by twenty men than two." [22]

The disadvantages of the column were, according to Bosroger: (1) the slaughter which hostile artillery executed upon such deep files; (2) the difficulty of maintaining order in the interior of so deep a body; and (3) the lengthening of its files in marching which prevented the rear from stopping simultaneously with the head, and also from turning to march by either flank without confusion. Whatever other imperfections it might have were common to other formations and could not be imputed to the column as an object of particular censure. Bosroger thought that the advantages of the column outweighed the disadvantages.

There were two general ways proposed for the formation of columns. The first was by doubling the files. This he rejected. The second was by placing the companies of a battalion one behind the other, which always gave the same depth of twenty-four and a front which varied with the companies' strength. Bosroger did not like this either, for the spaces left between the divisions of the column made it a marching column.[23] He also declared that the officers of each battalion formed two files which might be carried off by a couple of cannon shots. No troops should be exposed to such an eventuality. He complained further that the resulting columns were too large and took an immense time to form. They left gaps through which the enemy might penetrate to surround and attack them on every side. Moreover, such large bodies were not necessary to break the opposing line for it could not resist a formation half as deep as the proposed twenty-four man files.[24]

Having rejected the columns which had previously been proposed, Bosroger proceeded first to set up a series of principles for forming columns, and then to set forth his own method of doing so. First, the head and sides of a column must have an invariable proportion to each other, so that however the size of the companies and consequently the size of the column varied it would always have the properties of a column, i.e., a depth in excess of its front. Second, all the parts of the column must be so disposed that the officers could preserve order and regularity within it, and so that no confusion could result from its density, from the difficulty of communicating orders, or from the obstacles which prevented the officers from continuous observation of the men. Third, the companies must be so arranged that after having pierced the enemy's line, some could roll up the flanks exposed by the rupture. Fourth, the column must be able to form so near the enemy that it could not suffer from their artillery, and have the advantage of such speed that it could not be attacked during ployment, and of such arrangement that mutual aid could be given in case it should be attacked.

There were two different kinds of columns according to Bosroger. There were columns of simple files, that is to say, composed of companies on a depth of three, thereby providing a depth of three or six men greater than its front. There were also columns of double files composed of companies on a depth of six which resulted in columns whose depth was six or twelve men greater than their front. His larger columns would also be of two kinds since they were formed of four smaller ones of one or the other of the above types. This would not cause complications, according to Bosroger, for they passed successively from the simplest to the most complex by regular degrees in his maneuvers.[25]

Since companies were never at full strength in war times, the same maneuvers sometimes resulted in columns and sometimes in phalanxes. He based his maneuvers on a strength of thirty-six men per company instead of the nominal sixty-three. The companies should always have that many. If there were more they should be sent to the left at the moment of forming column and ranged in platoons or other divisions. If there were not enough for this purpose, at the moment of forming column, the surplus could be sent to the front to fire a few shots as skirmishers. They could then retire behind the column upon signal, or they could be sent there in the first place, as the commander deemed best. Under these conditions, a column of single files might be formed at any time from three companies in four seconds! [26]

Bosroger's method of forming column was: "Let the middle [company 1] front the enemy, if it is to keep its ground while the two others [2, 3], on the right and left are to make a turn and draw up in a square behind the wings of the company in front." [27] (See Figure 29.) [28] If there was any fear of being surrounded then

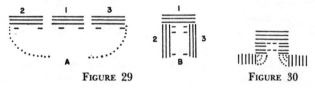

FIGURE 29   FIGURE 30

a fourth company could close in the rear. This column might be formed, Bosroger asserted, without stopping while advancing toward the enemy. The maneuver might actually be delayed until one was within fifteen paces of the enemy! In such a case, the companies which were to form the heads of the columns continued the advance at the word of command, while those that were to form the sides moved to right and left, respectively, and then made a quarter-wheel by files, placing themselves in a square, as described above, behind the lead companies, and continuing the advance at the same rate of speed.[29] (See Figure 30.) [30]

It was Bosroger's contention that his column fulfilled all of the four principles of a column which he had expounded. Whatever the number in the companies, they would always form a column if they were equal in size. The six officers acting in the space between the ranks would be able to preserve order within the column. The companies could attack the flanks of the breach by making only one motion, a facing. Finally, the little time required for the column's formation left the enemy no time to attack it during ployment nor to annoy it with artillery before it was upon the hostile line. Some might object that not all the files would be thirteen or sixteen deep. He admitted that four would be only three deep, but he thought that since the file closers were directly behind them that would perhaps make them superior to those which were sixteen deep.[31]

There are a number of dubious features about Bosroger's columns and tactics. It would seem extremely doubtful that the ployment could be accomplished in four seconds, whatever geometry might indicate. The movement involved a facing followed by a right-wheel by threes for twelve ranks. It would take more than four seconds just to give the commands. It is even more dubious to form the columns at a distance of only fifteen paces from the enemy. Not even Mesnil-Durand was so audacious. From all appearances, Bosroger would advance in line until ployment, since his companies were all on a level until then. This would presumably involve a fire action. It certainly would on the part of the defenders. It must be assumed that the defensive troops were putting up a last-ditch resistance, otherwise it would not be necessary to form columns at all at the late moment which Bosroger proposed. This meant that the ployment would be made at point-blank range under the heavy rolling volleys of the enemy. It is most doubtful, to say the least, that any discipline would be sufficient to enable troops to carry out even this simple maneuver under such a fire, even if the enemy did not press forward upon them while it was being executed. It is also doubtful, furthermore, that the lead companies would push forward with that impulsion, which the advocates of the *ordre profond* extolled so much, when they could not be sure that the column was forming behind them according to schedule.

It would seem that Bosroger denied the chief advantages of columns to his tactics by the long delay in ployment. The other advocates of columns never tired of telling how impossible it was for lines to advance without opening and wavering, and how rapidly columns could move upon the enemy. Bosroger must be in line to form his columns, and thus would appear to have to advance in line, which his fellow partisans claimed was impossible without heavy loss and disorder. If his lines were in disorder, it would be even less probable that he could form his columns within his scanty time limit. Since his front rank would be only three paces from the enemy when the column was completed, and since only half of the files would be deeper than those of the enemy, it is difficult to see what advantages would be gained over remaining in line right to the final clash.

Bosroger was caught in the dilemma of trying to avoid the heavy losses that artillery could inflict upon columns. Hence, his

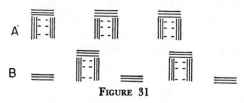

FIGURE 31

delay in forming his attack columns, but his attempted compromise failed to accomplish its purpose. In trying to rest his tactics upon the advantages of both formations, he fell between two stools.

For a full battalion, Bosroger gave two formations. A battalion was composed of nine companies counting the grenadiers. It might form three columns each of three companies which he called bastion-columns (see Figure 31A). It might also form two columns with three companies in line, one between the columns and the others on the flanks which he called bastion-like-columns (see Figure 31B).[32]

To form columns of double files required companies twice the size of those needed to form columns of single files, that is, companies seventy-two strong. To form such columns one first formed single file columns. Then the side companies placed themselves back to back behind the center company. The companies then doubled and closed their files; the first on its center and the other two on it, leaving, however, a distance of a pace between them and their adjacent flanks where the file closers could stand. Those of the two side companies went to the rear of the column.[33] (See Figure 32.)[34] The resulting column had the same front as the single file column, namely, twelve men, while its depth was only slightly greater, being eighteen instead of fifteen men.

Bosroger claimed that it did not expose the troops since, if the commander judged it dangerous to continue the maneuver, he might suspend it after completing the formation of the single file column.

The advantages of this formation were that it gave a solid column and concentrated twice the number of men on the same

FIGURE 32

ground. Bosroger preferred the single file column. There were certainly some additional difficulties which the double file columns had, over and above those attached to the single ones. The chief of these was that companies twice as large were required to form the former type as to form the latter. Quite apart from the fact that the normal company at full strength had only sixty-three men, the normal wastage of war would prevent their ever being at the required strength in the field unless the companies had a normal complement well in excess of the seventy-two required for the formation. It would seem that it could only be formed by using six companies of thirty-six instead of three larger ones. This would in turn leave three excess companies in each battalion.

It is evident, from the foregoing discussion, that Bosroger's tactics leave much to be desired. It would seem, although he appeared to be much less doctrinaire than his contemporary fellow partisans, particularly Mesnil-Durand, that his tactics were even less practical.

The essential parts of Bosroger's system which pertain to the controversy under discussion are included in the account given above. Like all the partisans of the *ordre profond,* he felt that the tactical changes brought about by the improvement in firearms were not justified.

Our regulations are much inferior to the phalanx and have nothing but the single effect of firearms to counterbalance all its advantages. The effect, however, of firearms is an artificial power, and does not originally belong to the manner of disciplining troops, the sole aim of which should be to employ men's natural action. It is man, therefore, and not this fire, which is to be considered as the principal agent; from hence we may, I think infer that, this method is very much inferior to the phalanx, and still more so to the Roman arrangement, which so far surpassed that of Greece.[35]

It is apparent from this quotation that Bosroger adhered to the ideas of the advocates of the *ordre profond* that tactics was primarily a matter of geometry and should be governed by it rather than by the properties of the weapons employed.

XII

Du Teil

The chapters of the *Essai général* which Guibert devoted to artillery were supplemented and amplified by a very influential book, *De l'usage de l'artillerie nouvelle dans la guerre de campagne,* published in 1778, by the Chevalier Jean du Teil (1738-1820), a distinguished officer of the Royal Artillery. He, and his older brother, Baron Joseph du Teil, also a distinguished artillery officer, were closely connected with the early phases of the career of Napoleon Bonaparte. Jean had been an officer in the Regiment of La Fère into which Napoleon was commissioned in 1785, and it would seem a safe inference that his doctrines were influential there. This regiment was sent, in 1788, to the artillery school at Auxonne, then commanded by the baron. There Napoleon became one of the baron's favorite pupils. Some years later he spent a holiday at the baron's chateau discussing military questions with him. Liddell Hart declares that direct inference would indicate that Napoleon studied Bourcet's manuscript in Baron du Teil's library, as the latter came from the same district and had served with Bourcet in Broglie's army in Germany during the Seven Years' War.[1]

This visit to the elder Du Teil's by Napoleon took place shortly before his Corsican adventures in the early part of the Revolution. On his return to France after the expulsion of his family from Corsica, Napoleon found the younger Du Teil in command of the artillery of the Army of Italy. The latter made him his assistant, and it was in this role that Napoleon had his first opportunity to play an important part, commanding the artillery at the siege of Toulon.

The influence of the Du Teils upon Napoleon is thus clear and direct. Napoleon was trained by them and opened his career under their auspices. The employment of artillery related in his memorandum on the defense of Corsica and other early writings, and which was practiced at the siege of Toulon and in his later campaigns, was based upon the theories of the younger Du Teil. To those theories it is now necessary to turn.

Du Teil opened by declaring that the great improvements recently made in the French artillery had so increased the rapidity of its movement and service, that it was more than ever necessary to study the best use to be made of ordinance in field warfare.

One will see that these changes have rendered the tactics of artillery more skillful, its principles more enlightened, more susceptible to being developed, and to being adapted to all the actions of war. In considering the relations which it can have with the tactics of infantry, one can judge that, relying upon each other, they become formidable, the one by the other. It results from this union and from this reciprocal support, that our enemies will triumph with difficulty over these great advantages, whose harmony so evidently constitutes the strength of armies.[2]

Du Teil was a strong advocate of mobility in warfare. In this, he followed Guibert closely which is not surprising since he leaned heavily upon the latter, as he acknowledged in a footnote. The ideas of Guibert about artillery agreed closely with those of Du Teil except in one important aspect. Guibert was of the old opinion that artillery was an auxiliary of the infantry and not an independent arm itself. At least, he was of this opinion when he wrote the *Essai général*. Du Teil recognized, on the other hand, that the great improvement which had been carried out in the artillery enabled it to take its place as a fully independent arm. He, therefore, coupled Guibert's work with the writings of Mesnil-Durand and Maizeroy, and condemned their opinion that a numerous artillery was a serious inconvenience and handicap to an army.[3] Guibert was fearful that a great mass of guns and a huge ammunition train would destroy mobility. The latter, it will be remembered, was his vital concern. Du Teil recognized that the reforms had so greatly increased the mobility of the artillery itself, that it was not necessary to reduce its numbers. On the contrary, he recognized that this mobility would permit more artillery to be used and provide more fire power. In general, however, there is a strikingly close parallel between the

ideas of Du Teil and Guibert which is clearly apparent upon reading the two works.

Du Teil declared that it was not surprising that, when Vauban and Coehorn were vying with each other, artillery's role should be considered solely that of siege warfare. Things were different in his day. "But it is true . . . that the destiny of fortresses almost always depends upon that of battles, that they [fortresses] ought to be considered only accessories, that finally the system of war ought to be changed, and that it consist in having armies well *constituted*, mobile and *maneuverable*. It is necessary that the artillery participate in these great changes, and that one distinguish field artillery from siege." [4]

He insisted that the changes made in the French artillery were not due to mere imitation but were the result of tactical requirements. All officers needed to know about these changes and about the execution of artillery, because they should have the greatest confidence in this, which should "second them, support them, and contribute to victory" as much as either of the other arms.[5]

In dealing with the changes made by Gribeauval in the French artillery, Du Teil discussed the Strassbourg tests. Du Teil declared that Gribeauval's changes diminished neither the range nor the accuracy of guns in the field. Even the four-pounder was shown at Strassbourg to have a range of eleven hundred yards at three degrees of elevation. That range, he declared, was so great that the eye can scarcely direct the shots with accuracy, but the multiplicity of shots will nevertheless cause the enemy anxiety.[6]

As a result of the improvements in the carriages, the new guns rolled much easier. A four-pounder could be hauled easily by four or even three horses. It could be handled readily by eight men using braces and levers. They could change position easily and even follow infantry on favorable ground. Four horses or eleven men could move an eight-pounder without difficulty, while six horses or fifteen men could do the same for a twelve-pounder. This ability to manhandle the guns allowed one to leave the horses in shelter, a very important consideration because of the confusion which they caused when in the line. Means had been provided whereby the guns could cross streams or ditches as easily as a small troop of cavalry "and cannonade in marching as quickly as the infantry can withdraw at the double." [7] He went on to speak of other improvements which increased the mobility and accuracy of the guns and cut down wear and tear on the roads.[8]

Having described the new artillery, Du Teil turned to the heart of his subject, the emplacement and the service of the guns, which he defined as follows:

The execution of artillery is the art of emplacing it, of directing its fire, of doing the greatest possible harm to the enemy, and of giving the greatest possible protection to the troops that it sustains. Troops and artillery ought to protect each other. It is indispensible for the artillery to know the tactics of the troops, or at least the results of their principal movements, and the effect, more or less great, which it ought to produce on any maneuver, judging its [the maneuver's] importance, and of the necessity of accelerating its fire or of changing position. It is not less important that infantry and cavalry officers, who have to command all arms, and by consequence artillery, should know the range of the various guns, the manner of emplacing them, and the general results of their execution.[9]

Du Teil laid down again five hundred *toises* as the maximum range, saying that, at ranges beyond this, objects became too indistinct for fire to be at all accurate. This did not mean that guns could not be fired beyond these ranges for a twelve-pounder could carry nineteen hundred yards at six degrees elevation. The eight's and four's could carry almost as far. Eleven hundred remained, however, the maximum effective range in war. For howitzers the most convenient range was one thousand yards at four degrees elevation which provided four or five ricochets on favorable ground. At greater elevations there was no ricochet and one lost the greatest effect of one's shots.[10] Du Teil was very insistent upon the importance of ricochet fire, and he declared later on that artillery should be placed so as to procure a grazing fire whenever possible. A slight elevation would be better than a great one, for the latter produced a plunging fire in which the shots tended to bury themselves rather than ricochet. This reduced the effect of solid shot very much. The closer the enemy came to a battery on a high elevation, moreover, the less he had to fear.[11]

If it was the general's intention to march on the enemy to attack him, said Du Teil, then both troops and artillery should march with the greatest possible rapidity, making use of all available cover. This would frequently surprise and disconcert the enemy. As soon as the artillery got within five hundred to one thousand yards range, it should go into action. It should impose upon the enemy by its more accurate and decisive fire. It was claimed by some that longer guns of heavier caliber would, in such a situation, have the advantage over those of less caliber. This was not the case, said Du Teil, for the latter fired more rapidly. There was no doubt, he claimed, that four-pounders arriving at a gallop, and firing three or four shots to one, would have the advantage over larger guns even if they were twenty-four-pounders. Firing at a good range, they would be sufficient to kill the gunners and horses and to dismount the guns.[12]

In such an attack, the best manner to dispose one's batteries was that which did the greatest damage to the foe. They should be placed so as to bring the largest number of troops under their fire, for a ball did not cease to be deadly until it had lost its force. If it missed the first-line troops, it might injure the reserve by ricochet.[13] This could best be accomplished by placing batteries so as to bear obliquely upon the enemy, if it were possible without being "battered with havoc" in return. However, when one was opposing a column, it was much better to place the battery head on, since one had the advantage of the maximum depth of target in that way. Guns so placed did not have to change direction as they did from a flank position. Their fire was, therefore, more easily adjusted, more rapid, and more deadly. As for battalion guns, they should not limit themselves to firing straight ahead, but whenever possible without too greatly increasing their range, they should cross their fire. Du Teil declared that the infantry should also make use of this principle, long known to the artillery. He disagreed specifically with Guibert, however, saying that infantry could not accomplish this by files, because their arms were not long enough and their files and ranks were not main-

tained with enough order in combat to permit it. It could be
done if a part of the front was obliqued to the remainder.[14]

Du Teil went on in the most famous quotation from his work
to deal with the foundation of his doctrine. "It is necessary to
multiply the artillery on the points of attack which ought to
decide the victory, relieving the batteries which have suffered,
replacing them by others, without the enemy's being able to
notice it, nor to prevail from an advantage which redoubles his
ardor, and discourages your troops. The artillery thus sustained
and multiplied with intelligence, procures decisive results." [15]
This idea Du Teil repeated over and over again—the concentration of artillery so as to procure decisive results. Speaking somewhat further on of the employment of artillery for defending or
attacking entrenched positions, he declared that the principles
were the same as for the open field. He asked rhetorically, "Does
it not follow further, that it is necessary to concentrate on the
principal points and upon the weak parts which are most threatened, the greatest quantity of fire?" [16] Again he laid down the
principle for attacking an entrenched position, a basic rule which
applied to all attacks. "It is necessary to assemble the greatest
number of troops, and a great quantity of artillery, on the points
where one wishes to force the enemy, while one threatens attacks
upon the others. One will impose upon him by movements and
false attacks." [17] The bombardment had for its purpose to demolish the defenses and unsettle the troops of the enemy. When
this had been accomplished, the moment for the infantry assault
had come, and "the victory which the artillery has prepared, then
depends only upon the courage of the troops." [18]

In these passages is set forth clearly the doctrine which
Napoleon came more and more to apply, especially after the
quality of his troops began to deteriorate following his break-up
of the First Grand Army in 1808. It is especially noticeable at
Wagram and the great battles which followed, when it was no
longer Ney or Murat but Drouot and Sénarmont who took the
first place as the most important lieutenants.[19] The doctrine
simply stated is that the attack must be prepared by overthrowing
the defenses and demoralizing the defending troops before the

infantry assault can be launched. It is the role of the artillery to make this preparation according to Du Teil. No clearer case of direct influence can be seen anywhere than that connecting Du Teil with Napoleon. The only point which seems peculiar is that Napoleon, who applied these ideas so clearly at Toulon, took so long to apply them on the battlefield.[20] The answer to that seems to be that his early armies were so superior in quality, and his tactics and strategy enabled him to be so decisively superior at the point of decision, that he did not need anything more for victory. As his opponents closed the gap tactically, and to some extent strategically, at the same time that their resources in men grew, Napoleon lost the advantage of numbers. The quality of his troops declined at the same time. Thus it became more and more necessary for him to rely upon artillery to procure the victories for which the old methods were either insufficient or lacking. It is worth noting that none of these later victories were as decisive as those of the earlier campaigns.

Du Teil declared in connection with the service of guns that "the conservation of munitions is one of the most important objectives in the execution of artillery." [21] Further on he declared, "The principal rules for the serving of artillery were to proportion the fire to the importance of the objective, to husband one's munitions, and conserve them for essential and decisive moments." [22] He declared that troops always complained because the guns did not fire enough, but the officers of other arms should in the future leave off complaining because the guns did not fire all the time and cease disturbing artillery officers in this way. If this principle should be abandoned, the result might well be a lack of ammunition at a critical moment when victory was in balance. Troops remain unconvinced in spite of all this. They should consider the fact that only at great expense, and by so increasing the ammunition trains as to cut down seriously the army's mobility, could one increase the ammunition beyond two hundred rounds per gun and sixty per man for the infantry. The former would not last two hours at two rounds per minute.[23]

Du Teil ran counter to Napoleon's ideas in this matter, for the latter put himself on record in the diametrically opposite sense. He complained that the artillery did not fire enough, that it was an axiom of war that one should not lack ammunition, and that the artillery should fire continuously without calculating expenditure. A gun should always have three hundred rounds with it according to Napoleon. This would be enough for two battles.

The main objective of artillery should be the enemy's troops and not his artillery. There were only two occasions when one was justified in turning one's guns upon those of one's opponents. They were when it was impossible to fire on the hostile troops or when the hostile artillery was having too disquieting an effect upon the troops which one protected. Artillery duels were profitless and should be avoided except in these two cases. It was a useless consumption of ammunition to try and overthrow a battery. Even if one succeeded, he had accomplished nothing, as the troops would still be there to conquer.[24]

Another important general principle set forth by Du Teil was that all of one's guns should never be put in battery unless they could be reinforced from the reserve, for once the enemy knew how many guns were opposed to him, he could concentrate more in his turn against them in order to secure superiority. This, said Du Teil, corresponds to the principle of not disclosing the kind and number of ones troops unless one wished to delude his enemy by a false disposition. Common sense should be used in applying these principles, for obviously one must not allow himself to be beaten in detail.[25] In the same way, batteries should avoid taking position too soon, when they are supporting the true attack, in order not to aid the enemy by giving him time for his counter-dispositions by disclosing the real point of attack too early.[26] Too obvious a collection of munitions frequently discloses the importance of an attack, whether it is real or false, and the number of troops to be employed. The troops should never be posted behind the batteries, as this offers the enemy two targets at once.[27]

It is interesting to note that in discussing the tactics of artillery, to which he added little, he declaimed against an abuse, a survival of old practice which illustrates the spirit of formality still surviving in military practice of his day. This was the custom of always placing the guns of the park with their muzzles pointed towards the enemy, as if, in that position, they were ready to resist him. This was a waste of time, and hence a cause of delay not only in the movements of the park, but in those of the whole army.[28]

Du Teil also discussed a number of detailed subjects, such as the use of artillery in mountain warfare, in crossing rivers, the use of field artillery in sieges, etc. These discussions do not add to the basic doctrines. The importance of these doctrines is obvious not only because of their repercussions upon practice in the great wars which followed their publication by a few years, but also for their general validity. Allowing for the changes brought about by modern ammunition, the basic ideas are still sound.

Tactics at the End of the Eighteenth Century
and during the Great Wars

The result of the maneuvers made at the Camp of Vaussieux was the general discrediting of the system of Mesnil-Durand. Most of the officers were decidedly opposed to it in spite of the continued support of Marshal Broglie. The majority began to come together on the middle ground just as had been the case before Mesnil-Durand revived the massive column for combat in the middle 1750's. All of these moderate officers agreed in rejecting the column of Mesnil-Durand with his exclusiveness and doctrinaire ideas on the one hand and the quite as exclusive predilection of the regulations and ordinances of 1774, 1775, and 1776 on the other. A number of lesser writers advocated a middle ground. Among these was a Baron de Traverse who perhaps best expressed the compromise in his *mémoire, Sur les maneuvres de l'infanterie.*[1] His position was that it is necessary to march and maneuver in column, to advance to the attack in line, and finally to charge home in column of attack. He had, therefore, a greater balance between the two schools than did Castries, Puységur, or Guibert who inclined to some extent toward one side or the other.

In another matter, Traverse expressed well the general ideas of the period. He advocated rapidity in the army's movements and so recommended that the army be divided into several parts each of which could quickly change from one formation to another.[2] This advocacy of the divisional system derived, of course, from Broglie's instruction of 1760 and was accepted almost unanimously in the Army.

One result was to diminish greatly the importance of Pirch's principles of alinement and points of view. This, in turn, resulted in the gradual appearance of doubts about them, even though, but a few short years before, they had been received with enthusiasm and had formed the basis of three successive drill regulations. Most officers followed Guibert in maintaining that regularity in alinement was an ideal incapable of achievement. For a number of years, however, there were some who still believed it to be attainable and even advocated the use of a surveyor's square for attaining it. A great number of regiments adopted it. "Nevertheless, they quickly grew tired of the use of topographical apparatus in the course of maneuvers, and they prefer to declare that, decidedly, it is impossible to regulate with exactness the march of a long line in battle." [3] The Army became content to concentrate on maintaining intervals and marching on the same level by means of a regular step sustained without accelerating or slowing.

This opinion was already widespread when General von Saldern's *Éléments de la tactique de l'infanterie* appeared in French about 1783. This work made known to French officers that the defects of the principles of points of view led to their being abandoned in Prussia just when Pirch was introducing them in France. As this book became known, it apparently stimulated a still greater dissatisfaction with the existing ordinance. An important *mémoire, Résumé des principes de tactique du général de Saldern,* was written by a German officer in French service. Colin attributed to this *mémoire* the abandoning of Pirch's principles and the determination to draw up a new ordinance.[4] According to this *mémoire,* the essential thing in marching was not to maintain all the battalions on exactly the same level but to maintain the intervals, so as to have room for the battalion guns, and to put all of one's men in action without ever having to break off files.[5] This idea was already current in the Army. The provisional instruction of 1788, which set forth new drill regulations, was much influenced by this document, containing as it did the chief dispositions and even some of the very words of the *mémoire.*[6]

For several years, there had been discussion of suppressing the third rank of infantry. This discussion was expressive of a tendency in the opposite direction from the ideas of the extreme partisans of the *ordre profond.* Mesnil-Durand had already proposed this for his chasseurs, that is, those of his troops who fought

by fire. Frederick had frequently ranged his men on two ranks.[7]
A number of French officers began to think that a formation in
two ranks was logical for fire action, since it was generally recognized that the fire of the third rank was not wholly effective. In
the years immediately following, this formation began to appear
officially in the ordinances.

The result of all these tendencies and *mémoires* was the determination to draw up a new ordinance to replace that which
had been in force for the last twelve years. The Provisional Ordinance of 1788 was very different from those of 1774, 1775, and
1776 which had preceded it. It summed up all the progress which
had been made since the Seven Years' War. It was hastily drawn
up, however, and "soon succumbed under the weight of innumer-
able criticisms of detail." [8]

The Council of War, which was instituted in 1787, delegated
to two of its members, the Comte de Puységur and the Duc de
Guines, the task of drawing up a new ordinance of infantry.
Both were partisans of the *ordre profond*. Ten regiments were
assigned to them, which allowed them to experiment with the
proposed maneuvers as they were formulated. Within a few days,
the Council received and approved that part of the instruction on
the school of the soldier. This fixed the ordinary pace at seventy-
six two-foot paces per minute and the accelerated pace at one
hundred ten.

The Council also decreed that fire by command be executed
with the first rank kneeling. It reestablished the fire by platoons.
It ordered that the soldier be trained to execute oblique fire
which was to be used only when crossfire could not be obtained by
the direction of the troops. It further decreed that in fire by
files (at will) only the first two ranks should fire. The third rank
was to remain still and replace the soldiers of the front ranks as
they were killed or wounded. This was certainly an unrealistic
provision for one can hardly imagine men standing motionless
under fire, doing nothing. Moreover, it deprived the battalion of
one-third of its fire power.

The completed instruction was issued on May 20, 1788. The
way in which it was organized indicated that it was drawn up with

the training of troops primarily in view. "They [the editors] did not limit themselves to setting forth the formations and maneuvers, but even the manner of instructing in them, not fearing repetitions, dividing the ordinance into schools and into lessons, specifying what ought to be done in each, and how one ought to do it." [9] It might be added, that this pattern was followed in the ordinance which replaced that of 1788.

As is quite evident from the foregoing, Guibert was no more the editor of this ordinance than he was of the preceding ones. His influence was very strong, however, for it was his tactics which were adopted and became official. The ordinance went back for inspiration to that of 1769 for light troops, drawn up by Guibert's father, rather than to the intermediary ones. It did not abandon entirely the principles of alinement which had dominated the last three drill regulations, but they were modified and much reduced, being relegated to a couple dealing with the march in column and in line. On the other hand, the ordinance adopted the columns of Guibert. It specified that evolutions of several battalions would most frequently be carried out by battalions in mass, though evolutions in line, sometimes imposed by conditions, were not excluded.

The elementary movements were perfected and simplified. The platoons were given more flexibility by making them march frequently by the flank, deploy by files, and so on. Wheelings were to be made by fixed or moving pivots as might be required. The ordinance adopted a column open at half intervals in place of the fully opened and closed columns which had some of the advantages of both. It was short enough and yet more flexible than the closed column.

An even greater innovation was the passage from three ranks to two, which enabled a general on occasion to assume the latter formation. This evolution would seem to indicate a recognition of the unreality of the provision regarding fire at will which, although it should be the most frequently employed, condemned the third rank to complete immobility. Fire would be either direct or oblique, executed either standing or marching, and in particular during a battalion's change of front.

The evolutions of several battalions could be executed, as already indicated, either by deployed battalions or in closed columns. A line of battalions could be ployed into close column in either of two ways. If the number of battalions was not too great, then all of them could ploy at once on a given division of one of them as though only one battalion were involved. Otherwise each battalion first ployed into closed column, and then formed on the indicated one by square movements, making a column of masses with four-pace intervals. The ordinance kept the usual two deployments, by the flank from fully open columns, and ahead from closed columns. In the latter case, one deployed the column by massed battalions, and then each battalion individually. The march in line was to be executed by observing the precautions already discussed. One should strive to keep a convenient point of direction, but it was of utmost importance to maintain the intervals and to keep on a level with the guide battalion. Changes of front were executed as in the Ordinance of 1776, where each battalion in column of full intervals marched forward in echelon.

The Ordinance of 1788 was never really put into effect for the events of 1789 put an end to the proceedings. Marshal Broglie became minister of war and suppressed the Council of War, bringing the work to an end. The ordinance fell into oblivion. A large number of criticisms were formulated on the details of the ordinance, especially upon those concerning the march of a line of several battalions in battle. There was hardly any attention paid to tactics during the next two years, but the threat of invasion in 1791 turned thoughts back to it. One would think that little change would occur, but the two ordinances which appeared in 1791 took another step in the direction of the *ordre profond* by adopting the column of attack.[10]

When the National Guard was formed in 1789, it was not drilled according to the Provisional Ordinance of 1788. Instead the Ordinance of 1776 was reedited for this purpose. It soon became apparent that the "meticulous rules of Pirch" and complicated commands of the ordinance were not satisfactory for an improvised militia. The military committee, instituted on October 2, 1789, was charged with drawing up a simpler instruction for the National Guard. Colonel Vicomte de Noailles of the Chasseurs d'Alsace presided over the committee and was the dominant spirit in the instruction which appeared on January 1, 1791. Although the majority of the committee were partisans of the *ordre profond,* they declared in their introduction, "The habitual formation of the National Guard will be on two ranks." [11]

The introduction was of great importance, for it clearly set forth the compromise which had been worked out in French tactical doctrines. It reads in part:

Without entering here into the question which is raised between the partisans of the *ordre mince* and those of the *ordre profond.* . . . We do not hesitate to establish that the march in column is that which the National Guards ought to prefer. They ought to pounce upon the enemy at the instant the point of attack is determined and conserve thus the incontestable advantage of the French in hand to hand combat.

After having indicated the attack in column as the most favorable for the battalions of National Guards, we do not, nevertheless, exclude the deployed order; we have sought only to simplify it.[12]

Although the editors of the new ordinance declared formally in favor of the attack in the *ordre profond* for the bayonet assault, they did not turn to the system of Mesnil-Durand for their model. They borrowed their methods of maneuver from Guibert instead. Moreover, they gave a large place to evolutions in line although they did not believe in the superiority of the *ordre mince* for combat.

Most of the maneuvers were drawn from the previous or-dinance and simplified, but Noailles added to them the column of attack "on the center" which was almost identical with that of the Ordinance of 1766.[13] It was lighter and more flexible than that of Mesnil-Durand which was tried at Vaussieux, because it involved one battalion only. For this reason, all that has been said condemning the central deployment does not apply to the column of attack of 1791. Being the most rapid method of ploy-ment and deployment it was invaluable at the critical moment of the bayonet attack. It will be remembered that Guibert's system

made use of ployment on the central division as well as each of
the other divisions and that it was the quickest way of using his
method. Noaille's column of attack used Guibert's method. The
third, second, and first platoons ployed behind the fourth while
the sixth, seventh, and eighth ployed behind the fifth, thus giving
a column of divisions.[14]

The work of the Committee of War was not completed with
the issuance of the Ordinance for the National Guard. It proceeded then to draw up a new ordinance for the regular infantry.
This was issued on August 1, 1791, and was by far the most important of eighteenth-century regulations. It remained in force
throughout the period of the Revolution, that of Napoleon, and
for many years thereafter, being replaced only in 1831 under the
July Monarchy. It was the culmination of all the intellectual
fermentation of the French Army during the century, fixing tactics
after the many variations of preceding regulations upon the intermediate ground represented by the tactics of Guibert. It contained the essentials of his system, columns for maneuver, line for
combat, while retaining the evolutions of the line of earlier regulations without insisting on the concern for alinement and regularity which had characterized these. These evolutions, vehe-
mently denounced by many as impractical for war, were all,
nevertheless, actually employed with all their variations on the
battlefields of the great wars from 1792 to 1815. It is, therefore,
necessary to examine the ordinance in some detail.

There have been misconceptions about it, as there have been
about so many aspects of eighteenth-century tactics. Of all the
erroneous opinions held about the latter, the most serious and
most common was that which held that the Ordinance of 1791
was the work of the partisans of the *ordre mince*. Colin quoted
a passage as being typical of this point of view. "The regulation
of 1791, which lasted nearly a century, was hardly more than a
reproduction of the regulation of 1776, elaborated after the Seven
Years' War under the influence of Prussian methods; it was accordingly the continuation of Prussian tactics in all its forms." [15]
He attacked this and similar views, recalling how the Ordinance
of 1776 followed the provisional instructions of 1774 and 1775 in

conforming strictly to Pirch's principles,[16] whereas that of 1791, like those immediately preceding, reduced them to almost nothing. He declared that the Ordinance of August 1, 1791, presented the greatest analogy to those of 1788 and January 1, 1791, while differing profoundly from that of 1776. That difference is apparent in an analysis of the Ordinance of 1791. He declared that the reason the evolutions of the line formed so large a part of the ordinance was not that the editors of 1791 felt that these evolutions had a greater importance than did the editors of 1788. Rather the former, intending to give a complete regulation, went into great detail in all matters. Since the evolutions of the line are the most complex and difficult of all maneuvers, this gave rise to "a cloud of explanations." The ordinance added no new maneuvers to those of 1788 but did go into much greater detail.[17] To this may be added the observation that this ordinance was the basis of the Revolutionary and Napoleonic tactics. Could anyone mistake the varied and flexible tactics of those wars with the formalism of Prussian tactics which Pirch and his followers represented?

The men who drew up the Ordinance of August 1, 1791, had worked with Noailles on that of January 1. They were partisans of the *ordre profond,* but by 1791 these partisans had rejected the system of Mesnil-Durand with its complications and limitations. They had come to full agreement with Guibert, accepting his system of columns and of ployment and deployment. They had come to see that the linear formation was not exceptional and, therefore, that the march and evolution of the line could not be excluded from the regulation. "In truth, it seems that in 1791, there was between the partisans of the *ordre profond* and those of the *ordre mince* only a difference of appreciation of the relative frequency of attacks in line and in column in combat, no one denying, moreover, that both would often be employed. The question reduced to these terms would be definitely resolved on the field of battle." [18]

The Ordinance of 1791, although drawn up by partisans of the *ordre profond,* thus represented the compromise ideas which had come to prevail as a result of the controversy between the two orders. One of its chief differences from the previous ordinances was its greater attention to detail; its more minute wording gave longer and clearer explanations of the subjects covered. Concerning this detailed content, Colin pointed out that it is necessary to consider the situation in the Army when the regulations of latter part of the eighteenth century were drawn up. It was necessary to establish order, precision, and discipline in troops which had been incapable of rapid deployment at Rossbach. Broglie's regulation of 1764 had first set the general style for modern regulations, and some of the formalism, particularly in the school of the soldier, survived from it. Generally speaking, the problem of the later regulations was not so much that of giving new formations and maneuvers as that of giving sound principles and practical procedures for assuring such matters as cohesion, maintenance of distances and direction, alinement of major units, etc. The series of regulations beginning with 1750 led down to those of 1788 and 1791 "establishing with all the detail necessary, those thousand precautions which have become so familiar to us." It is possible when one becomes familiar with them and forms habits and traditions based upon them to abridge them. Then they were essential, and it was this very detail which was responsible for the "rare perfection" with which the volunteer battalions maneuvered at Jemappes. It was even due in part to the same detail that improvised officers became good instructors so soon. "It is in comparing Rossbach and Jemappes that one can appreciate the work of the tacticians and instructors of the time of Louis XVI." [19]

The ordinance retained the organization of French infantry regiments given by Choiseul's ordinance in 1762. There were two battalions to each regiment. Each battalion was composed of eight companies of infantry (fusiliers) and one of grenadiers. The companies were identical with the platoons which were numbered in order from right to left. The grenadier companies were stationed on the outer flanks of their battalions, to the right of the first or right battalion, and to the left of the second. When the battalion drilled alone its grenadier company remained attached to it, but when the regiment drilled together, the second grenadier company joined the first forming on its left. Each battalion was divided into two wings or demi-battalions. Each company was divided into two sections, two companies together formed a division.[20]

The ordinance declared that on a peace footing the troops would be drawn up on two ranks. This was done because it was desirable that the troops occupy approximately the same ground as when formed in three ranks on a war footing. The suppression of the formation on two ranks as a field formation was another major difference from the previous regulations. One can only say that it was a retrograde step, for practically all soldiers agreed that the fire of the third rank was not effective, particularly when the troops were firing at will. Some expressed themselves in even more condemnatory terms. Nor were any of the methods to employ the third rank, such as having them load fusils for the second rank, ever very successful.

This ordinance, like the preceding ones, was divided into "schools" and "lessons." There were three schools; those of the soldier, the platoon, and the battalion. The ordinance was very explicit in stressing the importance of instructing the troops. The colonel, or in his absence the officer commanding, was made responsible for the instruction of the regiment. All officers must know all three schools and be able to command and explain them. All noncommissioned officers must be able to do the same for the first two.[21]

In line with this, Section II of the ordinance, the school of the soldier, pointed out the importance of this basic part of the training to all which followed. The instruction of recruits, it declared, was closely connected with, and had a strong influence on, the discipline of companies. Upon this depended, in turn, that of battalions. The "utmost care and attention" was enjoined upon all superior officers in this matter with the adjutants being particularly required, by turn, to attend this drill constantly. The captains were declared responsible to the colonels for the training of their recruits and "will, by no means, neglect it." [22] In short, the ordinance spared no pains to insure a thorough instruction of all troops, individually and collectively, and went into minute detail as to how it was to be done.

The quick step was reduced from one hundred ten to one hundred paces per minute, although it was permitted to increase this to one hundred twenty when charging under fire. The regular step, used for drilling, was retained at seventy-six. This subject was long under discussion, in fact, right through the great wars. General Schauenbourg, who had a good reputation as an instructor of troops, while commanding the Army of Helvetia in 1798, retained the seventy-six pace step but prescribed a route step of ninety paces per minute. General Meunier also favored ninety, but wished to keep the one hundred twenty for its prescribed purpose. He proposed it in 1791, and it was adopted by General Custine from experience in 1793. General Fririon, writing in 1822, wished the faster rate to replace the seventy-six as the regular step. He denied the regulation's claim that it could be maintained for any length of time only at the expense of cohesion. He insisted that lack of experience was the real cause and that, if troops were drilled frequently in it, they could double seventy-six. The real importance of all this lay in the field of maneuver, for speed in maneuvering on the battlefield was a vital factor in victory. If one army could complete a maneuver in say two-thirds the time it took its opponent, the latter would obviously have little chance of countering it.[23]

The most important subject in Section III, "School of the Platoon," was the methods of fire. The ordinance provided that it must be done on three ranks.[24] There were two kinds of fire permitted, that by salvos (*feu de peloton, feu de bataillon*, etc.) [25] and the fire of two ranks at will.[26] In the former, the entire unit fired together on command. The latter was more complicated. Only the first two ranks fired. The third rank was to load and pass its fusils forward to the second rank. This latter, however, was always to fire the same fusil twice except for the first time. The first file opened fire with the second file presenting its fusils the instant the first fired. A rolling fire was produced by the initial discharge, after which the men loaded and fired individually without waiting for the others.

Both the return to three ranks and the suppression of most types of fire were long the subject of discussion and of widespread dissatisfaction within the Army. This was true of the *feu de chaussée*, which was reestablished by General Schauenbourg's instruction as it had been in the Regulation of 1788, and the *feu de rang*. General Meunier favored the former for retreating and General Duhesme expressed the same opinion.[27]

It was generally admitted that the first of the two types of fire sanctioned by the ordinance was never used in war. Foreign armies claimed to make good use of it and also of the *feu de rang*, the latter especially when in square formation. Each rank fired consecutively and consequently could not be caught without fire by cavalry.[28]

The French Army, however, used only the *feu de deux rangs*. Colin insisted that even this was never performed as prescribed by the ordinance. He cited General Fririon for support. The latter declared that he never saw a French first rank kneel, as laid down by the ordinance, and that it was impossible to keep a French third rank impassive under fire. They also insisted on firing, if only in the air so as not to injure their comrades. "It is thus evident that, in fire, the third rank, or a third of the unit, is worthless."[29]

Marshal Saint-Cyr expressed himself to the same effect,[30] saying that they would fire even when formed on four to six ranks and that without waiting for the command if it was too long delayed. This was supported further by Captain Tanski, a veteran of the Grand Army, who declared[31] that a soldier did not have enough confidence in another's fusil to rely upon it. He noted several times that soldiers only pretended to change fusils.

Saint-Cyr declared[32] that one-quarter of combat losses were due to wounds inflicted by the third rank upon the first two, and that the proportion was even greater when the troops were largely recruits as at the battles of Lützen and Bautzen. According to the Marshal, Napoleon had believed that these wounds were due to self-maiming, but that having been brought round by the marshal to the above view, Napoleon suppressed the third rank. Colin doubted Saint-Cyr's story. It was very strange, he said, for this to have gone on for twenty years, especially when battalions had frequently fought with two-thirds recruits.

Tanski also opposed Saint-Cyr. He declared that he had fought in second rank as much as in third and had never been wounded, nor heard of any who had. If Saint-Cyr's charge had been true, it would not have been tolerated so long. He preferred to believe that in Napoleon's last campaigns unwilling conscripts mutilated themselves in hope of discharge rather than that soldiers had so long failed to note so easily verifiable a fact. Tanski thought that Napoleon was led to suppress the third rank because of inferiority of numbers and the necessity to occupy equal fronts with his opponents.[33] Tanski's conjecture was supported by General Chambray who asserted:

In the French Army, when losses had rendered battalions too weak, one formed them on two ranks. Two days before the battle of Leypsick, Napoleon ordered the formation of the infantry on two ranks; and until the end of the war, a part of the infantry was formed in this way, while the other continued to form on three ranks.[34]

Marshal Marmont and Napoleon himself opposed the third rank as well as Chambray, who declared further:

The principal reason that one gives in favor of the formation on three ranks is that infantry, having more depth in such a case, has more solidity for resisting the charges of infantry and cavalry. That reason is really specious. Actually, it has been seen that infantry . . . never meets at the bayonet; it has then to consider only fire and the influence of the cadre. The influence of the cadre is greater when there are only two ranks to watch instead of three. The same consideration applies to cavalry charges which are always repulsed by fire, when the infantry is firm and when it [the cavalry] charges it from the front.[35]

The opinion of the soldiers on the third rank was nearly unanimous. Some, however, would keep it for special purposes. Marshal Ney [36] liked it as a reserve force. He also testified to the dislike which the troops had for the *feu de deux rangs* as prescribed. This dislike disappeared when the third rank did not fire but was held for use as a reserve. General Brenier, writing between 1825 and 1830,[37] admitted all the arguments for two ranks; nevertheless, he desired to retain the third rank for use as skirmishers. The only partisan of the third rank in the French Army after the great wars was General Meunier, although General Pelet was undecided and kept it provisionally. Thus the survivors of the wars who expressed themselves were, with these exceptions, all partisans of the formation on two ranks.[88]

All of this supports the conclusion, therefore, that the return of the ordinance to the formation on three ranks was definitely a retrograde step. The question that remains is why, in the face of such a large preponderance of opinion, that formation was retained almost to the end of the long wars which followed. It seems difficult to assume that lack of time in a period of war was alone responsible. The change was a fairly simple one, and could have been accomplished without even bothering to make a formal change in the ordinance. It would not have involved changing maneuvers or evolutions.

Section IV of the ordinance dealt with the school of the battalion. The formation of columns both open and closed was contained in Part II. Open columns were to be formed in the usual manner, breaking the line by simultaneous quarter-wheels when formed forward and filing into column to the rear when formed to the rear.[39] Closed columns were formed by the method of Guibert, the diagonal filing into position in column, usually by platoons.[40]

Route columns were the subject of Part III [41] of the ordinance which emphasized the necessity of sound and accurate instruction concerning them in order that troops could deploy rapidly if suddenly attacked on the march.

A special maneuver, the *prompte manoeuvre*, was restored by the Ordinance of 1791.[42] It had as its purpose the rapid completion of a column turn of an open column when that became necessary. Thus, for example, if an open column, engaged in a turn, had suddenly to form a line, the *prompte manoeuvre* would enable it to shorten the time necessary for the column to take the new direction. To perform it, all the companies which had not yet made the turn would face to the right, assume the quick step, and, led by their captains, march by files on the shortest distance to place themselves successively in column. See Figure 33.

A closed column could change front by filing either to the right or left onto the new line instead of making a column turn for the purpose.[43] This movement allowed it to change front without advancing.

In Part IV of the school of the battalion, the ordinance dealt with methods of forming lines from open, half-open, and closed

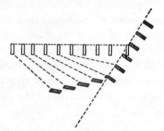

FIGURE 33

columns. Four methods of forming line with open columns were recognized. There was the standard simultaneous left quarter-wheel into line when the column arrived at the left of its position in line.[44] There was the processional movement of successive right-wheels into line as each company cleared the unit ahead of it.[45] This was for use when the column arrived at the right of its ground. Both of these methods were preceded by column turns in order to place the columns parallel to the line to be occupied. Both were standard maneuvers long used for forming lines from open columns.

There was, further, the simultaneous left-half-quarter-wheel followed by an oblique march and successive right-half-quarter-wheels by each company on arriving at the line.[46] This method was also for use when the column arrived at the right of its position. It had the advantage of not requiring the column to be parallel to the proposed line. It could be performed with the column perpendicular or at an angle to it. See Figure 34B.

The fourth method was for use when the column arrived in

front of the line it was to occupy instead of the rear. In such a case the column was halted, and the leading company counter-marched to the left into line. The remaining companies faced to the right and filed into line by their right flanks.[47] This formed a line with all units in the right order from right to left; a line which made front to the direction from which the troops had come. See Figure 34A.

A column open at half intervals formed a line by means of the same four methods.[48] It employed the second and fourth methods exactly as a column which was open at full intervals. To make

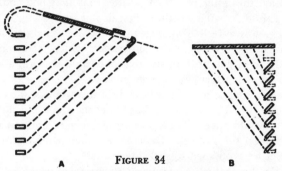

A   FIGURE 34   B

use of the first and third methods, however, it had to open to full intervals. Closed columns were to deploy into line by Guibert's method.[49] The columns were to be perpendicular to the line of deployment before starting the maneuver.

Of the battalion evolutions in line, the only one which needs to be noted is the passage of two lines through each other. As the retreating first battalion neared the second (at twenty paces), all the companies faced to the left. Each company then quarter-wheeled to the right by files which formed columns of three-men fronts which continued the advance toward the second line. The latter doubled files by sections (half-companies) which formed a line with section intervals. The columns of the first line passed through these intervals and then formed a line in the rear by simultaneous left quarter-wheels. The second line, now the first, then undoubled its sections.[50]

The column of attack was formed by central deployment, the

companies of each wing filing behind the two central ones. This ployment was performed standing fast. The deployment was performed in the reverse except that it was done by square rather than diagonal movements.[51] This column differed little from the regular closed column of divisions which most generals felt to be sufficient. General Meunier still preferred the column of attack as late as 1803, but he, too, seems to have abandoned his partisanship for it under the Empire. General Pelet showed that this column, simple as it appeared, had disadvantages which nullified it advantages. He was supported by Generals Morand and Chambray, the latter of whom pointed out that one could not form a column of attack without first deploying.[52]

There was a feeling among a number of generals that the Ordinance of 1791 had many movements which were too complicated and of doubtful utility; that one could perform all essential moves with a few basic movements.

The Ordinance of 1791 followed Guibert in not proscribing inversions of platoons within a battalion, though it did not go as far as he would have. There was a difference of opinion within the Army on the subject. Generals Mathieu Dumas, Meunier, and Pelet were opposed to such inversion.[53]

While the ordinance permitted inversion of platoons, it did not do so for inversion of ranks. A great deal of discussion was carried on as to the basis for assigning men to particular ranks. The ordinance required that troops countermarch whenever they had to make face to the rear. This was a lengthy maneuver requiring much time. It would have been much simplier in such circumstances merely to have deployed into line and then have the line about-face. General Pelet's *Manoeuvres d'un corps d'armée d'infanterie* supported this contention. The general wrote that he had seen this maneuver done many times almost in spite of those who had used it. He himself used it during the retreat from Leipsig to Erfurt in 1813 and also in 1814. It should be understood that this was a temporary measure into which one was forced by circumstances.[54]

On the whole, there was a general satisfaction with the means of ploying and deploying set forth by the ordinance. As Guibert had foreseen, the column of divisions became the basic formation for maneuvering. It was used by battalions as they entered the battlefield, enabling them to move easily to any point, to change the battle order, or the direction of the front. It was simple and easy to handle. The only handicap was the exclusive requirement of the ordinance that it change front from a halt.[55]

The fifth and final section of the ordinance dealt with the evolutions of the line. For purposes of instruction, it assumed a line of eight battalions although the same principles applied to any number. The evolutions proper started with Part II, which dealt with forming columns from line.[56] The methods were the same as for a single battalion which led to the first subject of criticism, namely, the ploying of a line of battalions into a closed column. Every platoon got under way at the same time and moved diagonally to its place in the column. It is obvious that, even with a deployment on the center, the platoons toward the extremities of the line would have a long distance to go. The ployment consequently would take some time to complete. General Schauenbourg declared this maneuver unreasonable and wished each battalion to ploy first and then move to its place in column, while General Meunier proposed that in a column of twelve or more battalions ployment first be executed by brigades of four battalions.[57]

In order to deploy several battalions from a closed column of divisions, each battalion moved out of column by a flank march to right or left, depending upon whether it was before or behind the battalion upon which the deployment was regulated. As each battalion was uncovered, it moved up to the line of deployment. The result was a line of battalions each in column of divisions. In the second part, all the battalions moved outward as a whole by flank marches until they had taken the necessary room for their respective deployments which were then done *à la Guibert*.[58]

Part V, the final part of the fifth section, closed the ordinance by dealing with marches in line and changes of front. These evolutions became progressively more complex and difficult towards the end of the ordinance. It was this part of the regulation which led to the misconception that it represented a complete victory for the partisans of linear tactics—a mere reediting of the Ordinance of 1776.

This final part opened with the rules for marching in line.[59] The six pages devoted to giving rules for this represented all that remained of Pirch's principles which had dominated the regulations of the seventies. These pages concentrated primarily upon the maintenance of the intervals between battalions. The essentials, according to the regulation, were accurate direction on the part of the color-bearer and uniformity of step. This article was vigorously criticized for the reason that off the parade ground no one would have either the occasion or the ability to execute this maneuver. The answer given to this criticism was that one could not devote too much time to accustoming the men to march in order of battle in peacetime and to marching rapidly in that formation so as to receive fewer shots.[60]

The most complex of the evolutions described was changing front for one or two lines.[61] For a single line of eight battalions to change front on the center of the line, fifth battalion, the battalions to the left of the regulating battalion, sixth, seventh, and eighth, formed an open column and then formed on the new line by the third method of forming line from open column.[62] The first three battalions of the line, which were to the right of the regulating battalion, also formed an open column and then formed on the new line by the fourth method of forming line from open columns.[63] The fifth and fourth battalions had special movements. The commanding general placed the first company of the fifth battalion and the eighth company of the fourth battalion individually upon the line of the new front. They acted as markers. Each of the remaining companies of the fifth battalion took part in the general movement by making a half-right-quarter-wheel, marching forward, and making a second right-half-quarter-wheel into line as soon as its right flank arrived on the line. The remaining companies of the fourth battalion formed line to the rear, apparently by about-facing and doing the same as the fifth battalion, then about-facing again.

When two lines changed front perpendicularly forward on the

right, it was done by breaking the battalions forward by right quarter-wheels of companies. This movement resulted in two open columns of companies along the old lines. The first battalion of the old line formed a line forward on its leading company (third method) while the other battalions disengaged their columns to go and arrive opposite the right of their new ground. They then did the same. The second line did the same as the first line except that the first battalion formed line to the rear. The new second line outflanked the new first line by two battalions on the right as a result of this evolution, and was in turn outflanked to the same extent on the left. In other words, the second line was displaced to the right by a two-battalion front. This evolution could be performed to the rear, or both forward and rearward at once on a central pivot instead of a flank pivot.

The change of front for a single line was relatively simple, but that of a second line involved serious complications. The difficulty was that either one could not maintain the interval between the two lines or else the second one was displaced to the right. The only way this latter could be avoided would be to have the second line pivot around an exterior point which was impossible by any known maneuver. Consequently, the idea of having the two lines corresponding exactly in regard to position after this evolution was given up.[64]

It has been held, that with this and the following evolutions, one is in the realm of Frederician rather than Napoleonic tactics, and these maneuvers have been criticized for a meticulousness which made them impracticable for the battlefield. This is not so. Marshal Lannes executed changes of front according to the ordinance at Austerlitz and also at Jena with one or two divisions while under fire.[65]

Part V of Section V concluded with movements in echelon,[66] retreat in checker formation,[67] the passage of two lines,[68] and the formation in rectangle.[69] The passage of two lines, which was executed as for a single battalion, led to much controversy. Subsequent generations considered it a monstrosity, but it was actually a very simple maneuver.[70] Colonel Dautane maintained [71] that forming columns would not serve the purpose because their ployment and deployment was too long and too dangerous. The passage of lines did serve the purpose, for even if the first line was in full rout, some seconds would be required to pass the second line, and the latter could make full fire as soon as it was unmasked. The first line could then reform under this shelter.

General Brenier criticized [72] strongly the statement of General Schauenbourg that this movement was too complicated for orderly execution even on the parade ground. He went on to say that, while he was not an exclusive partisan of this method, he had employed it on the battlefield. At the battle of Verona in 1799, where he commanded the Sixty-Third Regiment of the Line, he was compelled to retreat. In doing so, he passed through the Thirty-Third of the Line in the manner of the ordinance, and reformed behind it. This maneuver took place as if on parade, although executed under a heavy and deadly fire. Colin concluded from this, "that to our great surprise, this passage of lines so disparaged, so ridiculed, was not a folly of the regulation. It was really applied in war. One has judged it important enough to debate the details of it for a long time." [73] Brenier insisted that even if the first line was in too great disorder to execute the maneuver in orderly fashion, the men would still go to the intervals of the second. If the latter held firm, the first line would soon reform.

In the years after the great wars were finished, there were many general criticisms of the Ordinance of 1791. Some felt that it was too formal and that it retained too much of the character of the eighteenth century. Others felt that it showed much too great a preference for linear tactics. Still others praised it, having only a few specific criticisms.

The most vehement representative of the first group was Marshal Saint-Cyr. He maintained that the editors of the ordinance were men who, though trained, had little practical experience of war. The ordinance made troops shine in maneuvers, but it could not be applied in war. Its dispositions could not be executed rapidly and, consequently, not before an enemy. This led to no maneuvering at all. The first campaigns were conducted almost entirely as a war of skirmishers. The novelty of this won some successes at first, but as officers gained experience, they came to form their troops more regularly. To do this, they came to use those parts of the ordinance which were "least vicious" and could be used before the enemy.[74]

General Pelet supported Saint-Cyr, but without being so sweeping.[75] He declared that if war had not come so soon the ordinance would have lasted, in all probability, no longer than that of 1788 which was preferable in some respects. Each of its articles was attacked and changes and improvements were suggested, but no time was available during the continuous fighting to make the changes recognized as necessary. He said, elsewhere,[76] that the movements prescribed had not always been executed according to regulations, but rather, according to the needs of the moment. Other maneuvers, not foreseen by the regulation, had been badly executed because officers, tied to the letter of the ordinance, were not able to improvise natural means of execution quickly enough. Strict observance of the regulation sometimes led to checks, he declared, because its dispositions were neither rapid nor solid enough. Battles were lost because the theory of great movements was not fixed and generals did not know how to supply one.

These criticisms would seem to lay at the door of the ordinance matters for which it was not responsible. In answer to Saint-Cyr's assertion that its maneuvers could not be applied in war, one can cite the stubborn fact that they were, even those most bitterly assailed. Even he admitted that parts of the regulation formed the tactics used by the troops as they became accustomed to war. The reason for lack of maneuver in the early campaigns, those of 1793, but not those of 1792 as Jemappes clearly shows, was due to the large number of raw troops supplied by the *levée en masse* and the large proportion of inexperienced officers. It was not the fault of the ordinance.

As to the claim of Pelet, if it was true that changes were recognized as necessary, and the improvements had been already suggested, it is strange that they were not carried out. It does not seem possible to lay the blame on continuous fighting for there were no major campaigns from the end of 1800 until the fall of 1805. For many months of that period the First Grand Army was assembled and in training upon the Channel Coast, presenting an excellent opportunity for trying out those "necessary improvements." The Camp of Vaussieux offered a clear precedent. Moreover, it was more than fifteen years after the close of the great wars before this supposedly unsatisfactory ordinance was changed, and then only slightly.

Not all agreed that the regulation was too complicated. General Fririon did not judge it so. He insisted [77] that the maneuvers and evolutions of the line "are so simple, so easy, so within the capacity of everyone, that the announcement of the command suffices to make them understood and executed."

In contrast to this stand was the position of General Mathieu Dumas who agreed with Saint-Cyr that the maneuvers of the ordinance could not be executed in war with all the precision and formality required. Far more moderate than Saint-Cyr, however, he did not make this a criticism for he continued: "That ordinance is not only the best known, but moreover, the most appropriate to the national character; *it suffices for everything without confining to a scrupulous accuracy in the details of execution; it assures the results of maneuvers, and provides means of preventing inversions and all kinds of confusion.*" [78] This statement indicates that Mathieu Dumas understood much better than Saint-Cyr the simple fact that a drill regulation could not be applied upon the battlefield without any modification from parade ground procedures. This is a fact true of all regulations of that time and not just that of 1791.

Many condemned the ordinance for containing too many useless maneuvers. Among these was General Duhesme who declared that the ordinance, drawn up before the Revolution, was based upon Frederick II's camp maneuvers by men who had no experience in war. He asked: when were these maneuvers ever executed in war? when would the ground permit them? what battalion chief had executed such maneuvers as changes of front, passage of lines, and facing to the rear in battle, according to the ordinance? All the maneuvers Duhesme desired were the simultaneous left-wheel into line, the formation of line ahead from open column, closing the battalion *en masse*, deploying the battalion, marching in line, forming and deploying the column of attack, and rallying. A battalion could ignore all other maneuvers and make all changes of front in closed massed columns.[79]

General Pelet was not so comprehensive in his desire to suppress or modify the provisions of the ordinance, but he did wish to do so in so far as the evolutions of the line were concerned. He declared that they had been established for a surface as flat as paper, that some were defective and others incapable of execution, that modifications necessitated by terrain were not foreseen. Maneuvers in time of peace, he asserted, ought to be the study and image of those that would be used in war.[80]

A suitable answer to this was given by a Commandant Roguet who wrote:

Drills cannot resemble the actions of the battlefield. Frederick II, who maneuvered most of all the great generals, and Napoleon have never thought to establish that similarity. In peace time, one devotes oneself to regularity, to precision and the uniformity of movements, to the strict and constant observation of all the principles, but new elements supervene in action. The morale of the two forces, the character of the nations and of the commanders and above all, the influence of the battlefield on these latter complicate the question.[81]

Roguet went on to say that regulations were only the grammar of tacticians, laying down rules which formed the basis for the combinations they made in the presence of the enemy. He declared that experienced officers held that the maneuvers of the school of the battalion were the most useful, and that the evolutions of the line were most frequently impractical before the enemy. The latter were, nevertheless, precious, because they gave troops an idea of order and uniformity. Trained in order and precision, troops rarely fall into disorder, "that eternal cause of great disasters."

Here one has a just appreciation of the role of a drill regulation in the warfare of that day. Officers who expected to be able to apply such a regulation literally in combat, or who expected to obtain a regulation which could be so applied, were following a

will-o'-the-wisp. Peace time training is for the purpose of fitting
troops—officers and men alike—to meet the situations of war, not
for giving the solution to every problem which can occur. The
surprising fact is that even the most complex evolutions of the
Ordinance of 1791 fitted actual conditions well enough, as has
been indicated, to find occasion for application.

Colin also has answers to Pelet's assertions. He asks, how did
the latter propose to regulate the alinements or conversions of a
division of eight or twelve battalions so as to fit the terrain better
than did the ordinance? Or rather, he asks, what was there in the
ordinance which did not fit the most varied terrain? Hadn't
Frederick the Great used lines on all kinds of ground? The real
truth was, Colin declared, that Pelet didn't desire maneuvers in
line. He let this secret out in proposing a line of battalions in
which he agreed with General Morand.[82] Pelet wrote, "It is not
only the total ignoring of the influence of terrain and the geometrical regularity with which one can reproach the Ordinance of
1791. Its editors have sacrificed all to the *ordre mince,* that the
eloquent Guibert had made to triumph." [83] This last is not only
unjust to Guibert, it is typical of the misunderstanding of his
writing not only in his own day but later. Pelet had either not
read Guibert, or else had not done so with attention and understanding, for anyone who has will clearly see that Guibert was
not an exclusive partisan of linear tactics. He was the first to set
forth a simple system of column tactics. He advocated *the column
for maneuver,* the line for combat.

Pelet wrote elsewhere [84] that it was tactics which gained battles,
and that other things, such as morale, being equal, the army
which maneuvered with the greater precision and rapidity would
win over superiority of numbers. He went on to mention a
variety of maneuvers which had been employed in the grand
tactics of the imperial battles. Many of these maneuvers, as
Colin justly remarked, were of the *ordre mince.* The latter declared that Pelet reached superior rank only in the last years of
the Empire, and his tactical impressions were gained in those
battles where the French infantry struggled with difficulty
against the great superiority of the Allied cavalry.

This experience caused Pelet to foresee a change in war designed to enable infantry to fight on even terms with the other arms and caused him to move away from the *ordre mince*. It is what caused him to write, "It is necessary to occupy oneself above all with the vivacity of the attacks and the progress that foreign cavalry, as well as artillery, has made. It is under the blows of these perfected arms that infantry ought to prepare itself to maneuver in open plains where they can display their velocity. This new circumstance takes from the partsians of the regulation the sole supposition upon which they can execute its movements, alternately heavy and disconnected." [85]

There is nothing new about these ideas or problems. It is a manifestation of one of the arguments which Mesnil-Durand and the other advocates of the *ordre profond* had used to justify their theories. They had maintained that the *ordre mince* was incapable of resisting cavalry and that their formations could. What is surprising is that Pelet after twenty-five years of warfare should revive it, especially after British experience and triumphs with the order on two ranks and with their musketry fire. There was no longer the slightest excuse for doubting the efficacy of fire. The only explanation is that Pelet wished to erect a general theory of war upon the special circumstances of 1813 and subsequent campaigns, in which, as a result of the disaster of 1812, the French were decidedly inferior in cavalry. To do so is certainly a faulty and highly dangerous practice, but a fault which all but the most profound military minds are apt to commit. The partisans of the *ordre profond* in 1828 as in 1770 could justify their theories only by "an imaginary transformation of the conditions of war." [86]

An opinion quite contrary to Pelet's, one that corresponded almost exactly to Guibert's theories, was held by General Brenier. Brenier wrote [87] that, while he did not hold exclusively to either system, he believed it necessary to arrive on the field in columns. Once there, it was necessary to deploy as soon as possible so as to form a line of fire opposed to the enemy. The reserves, or second line if one wished that term, should be held in column ready to move at once wherever needed. Brenier and General Morand differ from Guibert only in wishing to limit columns to one battalion while Guibert wanted as many battalions per column as seemed appropriate.

Finally General Morand pointed out that the battalion maneuvers of the ordinance (which were those of Guibert) were so simple and regular that one need not ponder over what combinations were necessary to carry out one's intentions. A man of limited ability could dispose and maneuver his battalion as well as the ablest officer. "For, since the battalion maneuvers constantly in the same order, that is to say in column, it moves, *as if it were an individual* on the point which it ought to occupy. It ought to arrive there by the shortest route. Its chief need not make a choice between several ways of performing that movement, and the company officers can never hesitate nor be mistaken." [88]

Commenting upon this passage of Morand's, Colin declares that it makes the great simplicity of maneuvers in battalion columns stand out. At the same time, it shows the impossibility and uselessness of trying to regulate them, for these "little masses" can move like individuals by indication and do not need formal evolutions.[89]

For many years there existed a great misconception concerning the tactics employed by the French Armies during the Wars of the Revolution. At least this was true in the English-speaking world, but also to some extent in France. This misconception is clearly expressed by Sir Charles Oman in his chapter on "Column and Line in the Peninsula." [90] The remarkable fact is that he should retain this idea more than twenty years after it was exploded.

Oman started out with a sound exposition of eighteenth-century tactics, pointing out that normally the objective was to smash one of the hostile wings by outflanking it or overwhelming it with superior numbers, while containing the rest of the enemy with equal or inferior numbers depending upon one's strength. He pointed out that the decisive blow was usually delivered by a superior mass of cavalry which, once it had defeated that of the enemy, could hurl itself upon the flank and rear of the uncovered infantry.[91]

Such battles ended with the outbreak of the Wars of the French Revolution. Allied generals trained in the old school tried to reproduce battles of this kind, and their first French opponents obliged them. Soon the armies of the Republic were composed of raw troops demoralized by the removal or desertion of the bulk of their officers. The cadres of the units were small and hundreds of units had no cadres at all. These forces were inferior in tactics, maneuvering, and fire discipline to the well-drilled battalions of the Allies and suffered a series of disgraceful defeats at the hands of inferior numbers. The generals of the Republic thereupon improvised a new system of tactics, evolved from a consciousness of an overwhelming superiority of numbers and a determination to swamp the more maneuverable troops of the enemy by hurling huge masses upon them regardless of losses. This "improvised" system of tactics consisted of a very thick skirmishing line which sheltered and concealed a row of columns of the heaviest sort. The purpose of the former was to engage and occupy the enemy to such an extent that the latter would reach striking distance with little loss. The columns were then hurled upon the hostile first line with the purpose of breaking it by their mere impetus and weight, the idea being that they would endure the losses entailed in their short period under fire without losing their élan or their impetus.[92]

The skirmishers "frankly abandoned any attempt at orderly movement, took refuge behind cover of all sorts, but were so numerous that they could always drive in the very thin skirmishing line of the enemy and get closely engaged with his whole front." [93] The volleys of the enemy did little damage to these swarms since they took cover and did not offer much of a target. If attacked by the bayonet, they gave way only to return as soon as the hostile line halted.

Oman goes on to describe the French columns of companies and divisions, and then says: "But such a column, when properly sheathed by the skirmishing line till the last moment, generally came with a very effective rush against the heavily engaged and often already depleted line of allied troops opposed to it. It is equally clear that *without* its screen of *tirailleurs* it would have been a very clumsy and expensive instrument of war, since it combined the minimum of shooting power with the maximum of vulnerability." [94]

What is the misconception here? It is that the Revolutionary armies of 1793 and 1794 habitually fought in column, and that the column remained the fighting formation right through the Empire. The account of the use of skirmishers is essentially correct though the interpretation of their purpose is not.[95] It has been demonstrated that Guibert's tactical theories came to dominate the French Army, and that the column was *not* a combat formation in his eyes except in the special case of a combat of posts. It remains then to examine the actual tactics of the Revolutionary Armies.

Captain Colin made a thorough study of the sources which remain on the elementary tactics of the battles of the Revolution. He pointed out that indications concerning these tactics are rare but sufficient to enable one to make a résumé. The officers of the Royal Army of 1791 knew of and had participated in the controversy of which Guibert and Mesnil-Durand were the chief protagonists, and they had formed a mixed opinion. "In all cases, the great majority admitted the use of the formation in line for musketry combat, and the column of attack or of mass for attacks on posts, villages, entrenchments, etc." [96]

In the first great battle of the war, Jemappes in 1792, the reports show that assaults in column were ordered by General Dumouriez on the village of Quaregnon. During the battle also, the troops of General Ferrand, ten battalions strong, deployed in front of forty guns at quarter cannon range, performing the maneuver as if on parade according to the testimony of both Ferrand and Dumouriez.[97] The French Army in this battle was composed, however, of line troops of the Royal Army and of Volunteers of 1791 who had had a year's training under the ordinance. That they maneuvered so well under fire in contrast to the performance at Rossbach in 1757 is testimony to the tactical progress made in the French Army since the Seven Years' War.

Jemappes was not typical, however, for Colin says that, after the first use of columns there, both columns of attack and of masses were abandoned for some time, at least no trace of them can be found in 1793 and 1794. This contradicts directly the old idea which Oman retained more than a quarter-century after Colin wrote. The latter amassed at length the evidence which supports this contention.[98] He then concluded:

In summary, one makes use almost exclusively of combat by fire, whether in line, whether as skirmishers, and in the rare circumstances where one moves forward crossing bayonets, it is still in deployed line, after the enemy has been put in retreat. . . .

One never engages an action without detaching from each battalion a number of skirmishers fixed by the general (30, 50, or 100 per battalion). . . . The skirmishers of the whole brigade or division are assembled in a kind of troop, free to operate outside of the front on a determined point, whether in defending a wood, a village, a mill which serve as points of support for our flanks, whether in annoying those of the enemy.[99]

Colin directly contradicted Oman's claim that the French skirmish line always heavily outnumbered that of the Allies. He declared that the Austrians always had more skirmishers than the French during the Wars of the French Revolution and cited General Duhesme to that effect.[100] He also quoted a remark of Brossier [101] on the crowd of skirmishers which ordinarily accompanied an Austrian attack as late as 1800. He quoted Duhesme again as saying that owing to defeats for lack of skirmishers, the least trained troops were so used until, towards the end of 1793, the French had only light infantry; they maneuvered no more in line; that only a few battalions were brigaded together; that it would be difficult to make four battalions maneuver together; and that even the oldest regiments scarcely knew the school of the battalion. Duhesme went on to say that when it was necessary to attack a post, part of the troops were detached as skirmishers, and the rest marched in battle (in line) "getting under way afterwards on the run without maintaining the ranks." [102]

This was not accurate, Colin declared, for it did not apply to the Armies of the Rhine, the Moselle, the Alps, and the Pyrenees which were accustomed to maneuvers from the beginning of the war. It was applicable to the Army of the North in which Duhesme served, but even that army was not as badly off as he remembered it in 1806. Colin continues:

We can conclude nevertheless, from the recollections of General Duhesme, that these troops, less homogeneous, unquestionably, than those of Jemappes had to be engaged as skirmishers or in line rather than in columns because of their inexperience or their lack of solidity. It is in fact a strange error to suppose that ardor and inexperience have been able to bring troops of infantry to adopt the formation in column of attack. The battalions which have received no training are assimilated first to the light troops, grown rare, and they are in the minority. The others are formed in line.[103]

This again clearly denies the old idea of Revolutionary tactics not only as to the use of the column and the reason for it, but also in regard to skirmishers. They had been a standard part of the French Army for years. The increase in their numbers was due to the increase in proportion of untrained troops particularly in the Army of the North, which was the army opposed by the British incidentally, and not to the need to protect and screen the columns of attack as Oman has it. Colin continued by asking in what the inexperience of the troops consisted since their cadres remained much the same as in 1792. The proportion of recruits was about one-third, which contradicts Oman's statement that hundreds of units had no cadres at all. The recruits had only to march ahead, stop, face to right and left with their comrades. Those of 1813 did it perfectly and so did those of 1793 and 1794. Their deficiency was in solidity in combat, for the cadres did not have enough stability to maintain their recruits as did those of 1813 who were supported by a strong discipline and *esprit de corps*.[104] The real reason for lack of maneuverability on a large scale was the lack of capacity of most generals. Brigade, division, and even corps commanders were, largely, incapable in those early years.[105]

Captain Becke of the British Army, writing in 1909, accepted the position of Colin. He felt that the bulk of the experienced officers favored neither lines nor heavy massed columns for maneuver but favored small mobile columns of companies or doubled-companies (divisions). Advancing at deploying intervals these could deploy and develop their fire power on reaching decisive range. "For crossing a battlefield strewn with the *débris* of previous attacks this was undoubtedly a very practical solution; for the line formation of Frederick was entirely unsuited to such an advance." [106] He continued by saying that most authorities agreed that columns were the suitable formation for use behind the firing line, and the line for the development of fire. The former was thus a maneuver formation, and the latter a combat formation.

Returning to this subject further on in his work, he declared that there is apparently no trace of columns of *attack* in 1793 and 1794. The light infantry was used as skirmishers, the line infantry deployed for actual fighting, but used columns for maneuvering and for formations of readiness. The shallow formation, he felt, was best for the raw troops and inexperienced generals of the Revolutionary armies. He continued:

As a matter of fact the raw troops of the earlier Revolutionary armies could never have managed a long advance in line; and, again as an attack failed and the *débris* came reeling back on top of the succeeding lines, these, had they been rigid lines must have been hopelessly broken; but by advancing in lines of battalion columns intervals were left for the *débris* to swirl through without upsetting the advance of fresh troops, and under cover of the skirmishers, who always covered all attacks, the battalions could reach decisive range, and deploy into a ragged line to the best of their ability and develop their fire action at the psychological moment.

Doubtless the obscure view of a battlefield seen through a dense pall of smoke made it difficult for onlookers to observe what actually happened on the French side, and this can only be accurately gleaned from reports furnished by unit commanders of the troops engaged.

Again, as Colonel Maude says, the French deployments were not made with that parade-like precision to which Continental officers were then accustomed; and their minds had been misled by the numerous pamphlets advocating advances *en débandade* and also numerous others advocating deep formations; and hence they were readily led into the wrong path. But there can be no reason now for us to misread the past and its history any longer.[107]

This was written twenty years before Oman did exactly that. He most certainly did not do what Becke recommends and Colin did, namely, go back to the reports of the unit commanders of the time. It would appear from the foregoing that Colonel Maude, the future conqueror of Bagdad, and one of the most scholarly officers of the British Army in the opening years of the present century, had either also accepted Colin's position or arrived at it independently.

Only in 1796 did the *ordre profond* appear when it was used along with line formations in Germany. It appeared in Italy about the same time (end of 1795) as the result of the Instruction of General Schérer, a pupil of Marshal Broglie and predecessor of General Bonaparte. It proposed that a division of four demi-brigades of line infantry and one of light infantry would form an attack as follows: the three battalions of the latter formed on two ranks, spread out enough to cover the front of the twelve battalions of the former formed in battalion columns of divisions at three-pace intervals; light infantry 150 paces in front of the line infantry. The light infantry was to fire until it reached a range of fifty paces, and if the enemy held firm it was to redouble its fire. The line infantry was to pass through the light infantry, which was to form by platoons in the intervals between columns, and attack with the bayonet.[108]

This is pure Mesnil-Durand, being his form of attack practically to the letter. Schérer apparently had difficulty getting his divisional generals to adopt it for he used Mesnil-Durand's arguments in its behalf. In spite of this, General Massena's division fought in line at Montenotte the next year, and the line was used elsewhere in Italy, at Castiglione, La Favorita, and Rivoli, although the ground generally favored the *ordre profond*. Finally, almost immediately after the *ordre profond* appeared in the French armies, Bonaparte introduced his favorite formation, Guibert's *ordre mixte*, which was used whenever he intervened tactically in a battle, as at the Tagliamento in 1797, and which he still favored in exile at St. Helena, twenty years later.[109] At the battle of the Tagliamento, two divisions deployed the second battalions of the demi-brigades while the first and third battalions were held in closed columns on the wings of the second as supports.

Napoleon rarely intervened in the tactical handling of his troops. Oman was inclined to condemn him for this, pointing out that some of his battles, specifically Marengo and Waterloo, were badly fought tactically. He said, "Formations and movements were sometimes made under his eye which would have made Frederick the Great foam with rage." [110] This is perfectly true, as witness the case of Marshal Ney's corps at Friedland. When Napoleon left the tactical initiative to his subordinates the results were sometimes deplorable. At Friedland General Marchand moved to the attack with his entire division in one long column of sections while Ney's other divisional general moved his in one long line over 1,200 yards in length.[111] The result was very unsuccessful as might be expected.

Oman went on to say that Napoleon was essentially a strategist rather than a tactician, and, having an almost infallible strategic insight, he brought his troops nearly always to the right spot, where they usually did their duty even though tactical blunders sometimes levied an excessive cost for success.[112] This is generally true, as the example just given illustrates. The implication is, however, that Napoleon should have retained tactical control of troops after the manner of Frederick, and that it was due to his tactical deficiencies that he did not do so. This is unjust. The armies which Napoleon commanded were composed, first of several divisions, later of several corps. They were not tactical units as were Frederick's armies which usually maneuvered and fought as a whole. An essential part of the divisional system, and the organization in corps is merely an expansion of it, is to free the commander-in-chief from the necessity of fighting his army. Each division or corps commander fights his own troops, and once he has had his role and objective in the battle given to him, should be left to carry it out on his own initiative. A cardinal military principle is that an order should tell an officer what to do, not how to do it. His training and experience should tell him the latter. Napoleon was justified, therefore, in generally leaving tactical matters to his subordinates.

When this custom led to blunders such as those of Friedland, Napoleon occasionally intervened in person. When he did so, he invariably prescribed the *ordre mixte*. The battalions in column were not intended to take part in a fire action, as Oman seems to think, with his comparison of the *ordre mixte's* fire power with that of line and column. They were in support of the deployed battalions, ready to exploit the success, if and when gained, to renew the attack in case of a repulse, to fill a gap, or to make front in a new direction. The *ordre mixte* was a flexible formation subject to many variations and not "a heavy formation at best." All in all, the facts support Colin's judgment of Napoleon as a tactican rather than Oman's. "Whatever Marmont and Gouvion-Saint-Cyr may have said, Napoleon is, in this as in everything else, in the fullest acceptation of the word, the master of his generals; but in his absence errors are multiplied and have extremely serious consequences." [113]

In the battles of the Empire, the most varied tactics were used. At Austerlitz, Napoleon prescribed the *ordre mixte* for the decisive attack upon the heights of Pratzen though it was not fully adhered to. At Jena, Marshal Lannes's corps maneuvered both in line and column, although the line predominated, while Marshal Soult maneuvered in column. Marshal Davout used very diverse formations at Auerstadt though columns predominated. Very varied formations were used in 1809 including the monstrous column of General Macdonald at Wagram. Nothing is known of the tactics of the campaign of 1812, although it is claimed that the *ordre mixte* was used in the attack upon the great battery at Borodino. In 1813, the Allies had great superiority in cavalry and this led to the use of massive formations, especially at Lützen where regimental columns apparently were used.[114]

In all cases, however, it must be remembered that these were formations for maneuver, not for fire combat. The evidence all points to the fact that the French Army deployed for combat like all others. Where assaults took place in column, it seems certain that the troops went forward in that formation for the purpose of exploiting a gap made by artillery in the enemy's lines. The heavier formations appear only after the First Grand Army had been broken up in 1808 to provide troops for Spain. Thereafter the quality of Napoleon's troops was not up to the standard of 1805-7, at least for his armies as a whole. It was during this period, from 1809 on, that the artillery came more and more to occupy a dominant position in battle, preparing the victory which the infantry was to exploit. In cases where it had blown a gap in the enemy's line, the infantry would need to penetrate it as soon as possible, and would advance in columns, but where regular combat by fire, the only kind regularly employed by infantry at this time, was engaged, it was necessary to deploy, and this was done.

Napoleon was quite as well aware of the role of fire power in battle as any British soldier and understood the tactical facts connected with it. The whole problem has no clearer statement anywhere than that in the comparison of ancient and modern warfare which forms the observations on Caesar's fifth campaign in Gaul in Chapter V of the *Précis des Guerres de Jules César* which Napoleon wrote on St. Helena.

Napoleon had discussed the Roman use of the fortified camp and the highly successful results it so frequently procured for them. He then asked, "Why then has a rule so wise, so fruitful in great results, been abandoned by modern generals? Because offensive arms have changed in nature. Hand arms were the principal arms of the ancients. . . . The principal arm of modern armies is the missile arm, the fusil, that arm is superior to any that men have ever invented." [115] A few sentences on he says, "Since the principal arm of the ancients was the sword or the pike, their habitual formation has been the *ordre profond*. . . .[116] Since the principal arm of the moderns is the missile arm, their habitual order ought to be the *ordre mince* which alone permits them to put all their missile machines in play." [117] He continued by comparing ancient and modern armies, and then said:

The tactics of modern armies is founded upon two principles: 1st, that they ought to occupy a front which permits them to put all their missile weapons in action with advantage; 2nd, that they ought to prefer above everything the advantage of occupying positions which dominate, prolong, enfilade the enemy lines, to the advantage of being covered by a ditch, a parapet or any other example of field works.

The nature of the arms decides the composition of the armies, of the plans of campaign, of marches, of positions, of camping, of orders of battle, of the outline and profile of fortified places; which places a constant opposition between the system of war of the ancients and that of the moderns. The ancient arms require the *ordre profond;* the modern, the *ordre mince;* the one, fortresses strongly projecting, having high towers and walls; the others low lying fortresses, covered by a glacis of earth, which masks the masonry; the first, contracted camps, where the men, the animals, and the magazines were assembled as in a city; the others, extended positions.[118]

Here is clearly stated the basic principle about the tactical requirements of firearms, and incidently, a refutation by the greatest modern master of war of the false idea of Folard, Mesnil-Durand, and Maizeroy that tactics is a question merely of geometry unaffected by the basic arms employed. Napoleon expressed similar ideas elsewhere and at other times. It is quite clear that he understood what is after all the first principle of warfare, however much it may have been denied by the military ideologues of the Enlightenment.

Even Oman had to admit that Napoleon was aware of the inadequacy of the column as a combat formation. He quoted from General Foy's *Mémoires* a part of a conversation that the general had with the emperor in which the latter said, "Even in a plain, columns will smash lines only when they are supported by the fire of a very superior artillery which prepares the attack." [119] Oman then went on to say that Napoleon's attacks were prepared by crushing artillery fire on the point which he intended to attack, and which he, an old artillery officer, well knew how to direct. He thought that this preparation by concentrated batteries was for shielding his columns, and that he relied upon it rather than upon a heavy skirmish line for the purpose. He believed that the use of skirmishers greatly declined in the imperial period. He could recall no case of whole battalions breaking up into skirmishers, such as frequently happened in 1793 and 1794, in any of the battles of the Peninsula, and he thought it did not happen often, if ever, in any of the imperial battles.

Concerning this last point, this very action occurred at the battle of Thann in 1809. The corps of Marshal Davout which fought that battle was composed of veteran troops of the First Grand Army. Several regiments broke up completely into skirmishers as they drove the Austrians back in the broken ground above Thann.

The relation between the use of columns and heavy artillery preparation has already been mentioned, but nevertheless, Oman went on to say that whatever Napoleon's theoretical preferences were his great battle strokes were apparently generally made in very gross and heavy masses, the worst instances being those of General Macdonald at Wagram and General d'Erlon at Waterloo.

He has there picked *the* two cases of *attack* in column which can be shown. Neither of these is typical. The famous or "monstrous" column of Macdonald was, according to Colin, "a caricature of the *ordre mixte,* not capable of procuring the same advantages as the formations of the Tagliamento and Austerlitz. It presented two lines of four deployed battalions of which each wing was sustained by a column of four or five battalions in mass." [120] Napoleon let it pass and this led to the still more monstrous column of Waterloo. Macdonald's column was merely a formation improvised, somehow, to meet a cavalry charge at point-blank range.[121]

Becke also called this column a monstrosity, strongly resembling the hollow square which the British involuntarily formed at Fontenoy in order to protect their flanks from Saxe's crossfire and counterattacks. He asked if one should deduce that Cumberland was attacking in hollow square. He declared that many of the deductions and conclusions on French attack formations between 1793 and 1815, owing to their being caught in column, rest on no more solid ground. He agreed with Colin that Macdonald's column was "somewhat of a travesty" of the *ordre mixte.* "But even so it was hardly intended to break the Austrian line by sheer momentum and moral effect; and Macdonald (a very experienced officer) probably used it to lead his corps through the apparently already shattered Austrian line and bring it out *in hand* on the far side ready to meet any eventuality. The eccentric formation failed and was never repeated." [122]

This last is not exact, for D'Erlon's column was somewhat similar. In any case, Oman was not justified in drawing any general conclusions from these two isolated examples. Neither was typical, either of Napoleon's personal tactics, or of the general practice of the army. Macdonald's would appear to have been improvised to meet a sudden crisis. As for Waterloo, Napoleon did not exercise tactical control, for with the arrival of Bülow on the field, he was concerned with stopping the Prussian advance. These are examples of tactical blunders committed by his lieutenants. Oman says that neither of these two examples were ordered or authorized by Napoleon, but he asserts that it is clear that in many other cases the advance in solid undeployed masses was permitted or approved by him. This presents two problems for if Oman means attack he cites no other cases, while if he merely means advance, that is quite correct, it being the whole basis of French tactics to keep the troops undeployed until they reached decisive range for combat.

The Peninsular War represents a somewhat special case tactically. Oman has a reputation in that field because of the great work which forms his masterpiece. The essay under consideration has that war for its central topic. Yet here too the evidence would appear to indicate that Oman was hypnotized by the idea of attack in column.

He declared that the British prejudice in favor of the line was retained; that they held to the idea that the column was clumsy and expensive; that infantry should win by rapidity and accuracy of fire; that every musket not actually on the firing line was wasted. Their answer to the *ordre mixte* was to reduce the ranks from three to two, since the fire of the third rank was dangerous and ineffective. He declared that it was uncertain when this change was made, but that it was certainly in common use before the Egyptian Campaign of 1801 and that the ordinance of that

year made it common.[123]   Becke said that this formation on two
ranks had to be specifically ordered by General Wellesley when he
landed in Portugal in 1808.   He also said that British regulations
still required a three-deep formation until 1824 when the two-
deep formation received official sanction in the Field Exercise.[124]
Becke is correct here, for it was 1824 and not 1801 when the
official sanction was given.

Oman admitted that it would convey a false impression, although essentially true, to say that Wellesley went out to Portugal
simply to beat the column with the line.   Rather, he said, he went
to try his conception of how the line with its peculiarities and
limitations could be employed.   This conception was that the
line must not be exposed until the actual moment of conflict; that
it must have a skirmish line powerful enough to keep off the
enemy's until that moment; that its flanks must be properly
covered either by the nature of the ground or by cavalry and
artillery.

This latter contention is true, but it does not follow that it
was essentially true that he went out to beat the column with the
line.   What it actually indicates is that Wellesley had pondered
the earlier campaigns deeply and had come to correct conclusions
concerning them, namely, that the preparation for attack by the
French through the fire of skirmishers and artillery so unsettled
the hostile troops that they usually could not withstand the
French attack when it was skillfully handled.   Wellesley, therefore, developed his conception to prevent that happening to his
line.   Oman declared that in all his earlier battles each of these
conditions was carefully secured.

The latter went on to deal with one of Wellington's
(Wellesley's) greatest military assets, the extraordinary capacity he
had for the tactical employment of ground.   This enabled him to
show the enemy only his skirmishers and usually his artillery,
which had to be in position from the beginning since it went into
action long before the infantry conflict began.   This led his opponents to misjudge his position time and again with disastrous
results to themselves.   His ideal position was a glacis of rising
ground with a plateau or dip behind it.   His infantry would be

withdrawn from the skyline, being placed just behind the crest if the position was a ridge, or some hundreds of yards back from the edge, if a plateau. The troops stood or lay down until time for their action, thus being screened from all artillery fire since howitzers were not frequently used in the field in those days, and not at all for indirect fire. They advanced to their fighting position only when the contact with the line infantry was about to begin.[125]

Becke, in this connection, remarked that Colonel Maude pointed out to him that Wellington was fortunate in that his troops were almost the only ones which in those days could be trusted to stand firm and await impassively behind the brow of a ridge for the enemy assault. This helps to account, he declares, for Field Marshal Blücher's taking up a position on the near side of a slope at Ligny and for his remark, "My lads like to see their enemies." [126] Wellington's "caustic" comment was, "Damnably mauled these fellows will be, every man visible to the enemy." [127]

Thus Wellington's tactical use of ground secured his line against the opposing artillery and enabled him over and over again to secure tactical surprise as at Vimeiro, Busaco, and Salamanca. There were still the French skirmishers from whom the line must be protected. Wellington secured this protection by establishing for himself a skirmish line so thick and powerful that it was able to keep off the French skirmishers and prevent them from unsettling his line.

It was the French infantry of the line which suffered from skirmish fire. This heavy skirmish line smothered that of the French "and forced the hostile column to commit itself to the main fight without any protective sheathing." [128] Oman's conception of French tactics in the Peninsula is: that after a preliminary artillery duel and unsuccessful skirmish fight, the French columns advanced to the assault having to drive in the British skirmish line, suffering severely in the process; that the columns· then ran up against the intact British line and were invariably worsted in the fire action which followed.

Turning to Colin's treatment of Peninsular tactics, one finds an interesting development. Writing in 1902 he remarked on the too exclusive use of the *ordre profond* in Spain and quoted Napier and especially Oman on its inadequacies versus the British line.[129]   At this time, he quite obviously had not given to the tactics of the Peninsular War the study which he had to the other theatres.   In 1911, he had something quite different to say. He remarked on Wellington's tactics, his wonderful use of ground, and his use of two ranks with one-third employed as skirmishers who fell back on the flanks.   "The French, according to their wont, move forward in small columns preceded by skirmishers; but suddenly the formidable discharge of the British stops them at the moment when they wish to deploy.   It is soon nothing but a disordered mob which is whirled round and thrown back before the counter-attack." [130]

Becke was more specific.   He said:

In the Peninsular War (1808-14) the French troops opposing the British in battle were not under the Emperor's eye, and were led by their Marshals.   Under these conditions they conspicuously failed to make head against Wellington's two deep British line. . . .   In many cases the French had literally owing to the skill Wellington showed in taking up a position—to take the bull by the horns.   Hence, on reaching the crest of the plateau, they were often taken by surprise, and ere they could deploy were attacked by the unshaken British line, which mangled the front of the French formation with fire as it strove to struggle out into line, and then advance promptly with the bayonet to complete the decision.   The French, of course, were using columns as formations of manoeuvre, and had missed the psychological moment when they should have, and could have still, deployed, and thus were caught at a disadvantage.   The British two-deep line naturally out-flanked the French (if the latter failed to accomplish the deployment) enfiladed them and crushed them with fire.   And that the French in the Iberian peninsula were often caught in the column formation ere they deployed is undisputed.   In such cases, Wellington's fire forma-tion gave the British a great superiority, and the fight invariably went well for his army.[131]

And again further on:

Owing to the frequency with which the French were surprised in columns in the Peninsula and for other reasons . . . , an idea was prevalent that the "column" was the French attack formation.   The evidence now to hand would appear to show this was not the case. Naturally Napoleon and his Marshals were neither "mules" nor

"Dullards", further they possessed an unrivalled experience of war; and we cannot, therefore, be surprised to find that they did not wish to neutralize the fire-power of seven-eighths of their infantry, at the crisis of an action, by using the column as an attack formation, for they one and all subscribed to the principle that battles are won by fire, or, as Napoleon put it, *"l'arme à feu est tout; le reste est peu de chose."* A study of the subject brings out that the French tactical procedure was in accord with this saying.[132]

And lastly:

On the other hand, the French having very often difficult ground to cross, naturally did so in column formations, covered always by their skirmishers, and thanks to the skill with which Wellington took up his positions, were often deceived as to their extent, and the dispositions of the British, and hence were caught in column, ere they could deploy. . . .

But had Wellington been confronted by Napoleon in Spain, we should in all probability have heard much less of column and line. Wellington was no match for the Emperor as Waterloo proved; and had not the Prussians intervened there in crushing strength, the Emperor must have won a decisive victory, and proved the superiority of his tactical methods.[133]

This final judgment is given for what it is worth in regard to Waterloo. It is subject to dispute, but in Spain at least it is certainly true. Wellington realized it himself, at least on occasion, as when he remarked after Fuentes d'Onoro, "If Boney had been here, we should have been beaten."

This analysis of French tactics is clear and correct, as even Oman supports it. The latter had to admit it in fact, for he said one will ask why the French did not deploy, and that the answer is that they did try to "sometimes," but that it was always too late when they were under fire and heavily engaged, and that it usually led only to their greater confusion. He cited an attempt at Albuera where, as soon as one-third of a company got out from the column, they would immediately run back. But, he says, the French generally did not seek to deploy, primarily because they were strongly convinced that the column was the proper striking force to carry a given point.

Thus Oman gives the impression that French attempts to deploy were more or less imitative when the French found that their own tactics had failed. To accept this one has to assume that the French adopted in Spain a system of tactics which they did not employ elsewhere; that they persisted in this with hard-headed stupidity through failure after failure; that they sometimes tried to imitate their vanquishers in the heat of action; and finally that no one of authority was able to figure out what was wrong. This is true for he quoted a number of comments on the British by French generals and then said that none of them made a mention of line or column or seems to have reached the conclusion that it was their tactical formation which made victory impossible.[134] This is a most damning admission, for far from supporting his thesis, it demolishes it. None of them reached the conclusion that French defeats were due to their tactical formation, because none of them conceived of the column as an attack formation. Those defeats were due to the reasons assigned by Generals Reille and Foy, whom Oman quoted, namely, Wellington's tactical superiority to his opponents and the constancy and splendid fire discipline of the British infantry.

Finally, while it is correct to say that the French, or many of them, were convinced that the column was the proper striking force to carry a post, that is not to say that they meant to wage battles in column. The French had long accepted the column for an attack upon a post, by which they meant a fortified wood, village, or similar strong point. Guibert, who advocated the line for fire combat, accepted the column for this purpose. A regular fire action of that day was hardly practicable against such a post in which the defenders had cover while the assailants were exposed in the open. It was best to carry it by a rush in a *coup de main*, and the column was accepted for this purpose. That is a far cry from the fire combat of a pitched battle. One can only conclude that Becke's interpretation of Peninsular tactics is correct, and wonder why Oman, twenty years later, should go out of his way to reassert his old position, and that without bringing evidence which in any way refuted that interpretation. He was apparently unaware of it; at least, he ignored it.

The discussion can be closed with a last quotation from Colin on imperial tactics, for having stated, as already quoted, that

Napoleon was superior in tactics, as in all else, to his lieutenants, he says:

As for his marshals and his generals, they have applied from 1805 to 1813, on the battlefields of Germany, the most diverse formations. They are entirely eclectic, and, if Lannes appears to incline more voluntarily towards the *ordre mince,* Soult towards the *ordre profond,* these are only degrees.   One has seen columns closed to platoon intervals, to full interval, squares, deployed lines, skirmishers, changes of front, passage of lines, etc.   In brief, if the examples which come down to us are rare, one sees all the regulation of 1791 pass in review there, and one can say that no one of its parts has been superfluous; they have all been applied, even those which appear most strange to us.[135]

In conclusion, it can be said that in the controversies of the eighteenth century the military writers of France developed a system of tactics which, embodied finally in the Ordinance of 1791, consummated a long period of tactical improvement and played an important part in the triumphs of the wars which followed almost immediately.   They evolved also doctrines of artillery employment and of strategy which were essential elements of Napoleon's art of war.   Of these writers Guibert stands out above all the others, for he has an important place in the development of petty tactics, grand tactics, artillery doctrine, and strategy; he is the only one who figures in all.   Finally, Napoleon alone clearly took advantage of all that was thus made available.   Drawing from these varied sources, he welded them into a consistent practice far superior to any previously employed.

Notes

INTRODUCTION

1. Villate, "Le mouvement des idées militaires en France," *Revue d'histoire moderne*, X (1935), 228.

2. Colin, *La tactique et la discipline dans les armées de la révolution*, pp. x-xi.

3. The fusil is generally referred to as a musket in English—the latter word being loosely used in the English language. Fusil is used in this work to distinguish the flintlock firearm from the musket proper, an earlier weapon.

CHAPTER I: TACTICS OF THE EARLY EIGHTEENTH CENTURY

1. On Swiss tactics see Oman, *A History of the Art of War in the Middle Ages*, II, 253-80. Also his *A History of the Art of War in the Sixteenth Century*, pp. 63-73.

2. Colin, *L'infanterie au XVIIIe siècle. La tactique*, pp. 29-30.

3. A file is a line of men in formation perpendicular to the front of the formation, while a rank is, of course, a line parallel to the front of the formation.

4. Colin, *L'infanterie au XVIIIe siècle*, p. 32.

5. Quoted in *ibid.*, p. 28, from De Vault's *Mémoires relatif à la succession d'Espagne* (Paris, 1836-62).

6. More detailed accounts of eighteenth-century tactics can be found in Colin's *L'infanterie au XVIIIe siècle*, already referred to, and in Reboul, *Histoire militaire et navale*, Vol. I, which forms Vol. VII of Hanotaux, *Histoire de la nation française*. For briefer accounts, see also Revol, *Histoire de l'armée française* and Weygand, *Histoire de l'armée française*.

7. Feuquières, *Mémoires de M. le Marquis de Feuquières . . . , contenans ses maximes sur la guerre, etc.*, II, 24.

8. *Ibid.*, III, 176.

9. J. F. de Puységur, *Art de la guerre par principes et par règles*, I, 142.

10. *Ibid.*, I, 225.

11. *Ibid.*, I, 226-27.

12. *Ibid.*, I, 156-202.

13. *Ibid.*, I, 163.

14. The unit of maneuver in the battalion varied according to circumstances at this time but was seldom or never the same as the unit of organization, the company. The grenadiers always performed the maneuver separately, regardless of how many divisions the fusiliers formed.

15. This is adapted from Puységur's *Planche* II, facing p. 166 of Vol. I. The officers and drummers are omitted for simplification.

16. This figure is adapted from Puységur's *Planche* II, facing p. 176 of Vol. I.

17. This figure is adapted from Puységur's *Planche* VIII, facing p. 194 of Vol. I.

18. Puységur, *Art de la guerre,* I, 194-95.

19. *Ibid.,* I, 353-58.

20. *Ibid.,* I, 348-49.

21. *Ibid.,* I, 350-51.

22. This diagram was made from Puységur's *Planche* XIX.

CHAPTER II: THE MAKERS OF SYSTEMS

1. Folard, *Nouvelles decouvertes sur la guerre.* This work forms Vol. VII of the 1774 Amsterdam edition of Folard, *Histoire de Polybe . . . avec un commentaire* which was used in this study. Reference is to pp. 4-6.

2. *Ibid.,* p. 13.

3. *Ibid.,* p. 24.

4. Colin, *L'infanterie au XVIIIᵉ siècle,* p. 37.

5. Folard, *Traité de la colonne, la manière de la former, & de combattre dans cet ordre.* This is found in Vol. I of the edition referred to. Quotation is from pp. lii-liii.

6. Folard's italics.

7. Folard, *Traité de la colonne,* I, liv.

8. *Ibid.,* I, lv.

9. *Ibid.,* I, xciv.

10. *Ibid.,* I, lxxvi-lxxvii.

11. *Ibid.,* I, xcvi.

12. *Ibid.,* I, lvii. Folard's italics.

13. *Ibid.,* I, lvi.

14. In a deployed battalion, fire by rank consisted of the first rank firing, then the second, third, and fourth. The first was then supposed to be ready to fire again. Fire by platoon would be made by all ranks of the right platoon firing, followed successively by each platoon from right to left, the famous rolling volleys. It could be made by other subdivisions of the battalion. It was more intense and concentrated than fire by ranks.

15. Folard, *Traité de la colonne,* I, lxii-lxiii.

16. *Ibid.,* I, lx.

17. *Ibid.,* I, lxiii. On p. xcvii, he says that the length is eleven feet overall.

18. Folard, *Nouvelle découvertes,* pp. 46-47.

19. The mixture of arms is discussed in a *Dissertation où l'on examine, si l'usage où l'on est de mettre la Cavalerie sur les ailes, & l'Infanterie au centre, dans un bataille rangée est aussi bien fondé, qu'il est ancien & universel.* This can be found on pp. 42-74 of Vol. VII of the 1774 edition of Folard's works.

20. *Ibid.,* p. 65.

21. *Ibid.*

22. *Ibid.,* p. 67.

23. Folard, *Traité de la colonne,* I, lxiv ff.

24. Terson, *Lettre d'un officier au service des États Généraux sur le Polybe, de M. le Chevalier de FOLARD.* This letter appeared in 1730. Its author was an able French officer who died in the Dutch service. It appears in Vol. VII of the 1774 edition of Folard's works on pp. 75-78. The quotation is from p. 76.

25. These criticisms are contained in *Sentimens d'un homme de guerre sur le nouveau système du Chevalier de Folard.* It is by a Monsieur D. whom Folard declared to be General de Savornin. The four letters which compose it are published in Vol. VII of the 1774 edition of Folard's works, forming pp. 83-235, and are followed by Folard's reply which is also found as a preface to Vol. VI of the same edition.

26. Colin, *L'infanterie au XVIIIᵉ siècle,* p. 37.

27. The morale of troops was hardly discussed by other writers. The reason, as far as the doctrinaires are concerned, would seem to be their naive faith that their formations would, of themselves, remedy deficiencies in morale. Saxe, however, dealt frequently with measures designed to bolster morale in the various situations of war.

28. Liddell Hart, *The Ghost of Napoleon,* pp. 28-31.

29. Saxe, *Mes rêveries,* I, 1.

30. *Ibid.,* I, 2-3.

31. *Ibid.,* I, 9.

32. *Ibid.,* I, 29.

33. *Ibid.,* I, 32-33.

34. *Ibid.,* I, 37.

35. *Ibid.,* I, 41-43.

36. This system is discussed by Saxe in Chapter II of *Mes rêveries,* I, 46-76.

37. *Ibid.,* I, 73-74.

38. *Ibid.,* I, 77-119.

39. T. R. Phillips, in his translation of Saxe, calls them rifled, breech-loading carbines. See Phillips, *Roots of Strategy.*
40. Saxe, *Mes rêveries,* I, 88.
41. *Ibid.,* I, 122-23.
42. Speaking of the method of fire training employed in his regiment by Saxe, who was then a colonel, Folard, in the late 1720's, made a remarkable prophesy concerning him long before he had won his great fame. "That which I have just said is excellent; but it is necessary to train troops to fire according to the method which the Comte de Saxe has introduced in his regiment: a method which I find excellent, as well as its inventor who is one of the greatest geniuses for war that I have known, and one will see in the first war that I am not mistaken in what I think." Folard, *Histoire de Polybe,* III, 291.
43. Saxe, *Mes rêveries,* I, 126.
44. *Ibid.,* I, 144.
45. Liddell Hart, *The Ghost of Napoleon,* p. 34.
46. Saxe, *Mes rêveries,* I, 145.
47. *Ibid.,* II, 16-17.
48. See Fortescue, *A History of the British Army,* Vol. II, Chapters V, VI, and VII.
49. Saxe, *Mes rêveries,* II, 73-75.
50. *Ibid.,* II, 85-94.
51. Liddell Hart, *The Ghost of Napoleon,* p. 47.
52. Fortescue, *A History of the British Army,* II, 160-62.
53. Saxe, *Mes rêveries,* II, 96-97.
54. *Ibid.,* II, 98.
55. *Ibid.,* II, 95 and 130.
56. *Ibid.,* II, 146. The discussion of the general is on pp. 142-48.
57. *Ibid.,* II, 148-49.
58. Liddell Hart, *The Ghost of Napoleon,* pp. 29-31.
59. Saxe's italics.
60. Saxe, *Mes rêveries,* II, 149.
61. *Ibid.,* II, 150-51.
62. Mesnil-Durand, *Projet d'un ordre françois en tactique.* This discussion occupies pp. 1-43.
63. *Ibid.,* p. 11.
64. *Ibid.,* pp. 44-47.
65. *Ibid.,* pp. 51-67.
66. *Ibid.,* pp. 75 ff.
67. *Ibid.,* pp. 68-75.
68. *Ibid.,* pp. 81-82.
69. *Ibid.,* pp. 91-92.
70. *Ibid.,* pp. 96-121.
71. *Ibid.,* pp. 177-87.

72. *Ibid.*, p. 121.
73. *Ibid.*, p. 398. The exact quotation is: "For there is no cannon loaded with case shot or otherwise, which approaches the effect of a catapult, which belches forth on a heavy phalanx 100 pounds of stone, balls, or arrows, and sometimes very much more."
74. *Ibid.*, pp. 230-40.
75. *Ibid.*, Chapters XI, XII, and XIII.
76. Colin, *L'infanterie au XVIII* siècle, p. 63.
77. Mesnil-Durand, *Projet d'un ordre*, p. 274.
78. *Ibid.*, p. 431.
79. *Ibid.*, p. 434.
80. Colin, *L'infanterie au XVIII* siècle, p. 62.
81. *Ibid.*, p. 65.
82. Mesnil-Durand, *Suite du projet d'un ordre françois en tactique*, p. 11.
83. *Ibid.*, p. 12.
84. *Ibid.*, pp. 10-11.
85. *Ibid.*, p. 33.
86. *Ibid.*
87. *Ibid.*, pp. 33-34.
88. *Ibid.*, p. 35.
89. *Ibid.*, pp. 36-37.
90. *Ibid.*, p. 48.
91. Colin, *L'infanterie au XVIII* siècle, p. 67.

CHAPTER III: TACTICAL DEVELOPMENTS OF THE
FIRST HALF OF THE CENTURY

1. Colin, *L'infanterie au XVIII* siècle, p. 32.
2. *Ibid.*, pp. 34-35.
3. *Ibid.*, pp. 38-39.
4. Colin, *La tactique et la discipline*, pp. xi-xii.
5. Villate, "Le mouvement des idées militaires en France," *Revue d'histoire moderne*, X (1935), 245.
6. *Instruction sur l'exercice de l'infanterie du 29 juin, 1753*, Archives du Ministère de Guerre, A[1b] 1175, No. 46, pp. 32-38.
7. Colin, *L'infanterie au XVIII* siècle, p. 44.
8. *Ibid.*, pp. 44-45.
9. *Instruction sur l'exercice de l'infanterie du 14 mai, 1754*, Archives du Ministère de Guerre, A[1b] 1175, No. 47, pp. 64-70.
10. C. de Puységur, *Observations sur l'instruction du 14 mai, 1754, etc.*, Archives du Ministère de Guerre, Carton No. 1706.
11. See Colin, *L'infanterie au XVIII* siècle, p. 42.
12. *Ibid.*, p. 46.
13. Fortescue, *A History of the British Army*, II, 116.

14. Colin, *L'infanterie au XVIIIe siècle*, p. 30.

15. *Ibid.*, p. 47.

16. *Ibid.*, pp. 47-49.

17. See *ibid.*, pp. 50-51. Bombelles (1681-1760) was, as Colin points out, neither an innovator nor a utopian, but a celebrated practical tactician recommending what he had seen successfully used in war.

18. *Ibid.*, p. 51. Reboul also reported this. See Reboul, "Histoire militaire et navale," in Hanotaux, ed., *Histoire de la nation française*, VII, 501. Against this French version, it is only fair to give that of the British. Fortescue declared that Ingoldsby was supposed to reduce the Redoubt d'Eu, but misinterpreting his instructions, hesitated and never delivered his attack at all. Instead he joined in Cumberland's main attack against the left of the French position and shared its fate. He was court-martialed for his behavior, but acquitted of all but an error of judgment. See Fortescue, *A History of the British Army*, II, 113-14 and 119-20.

19. Colin, *L'infanterie au XVIIIe siècle*, pp. 52-53.

20. See *ibid.*, pp. 53-54.

21. See *ibid.*, p. 54.

22. See *ibid.*, p. 55. Quoted from Sparre, *Instructions militaires*, p. 48.

23. See *ibid.*, p. 55.

24. *Ibid.*, p. 56.

25. Reboul, "Histoire militaire et navale," in Hanotaux, ed., *Histoire de la nation française*, VII, 501.

26. *Ibid.*, VII, 495.

27. *Ibid.*, VII, 502.

28. Colin, *L'infanterie au XVIIIe siècle*, p. 69.

29. *Ibid.*, p. 70.

30. *Ibid.*

31. *Ibid.*, pp. 71-72.

32. *Ibid.*, pp. 73-80.

33. *Ibid.*, p. 73.

34. *Ibid.*, p. 74.

35. *Ibid.*, p. 80.

36. Broglie, *Instruction pour l'Armée du Roy commandée par M. le Maréchal de Broglie, 1760.* Archives Nationales, Guerre, A¹ 3550.

37. *Observations sur l'armée française en Allemagne.* Archives du Ministère de guerre, series of Mémoires et Reconnaissances, Carton No. 1710.

38. Colin, *L'infanterie au XVIIIe siècle*, pp. 86-87.

39. *Ordonnance du Roi concernant l'infanterie française*, Dec. 10, 1762. To be found in *Recueil d'ordonnances militaire*, Vol. I, 1762-1763.

40. *Ordonnance du Roi concernant la cavalerie*, Dec. 21, 1762. *Ordonnance du Roi concernant les dragons*, Dec. 21, 1762. To be found in *Recueil d'ordonnances militaire*, Vol. I, 1762-1763.

41. *Ordonnance du Roi concernant les troupes légères*, March 1, 1763. To be found in *Recueil d'ordonnances militaire*, Vol. I, 1762-1763.

42. Colin, *L'infanterie au XVIIIᵉ siècle*, pp. 86-89.

43. See *ibid.*, pp. 89-90.

44. L. P. de Puységur, *Nottes sur l'ordonnance du Roy du 20 mars, 1764 pour régler l'exercise de l'infanterie*, Archives du Ministère de Guerre, Carton No. 1710.

45. See Colin, *L'infanterie au XVIIIᵉ siècle*, pp. 91-92.

46. *Ibid.*, p. 93.

47. *Ordonnance du Roi pour régler l'exercice de l'infanterie du 1ᵉʳ janvier, 1766.* To be found in *Recueil d'ordonnances militaire*, Vol. II, 1764-1766. The first eleven titles occupy pp. 2-90.

48. *Ibid.*, II, 42-43.

49. *Ibid.*, II, 46.

50. *Ibid.*, II, 37.

51. The text of the ordinance declares that the second wheel of the right sections should be to the left. This must be an error for a right section makes, as stipulated in the ordinance, a left wheel at the start. If it makes a second left wheel on reaching the second ground, it would face to the rear and not to the front as required.

52. *Ordonnance . . . de 1ᵉʳ janvier, 1766*, Title XV, Article II, pp. 132-43.

53. In Figure 17, A represents the battalion at the moment when the first wheel has been completed. B represents it at the moment when the fourth sections from the center have half completed their second wheel. For the sake of clarity and simplicity, the figure represents an open column. The column of attack was a closed column with a two-pace interval between platoons. The platoons would take up the half-step until they had successively closed to that distance. The grenadiers in B are not in comparative position since the ordinance merely says that they are to march rapidly.

54. Colin, *L'infanterie ʳu XVIIIᵉ siècle*, p. 94.

55. *Ordonnance . . . uᵤ 1ᵉʳ janvier, 1766*, Title XV, Article III, pp. 143-46.

56. *Ibid.*, Title XV, Article III, pp. 142-43.

57. *Ibid.*, Title XVI, Articles I and II, pp. 147-49.

58. *Ibid.*, Title XVI, Article III, pp. 148-51.

59. *Ibid.*, Title XIV, pp. 118-31. Colin says that a second additional type of fire, *feu de rang*, was adopted. This was a complicated system which called for an exchange of fusils by the second and third

ranks after every second discharge, except the first time, when it was after only one. Colin, *L'infanterie au XVIIIe siècle,* p. 95.

60. Colin, *L'infanterie au XVIIIe siècle,* p. 96.

61. *Ibid.,* p. 98.

CHAPTER IV: GUIBERT

1. Colin, *L'infanterie au XVIIIe siècle,* p. 109.

2. *Ibid.*

3. Guibert, *Essai général de tactique,* II, 136-37.   The edition of this work used by the author was that published in Liége in 1775.

4. Guibert's work also evoked both acclaim and condemnation in print.   Voltaire was enthusiastic about the *Essai* and wrote a laudatory poem, *La tactique,* in which he declared Guibert to be "already worthy perhaps to command in the art of which he is master."   The Prince de Ligne declared Guibert's book to be "the best in my library."   On the other hand, the Marquis de Sylva in his *Remarques sur quelques articles de l'Essai général de tactique de Guibert avec des considerations sur le presente guerre entre les Russes et les Turcs* (Turin, 1773) found matters to criticize, as did several other writers. See Jähns, *Geschichte der Kriegswissenschaften vornehmlich in Deutschland,* III, 2068-69.

5. Toulongeon, *Notice historique sur Jacques Antoine Hypolite de Guibert.*   This forms the preface for the edition of Guibert's *Journal d'un voyage en Allemagne,* published in Paris in 1803.   It was also separately published as *Éloge veridique de Guibert.*   For reference see the former, p. 10.

6. In this connection, Mme. de Stael wrote in *Éloge de Monsieur de Guibert,* "Finally M. de Guibert wrote his projects and his ideas before being able to carry them out, and, better known to his enemies than to the public, he created obstacles to his career before having acquired the power which could enable him to surmount them." *Oeuvres posthumes de Madame la Baronne de Staël-Holstein,* p. 418.

7. Guibert, *Essai général de tactique,* I, vii-viii.   This work will henceforth be referred to simply as *Essai.*

8. *Essai,* I, xiii-xiv.

9. *Ibid.,* I, xix.

10. *Ibid.,* I, xxxi.

11. *Ibid.,* I, xxxvi-xlii.

12. *Ibid.,* I, xliii.

13. *Ibid.,* I, xlv.

14. R. R. Palmer in Chapter 3 of Earle, ed., *Makers of Modern Strategy,* p. 64.

15. It is noticeable that the name of Marlborough is excluded. Along with most of the French writers of this time, Guibert does not

cite him as an example. When they need examples to illustrate their theories they draw upon the campaigns of all generals but him. The very few like Feuquières who do, usually give Eugene most of the credit, not only for his own, but also for Marlborough's achievements. It is difficult to account for this. Possibly the defeats which Marlborough inflicted upon the French were too painful and they preferred not to recall them.

16. Colin, *The Transformations of War*, p. 197. The only edition of this work available to the author was the translation by L. H. R. Pope-Hennessy.

17. *Essai*, I, lvii.

18. *Ibid.*, I, lxviii. Guibert's italics.

19. *Ibid.*, I, 6.

20. *Ibid.*, I, 10.

21. Colin, *L'infanterie au XVIII⁰ siècle*, pp. 121-22.

22. *Essai*, I, 32. Author's italics.

23. *Ibid.*, I, 33.

24. *Ibid.*, I, 50-69.

25. This is without doubt a reference to the battle of Chotusitz about which Rostaing reported such figures.

26. This would seem to contradict his earlier and sound statement that one must gain fire superiority before advancing.

27. This refers only to a line of troops and should not be understood to refer to skirmishers, nor to the volley which many officers had their men deliver at forty paces before closing with the enemy.

28. *Essai*, I, 70 ff.

29. *Ibid.*, I, 91.

30. *Ibid.*, I, 94.

31. *Ibid.*, I, 94 ff.

32. It is curious that while Guibert proposes to organize his battalion on the basis of three, giving nine fusilier companies, he uses a battalion consisting of eight fusilier companies plus two élite companies, a grenadier company on the right flank and a chasseur company on the left. Apparently he wished his demonstrations to make use of the existing battalion, in order to make their practicality clear.

33. *Essai*, I, 111-15. Also Guibert, *Projet d'instruction sur les deploymens de l'infanterie*. Archives du Ministère de Guerre, Carton No. 1711 of the series of Mémoires et Reconnaissances, pp. 4-12.

34. Colin, *L'infanterie au XVIII⁰ siècle*, p. 120.

35. *Ibid.*, p. 121.

36. *Essai*, I, 117.

37. Quoted from Oman, *Studies in the Napoleonic Wars*, pp. 55-56. He in turn quotes it from General Trochu's *Armée Française en 1867*.

38. See p. 116 *supra*.

39. Colin, *L'infanterie au XVIIIe siècle*, p. 124.

40. *Essai*, I, 123.

41. *Ibid.*, I, 116-29.

42. *Ibid.*, I, 129 ff. See also Guibert, *Projet d'instruction*, pp. 24-32.

43. Colin, *L'infanterie au XVIIIe siècle*, p. 130.

44. *Essai*, I, 173.

45. *Ibid.*, I, 176.

46. *Ibid.*, I, 181-83.

47. *Ibid.*, I, 184-88.

48. *Ibid.*, I, 189-95.

49. In his demonstrations for cavalry, Guibert used the then existing regiment of four squadrons rather than one such as he preferred.

50. *Essai*, I, 196-97.

51. *Ibid.*, I, 199.

52. *Ibid.*, I, 202-4.

53. *Ibid.*, I, 205-14.

54. *Ibid.*, I, 215-21.

55. *Ibid.*, I, 222-23.

56. *Ibid.*, I, 223.

57. Actually they were chasseurs, élite light infantry. The term was later applied also to light cavalry of French origin, as distinct from hussars which were originally foreign regiments.

58. *Essai*, I, 330.

59. Villate, "Le mouvement des idées militaires en France," *Revue d'histoire moderne*, X (1935), 253.

60. Reboul, "Histoire militaire et navale," in Hanotaux, ed., *Histoire de la nation française*, VII, 556.

61. Villate, "Le mouvement des idées militaires en France," *Revue d'histoire moderne*, X (1935), 253.

62. *Ibid.*, p. 254.

63. See *ibid.*, pp. 254-55.

64. *Essai*, I, 233.

65. *Ibid.*, I, 234. Guibert's italics.

66. *Ibid.*, I, 235-36.

67. *Ibid.*, I, 243-46.

68. *Ibid.*, I, 249-50.

69. *Ibid.*, I, 251-52.

70. *Ibid.*, I, 262.

71. Villate, "Le mouvement des idées militaires en France," *Revue d'histoire moderne*, X (1935), 256.

72. *Essai*, I, 264-72.

73. *Essai*, II, "Avant-propos," 6.
74. Liddell Hart, *The Ghost of Napoleon*, pp. 74-75.
75. *Essai*, II, 2.
76. *Ibid.*, II, 12-29.
77. *Ibid.*, II, 32-37.
78. *Ibid.*, II, 78.
79. *Ibid.*, II, 43-44.
80. *Ibid.*, II, 49-50.
81. The discussion of orders of battle is found in *Essai*, II, 45-61.
82. Liddell-Hart, *The Ghost of Napoleon*, p. 82.
83. *Essai*, II, 58-59.
84. *Ibid.*, II, 61-62.
85. *Ibid.*, II, 70-76.
86. Guibert would form a chasseur company, or a second company of grenadiers, in order to give his battalions sufficient strength. A further reason which he gave was that the system followed in his day of having only one wing of a battalion composed of élite troops was "an evil." The élite companies of a brigade would form a battalion when assembled for special service.
87. *Essai*, II, 81-130.
88. *Ibid.*, II, 132.
89. *Ibid.*, II, 178-80.
90. Liddell Hart, *The Ghost of Napoleon*, p. 85.
91. *Essai*, II, 215.
92. *Ibid.*, II, 140.
93. *Ibid.*, II, 137-65.
94. In this discussion and comparison, the author excludes Bourcet, yet to be discussed, and Feuquières, who cannot be classified as tactical writers.

CHAPTER V: BOURCET

1. Wilkinson, *The French Army before Napoleon*, p. 34.
2. Bourcet, *Principes de la guerre de montagnes*, pp. 61-62.
3. *Ibid.*, pp. 86-87.
4. *Ibid.*, p. 87.
5. *Ibid.*, pp. 68-74.
6. *Ibid.*, p. 87.
7. Author's italics.
8. Bourcet, *Principes de la guerre de montagnes*, p. 88.
9. *Ibid.*, pp. 88-89.
10. *Ibid.*, pp. 103-4.
11. *Ibid.*, pp. 94-96.
12. *Ibid.*, pp. 90-92.

13. *Ibid.*, pp. 97-98.
14. *Ibid.*, pp. 127-28.
15. *Ibid.*, pp. 138-39.

CHAPTER VI: JOLY DE MAIZEROY

1. Maizeroy, *La tactique discutée et reduite à ses veritables loix,* p. vii.
2. *Ibid.*, pp. xii-xiii.   Maizeroy's italics.
3. Colin, *L'infanterie au XVIIIᵉ siècle,* p. 189.
4. Maizeroy, *Cours de tactique, théorique, practique, et historique,* I, xxii-xxiii.   The edition used in this study was that published in four volumes in Paris in 1785.   The first two volumes contain the original work published in 1766.   Vol. III was originally published separately in 1767 as *Traité de tactique*.   Vol. IV was originally published separately as *La tactique discutée et reduite à ses veritables loix* in 1773.   The *Cours de tactique* will hereafter be referred to as *Cours*.
5. Colin, *L'infanterie au XVIIIᵉ siècle,* p. 191.
6. *Cours,* II, 190.
7. *Ibid.*, I, 123.
8. *Ibid.*, IV, 88.   Also *La tactique discutée,* p. 88.
9. *Cours,* IV, 13.   Also *La tactique discutée,* p. 13.
10. *Cours,* IV, 14-17.   Also *La tactique discutée,* pp. 14-17.
11. *Cours.* II, 187-88.
12. *Ibid.*, IV, 19.   Also *La tactique discutée,* p. 19.
13. *Cours,* IV, 21-24.   Also *La tactique discutée,* pp. 21-24.
14. Maizeroy discussed the Pythagorean concept of numbers briefly on pp. 21-22 of Vol. IV of the *Cours* and of *La tactique discutée*.
15. *Cours,* II, 188-90.
16. *Ibid.*, III, 255-56.
17. *Ibid.*, II, 189.
18. Maizeroy surprisingly advocated the wearing of breastplates by infantry as well as by cavalry.   He declared breatplates to be indispensable for infantry and was vigorously contemptuous of soft and delicate people who feared their weight.   Yet the only advantage he adduced was that they would increase courage.   It is peculiar that Maizeroy, who recognized the anachronism involved in restoring the pike, should advocate the still greater anachronism of restoring defensive armor and that without any convincing arguments.
19. *Cours,* III, 266.
20. Maizeroy, *La tactique discutée,* pp. 393-94.
21. He had previously declared that these intervals were only twenty paces.
22. *Cours,* II, 192-93.

23. Colin, *L'infanterie au XVIIIe siècle*, p. 193.

24. *Cours*, II, 176 for the first quotation and p. 198 for the second.

25. *Ibid.*, III, 259.

26. *Ibid.*, III, 432-33. Maizeroy concluded his discussion of marches with a proposal for the limitation of arms to diminish the evils which result from the quarrels of states. Could the states not, he asked, reduce their troops to the smallest possible number and fix their relative strength on the basis of each state's power? War is only a game like all things of this life, he declared, and all that is needed is to fix its rules. Ridiculous as this idea may seem, he declared, it is fully as possible as the Abbé de Saint-Pierre's European Congress. *Cours*, III, 482.

27. *Ibid.*, I, 204-5.

28. *Ibid.*, IV, 185. Also *La tactique discutée*, p. 185. Author's italics.

CHAPTER VII: PIRCH

1. Colin, *L'infanterie au XVIIIe siècle*, p. 136.

2. *Ibid.*, p. 137.

3. *Ibid.*, pp. 137-38.

4. *Ibid.*, p. 138.

5. *Ibid.*, p. 150.

6. Pirch, *Mémoire raisonné sur les parties les plus essentielles de la tactique*. Archives du Ministère de Guerre, Carton No. 1712, of the series of Mémoires et Reconnaissances, p. 8.

7. *Ibid.*, p. 10.

8. Colin, *L'infanterie au XVIIIe siècle*, p. 111.

9. Pirch, *Mémoire raisonné*, p. 22. Pirch's italics.

10. Colin, *L'infanterie au XVIIIe siècle*, p. 158.

11. *Ibid.*

12. *Ibid.*, pp. 159-60.

13. Montbarey, *Observations sur l'instruction provisoire*. Archives du Ministère de Guerre, Carton No. 1713 of the series of Mémoires et Reconnaissances, Pièce 13, p. 1.

14. *Ibid.*, p. 2.

15. *Ibid.*, p. 7.

16. Colin, *L'infanterie au XVIIIe siècle*, p. 167.

17. Nicolaî, *Observations sur l'instruction provisoire du 11 juin, 1774*. Archives du Ministère de Guerre, Carton No. 1713.

18. Clarac, *Réflexions sur quelques points de l'instruction du 11 juin, 1774*. Archives du Ministère de Guerre, Carton No. 1713.

19. Colin, *L'infanterie au XVIIIe siècle*, p. 171.

20. *Ibid.*

21. *Ordonnance du roi pour régler l'exercice de ses troupes d'infanterie du 1er juin, 1776.* Archives du Ministère de Guerre, A¹ᵇ, 1175, No. 60, pp. 70-74.

22. *Ibid.,* pp. 74-80.

23. *Ibid.,* pp. 100-101.

24. *Ibid.,* pp. 102-8 and 113-16.

25. *Ibid.,* pp. 108-12.

26. *Ibid.,* pp. 123-42.

27. *Ibid.,* pp. 167-72.

28. *Ibid.,* pp. 181-209.

29. *Ibid.,* pp. 211-12.

30. *Ibid.,* pp. 213-17.

31. See Colin, *L'infanterie au XVIIIᵉ siècle,* pp. 177-80.

CHAPTER VIII: MESNIL-DURAND'S NEW SYSTEM

1. Colin, *L'infanterie au XVIIIᵉ siècle,* p. 195.

2. Mesnil-Durand, *Fragments de tactique ou six mémoires,* pp. lvi-lvii. This work will hereafter be referred to simply as *Fragments.*

3. *Fragments,* p. liv-lxii.

4. Colin, *L'infanterie au XVIIIᵉ siècle,* p. 195.

5. *Fragments,* p. 17.

6. *Ibid.,* pp. 17-18.

7. *Ibid.,* pp. 18-19.

8. *Ibid.,* pp. 19-23.

9. These figures are from Colin and represent, apparently, the units from Mesnil-Durand's instruction for infantry drill which forms the subject of his Ninth *Mémoire.* They differ somewhat from the originals, especially in the position of the élite companies. These are, however, the forms which were proposed for actual use and which were tried out.

10. *Fragments,* pp. 24-31.

11. *Ibid.,* pp. 45-46.

12. *Ibid.,* pp. 32-42.

13. Colin, *L'infanterie au XVIIIᵉ siècle,* p. 196.

14. *Fragments,* pp. 108-23.

15. *Ibid.,* pp. 130-37.

16. *Ibid.,* pp. 138-65.

17. *Ibid.,* pp. 170-72.

18. *Ibid.,* pp. 172-81.

19. *Ibid.,* pp. 181-85.

20. Colin, *L'infanterie au XVIIIᵉ siècle,* p. 203.

21. Mesnil-Durand's method of citing passages from Guibert did violence to the latter's ideas at times. He drew passages from here and there and even, on occasion, drew together sentences from several

widely separated parts of Guibert's work in order to present what purported to be Guibert's opinion on a given subject.

22. *Fragments*, pp. 224-29.

23. Mesnil-Durand's smallness of spirit is indicated by his comments upon Guibert's account of his instruction by his father in military knowledge. Mesnil-Durand quoted the clause, "when I had once understood the elements of tactics. . . ." He criticized this at great length and concluded by saying that a young man, a child even, who understood the elements of tactics would be the first tactician of Europe and the best authors would be only lambs by comparison. Mesnil-Durand knew, as any reader of Guibert knows, that Guibert claimed only that he understood the basic principles of tactics, and not that he understood the subject in its entirety with all its ramifications. This attempt to prove conceit on his opponent's part is petty and merely reveals his own nature.

24. *Fragments*, pp. 288-98.

25. *Ibid.*, pp. 312-22.

26. *Ibid.*, pp. 322-29. There follows a long series of calculations on the amount of distance covered and the time necessary for the formation of the two obliques. Mesnil-Durand calculated that Guibert's oblique would require ninety-seven or ninety-eight minutes with the objective clear to the enemy for the whole time. His own oblique would take only thirty-four or thirty-five minutes with the objective clear for only three or four minutes. Dispensing with the preliminary moves upon which Guibert did not insist, Mesnil-Durand declared that the respective times would be sixty-four and one-half minutes and three and one-half minutes. There is obviously something faulty with the calculations or rather with the premises upon which they are based. *Fragments*, pp. 329-41.

27. *Ibid.*, pp. 342-70.

28. *Ibid.*, *Septième Mémoire*, pp. 1-5.

29. Tronson du Coudray replied to Mesnil-Durand's Seventh *Mémoire* with a work entitled *L'ordre profond et l'ordre mince considerées par rapport aux effets le l'artillerie*. He attacked the *ordre profond* (especially Mesnil-Durand's version) on the ground that it was so much more vulnerable than the *ordre mince* to artillery that it could not be used on the battlefield. He made an excellent case for his contention even though some of his supporting calculations were fanciful. Mesnil-Durand countered with *Réponse à la brochure intitulee: L'ordre profond et l'ordre mince considerée par rapport aux effets de l'artillerie*. Mesnil-Durand defended himself chiefly by re-iteration of arguments already advanced. He failed to break down the contentions of Tronson du Coudray except for the latter's supporting calculations.

30. Mesnil-Durand cited the author of a work called *L'essai sur l'usage de l'artillerie* as his authority.

31. *Fragments, Septième Mémoire*, pp. 11-17.

32. This argument was based upon scattered quotations taken from various sources including Tronson du Coudray's *L'artillerie nouvelle*. Most of these quotations do not support Mesnil-Durand's conclusion. He reached it by his frequent practice of pulling quotations out of context and giving them tortured interpretations inconsistent with their meaning. The idea that a four-pounder could kill only three, or at most four, men in a file was a convenient point for Mesnil-Durand. It would mean that a column would suffer no more from a four-pounder than a line, which was, of course, Mesnil-Durand's purpose. Both Tronson du Coudray and Guibert refuted this, the latter by saying that he had himself seen eight or nine men killed by a single shot.

33. *Fragments, Septième Mémoire*, pp. 19-23.

34. *Ibid.*, p. 36.

35. Footnote to Title XI, *Fragments, Neuvième Mémoire*, pp. 58-59.

36. Colin, *L'infanterie au XVIIIᵉ siècle*, pp. 200-201.

1. Colin, *L'infanterie au XVIIIᵉ siècle*, p. 214.

2. *Ibid.*

3. Wimpfen, *Relation de ce qui est passé au camp de Vaussieux*. Archives du Ministère de Guerre, Carton No. 1819 of the series of Mémoires et Reconnaissances, p. 2. This is the only complete and detailed contemporary account of the maneuvers of Vaussieux extant. It is necessary to keep in mind, however, that Wimpfen was an extremely partial witness, being strongly opposed to Mesnil-Durand's system.

4. *Instruction du maréchal de Broglie pour la première manoeuvre de Vaussieux*. Archives du Ministère de Guerre, Carton No. 1715, pièce 12 of the series of Mémoires et Reconnaissances, p. 3. The movements prescribed by Broglie are also given in Wimpfen's *Relation*, pp. 3-6.

5. Colin, *L'infanterie au XVIIIᵉ siècle*, p. 215. Quoted from Mesnil-Durand, *Examen de la première manoeuvre faite au camp de Vaussieux*.

6. *Ibid.*

7. *Instruction du maréchal de Broglie*, pp. 4-5. Also Wimpfen, *Relation*, pp. 4-5.

8. See Colin, *L'infanterie au XVIIIᵉ siècle*, p. 216.

9. *Ibid.*

10. *Instruction du maréchal de Broglie*, pp. 5-6. Also Wimpfen, *Relation*, pp. 5-6.
11. Wimpfen, *Relation*, p. 6.
12. *Ibid.*
13. *Ibid.*, pp. 7-8.
14. Colin gives the date as the 15th, *L'infanterie au XVIIIe siècle*, pp. 218-19.
15. Wimpfen, *Relation*, p. 8.
16. *Ibid.*, pp. 8-11.
17. Colin, *L'infanterie au XVIIIe siècle*, p. 219.
18. Wimpfen, *Relation*, pp. 11-12.
19. Colin gives the date as the 16th.
20. Wimpfen, *Relation*, pp. 13-14.
21. *Ibid.*, pp. 14-16.
22. Colin, *L'infanterie au XVIIIe siècle*, p. 222.
23. Wimpfen, *Relation*, pp. 16-17.
24. *Ibid.*, p. 19.
25. *Ibid.*, pp. 19-21.
26. *Ibid.*, pp. 21-22.
27. *Ibid.*, pp. 23-24.
28. See Colin, *L'infanterie au XVIIIe siècle*, pp. 226-27.
29. See *ibid.*, p. 227.
30. See *ibid.*, pp. 227-28.
31. *Ibid.*, pp. 229-30.
32. *Ibid.*, pp. 230-31.
33. Castries, *Observations de M. de Castries sur le projet d'instruction donné à l'infanterie*. Archives du Ministère de Guerre, Carton No. 1715, pièce 11 of the series of Mémoires et Reconnaissances.
34. *Ibid.*, p. 8.
35. *Ibid.*
36. *Ibid.*
37. *Ibid.*, pp. 8-9. Author's italics.
38. *Ibid.*, p. 9.
39. *Ibid.*
40. Puységur, *Avis demandé à M. le comte de Puységur sur le projet d'instruction pour l'exercice de l'infanterie*. Published by Colin in *L'infanterie au XVIIIe siècle*, pp. 238-42.
41. *Ibid.*
42. *Ibid.*

CHAPTER X: THE *Défense* OF GUIBERT

1. Guibert, *Défense du système de guerre moderne*. The edition used in this work was *Oeuvres militaires de Guibert publiées par sa*

veuve. The *Défense* is contained in Vols. III and IV of the collected works. It will be referred simply as *Défense* henceforth.

2. *Défense,* I, 208.

3. *Ibid.,* I, 208-9.

4. *Ibid.,* I, 179.

5. *Ibid.,* I, 247-59.

6. *Ibid.,* I, 260-62.

7. *Ibid.,* I, 265.

8. *Ibid.,* I, 269-75.

9. *Ibid.,* I, 280.

10. *Ibid.,* I, 296.

11. *Ibid.,* I, 304-8.

12. *Ibid.,* I, 308-11.

13. *Ibid.,* I, 320-24.

14. *Ibid.,* II, 38.

15. Colin, *The Transformations of War,* pp. 114-15.

16. *Ibid.,* pp. 117-20.

17. *Defense,* II, 48-53.

18. *Ibid.,* II, 55.

19. *Ibid.,* II, 55-58.

20. See Colin, *The Transformations of War,* p. 111.

21. *Défense,* II, 68.

22. *Ibid.,* II, 69-71.

23. An example is to be found in the orders sent to Massena by Berthier on April 17, 1809, in which is found the following: "You will march *Monsieur le Duc,* immediately after your advance guard in order to maneuver according to circumstances." Saski, *Campagne de 1809 in Allemagne et en Antriche,* II, 211-12. Massena's failure to heed these orders allowed Hiller to escape from what would otherwise have been a fatal trap at Landshut.

24. See Colin, *The Transformations of War,* p. 112.

25. *Défense,* II, 83-85.

26. *Ibid.,* II, 90-93.

27. *Ibid.,* II, 153-54.

28. *Ibid.,* II, 182.   Guibert's italics.

29. *Ibid.*   Guibert's italics.

30. *Ibid.,* II, 186.

31. *Ibid.*

32. *Ibid.,* II, 188-89.

33. *Ibid.,* II, 189.

34. *Ibid.,* II, 189-91.

35. *Ibid.,* II, 212.

36. *Ibid.,* II, 212-13.

37. *Ibid.,* II, 212-27.

38. *Ibid.*, II, 228-30.
39. *Ibid.*, II, 270-75.
40. Palmer in Earle, ed., *Makers of Modern Strategy*, pp. 62-68.
41. *Défense*, II, 270.
42. The same critic, dealing with Guibert's ideas on artillery, while declaring correctly that Guibert took a middle position favorable to Gribeauval on the new artillery, stated that "he never fully appreciated the work of contemporary artillery theorists, such as du Teil, who were using the new mobility of guns to achieve heavy concentration of fire." (p. 65). This seems a little strange considering that Guibert stressed the preparation of attacks by overthrowing or destroying parts of the hostile front with a concentrated artillery fire. Guibert also stressed the mobility of the new guns, believing that this mobility made possible a reduction in the quantity of guns. Moreover, du Teil himself, while not always agreeing with Guibert, paid the highest tribute to the *Essai général*, "A work which has immensely contributed to developing my ideas and my emulation." Du Teil, *De l'usage de l'artillerie nouvelle*, footnote, pp. 118-19.
43. Colin, *L'infanterie au XVIIIᵉ siècle*, p. 212.

CHAPTER XI: THE CONTROVERSY CONTINUES

1. Joly de Maizeroy, *Théorie de la Guerre*, pp. i-ii, henceforth referred to as *Théorie*.
2. *Théorie*, p. lxvi.
3. *Ibid.*, pp. lxxxv-lxxxvi.
4. Maizeroy refers to the tests made by four battalions at Metz in 1775 already discussed in Chapter IX. These tests were inconclusive. The far more extensive maneuvers at Vaussieux had not yet occurred when Maizeroy wrote.
5. The Introductory Discourse forms pp. i-lxiii of the *Théorie de la Guerre*.
6. *Théorie*, pp. 49-63.
7. *Ibid.*, pp. 115-21.
8. *Ibid.*, pp. 122-27.
9. *Ibid.*, pp. 127-31.
10. *Ibid.*, p. 141.
11. *Ibid.*, pp. 138-47.
12. *Ibid.*, pp. 174-93.
13. *Ibid.*, p. 237.
14. *Ibid.*, p. 247.
15. *Ibid.*, pp. 269-73.
16. *Ibid.*, p. 304.
17. *Ibid.*, pp. 304-5.
18. *Ibid.*, pp. 305-62.

19. Bosroger, *The Elementary Principles of Tactics with New Observations on the Military Art*, p. 52. Translated by an officer of the British Army. This was the only edition available to the author.

20. *Ibid.*, p. 56.

21. *Ibid.*

22. *Ibid.*, pp. 56-57.

23. "Or something worse," he says, "because the sections of the same platoons, or the platoons of the same divisions are no longer together but while they preserve this order." *Ibid.*, pp. 59-60. The meaning and force of this objection are not apparent.

24. *Ibid.*, pp. 58-61.

25. *Ibid.*, pp. 62-65.

26. *Ibid.*, pp. 67-68.

27. *Ibid.*, p. 69.

28. This is from Figures 1 and 2 of Bosroger's *Planche* II.

29. Bosroger, *Elementary Principles*, pp. 69-70.

30. This is Figure 3 of Bosroger's *Planche* II.

31. Bosroger, *Elementary Principles*, pp. 70-72. His figures are not clear for, with thirty-six men per company, there would be twelve men per rank. This would make the deep files of fifteen men and would leave six files of three men only, not counting file closers, according to the present author's calculations.

32. *Ibid.*, pp. 72-74.

33. *Ibid.*, pp. 87-88.

34. These are Figures 4 and 5 of Bosroger's *Planche* V.

35. Bosroger, *Elementary Principles*, pp. 140-41.

CHAPTER XII: DU TEIL

1. Liddell Hart, *The Ghost of Napoleon*, p. 80.

2. Du Teil, *De l'usage de l'artillerie nouvelle dans la guerre de campagnes, connoissance nécessaire aux officiers destinés a commander toutes les armées.* The edition used by the author was published at Paris, Limoges, and Nancy in 1924, pp. i-ii.

3. *Ibid.*, p. iii.

4. *Ibid.*, p. 2. Du Teil's italics.

5. *Ibid.*, pp. 3-4.

6. *Ibid.*, pp. 7-8.

7. *Ibid.*, p. 11.

8. *Ibid.*, pp. 14-25.

9. *Ibid.*, p. 26.

10. *Ibid.*, pp. 27-29.

11. *Ibid.*, p. 40. See also pp. 115-18.

12. *Ibid.*, pp. 31-32.

13. *Ibid.*, pp. 33-34.

14. *Ibid.*, pp. 34-36.
15. *Ibid.*, pp. 36-37.
16. *Ibid.*, p. 57.
17. *Ibid.*, pp. 61-62.
18. *Ibid.*, p. 65.
19. Colin, *The Transformations of War*, p. 26.
20. Liddell Hart, *The Ghost of Napoleon*, p. 79.
21. Du Teil, *De l'usage*, p. 39.
22. *Ibid.*, p. 51.
23. *Ibid.*, pp. 51-52.
24. *Ibid.*, pp. 50-51.
25. *Ibid.*, p. 44.
26. *Ibid.*, p. 63.
27. *Ibid.*, p. 45.
28. *Ibid.*, p. 105.

CHAPTER XIII: TACTICS AT THE END OF THE EIGHTEENTH CENTURY AND DURING THE GREAT WARS

1. Traverse, *Sur les manoeuvres de l'infanterie.* Archives du Ministère de Guerre, Carton No. 1713.
2. *Ibid.*
3. Colin, *L'infanterie au XVIIIᵉ siècle*, p. 248.
4. *Ibid.*
5. *Resumé des principes de tactique du général de Saldern.* Archives du Ministère de Guerre, Carton No. 1779.
6. Colin, *L'infanterie au XVIIIᵉ siècle*, p. 252.
7. *Ibid.*, p. 253.
8. *Ibid.*, p. 254.
9. *Ibid.*, pp. 255-56.
10. *Ibid.*, pp. 254-59.
11. *Ibid.*, pp. 259-60. The Introduction is quoted by Colin on p. 260.
12. See *ibid.*, p. 261.
13. See *supra*, p. 101.
14. Colin, *L'infanterie au XVIIIᵉ siècle*, pp. 262-63. One of the most ingenious devices of Noailles was to identify changes of front with deployment of a column which cut in half the space necessary to explain it. It was done by forming the line in columns which then marched by a simple column wheel onto the new line and deployed.
15. *Ibid.*, p. 264. Quoted by Colin with reference only as from one of the most recent histories of tactics.
16. See *supra*, p. 205.
17. Colin, *L'infanterie au XVIIIᵉ siècle*, pp. 264-65.

18. *Ibid.*, p. 265.
19. Colin, *La tactique et la discipline dans les armées de la revolution,* pp. xi-xii.
20. Macdonald, *Rules and Regulations for the Field Exercise and Manoeuvres of the French Infantry (Being the Ordonnance of 1er Aout, 1791),* pp. 1-4. This is the edition of the ordinance available to the author. All references will be under the translator's name.
21. *Ibid.*, pp. 8-9.
22. *Ibid.*, p. 10.
23. Colin, *La tactique et la discipline,* pp. xiv-xvi.
24. Macdonald, *Rules and Regulations,* p. 65.
25. *Ibid.*, pp. 72-73.
26. *Ibid.*, pp. 73-74.
27. Duhesme, *Essai sur l'infanterie-légère,* p. 178.   Quoted by Colin, in *La tactique et la discipline,* pp. xvii-xviii.
28. Colin, *La tactique et la discipline,* p. xviii.
29. Fririon, *Considerations sur l'infanterie française,* p. 47.   See Colin, *La tactique et la discipline,* p. xix.
30. Gouvion Saint-Cyr, *Mémoires sur les campagnes des Armées du Rhin et du Rhin-et-Moselle, de 1792 jusqu'a la paix de Campo-Formio,* I, xliv-xlv.
31. Tanski, "Notes sur le supplement à Ordonnance du 4 mars, 1831 inséré dans le *Spectateur militaire* du mois de janvier, 1832 par le général Loverdo," *Spectateur militaire,* XIII (1832), 397.
32. Saint-Cyr, *Mémoires,* I, xliv (footnote).
33. Tanski, "Notes sur le supplement à Ordonnance du 4 mars, 1831 . . . ," *Spectateur militaire,* XIII (1832), 395-96.
34. Chambray, *De l'infanterie,* p. 12.
35. *Ibid.*, pp. 23-24.
36. Ney, *Mémoires du maréchal Ney,* II, 402.
37. Brenier, "A messieurs les rédacteurs du *Spectateur militaire,*" *Spectateur militaire,* II (1827), 472.
38. Colin, *La tactique et la discipline,* p. xxvi.
39. Macdonald, *Rules and Regulations,* pp. 135-40.
40. *Ibid.*, pp. 141-47.   For illustration see Figure 20.
41. *Ibid.*, pp. 154-64.
42. *Ibid.*, pp. 166-69.
43. *Ibid.*, pp. 174-77.
44. *Ibid.*, pp. 186-88.   See Figure 15.
45. *Ibid.*, pp. 188-92.   See Figure 2.
46. *Ibid.*, pp. 192-96.
47. *Ibid.*, pp. 196-98.
48. *Ibid.*, pp. 200-202.
49. *Ibid.*, pp. 202-8.

50. *Ibid.*, pp. 235-51.

51. *Ibid.*, pp. 259-63.

52. Pelet, "Essai sur les manoeuvres d'un corps d'armée d'infanterie," *Spectateur militaire*, VI (1828-29), 119. Chambray, *De l'infanterie*, pp. 25-26. Morand, *De l'armee selon la Charte*, pp. 143 and 147. The last citation quoted by Colin in *La tactique et la discipline* in his discussion on pp. xxxii-xxxv. General Meunier discussed the column of attack in his *Dissertation sur l'ordonnance de l'infanterie* (Paris, 1805), and in his *Evolutions par brigades* (Paris, 1814), according to Pelet.

53. Colin, *La tactique et la discipline*, pp. xxxvii-xxxix.

54. *Ibid.*, p. xxxviii.

55. *Ibid.*, p. xxxix-xl.

56. Macdonald, *Rules and Regulations*, pp. 278-85.

57. Colin, *La tactique et la discipline*, p. xlvi.

58. Macdonald, *Rules and Regulations*, pp. 320-34.

59. *Ibid.*, pp. 334-41.

60. Colin, *La tactique et la discipline*, pp. xlvii-xlviii.

61. Macdonald, *Rules and Regulations*, pp. 362-80.

62. See *supra*, p. 314 and Figure 35B.

63. See *supra*, pp. 314-15 and Figure 35A.

64. Colin, *La tactique et la discipline*, pp. lxviii-l.

65. *Ibid.*, p. l.

66. Macdonald, *Rules and Regulations*, pp. 380-89.

67. *Ibid.*, pp. 389-91.

68. *Ibid.*, pp. 391-94.

69. *Ibid.*, pp. 394-402.

70. See *supra*, p. 315.

71. Dautane, "Réponse du colonel du 3ᵉ régiment d'infanterie de ligne aux observations de M. le maréchal-de-camp . . . ," *Spectateur militaire*, VIII (1829-30), 342-43.

72. Brenier, "Observations sur le passage des lignes," *Spectateur militaire*, VIII (1829-30), 47-48.

73. Colin, *La tactique et la discipline*, pp. lii-liii.

74. Saint-Cyr, *Mémoires*, I, xliii.

75. Pelet, "Essai sur les manoeuvres d'un corps d'armée d'infanterie," *Spectateur militaire*, VI (1828-29), 111.

76. *Ibid.*, *Spectateur militaire*, IV (1828), 317.

77. Fririon, *Considerations sur l'infanterie française*, p. 53. Quoted by Colin, *La tactique et la discipline*, p. lv.

78. Mathieu Dumas, *Précis des événements militaires, ou essais historiques sur les campagnes de 1799 à 1814*, XII, 30-31. Mathieu Dumas's italics.

79. Duhesme, *Essai sur l'infanterie légère*, p. 177. Quoted by Colin, *La tactique et la discipline*, pp. lvi-lvii.

80. Pelet, "De la division," *Spectateur militaire*, II (1827), 278-79.

81. Roguet, "Etudes sur l'ordre perpendiculaire," *Spectateur militaire*, XVIII (1834-35), 508.

82. Colin, *La tactique et la discipline*, p. lix.

83. Pelet, "Essai sur les manoeuvres d'un corps d'armée d'infanterie," *Spectateur militaire*, VI (1828-29), 111.

84. *Ibid., Spectateur militaire*, IV (1828), 316.

85. *Ibid., Spectateur militaire*, VI (1828-29), 113.

86. Colin, *La tactique et la discipline*, p. lx.

87. Brenier, "À messieurs les rédacteurs du *Spectateur militaire*," *Spectateur militaire*, II (1827), 477.

88. Morand, *De l'armee selon la Charte*, p. 151. Quoted by Colin in *La tactique et la discipline*, p. lxii. Colin's italics.

89. Colin, *La tactique et la discipline*, p. lxii.

90. Oman, *Studies in the Napoleonic Wars*, Chapter V, pp. 82-108.

91. *Ibid.*, p. 85.

92. *Ibid.*, pp. 85-87.

93. *Ibid.*, p. 87.

94. *Ibid.*, pp. 88-89. Oman's italics.

95. Oman apparently made little or no use of French works on this period and was not familiar with French military theory of the time, or he would not have said that Republican generals improvised a system, all the essential elements of which can be found in the works of Mesnil-Durand, both as to formations and purposes. It seems to the present author that he gives away this failure to consult French sources and authorities by citing, as his main supporting quotation, the following from an anonymous British pamphlet of 1802, *Character of the Armies of the Various European Powers in 1802*. "The French Army was composed of troops of the line without order, and of raw and inexperienced volunteers. They experienced defeats in the beginning, but war in the meantime was forming both officers and soldiers. In an open country they took to forming their armies in columns instead of lines, which they could preserve without difficulty. They reduced battles to attacks upon certain points where brigade succeeded brigade, and fresh troops supplied the place of those who were driven back, till they were able to force the post and make the enemy give way. They were fully aware that they could not give battle in regular order, and sought to reduce engagements to important affairs of posts. This plan has succeeded. They look upon losses as nothing, provided that they succeed in the end; they set little value upon their men, because they have the certainty of being able

to replace them, and the customary superiority of their numbers affords them an advantage which can only be counterbalanced by great skill, conduct, and activity." This passage is essentially correct, except for the idea of employing columns in combat. It is, however, remarkable that Oman cites no French authorities in support of his position. This failure would appear due to the long acceptance of the concept he expounds.

96. Colin, *La tactique et la discipline*, p. lxiii.

97. *Ibid.*, pp. lxiii-lxiv.

98. *Ibid.*, pp. lxv-lxvii.

99. *Ibid.*, pp. lxvii-lxviii.

100. Duhesme, *Essai sur l'infanterie légère*, p. 85. Quoted by Colin, *La tactique et la discipline*, p. lxviii.

101. See Colin, *La tactique et la discipline*, p. lxviii.

102. Duhesme, *Essai sur l'infanterie légère*, p. 90. Quoted by Colin, *La tactique et la discipline*, p. lxix.

103. Colin, *La tactique et la discipline*, p. lxix.

104. *Ibid.*, pp. lxx-lxxi.

105. *Ibid.*, pp. lxxi-lxxii.

106. Becke, *An Introduction to the History of Tactics, 1740-1905*, p. 15.

107. *Ibid.*, pp. 72-73.

108. See Colin, *La tactique et la discipline*, p. lxxxv.

109. *Ibid.*, p. lxxv.

110. Oman, *Studies in the Napoleonic Wars*, p. 91.

111. Colin, *The Transformations of War*, p. 23.

112. Oman, *Studies in the Napoleonic Wars*, p. 91.

113. Colin, *The Transformations of War*, p. 24. See also his *La tactique et la discipline*, p. lxvi.

114. Colin, *La tactique et la discipline*, pp. lxxxiv-lxlii.

115. *Correspondance de Napoleon Ier publiée par ordre de l'Empereur Napoléon III*, XXXII, 27.

116. *Ibid.*

117. *Ibid.*, p. 28.

118. *Ibid.*, p. 30.

119. Oman, *Studies in the Napoleonic Wars*, p. 92. Quoted from p. 107 of Foy's *Mémoires*.

120. Colin, *La tactique et la discipline*, pp. lxl-lxli.

121. Colin, *The Transformations of War*, p. 23.

122. Becke, *An Introduction to the History of Tactics, 1740-1905*, p. 76.

123. Oman, *Studies in the Napoleonic Wars*, pp. 96-97.

124. Becke, *An Introduction to the History of Tactics, 1740-1905*, p. 26.

125. Oman, *Studies in the Napoleonic Wars*, pp. 99-100.

126. Becke, *An Introduction to the History of Tactics, 1740-1905*, p. 77.

127. Oman, *Studies in the Napoleonic Wars*, p. 100.

128. *Ibid.*, p. 102

129. Colin, *La tactique et la discipline*, pp. lxlii-lxlv.

130. Colin, *The Transformations of War*, p. 24.

131. Becke, *An Introduction to the History of Tactics, 1740-1905*, pp. 26-27.

132. *Ibid.*, p. 71.

133. *Ibid.*, pp. 77 and 78.

134. Oman, *Studies in the Napoleonic Wars*, p. 108.

135. Colin, *La tactique et la discipline*, pp. lxlvi-lxlvii.

Bibliography

Bacquet, Captain. L'infanterie au XVIIIe siècle. L'organization. Paris, 1907.

Becke, Archibald Frank. An Introduction to the History of Tactics, 1740-1905. London, 1909.

Berthier, Alexandre. Journal de la campagne d'Amérique 10 mai 1780-26 août 1781. Edited by Gilbert Chinard. Washington, 1951.

Bosroger, Leroy de. The Elementary Principles of Tactics with New Observations on the Military Art. Translated by an officer of the British Army. London, 1771.

Bourcet, Pierre de. Principes de la guerre de montagnes. Paris, 1888. Written between 1764 and 1771.

Brenier, Antoine-François. "À messieurs les redacteurs du Spectateur Militaire," Spectateur Militaire, Vol. II, 1827.

—— "Observations sur les passages des lignes," Spectateur Militaire, Vol. VIII, 1829-30.

Broglie, Victor-François de. Instruction du maréchal de Broglie pour la première manoeuvre de Vaussieux. Archives du Ministère de Guerre, Carton No. 1715, pièce 12.

—— Instruction pour l'armée du Roy commandée par M. le Maréchal de Broglie, 1760. Archives Nationales, Guerre A^I 3550.

Castries, Charles-Eugene-Gabriel de La Croix de. Observations de M. de Castries sur le projet d'instruction donne a l'infanterie. Archives du Ministère de Guerre, Carton No. 1715, pièce 11.

Chambray, Georges de. De l'infanterie. Paris, 1824.

Clarac, Brigadier de. Réflexions sur quelques points de l'instruction du 11 juin, 1774. Archives du Ministère de Guerre, Carton No. 1713.

Colin, Jean-Lambert-Alphonse. La tactique et la discipline dans les armées de la révolution. Correspondance du Général Schauenbourg du 4 avril au 2 août, 1793. Paris, 1902.

—— L'infanterie au XVIIIe siècle. La tactique. Paris, 1907.

—— The Transformations of War. L. M. R. Pope-Henessy, translator. London, 1912.

Coudray, Tronson du. L'ordre profond et l'ordre mince considerées par rapport aux effets de l'artillerie. Metz, 1776.

Dautane, Colonel. "Réponse du colonel du 3ᵉ regiment d'infanterie de ligne aux observations de M. le maréchal-de-camp . . . ," *Spectateur militaire,* Vol. VIII, 1829-30.

Dodge, Theodore Ayrault. Napoleon. 4 vols. Cambridge, Mass., 1904-7.

Du Teil, Jean. De l'usage de l'artillerie nouvelle dans la guerre de campagne, connoissance nécessaire aux destinés de commander toutes les armées. Paris, Limoges, and Nancy, 1924. First published in 1778.

Earle, Edward Meade, ed. Makers of Modern Strategy. Princeton, 1944.

Feuquières, Antoine de. Mémoires de M. le Marquis de Feuquières, lieutenant général des armées du roi, contenans ses maximes sur la guerre, etc. 4 vols. London and Paris, 1737. First published in 1711.

Folard, Jean-Charles de. Dissertation ou l'on examine, si l'usage ou l'on est de mettre la Cavalerie sur les ailes, & l'Infanterie au centre, dans un bataile rangée est aussi bien fonde, qu'il est ancien & universal. Amsterdam, 1774.

—— Histoire de Polybe . . . avec un commentaire. 6 vols. Amsterdam, 1774. First published in 1727-30.

—— Nouvelles découvertes sur la guerre. Amsterdam, 1774. First published in 1724.

—— Traité de la colonne, la manière de la former & de combattre dans cet ordre. Amsterdam, 1774. First published in 1727.

Fortescue, J. W. A History of the British Army. 13 vols. 2d ed., London, 1910.

Guibert, Jacques-Antoine-Hypolite de. Défense du système de guerre moderne. 2 vols. Paris, 1803. First published in 1779.

—— Essai général de tactique. 2 vols. Liege, 1775. First published in 1772.

—— Journal d'un voyage en Allemagne. Paris, 1803.

—— Projet d'instruction sur les deploymens de l'infanterie. Archives du Ministère de Guerre, Carton No. 1711.

Guichard (Guischardt), Charles. Mémoires militarires sur les Grecs et les Romains où l'on a fidélement retabli sur le texte de Polybe et des tacticiens Grecs et Latins. The Hague, 1758.

Instruction sur l'exercice de l'infanterie du 29 juin, 1753. Archives du Ministère de Guerre, A¹ᵇ 1175, No. 46.

Instruction sur l'exercice de l'infanterie du 14 mai, 1754. Archives du Ministère de Guerre, A¹ᵇ 1175, No. 47.

Jähns, Max. Geschichte der Kriegswissenschaften vornehmlich in Deutschland. 3 vols. Munich and Leipzig, 1891.

Liddell Hart, Basil H. The Ghost of Napoleon. New Haven, 1934.

Macdonald, John. Rules and Regulations for the Field Exercise and Manoeuvres of the French Infantry (Being the Ordonnance of 1er Août, 1791). London, 1806.

Maizeroy, Joly de. Cours de tactique, théorique, practique, et historique. 4 vols. Paris, 1785. First published in 1766 in 2 vols. with items three and one following successively included after separate publication.

—— La Tactique discutée et reduite à ses veritables loix. Paris, 1773.

—— Théorie de la guerre. Nancy, 1777.

—— Traité de tactique. Paris, 1767.

Mathieu Dumas, Guillaume. Précis des événéments militaires, ou essais historiques sur les campagnes de 1799 à 1814 avec cartes et plans. 19 vols. Paris, Strasbourg, London, 1800-1826.

Mesnil-Durand, François-Jean de Graindorge d'Orgeville de. Fragments de tactique ou six memories. Paris, 1774.

—— Projet d'un orde françois en tactique. Paris, 1755.

—— Réponse à la brochure intitulée: L'ordre mince et l'ordre profond considéré par rapport aux effets de l'artillerie. Amsterdam and Paris, 1776.

—— Suite du projet d'un ordre françois en tactique. Paris, 1758.

Montbarey, Alexandre-Marie-Léonor de Saint-Mauris de. Observations sur l'instruction provisoire. Archives du Ministère de Guerre, Carton No. 1713.

Napoleon. Correspondance de Napoléon Ier publiée par ordre de l'Empereur Napoléon III. 32 vols. Paris, 1858-70.

Ney, Michel. Mémoires du maréchal Ney. 2 vols. Paris and London, 1833.

Nicolaî, Antoine-Chretien de. Observations sur l'instruction provisoire du 11 juin, 1774. Archives du Ministère de Guerre, Carton No. 1713.

Observations sur l'armée française en Allemagne. Archives du Ministère de Guerre, series Mémoires et Reconnaissances, Carton No. 1710.

Oman, Sir Charles. A History of the Art of War in the Middle Ages. London, 1924.

—— A History of the Art of War in the Sixteenth Century. New York, 1937.

—— Studies in the Napoleonic Wars. London, 1929.

Ordonnance du Roi concernant l'infanterie française. December 10, 1762. Recueil d'ordonnances militaires, Vol. I, 1762-63. Paris.

Ordonnance du Roi concernant la cavalerie. December 21, 1762. Recueil d'ordonnances militaires, Vol. I, 1762-63. Paris.

Ordonnance du Roi concernant les dragons. December 21, 1762. Recueil d'ordonnances militaires, Vol. I, 1762-63. Paris.

Ordonnance du Roi concernant les troupes legeres. March 1, 1763. Recueil d'ordonnances militaires, Vol. I, 1762-63. Paris.

Ordonnance du Roi pour règler l'exercice de l'infanterie du 1er janvier, 1766. Recueil d'ordonnances militaires, Vol. II, 1764-66. Paris.

Ordonnance du Roi pour règler l'exercice de ses troupes d'infanterie du 1er juin, 1776. Archives du Ministère de Guerre, A1b 1175, No. 60.

Pelet, Jean-Jacques-Germain. "De la division," Spectateur militaire, Vol. II, 1827.

—— "Essai sur les manoeuores d'un corps d'armée d'infanterie," Spectateur militaire, Vols. IV, 1828, and VI, 1828-29.

Phillips, T. R. Roots of Strategy. Harrisburg, 1940. This is a translation of a number of military classics.

Pirch, Baron de. Memoire raisonné sur les parties les plus essentielles de la tactique. Archives du Ministère de Guerre, Carton No. 1712.

Puységur, Captain Chevalier de. Observations et critiques sur l'instruction du 14 mai, 1754. Archives du Ministère de Guerre, Carton No. 1706.

Puységur, Jacques-François de Chastenet de. Art de la guerre par principes et par règles. 2 vols. Paris, 1749.

Puységur, Louis-Pierre de Chastenet de. Avis demande à M. le comte de Puységur sur le projet d'instruction pour l'exercice de l'infanterie. Archives du Ministère de Guerre, Carton No. 1715. Published by Colin in his L'infanterie au XVIIIe siècle.

—— Nottes sur l'ordonnance du Roy du 20 mars, 1764 pour règler l'exercice de l'infanterie. Archives du Ministère de Guerre, Carton No. 1710.

Reboul, F. "Histoire militaire et navale," in Histoire de la nation française, Gabriel Hanotaux, editor. 15 vols. Paris, 1920-29.

Resumé des principes de tactique du général de Saldern. Archives du Ministère de Guerre, Carton No. 1779.

Revol, J. Histoire de l'armée française. Paris, 1929.

Rochambeau, Donatien-Marie-Joseph de Vimeur de. "The Journal of the Vicomte de Rochambeau." Translated by Lawrence Lee. Published in Jean-Edmond Weelen's Rochambeau, Father and Son. New York, 1936.

Roguet, Commandant. "Etudes sur l'ordre perpendiculaire," Spectateur militaire, Vol. XVIII, 1834-35.

Saint-Cyr, Gouvion. Mémoires sur les campagnes des Armées du Rhin et du Rhin-et-Moselle de 1792 à la paix de Campo-Formio. 4 vols. Paris, 1829.

Saski, Commandant. Campagne de 1809 en Allemagne et en Autriche. 3 vols. Paris and Nancy, 1899-1902.

Savornin, General de. Sentimens d'un homme de guerre sur le nouveau système de Chevalier de Folard. Amsterdam, 1774. First published anonymously but attributed by Folard to Savornin.

Saxe, Maurice de. Mes revêries. 2 vols. Amsterdam, 1757.

Staël, Anne-Louise-Germaine, Mme. de. "Éloge de Monsieur de Guibert," in Oeuvres posthumes de Madame la Baronne de Stael-Holstein. Paris, 1838.

Tanski, J. "Notes sur le supplément à Ordonnance du 4 mars, 1831, inséré dans le Spectateur militaire du mois de janvier, 1832 par le général Loverdo," Spectateur militaire, Vol. XIII, 1832.

Terson, Colonel. Lettre d'un officier au service des États Généraux sur le Polybe de M. le Chevalier de FOLARD. Amsterdam, 1774. First published in 1730.

Toulongeon, F. E. Éloge véridique de Guibert. Paris, 1790. This work was also published as a preface to Guibert's Journal d'un voyage en Allemagne, under the title "Notice historique sur Jacques Antoine Hypolite de Guibert."

Traverse, Baron de. Sur les manoeuvres de l'infanterie. Archives du Ministère de Guerre, Carton No. 1713.

Villate, R. "Le mouvement des idées militaires en France," Revue d'histoire moderne, Vol. X, New Series 4, No. 18, 1935.

Weygand, Maxime. Histoire de l'armée française. Paris, 1938.

Wilkinson, Spenser. The Defence of Piedmont. London, 1927.

—— The French Army before Napoleon. Oxford, 1915.

Wimpfen, Louis-Felix de. Relation de ce qui est passe au camp de Vaussieux. Archives du Ministère de Guerre, Carton No. 1819.

Index

Agincourt, battle of, 134
Albuera, battle of, 342
Argenteau, General d', Austrian Army, defeated at Montenotte, 256-57
Art de la guerre par principes et par règles (J. F. de Puységur), 16-25
Artillerie nouvelle, L' (Coudray), 228
Auerstädt, battle of, 334
Austerlitz, battle of, 319, 334, 337

Bautzen, battle of, 311
Beaulieu, General Jean de, Austrian Army, 142, 169, 256
Becke, Captain Archibald F., British Army, accepts Colin's views on French Revolutionary tactics, 330-32, 337; 339, 340, on Peninsular tactics, 341-42
Belgrade, battle of, 45
Belidor, Bernard F. de, 88; ballistic research of, 145
Belle-Isle, Charles de, Marshal of France, interest in artillery reform, 88-89; 145
Bergen, battle of, 92, 161
Bicocca, battle of, 8
Blenheim, battle of, *see* Höchstädt, battle of
Blücher, Field Marshal Gebhardt L. von, Prussian Army, 340
Bombelles, General Henri F. de, favors independent over regulated fire, 85; criticism of the Ordinance of *1755*, 86-87
Borodino, battle of, 334
Bosroger, Leroy de, declares his general agreement with Maizeroy, 283; declares himself a partisan of the *ordre profond*, 283-84; discusses characteristics of columns, 284; tactical system of, 284-87, 288-89; estimate of his tactics, 287-88, 289-90
Bourcet, General Pierre de, French Army, 174; role in the French Army, 175-76; on the conduct of offensive warfare, 176-79; on plans of campaign: offensive, 179-82, defensive, 182-83; on

special limitations upon mountain warfare, 183-84; influence of, 184; 256, 257, 291
Brenier, General Antoine F., French Army, 313; upholds passage of two lines of Ordinance of *1791*, 320; views on tactics in agreement with Guibert, 325
Broglie, Victor F., Marshal of France, 50, 75; able tactics at Bergen, 92; advocates chasseur companies for battalions, 92-93; issues Instruction of 1760 establishing divisional system, 94-95; inspires the *Observations sur l'armée française en Allemagne*, 95; 97, 98, 100, 107, 112; use of light troops, 143; 156, 161, 211; suports Mesnil-Durand's second system, 233; at Camp of Vaussieux, 234-40; condemned by Wimpfen, 242; comments upon Camp of Vaussieux, 243; 244; problem of his continued support of Mesnil-Durand's tactics, 245-46; 249, 258, 266, 291, 300, 304, 332
Brossier, General, French Army, 329
Bugeaud, Thomas R., Marshal of France, quoted on column attacks in the Peninsula, 125; 162
Bülow, General Friedrich W. von, Prussian Army, 338
Burgoyne, General Sir John, British Army, 264
Busaco, battle of, 340

Castiglione, battle of, 332
Castries, General Charles E. de, French Army, comments upon Mesnil-Durand's second system, 246-47; 300
Catherine II (the Great) of Russia, 263
Chabot, General de, French Army, 233, 239, 243
Chambray, General Georges de, French Army, quoted on the third rank, 312; 316
Charles XII of Sweden, 26, 59, 112

Seidlitz (Seydlitz), General Friedrich W. von, Prussian Army, 88

Sénarmont, General Henri, French Army, 153, 296

Skirmishers, Saxe's use of, 48-49; Mesnil-Durand employs, 66-67; use of, abandoned, 84-85; reappear under the Regency, 85; experimentation with, in camps of instruction, 85; use of light or irregular troops for, 86; regulated by Regulation of *1764*, 99; Mesnil-Durand's use of, for fire preparation, 211-12; Maizeroy relies on, for protection from artillery, 281; Oman and Colin on role of, in French Revolutionary tactics, 327-30; Wellington's solution of the problem of French skirmish tactics, 339, 340, 341

Soubise, Charles de, Marshal of France, 91

Soult, Nicolas J., Marshal of France, 334, 344

Spires, battle of, 13, 81

Suite du projet d'un ordre françois en tactique (Mesnil-Durand), 76-79

Sundershausen, battle of, 92

Sur les manoeuvres de l'infanterie (Traverse), 300

Swiss pike columns, tactics of, 7; methods of coping with, 7-8

Tactique discutée, La (Maizeroy), 185

Tagliamento, battle of the, 250, 332, 337

Tanski, Captain J., French Army, 311, 312

Terson, Colonel, Dutch Army, criticizes Folard's system, 39

Thann, battle of, 337

Théorie de la guerre (Maizeroy), 269-83

Torgau, battle of, 112, 255

Toulon, siege of, 291, 292, 297

Traité de la colonne (Folard), 27-34

Traverse, Baron de, 300

Turenne, Henri de, Marshal of France, 35, 84, 111, 141, 269, 282

Vallière, Jean F. de, reforms artillery in *1732*, 88; 89, 145, 228

Vallière, Joseph F. de (son of preceding), opposes reform of artillery, 145; 146, 147

Vauban, Sébastien de, Marshal of France, 111, 170, 172, 293

Vaux, Noël de, Marshal of France, 107

Verona, battle of, 320

Villars, Claude L. H. de, Marshal of France, 111, 282

Villate, R., 82, 147, 185

Vimeiro, battle of, 340

Wagram, battle of, 296, 334, 337

Washington, General George, 264

Waterloo, battle of, 333, 337, 338, 342

Wattignies, battle of, 256

Wellington, Duke of (General Sir Arthur Wellesley), 339, 340, 341, 342

Wilkinson, Spencer, quoted on Bourcet as a staff officer, 175-77

Wimpfen, General Louis F. de, French Army, 233; comments upon first maneuver at Vaussieux, 235-36; comments upon second maneuver, 236-37; comments upon third maneuver, 237, 238-39; comments upon fourth maneuver, 239-40; comments upon fifth maneuver, 240-41; comments upon sixth maneuver, 241; condemns Broglie, 242; castigates Mesnil-Durand, 242-43; 244, 246

Zorndorf, battle of, 162